◆HOMES IN ALBERTA◆

◆

HOMES
IN ALBERTA
Building, Trends,

and Design

1870–1967

◆

DONALD G. WETHERELL

IRENE R.A. KMET

A CO-PUBLICATION OF
The University of Alberta Press
Alberta Culture and Multiculturalism
Alberta Municipal Affairs

First published by
The University of Alberta Press,
Alberta Culture and Multiculturalism and
Alberta Municipal Affairs

Copyright © Donald Wetherell, Irene Kmet, Alberta Culture and
Multiculturalism, Alberta Municipal Affairs, 1991

The University of
Alberta Press
Athabasca Hall
Edmonton, Alberta
Canada T6G 2E8

ISBN 0-88864-223-7 cloth

CANADIAN CATALOGUING IN PUBLICATION DATA

Wetherell, Donald Grant, 1949–
    Homes in Alberta

    Includes bibliographical references and index.
    ISBN 0-88864-223-7

    1. Housing—Alberta—History. 2. Architecture,
Domestic—Alberta—History. 3. Alberta—
Social conditions. I. Kmet, Irene, 1950–
II. Title.
HD7305.A6W48 1991   363.5′097123   C91-091566-0

Typesetting by
The Typeworks,
Vancouver, BC,
Canada

Printed on acid-free
paper.

Printed by John Deyell Company, Lindsay, Ontario, Canada

◆

◆

◆ ◆ CONTENTS

In 1985 the Department of Alberta Culture and Multiculturalism and the Department of Housing jointly commissioned an independent study of the history of housing in Alberta. Following the amalgamation of the Department of Housing with Municipal Affairs in 1986, Alberta Municipal Affairs maintained its involvement with the project. The commitment by both departments to the project included giving us complete freedom to pursue the study in the manner we found appropriate.

As in all such projects, a great number of people provided assistance and guidance. Frits Pannekoek and Les Hurt of Alberta Culture and Multiculturalism and Linden Holmen of Alberta Municipal Affairs encouraged and supported the project throughout. Murray Rasmusson, Deputy Minister of Alberta's Department of Housing until 1986, gave the project its first impetus, and Carl Betke and Diana Thomas of Historic Sites Service each provided valuable guidance on various aspects of Alberta's architectural, civic, and political history. Kathryn Merrett's editorial skills are gratefully recognized, as are the editorial and design work of Mary Mahoney Robson and Joanne Poon of The University of Alberta Press.

John Saywell of York University, Christina Cameron of Parks Canada, and Tom Carter of the Institute of Urban Studies, University of Winnipeg, provided valuable advice at the beginning of the project, although they will recognize that their advice was not always followed. Maurice Clayton, an architect formerly with Canada Mortgage and Housing Corporation, shared his intimate knowledge of building practices and housing in Canada. The staff of various archives and libraries were, as always, generous with their attention to our research. We owe special thanks to Dave Leonard and Keith Stotyn of the Provincial Archives of Alberta, Trude McLaren of the University of Alberta Archives, June Honey and Helen Lerose of the City of Edmonton Archives, Doug Cass of the Glenbow Alberta Institute Archives, the staff of the Canadian Architectural Archives, and Jeannine Green and staff of the Bruce Peel Special Collections Library at the University of Alberta. The Alberta Association of Architects made their library in Edmonton available for our use and gave us permission to photocopy materials from their records at the Canadian Architectural Archives. Despite the assistance of so many, the research conclusions of this study are our responsibility alone.

This book has been published with the help of a grant from the Social Science Federation of Canada, using funds provided by the Social Sciences and Humanities Research Council of Canada. The Alberta Foundation for the Literary Arts also provided funds towards this publication.

◆ x

ACKNOWLEDGEMENTS

A house's shape, layout, and decoration, among other factors, combine to produce a certain overall effect, or design. In the history of buildings, design is often dealt with in terms of style, that is, as a combination of elements which over time become a recognizable, historical style. Often, however, the terms "type" or "form" are also used to describe the visual effect of a building. Nor is there historically consistent use of the terms "house" or "dwelling." In this book, these terms are used as follows.

DESIGN: The combination of shape, layout, decoration, and other factors that produce an overall effect.

DWELLING: A place of residence, not necessarily a house.

FORM: The essential and basic physical characteristics of a house. "Form" is used to classify certain commonly built houses which share essential physical characteristics, though not necessarily stylistic influences. Before 1945, the three most widely built forms of houses in Alberta were the bungalow, the foursquare, and the homestead; other forms emerged in later years, such as the split level of the 1960s.

STYLE: Historically recognized and defined styles, or decorations or ornaments of a house that are derived from such styles. "Style" is used in a narrow way to mean either decoration derived from historically recognized styles, or styles such as Tudor, Gothic and Spanish colonial.

TYPE: The purpose or function of the building. A dwelling is a type of building, as is a church or a factory. In terms of dwellings, there are numerous subtypes, such as a tipi, a single family detached house, a duplex, and an apartment block.

These definitions are consistent with an understanding that while some houses in Alberta were built to formal styles, more often only certain elements of these styles were applied, often inconsistently and randomly, as part of a broader process which met the social and economic demands that housing served.

◆ Staples and Company,
lumber dealers, Calgary.
Float in the Calgary Exhibition parade, 1908.
PAA B3194.

Housing is not merely shelter. Since the beginning of European settlement in Alberta in the nineteenth century, social attitudes, personal ambitions, and the impact of technological, economic, and social change have been revealed by the evolution of house designs, changes in methods and materials of construction, government policy and regulation of housing, and housing supply and conditions. In one sense, the house has been a place of great personal meaning, while, on a broader level, it has been tightly bound to almost all aspects of the history of the province.

Although the province of Alberta was not formed until 1905, European fur traders were active in the area from the late eighteenth century and established the first post at Fort Chipewyan in 1788. Later, posts were established in the parkbelt region, including Edmonton in 1795. Beginning in the 1840s, missionaries working in the region encouraged the emergence of a number of mixed blood settlements such as Lac Ste Anne in 1844, St. Albert in 1861, and Victoria in 1864. While the fur trade and the Christian missions focused settlement in the central and northern areas of the province, Canada's purchase of the Hudson's Bay Company territory in 1869/70 changed the destiny of the region and land surveys began. While the missions and fur trade posts remained prominent for some time, the establishment of North West Mounted Police (NWMP) posts at places like Fort Macleod in 1874 and Fort Calgary in 1875 and, most importantly, the routing of the Canadian Pacific Railway (CPR) through the southern part of the future province in the early 1880s eroded the traditional settlement pattern. While rail connection with eastern Canada was in place by 1883, settlement was slow to take off, partly because low international grain prices provided little incentive for agricultural settlement. European settlers in the Alberta region had increased from 1,100 in 1881 to 17,500 a decade later, most of whom lived in the southern region. The old settlments in the north languished until 1891, when Edmonton was connected by rail to Calgary.

The construction of railways provided an important part of the infrastructure necessary for future economic development. In the late 1890s European and Canadian migration to the prairie region increased dramatically. From this point until 1913, the population grew and the economy boomed. As two new transcontinental railways were constructed, new districts opened for settlement. In 1901 the population of the province reached about 73,000 and by 1911 it stood at almost 375,000.[1] While Edmonton and Calgary had been small service centres in 1901, by 1912 they were clearly dominant in Alberta's economic and social life and served respectively as the metropolises of the northern and southern halves of the province. In the midst of this growth, the Canadian government created the province of Alberta in 1905. Its population contained many ethnic groups, although English-speaking settlers were dominant in political, social, and economic life. Initially, people of Ontario origin were most powerful in shaping the province in the image of their former home. In 1884, a year after the railway had reached Calgary, one observer noted Calgary's transformation in a single year from "only a hamlet" to a town in "every sense the name implies in Ontario."[2]

The Alberta economy depended upon staple raw materials. Fur exports remained important into the twentieth century, but cattle exports had surpassed those of fur in the 1870s. Cattle gave way in turn to cereal crops by 1900 and to oil and gas after World War II. External markets drove all of these primary resource developments, a condition which, in combination with the nature of frontier settlement, created an unstable economy of speculative booms and depressions. By World War I the economy was in a down cycle, and although it recovered for a time in the 1920s, it collapsed in the late 1920s under the dual influence of the world economic depression and a severe drought. These events increased discontent with the national economy and created a sense of desperation about such climactic and economic instability.

Such resentments were built upon a tradition of political dissent in Alberta. In 1921 the United Farmers of Alberta (UFA) were elected; farmers hoped that this government, acting in the interests of the single most important group in the province, would correct the wrongs farmers believed they suffered under the national economy. The UFA held power until 1935 when, unable to respond to the calamity of the Depression, tired, and racked by scandal, it was defeated by the Social Credit movement of William Aberhart. The attraction of Social Credit lay in its promise to deal with Alberta's seemingly distinctive regional problems. While Social Credit's anti-banking theories (irresistible in a debtor agricultural economy) and Aberhart's insistence that the commoditization of money was evil contributed little to solving Alberta's problems, the province did see rapid economic growth from 1939 until 1945 because of World War II. This was especially important for those towns and cities in central and northern Alberta which were the staging points for construction of the Alaska Highway and the CANOL oil pipeline from Norman Wells to Whitehorse. With the discovery of oil at Leduc near Edmonton in 1947, a sustained 35 year period of economic expansion followed, characterized by Alberta's evolution into an urban society. In the 40 years before World War II, more than 60 percent of the population had been rural, but this dropped to less than 50 percent by 1951 and continued to decline. Calgary became the administrative centre of the oil industry. Edmonton benefited from the development of the oil resources of the province and from an increasing role in northern servicing and provincial administration. Both cities grew remarkably, entrenching their authority over their respective hinterlands.

Because settlement was tied so closely to the development of railways, commercially produced standard building materials were readily available to settlers. While many rural people built their first and often their second houses from cheaper, noncommercial materials like logs, those with sufficient capital, primarily in the cities, built permanent houses with machined materials. This use of standardized building materials and servicing components helped to integrate Alberta housing into the North American mainstream. Nor was the settlement frontier in Alberta isolated from North American commercial mass culture. Ideas about house design therefore tended to follow common North American models rather than demonstrate unique regional styles and construction practices. In Alberta, an individual's selection of a particular sort of house was part of a wider process of social and technological development. Deryk Holdsworth observed that "material culture is potentially more universal and its transfer less geographically focussed in the industrializing period."[3] Alberta was integrated into national and, in the case of house design, North American culture from the beginning of settlement in the late nineteenth century. At the same time, standard house design was not universal. A number of folk traditions were applied at the time of initial settlement, but such traditions were not adopted consistently in the province. Nor did they resist the trend to standardized North American house forms and styles, which the English-speaking culturally dominant group in Alberta favoured as "Canadian" housing.

The spread, or diffusion, of house styles and forms has been the subject of a number of studies.[4] One theory popular in the United States holds that housing styles spread from the upper classes and leaders of opinion down the social scale to middle and working classes. This theory of "social diffusion" has rarely been tested, but Robert Bastian concludes that such a "hierarchical" process did not apply in the spreading of at least one style.[5] According to another theory, housing styles and forms are responses to tradition and fashion: they do not follow function, but "spring from the past" in association with cultural traditions.[6] Each of these theories has a measure of validity for Alberta, although neither provides a wholly convincing explanation. The popular dream of upward social mobility meant that upper class housing, often built according to formal historical styles, always exerted a significant attraction for the prairie middle class and, in turn, these middle class styles influenced working class people. Yet a significant measure of autonomy of design prevailed in ordinary housing, indicated by the use of several house forms which, while not unique in class terms, were prevalent among ordinary housing. But appropriate models were unclear in a mass society, especially one subject to so much foreign influence. American fashions had an obvious attraction, although there was no agreement on specific preferable styles—be it the American east-coast colonial aesthetic, for example, or the ostentation of Hollywood stars. A "British" look also had followers, at least until World War II, with half-timbered, Tudor styles attracting the Canadian middle class which maintained an attachment to things English. Even so, such building styles, developed by architects for the rich or for large institutions, had limited application for ordinary housing. The evolution of architectural styles, meaning formal historical styles or the decoration derived from such styles, is only a small part of the history of housing.[7] Few people thought about their houses as "architecture" or as "art"; instead, they saw their houses largely in social, economic, and technological terms. In the latter case, services were as significant as style, and, in Alberta, the middle class was the largest group able to afford such modern services as plumbing and electricity.

Services were central in the evolution of housing from the nineteenth century in North America, and exerted a profound impact on the design, cost, and context of housing. The house became a focus for technological change and scientific advance. The use of electricity, the development of new materials, and revolutionary discoveries about the causes and the spread of disease in the late nineteenth century contributed to modifications in house design, and, just as importantly, justified the need for community systems to support the provision of services to the house. No longer just matters of comfort or aesthetics, electricity, ventilation, light, and sanitation came to be seen as essential to health and to the definition of adequate housing. Lewis Mumford noted that when connected to water and sewer systems, electrical lines, and roads, the house lost its "self sufficient isolation" and began to function as one part of a collective unit in which "the efficiency of the individual cell was now conditioned on the efficiency and economy of the whole. Well-equipped houses, without appropriately modified community plans, could achieve only a small part of their mechanical promise."[8] Such systems added appreciably to the cost of housing, to the cost and function of government, and came to define housing that incorporated such services as normative and adequate housing for the whole society. Thus, in a rural society like Alberta, the housing of its many farmers came to be automatically defined as inadequate. Twentieth century house servicing assumed an urban setting, making all housing questions implicitly urban in their reference.

House servicing was not only a matter of economic and mechanical organization. It was also quickly integrated with social and political assumptions. Even though installation of urban house services required collective organization and necessarily led to a loss of individual autonomy, this did not present a challenge to most existing social and political precepts. Instead, the modern serviced house came to reinforce many of them, especially that of private ownership of property. Private property was a basic tenet of life in Alberta and its importance was often demonstrated in housing. The ownership of a house provided more than personal security; as a symbol of independence, economic success, and social integration, it sustained deeply held personal and collective ambitions. In Canada, as in the rest of North America, the house played a fundamental role in beliefs about the virtues of self-improvement and individual responsibility.[9] Private ownership of property, in the form of houses, tended to blur class lines in a society in which ownership of property, no matter how humble, theoretically gave an individual a measure of social status and a stake in the status-quo. These notions were intensified in Alberta, where the ideal of home ownership played a significant part in the rhetoric surrounding pioneering and settlement. In such a context, the meaning of housing went well beyond the assertion of individual will and circumstance. Modern serviced housing was rapidly incorporated into definitions of social and individual success. Change became virtue and newness a sign of success, a social attitude that usually led people to accept uncritically the dictates of fashion and its association with newness. In the early stages of settlement, new buildings signalled permanency, economic and social growth, and the taming of the frontier, while, later, newness announced both personal and corporate financial and social success.

These attitudes were not, however, tied exclusively to the frontier and a quest for individual betterment. Undoubtedly, the services included in a house directly affected one's quality of life and expressed control of one's future. Beyond this, however, the meeting of these individual needs through technology integrated the modern house with the commonly held belief in the English-speaking world that society should steadily evolve towards better health, greater happiness, more wealth, and increased material comfort. According to this ideology, progress was not universal or random; it was the product of capitalism, science, and European civilization. And one way that progress was expressed and given reality in everyday life was through the planning, design, and technological infrastructure of the house. Thus, not only a potent social institution, demonstrating social integration and individual success, the house also manifested on a personal level the social, technological, and political values of one's civilization.

In Alberta housing, progress was often demonstrated by the use of the word "modern" which was used to describe the various changes brought about by numerous forces such as scientific discoveries and commercially directed fashions. Hence, things modern ranged from plumbing to currently popular fashions brought about by increasing commercialization, and all worked to define progress and give it practical meaning in everyday life. This mutually reinforcing pattern meant that housing could never be concerned only with architectural style. Rather, modernity drew on a number of basic assumptions that were manifested in services and the layout of houses: the values of science, private property, health, and comfort.

The house also played a central role in popular social theory, which saw the family as the basic social unit. While the Alberta family was socially autonomous, it contributed to social stability and coherence. As shelter for the family, the house took on meaning for the support of family life. According to prevailing gender roles, a woman's ideal place in society centred in the home.[10] Further, the idealized family, a tightly linked, happy, and controlled unit, could be reinforced through the way houses were laid out and made into "homes." The society's emphasis on the family invested housing with both private and public significance, but such thinking was not unique to Alberta or Canada. American and British social theorists made the same assumptions and Canadians often drew upon their writings to explain and assess the importance of the home in society.

Housing thus reflected many influences, ranging from often internationally based theory about the social significance of the house to more immediately direct factors such as the economy, population growth, class, ethnicity, income, and politics. Yet, despite its significance for revealing important aspects about everyday life and economic and political evolution, the history of housing in Canada is relatively undeveloped. In Richard Harris's words, "historical scholars have not recognized the importance of housing in modern Canada." Indeed, he argues that there is no "synthetic review of what is known, and no agenda that identifies what needs to be known about housing in Canada."[11] Moreover, as John Saywell noted in *Essays on the History of Residential Construction in Canada*, changing census definitions and other limitations of source materials are a problem for such a review.[12] Another difficulty is, of course, the immense scope of the topic. Our approach has been to explore broadly all aspects of housing in Alberta. By restricting the scope of study to a single province, a manageable focus can be found with which to analyse important aspects of Canadian housing history. Thus, we explore most significant aspects of housing in Alberta: housing conditions, tenure, affordability, availability of financing, government policy, and social implications, as well as design, structural, and architectural components. In the belief that the houses of middle class, working class, and farm people reveal most about Alberta's social and intellectual context, our emphasis is on the housing of ordinary people.

Because changes in house design are imprecise in ordinary domestic architecture, this study is organized around changes in economic conditions and government housing policy in Alberta rather than the evolution of house design. While government became an increasingly important force in housing in the first half of the twentieth century, general economic developments were even more significant in affecting housing conditions, the volume of house building, and standards of servicing and construction. The chapters have thus been arranged in four main sections reflecting the economic and political context of Alberta housing: the impact of settlement; the period between 1883 and the end of World War I; the years from 1919 to the end of World War II; and lastly, the developments from 1946 until 1967.[13]

SETTLEMENT

1700s – 1900s

Fort Chipewyan •

Fort McMurray •

Peace River
• Dunvegan
Fahler
• Grouard
Grand Prairie
Slave Lake

Swan Hills
Athabasca
Lac La Biche

Cold Lake •
Whitefish Lake
Bonnyville
Westlock
Smoky Lake
Barrhead
Redwater
Pakan
Wostok
Lac Ste. Anne St. Albert
Fort Saskatchewan
Stony Plain
Sherwood Park Vegreville
Edson
EDMONTON
Tofield
Lloydminster
Drayton Valley
Devon
Beaumont
Holden
Mannville
Leduc
Viking
Cadomin
Pigeon Lake
Wetaskiwin
Camrose
Wainwright
Jasper
Mountain Park
Sedgewick
Rimbey
Nordegg
Bingley
Lacombe
Eckville
Blackfalds
Stettler
Castor
Alhambra
RED DEER
Coronation
Sylvan Lake
Delburne
Consort
Penhold
Bowden
Innisfail
Olds
Hanna
Carstairs
Munson
Drumheller
Cereal
Morley
Cochrane
Rockyford
Exshaw
CALGARY
Turner Valley
Okotoks
Bassano
High River
Brooks
Nanton
Carlstadt
Claresholm
Medicine Hat
Coleman
Blairmore
LETHBRIDGE
Bellevue
Fort Macleod
Pincher Creek
Cardston

— Railroads circa 1942

0   50   100 km

ONE

Settlement and Early Housing in Alberta

The years between 1870 and 1913 are traditionally seen as Alberta's greatest settlement period. The material culture of the indigenous people still existed during this period, but between 1896 and 1913 the immigrant population increased rapidly, with most new settlers destined for rural areas. Settlement was not, however, evenly distributed because of the link between settlement and railways. The CPR connected Calgary, Medicine Hat, and part of southern Alberta to the national economy by 1883, while Red Deer and Edmonton were not similarly linked until 1891. Other parts of the province waited longer still. The area between Edmonton and Lloydminster did not have rail transportation until the early twentieth century and rail connection to the Peace River district was not established until 1916. The implications of such dispersed development are obvious. In areas without efficient, inexpensive transportation, settlement lagged and building materials such as milled lumber, shingles, windows, doors, and paper had to be produced locally, imported at considerable cost overland from the nearest railway point or manufacturing centre, or done without.

Uneven settlement meant that there was never a period in the history of Alberta when pioneer housing was uniform. Frame houses made of milled lumber, identical to those built in Ontario, were popular in one part of the province, while log or sod construction was employed in other areas. Even within a small area, housing was often diverse. In 1912 one could find sod houses, shanties, and gable roofed two-storey houses existing alongside one another in Hanna. This variety can best be understood in terms of the buildings' intended permanence. Generally, housing on the frontier almost always occurred in stages, the first of which was immediate temporary shelter, the second an improved but still temporary shelter, and finally a permanent house. In the early nineteenth century, settlers in Ontario had followed this sequence, from log shanty to log house and then to frame or brick construction.[1] Roughly the same process occurred in Alberta. Immediate shelter was provided by tents, dug-out houses, or shacks. Improved but still temporary housing added sod houses and log houses. Permanent houses were constructed of milled wood, brick or brick veneer, or, rarely, stone or cement.

Construction techniques and materials were not always a reliable way of distinguishing between the temporary and the permanent. Many people built log houses with the intention that they would serve as permanent housing for themselves and their families, a practice that continues today. Further, many could not immediately proceed to the next stage of shelter and continued to use shacks and log houses for extended periods of time. In one study of the history of Beaumont, it was found that although most people intended their log houses as temporary dwellings only, these houses remained in use on the average from seven to twelve years.[2] Nevertheless, contemporary thinking saw log houses as a necessary but backward form of construction. Generally, framed or brick houses were considered "modern" while log and other forms were seen as "primitive." The ease with which frame houses could be enlarged responded to owners' desires for personal, economic, and social improvement. Further, in a society that equated modernization with progress, money with social advancement, and manufactured products with economic development and growth, houses not constructed from commercially produced products were viewed as anachronistic. These views, an outgrowth of the transformation of the European world under industrialization and capitalism, were given added force in Alberta by the unique circumstances of the province's development.

When Canada annexed the Hudson's Bay Company lands in 1870, she extended her own laws and structures to the newly acquired lands. Over the next two decades, Canadian law was put in place, a

◆ During settlement, a single community contained a variety of permanent and temporary housing as this photograph of Hanna in 1912 illustrates. PAA A11944.

system of government was created and a police force was established. Rules for alienating land were implemented and the region was connected with Canada by a railroad, an achievement that promised the benefits of European science and technology to the west. The region would be economically and culturally integrated with the rest of Canada and Canadian manufactured products would equip and build Alberta houses. In the prairie west, the frontier was not so much a state of mind as one of place. When settlers arrived, their task was to fit their lives into an existing political system and to re-create the material and social worlds they had left behind. This re-creation took the best part of the years before World War I, and it was not achieved easily. The pioneering process was often brutal—between 1905 and 1930 the failure rate on homesteads in Alberta was an astounding 46 percent.[3] At least for the British and other English-speaking Canadian settlers, a cultural future nonetheless seemed clear, familiar, and attainable. For others, the new land required adaptation to a strange and frequently hostile culture. Even the way one related to the land was sometimes alien. Despite dreams of recreating the village life of their past, many Ukrainian settlers had to adapt to the spatial arrangement of farms demanded by the Canadian land survey system. Each farmyard was located on a separate quarter section of land, making the farm villages of Europe impossible, which, as John Lehr has observed in his study on Ukrainian settlement, reflected the "interests of the corporate and governmental elite of English Canada." The Ukrainian immigrant was forced to accommodate himself to "this institutional framework which bound his actions, determined the spatial layout of his landscape and molded his society in the new land."[4] Similarly, Mormon settlers in southern Alberta were obliged to reject their ideal of the nucleated village stipulated in the Plat of Zion in favour of settlement that fit the grid layout of the land.[5]

INDIGENOUS HOUSING

The housing and other practices of the indigenous people of the region were of almost no importance to the incoming settlers, whether they were English-speaking settlers from Ontario, Britain, or the United States, or non-English-speaking peoples from Europe. Indian cultural life soon became little more than an example of local and regional colour. The Indians' accommodation to the harsh climate, sparse resources, and the dramatic variability of the land was most often viewed with condescension rather than respect. Indian standards of housing were dramatically different from those of Europe since, like housing everywhere, they were related directly to political and social structures. Nomadism, combined with a non-centralized system of political and social life, required housing that was easy to transport and erect. Housing of the plains cultures was typified by buffalo hide tipis, while those who occupied the forested areas used moose or caribou hide tents or bowed roof huts. Thus, different technology, materials, and economic, cultural, and social practices led to types of shelter that were different than those of the European world. In many respects, these shelters had an excellence in their material form that related directly and effectively to Indian cultural needs and to the climate and resources of the region.

Plains Indian tipis were constructed of buffalo hide which was stretched around a conical framework of up to eighteen long poles. These poles rested on a basic framework of either three or four poles lashed together at the top. Two flaps on the outside near the top of the tipi "served as cowls for the smoke holes, each being adjusted by a pole in accordance with the direction of the wind. The doorway, which could be closed with a small flap, was a narrow aperture in the face of the tent; the fireplace was in the centre."[6] The poles were most often poplar, but for those who lived within reach of the foothills and the mountains, lodge pole pine was used. The interior of the tipi was usually open, although an inner curtain of hide, before which the head of the household sat, was sometimes suspended along the wall facing the door. Both the Blackfoot in the south and the Plains Cree, who by the mid nineteenth century occupied the area around Fort Edmonton and eastward into Saskatchewan, used this type of construction. The only structural difference between the two was that Blackfoot tipis used a basic frame of four poles as opposed to a three pole frame employed by the Cree.[7]

Blackfoot tipis increased in size as a result of European contact. Tipi size initially was limited by the maximum forty or fifty pound load that a dog travois could carry, or about one buffalo hide. In his study of the Blackfoot, Oscar Lewis calculated that "a six to eight skin tipi would probably tax their transportation facilities to the limit. Such a tipi would accommodate six to eight persons." By the mid eighteenth century, tipis had become larger, which "would have been impossible without the improved means of transportation supplied by the horse." In the early nineteenth century a further increase in tipi size occurred, stimulated by greater wealth from the fur trade and

◆ A Sarcee tipi in southern
Alberta, 1891-1904.
PAA B33.

◆ The use by native
peoples of traditional
dwelling types, but in-
corporating new manu-
factured materials, is
shown in this photo-
graph of an Indian settlement along the Atha-
basca River, 1914-1918.
PAA A11.532.

from an increase in polygamy. Average tipis now utilized as many as twelve skins and would accommodate up to ten people; even larger tipis were constructed by the wealthy.[8] Women made the tipis, gathering and peeling the poles for the framework and preparing and sewing the hides for the covering. Among both Blackfoot and Plains Cree, the tipi was owned by the women, whose permission was required if the cover was to be painted. Since the hides would last only about two years, and since they could only be prepared outside, much of women's work during the summer involved the maintenance of housing.[9]

The use of tipis among the Plains Indians never died out completely. Their use for ceremonial functions and limited summer housing has continued to the present, although canvas has usually been substituted for hide. Nonetheless, the missionaries, and later the Indian agents, encouraged Indians to live in houses. At Whitefish Lake, a Methodist mission settlement established in the 1850s, the missionaries built a house for the chief, and by 1884 it was reported that his example of living in a house had been followed by some members of his band, although many of the Cree there were still living in tipis.[10] At Morley, another mission area, Indians on the reserve were living in log houses in 1884.[11] Indian agents and missionaries encouraged Indians to use European types of housing because they saw the house and private property as an essential means of encouraging native people to adopt an agricultural economy and acquisitive habits. Personal pride in owning real property was accepted by Europeans as an important measure of acculturation. In 1884 it was observed that, among other examples of acculturation such as Christian schools, the Cree at Whitefish Lake were holding "property of all kinds. . . . separately."[12] European housing was seen not merely as an improvement in living conditions, but as an indication that Indians had changed their economy, social order, and world view.

Woodland Indians, such as the Slave and the Beaver, differed in their housing from Plains Indians, although there was a large transitional zone in the geographic centre of the province where plains forms were dominant. The French missionary, Emile Petitot, remarked in the late nineteenth century that in the far north tents were made from caribou or moose hide stretched over a conical framework of poles. The poles were lashed at the top where a hole was left to allow the smoke from the fire to escape. In other cases, the dwelling was dome shaped and the hide was used either with the hair on or off. Another popular approach was to build a shelter from spruce boughs or saplings fastened down at one end and bent over to form a hoop which was then covered with hides. It was probably used when the tribe was moving from one area to another. Like that of the Plains Indians, northern housing was undergoing change during the late nineteenth century. In 1887 Petitot observed that "the Dindjie [Loucheaux] and Dene [Chipewyan] have learned from white people how to build shacks."[13] Clearly, however, Indians in northern Alberta continued to use tents well into the twentieth century, especially for summer housing. While Indians to the south also continued to use tents, the near extermination of the buffalo, and the consequent loss of hides as a building material, was an important factor in the decrease of Indian traditional housing in central and southern Alberta.

FUR TRADE BUILDING PRACTICES

During the century after 1778, about one hundred fur trade posts were built in what was to become Alberta. Without exception, these were built of wood, with the same construction methods being used for all buildings, including shelter. Essentially, three ways of building with logs dominated in the fur trade period. Two of these were frame systems with logs laid horizontally while the other did not employ a frame system and utilized logs vertically.

Vertical log construction, also referred to as *en pile,* or stockade, was the simplest. Upright posts were set side by side in a trench, a method employed not only for pallisades but also for buildings. Although this approach was valued for the speed and ease with which buildings could be erected, its long term use was severely limited by the tendency of the roof to push the walls out. The two methods which used logs horizontally were more complicated. Both post on sill and post in ground were systems in which a frame was constructed and filled in with a curtain of logs. Unlike vertical log construction, the curtain of logs forming the walls in these frame systems was not a bearing element since the frame held up the building.[14]

In post on sill construction upright tenoned posts were fitted into a mortised sill. These upright posts were spaced every ten to twelve feet along the sill and were "continuously mortised or grooved on two sides." Squared logs with tenons on each end were "slid down into the grooves or mortises," creating a wall "log on log without. . . . nails or pegs." In post on ground construction, grooved uprights, identical to those used in post on sill construction, were set into the ground, rather than on a sill. The tenoned logs were then dropped into the grooves with the first row of logs resting directly on the ground.[15] Both of these frame systems created a building made up of panels of horizontal logs between upright posts. Because they needed no nails and only few pegs, and since large buildings could be built with short logs, these frame systems were practical for the prairies and the north. They also allowed a great deal of flexibility since the resulting buildings could be extended to reach any length.

Despite considerable debate among historians, it appears that no one building method was dominant in the region before the early nineteenth century. Buildings built before 1821, when the Northwest Company and the Hudson's Bay Company united, were most often intended to be temporary. The instability of the trade and the ferocious competition led to rapid construction and equally rapid abandonment of posts once an area was stripped of its resources or the trade shifted to some other area. In this environment, vertical log and post in ground construction methods were probably most often employed.[16] The end in 1821 of ruinous competition stabilized the trade, and the Hudson's Bay Company adopted post on sill construction as its usual method of building.

The origins of post on sill construction and the reasons for its adoption have also given rise to debate. It has been suggested that it was the "result of ignorance and inexperience which crystallized into a custom and then a rigid convention."[17] A more reasonable explanation is that the Nor'west traders brought the method to the prairies in the late eighteenth and early nineteenth centuries from the St. Lawrence Valley where it had been commonly used in the eighteenth century.[18] The Hudson's Bay Company further stimulated its use. While the Company brought masons, plasterers, and carpenters from England and Scotland, it imitated the Nor'westers and recruited Canadians for the crucial work of hewing and laying logs since, "as a rule, Canadians were better axemen."[19] Presumably, the Canadians employed the log construction method of the St. Lawrence with a skill that was not challenged by the Company's British employees.[20]

Since post on sill was a system of frame construction, it allowed the erection of large structures. Because the Hudson's Bay Company controlled trade within several million square miles and was an imperial power in its own right, it needed large buildings. The men's house at Fort Edmonton in 1846 measured over 150 feet in length and the "Big House," the central administration and trade building, was a three- and one-half story building with 10,000 square feet of floor

◆ A rare example of post on sill construction applied by the Diegells family, 1913.
PAA A.11.406.

space.[21] The Roman Catholic Church used corner notched log construction, but also made use of post on sill, at least for its most important buildings. The mission and convent in St. Albert, built in 1863, and the Bishop's residence, built in 1879, used post on sill construction.[22] Milled lumber, stone, and brick, the only other building materials that could be used at the time to erect such buildings, were either unavailable or impractical in an area without any roads. Post on sill construction had several other advantages: it made use of short lengths of log, required no expensive nails, and was durable. The resulting buildings did, however, tend to be cold since the panels usually shifted and created gaps between the logs. Although it was customary to plaster the outside with mud, the logs were sometimes left bare and new chinking was applied each fall in preparation for winter.[23] While post on sill was the best response to the needs of the time, changes in transportation and supply of building material led to its gradual abandonment by the Hudson's Bay Company by the late 1870s.[24] Even so, records indicate the sporadic use of post on sill construction as late as 1913 in Alberta.

METIS HOUSING

Fur trade posts and missions acted as a focus for settlement in the mid nineteenth century. Although there seems to have been no wooden houses outside the fort at Edmonton in the early 1850s, about 130 people lived within the pallisades.[25] However, settlements made up of detached houses began to develop around missions in the northern and central parts of the province. A number of French-speaking Metis had settled at Lac Ste Anne by about 1840; in 1844 Father Thibault established a mission there with the hope of encouraging the Metis to become more settled and agricultural.[26] At about the same time, Lac La Biche emerged as a mixed blood settlement, and by 1870 missionary activity at Whitefish Lake, Pigeon Lake, St. Albert, Victoria, and Dunvegan served as the nuclei of small mixed blood settlements. These settlements served as bases in a highly mobile lifestyle. The Metis combined the traditions of two cultures, using Indian tipis while travelling and European houses when at the home base. In 1858, James Hector of the Palliser Expedition described Metis tents near Edmonton as "merely Indian wigwams of buffalo skins sewed together and stretched over poles." These tents were likely modeled on the three pole system used by the Plains Cree.

Indeed, Hector stated that the Metis differed little from "the natives [Cree], except that their dress is all of European manufacture."[27]

The Metis, however, did represent something different and new in Alberta. The fact that they lived in European types of dwellings for at least part of the year defined them as a transitional group in the cultural development of the region. In 1858 Hector described the Lac Ste Anne settlement as two villages of thirty to forty houses each.[28] Fort Victoria in 1872 contained both the log houses of the mixed bloods and the tents of the Cree who had moved there during the winter. For the missionaries, the use of log houses by the Metis, as for Indians, meant the adoption of an agricultural lifestyle which was not merely a way of making a living but was, as George MacDougall at Fort Victoria believed, "one of the lessons of Christianity."[29]

The houses of the Metis were simple structures, built with bearing walls of horizontally laid log interlocked at the corners. Frame systems, such as post on sill construction, seem rarely to have been used by Alberta Metis for house construction. Victoria Callihoo recalled that during the 1870s the houses at St. Albert and Lac Ste Anne were constructed from local spruce. The logs were either squared or left round. The corners were joined with a dovetail or a round (or scribed) notch, and the logs were chinked with mud and grass. The houses were single storied, usually with two windows and one door. The roof was covered with large pieces of spruce bark cut in the spring. This bark was effective only if laid with the inner side to the elements. It was probably laid shingle style over rafters and held down with long poles tied onto the gable end of the house. The windows were made of scraped hide which, while not transparent, did let in some light. Logs were sawn lengthwise and laid cut side up for floors, although packed earth floors were common as well. Cut logs were also banded together with iron or wooden cross bars and used for doors.[30]

While the origin of Metis construction methods in Alberta is undocumented, it can be assumed that these methods came from Red River since they resemble descriptions of Metis housing there.[31] Whatever their origin, the Metis structures must have looked tidy. The squared logs and dovetailed corners produced a naturally clean finish that was emphasized by the custom of applying a thin coat of white-mud plaster to the outside. Yet their comforts cannot be extolled; the lack of stoves and the reliance on a corner fireplace for heating and cooking meant that they must have been cold.[32] In addition, the Metis did not use furniture and, given the difficulty of getting water and the overcrowding that was apparently common, sanitation was poor.

Between 1885 and 1900, Metis were often hired by white settlers to build log structures, and it seems that in parts of Alberta they were an early building fraternity. As late as 1894 at Blackfalds, "almost all the hewn and dovetailed log houses were put up by the same man, a French half-breed named Pouchon or Pouchet," and such was his reputation that "it was considered, even by many Canadians among our neighbours, partly resourceful ingenuity and partly arrogant conceit to think of doing one's own dovetailing." Only with large scale immigration after the turn of the century, and, presumably, with the wider use of round notched corners, did the individual settler begin to do his own log work.[33]

LOG CONSTRUCTION

Building with logs was familiar and acceptable to the increasing number of settlers who began to move to Alberta from Ontario and the United States towards the end of the nineteenth century. Although log construction was not traditional in Britain, it had a long tradition in northern continental Europe and was adopted immediately in North America with the beginning of settlement along the Atlantic coast and the St. Lawrence. This log building tradition was further refreshed and diffused by population movement in North America and the continuous arrival of immigrants from Europe. Although many of the later settlers coming to Alberta from Ontario left framed houses behind, they often used log construction for their first home on the frontier, returning to an earlier tradition in response to the immediate need for temporary housing.[34]

The traditions imported to the Northwest, like those already in use by the Metis, emphasized horizontal log construction, with bearing walls and notched corners. This became the dominant method of log construction in Alberta. In some cases, log was used in a different fashion. One house near Viking was built of poplar logs sawed into two foot lengths and then stacked and bound with clay to form the walls. There were precedents in Ontario and New York for this method, but it was so labour intensive that it was unsuitable for the frontier. Since most settlers needed the most practical shelter possible due to limited time, capital, and technical skills, they used horizontal log construction that made use of locally available timber. As John

Palliser had noted in 1858, much of this timber was too poor to export, but it "would serve the purpose of the settler and suffice to construct houses and furnish him with fuel."[35] Thus, in the early 1880s most people built log houses everywhere in the province, including the emerging urban centres like Calgary and Edmonton. In 1884, Fort Macleod was described as having an "uncouth look," a place that only recently had "begun to evolve itself from the chrysalis of barbarism. The buildings are log with mud roofs."[36] While the log era passed quickly in urban areas, it was much more persistent in rural areas, and the northern, central, and foothills areas of rural Alberta were very much a log house society before 1900. Blackfalds in the 1890s was described as a "community of log houses."[37]

Finding logs for housing was not always easy. Homesteaders who had timber on their land were able to use it as they wished, but building with logs was purely academic for those settling on the open plains in the eastern part of the province at the turn of the century. Logs were unavailable and settlers used milled lumber brought in by rail. Those located at the margins of wooded areas, at Fort Macleod for example, had no useable timber on their land but were permitted to cut it on nearby forested federal crown lands upon payment of a small fee. Permits were also issued to commercial lumber operations. The permit system was designed to regulate the use of an essential, and often scarce, commodity, and some form of regulation appears to have been needed. For example, by 1878 "most of the large trees" in the river bottom around Fort Macleod had been cut by local residents for cordwood and good building timber was already scarce.[38] Nonetheless, the federal regulation of timber enraged many settlers and, as early as 1882, the *Edmonton Bulletin* described the permit system as a pernicious policy that restricted settlement and economic growth. The amount of timber allowed was "not enough for the first shanty," or for fences, outbuildings, or other improvements. Moreover, the tax was said to be unfair, draining settlers' capital into federal coffers while returning nothing to the region. Six years later, the *Macleod Gazette* argued that timber should be "as free as the air," because the more timber a settler used, "the more valuable he is as a settler." The only acceptable regulation was to prevent timber falling into speculators' hands, any other was "bosh."[39]

The arguments over timber illustrate the prevalent view that the land was for the taking and any regulation standing in the way of economic growth should be done away with. Nonetheless, the settlers' demands were not unreasonable in some respects. Much of the wood which they took from crown lands in southwestern Alberta was dry fallen timber, and such harvesting was not a wasteful use of the resources of the region. This was recognized by an order in council in 1889 allowing settlers to take dry fallen timber of up to seven inches in diameter from crown lands without a permit. Even then, discontent remained, and it was said, quite erroneously, that such small timber was useless for building purposes. By the turn of the century, the controversy over crown land timber had, to all intents and purposes, died away. Permanent housing, built of machined lumber, had become dominant in the area and the regulations permitting free use of small dry timber adequately met local needs for fuel and fencing.[40]

While machined lumber was not uniformly available or affordable for all builders in the province in the early settlement years, the establishment of local sawmills in places such as Calgary, Edmonton, and Red Deer in the early 1880s ended the use of logs for houses in the emerging urban centres. The rapid adoption of machined lumber in these settlements illustrated the settlers' eagerness to implant a familiar material culture. Lumber supply from these mills was limited, however, and production for house building was almost always consumed in the immediate locale.[41] Further, the supplies necessary for framed construction were often impossible to obtain in the early years of settlement. In 1878, for example, the I.G. Baker store at Fort Macleod had a few window panes in stock but no window frames, and no other building materials were locally available.[42] By the 1890s, such limitations had been surmounted because of better transportation and the emergence of local manufacturers and importers of building supplies. Lumber could easily be imported from British Columbia, but it remained impractical for rural settlers who had relatively little capital or were distant from rail lines. This situation was exacerbated at the turn of the century in Alberta by the actions of a lumber trust which prevented competition and was said to have forced up the price of milled lumber. In 1902 it was observed that one factor in the prosperity of the Red Deer area was its "abundant supply of good building material," which, if not available, "would cause many to think seriously" about moving to the prairies given "the prohibitive prices of all kinds of building material."[43] Rough planking could be sawn by hand, but it was an expensive and time consuming task since such planks were produced by two men using a pit saw (sometimes called a whip saw) which was a long saw with a handle at each end. It was hard, slow work and good progress was reckoned to be 200 board feet a day.[44]

The limited supply and later the cost of milled lumber contrasted sharply with the availability of indigenous material and confirmed the appeal of log construction in rural areas. Even when rail connections were completed in the wooded parts of the province, log houses remained the settlers' first response. If one could obtain logs at no direct cost, the only cash outlay was for windows and hardware. In many cases, these houses continued in use well after the settlement period in the locality had ended. Their main drawback was that they were difficult to enlarge because of their bearing walls. They were warm in winter if properly chinked and banked with snow, and their use was often extended by covering the outside with siding and the interior with planking. Further, a log house could easily be put up and finished in one season and construction required little equipment other than an axe, hammer, saws, chisels, and an auger. Speed of construction can be ascertained by the knowledge that a good axeman could cut and square ten logs per day. Although it is difficult to estimate the number of logs needed, a very small shanty built of seven inch diameter timber would take about ninety logs.[45]

The basic structural elements were the same in all horizontal log construction, but construction techniques varied in response to the quality and availability of materials. Historian and poet Frank Gilbert Roe, whose family settled near Blackfalds, recalled that builders commonly used single length logs and cut out the windows and doors after the wall was up. Smaller lengths could be utilized as door or window frames to distribute the load. If short lengths were used in a blind wall (one without door or windows), a single pair of posts was sunk at its mid-point and the logs were lap-jointed between them. Similarly, if single length logs were unavailable for use as lintels above doors and windows or as the finishing plate for the wall, the logs were lap-jointed or otherwise fastened to make a strong plate to carry the roof rafters. If the logs were crooked, the natural bulges were placed upward so that they could sag downward and straighten themselves. If the bulge was great enough to distort the wall, saw cuts were made half way through the log at the point of the bulge to force it to sag downward when laid into the wall. The same procedure was used for round and squared logs although, in the latter case, small bulges could be hewed out of a log by a skilled axeman.[46]

The corners of these buildings were an important sign of a skillful builder. Although corners were joined in many ways in Europe, the most commonly used notching methods in Canada and in Alberta were dovetailing and round, or scribed, notching.[47] Generally, squared logs were dovetailed while round logs were round notched, but "there were no formal rules." In examining log buildings in the area west of Edmonton, William Wonders and Mark Rasmussen found that sometimes more than one type of notch was used on the same building. In theory, a well constructed log building did not require nailing, but, when available, spikes were frequently used to reinforce the corners. Some Ukrainian builders drilled holes vertically through two or three logs and inserted pegs to stabilize the walls.[48] Corners were finished tightly against the building, with dovetailed corners sawn flush to the wall and round notched corners sawn to leave only two to three inches of log protruding. Long log ends sticking out at the corners of a building were thought to indicate sloppy workmanship and, perhaps just as importantly, to be unworthy of a true pioneer. Frank Gilbert Roe called such practices "dude ranch architecture."[49]

Roe recalls that when sufficiently large logs were available, they were hewed on both the interior and exterior walls to make the walls a uniform thickness. When only smaller logs were available, the logs were laid into a wall in the round and then hewed with a broad axe to make them even. When logs were left round, they were usually peeled to prevent rot and to retain chinking which otherwise fell off with the bark as it dried. Chinking was essential to seal the building and techniques were as varied as the builders. Sometimes moss was laid on the log courses as the building went up, each log holding the moss beneath it in place, and additional moss was forced into the cracks once the building was finished. Rags, a clay-manure-straw plaster, and strips of lath, among other devices, were also used for chinking.[50] Again, there was no hard and fast rule and any suitable material that was at hand was used.

Foundations and roofs were also built in a variety of ways. Flat stones were frequently used for foundations, as were wooden blocks, but sometimes no foundation was laid at all, leading to rapid deterioration of the bottom part of the walls.[51] In the late nineteenth century, two common roofing methods were sod (popularly known as "government shingle") and overlapped boards, although wood shingles, and later asphalt roofing, were used if at all possible to provide a water tight covering. By 1900, the gable ends of pioneer log houses were often finished with sawn lumber, which, as Frank Gilbert Roe recalled, "rather spoiled the effect of a log house."[52] The exterior of these houses was usually left unfinished and the peeled logs were allowed to cure to a hard finish. In a few cases, English-speaking settlers covered the logs with a mud plaster which provided a smooth

◆ A well constructed house made of unpeeled logs ca. 1909. The poles projecting from the front were likely supports for an intended verandah, suggesting that the house was meant as a permanent home. PAA A3469.

Horticulture was important for some settlers, as the surroundings of the Ogden's slab shack at Bingley in 1911 illustrate. Note the cold frame in front.
◆ GAI NA 470-2.

◆ A rather ramshackle log house with a sod roof near Lloydminster. Not dated, probably about 1905. PAA A1247.

A nicely crafted log house with an Ontario style carpenter Gothic front dormer, early 1900s. PAA H-486.

surface that could be painted. In many other cases, the exterior of the house was whitewashed to make it presentable. Some settlers also planted shrubs and flowers around the house, which, it was said, should not be a great expense since "many could send to their former home and get shrubs and roots enough to make a beautiful flower garden."[53]

While there were a number of two-storey log houses, most were single storey structures with a gable roof. If there was sufficient headroom, the attic was used as a bedroom. The pitch of the roof depended upon the roofing material. Sod roofs required a shallow pitch to keep the sods in place, but if the sod was replaced with wood or shingle, the pitch could be increased to allow more attic room. The size of these houses was naturally limited by the length of log used; size varied from one area to another. Due to the timber shortage near Fort Macleod by the late 1870s, the house that the Maunsell brothers built there was "more like a pen than a house." Nonetheless, such log shanties were found everywhere in the province where log construction was used. Houses tended to be larger in west central Alberta, but even here no log house exceeded 35 feet on any side, and house sizes generally ranged from 12 feet square up to 20-by-35 feet. House size was further determined by roof span limitations. With a central interior brace from the ridge pole to the ceiling joist, a roof 12 to 16 feet long could be supported without bracing it to the floor. Anything beyond this size required the use of heavy bracing.[54] Labour also affected house size. As in Saskatchewan and North Dakota, building bees were uncommon in Alberta, except among Ukrainians. Houses were generally built by the owner and his family, an example of the individualism and isolation of prairie pioneer life. Moreover, since many settlers saw their log houses as temporary, their tendency in Alberta, as in Saskatchewan, was to build small. Most of these log houses consisted of one large room often partitioned with wood or cloth into a sleeping and a living area. In some cases, the interior walls were finished with sawn planking that could be papered or kalsomined. Floors were often packed earth, but they were dusty and often became infested with fleas from the family dog. Accordingly, floors were made from planking if possible, but often the earth was simply covered with linoleum.[55]

The variable quality of these log houses was perhaps related to whether or not the builder intended his log house to be temporary or permanent. Some were "marvels of beautiful workmanship, often built with nothing but an axe for a tool kit." Others were ramshackle affairs without much attempt at proper finishing and with ridge poles sticking out "at varying lengths just as they were built."[56] It is one of the cliches about prairie settlement that the settler's log house was "quite manifestly the poorest building on his place, his barns and stabling being noticeably superior." Frank Gilbert Roe explained that it was common for cash short settlers to squat on a homestead. Even without permanent residence on this land, "the putting up of even the bare walls of a shack was considered in local opinion to make the place one's own." Similarly, in 1893 it was noted that a common means of holding a homestead at Leduc was "turning a few sods and throwing a few logs together and calling it a habitable dwelling." This house, the first and most quickly built structure on the farm, often continued in longer use than was originally intended or hoped. Nevertheless, in many cases the farm house was clearly better than the barn or outbuildings. Contemporary photographs testify to the high standard of some log construction in Alberta. Well finished logs and the use of features such as verandahs suggest that such houses were intended to be more than temporary structures. On homesteads patented before 1920 in Athabasca, the average value of the house usually exceeded the average value of the barn by at least 25 percent, suggesting that the stories about the quality of farm houses in relation to barns were overstated.[57]

The use of log construction crossed almost all ethnic lines in the society. It commonly showed a great deal of inventiveness and variety, and one ethnic group often adopted some building techniques from other groups. Even so, ethnic influences on log building techniques were apparent in some cases. Scandinavians frequently used "squared beamed spruce, with multilayered walls and large multiroomed layout," while Ukrainians employed poplar in conjunction with lath and plastering.[58] Moreover, there sometimes was an ethnically-based difference in attitude towards housing built of log. Not all settlers saw them as temporary structures—Scandinavians in west central Alberta often built permanent log dwellings, as did Ukrainian settlers who replaced their first shelter with a log plaster house and, a short time later, if money allowed, replaced that with a larger log plaster house in the same style.[59] Indeed, these plastered log buildings were one of the most identifiable characteristics in Alberta of Ukrainian settlement.

Single traits are, however, insufficient to constitute an ethnic tradition in building. Vernacular or folk building traditions, including the log construction of North American English-speaking settlers, did not rely upon written rules but evolved as a result of practical experience. In connection with Ukrainian vernacular building, John Lehr argues that changes in building techniques occurred because of "basic shifts in the culture itself." As all cultural groups in Alberta were confronting a new environment, adaptation was inevitable. Thus, it is difficult to characterize a "folk" or vernacular building tradition. But, as Lehr notes in respect to Ukrainians, folk style "exists in the cumulation of features which are common to that style. Any one of these common attributes is, in isolation, not indicative of a Ukrainian background; it is the occurrence of all or some of them within one building" which produces a distinctive building tradition.[60] Best documented, the Ukrainian log building tradition in Alberta provides a good example of the application of an identifiable and widely used ethnic tradition.

Most Ukrainians who settled in Alberta before 1914 came from the Western Ukraine, and although there was considerable variation in their architecture, there were typical features such as "a southward orientation, a single storey, a rectangular two or three roomed plan; a central chimney; a gable, hipped gable, or hipped roof; and use of distinctive colours in decorative trim." Unlike Ukrainian houses in Manitoba, where post on sill and vertical log construction derived from Ukrainian tradition were two among many techniques employed, Ukrainians in Alberta used horizontal log construction almost exclusively. Lehr attributes this to "differences in the timber quality of each area at the time of settlement." Better timber in east central Alberta, in contrast to poorer timber in Manitoba, led Ukrainian settlers with "virtually identical" cultural heritage to use different methods.[61]

In Ukrainian log construction, logs were joined at the corners with round notching or dovetailing, and the general practice of using round notching on round logs and dovetailing on squared logs was followed by Ukrainian builders, just as it was by most other log builders. Except among some Bukowinians, the walls were covered inside and out with a plaster made of mud and straw.[62] Another building technique used poles. Frank Gilbert Roe observed that "Russian" settlers, as he called them, made "no pretence" of finding what English-speaking settlers would have called "good logs," theirs "were big straight green poles—four or five inches thick." These poles were "peeled in June (when such things must be done to make a good job) and built up with sufficient space between them to admit one's hand." The walls were sometimes stiffened with pegs inserted in holes drilled vertically through the logs. This skeleton was let dry for a year after which the walls were covered completely with a mud straw plaster which "was 'keyed' between the logs into a. . . . homogeneous mass, precisely as a plasterer keys his plaster behind the lath."[63]

Whether used over logs or poles, the application of plaster was a high art. While there were different approaches, the plaster finish usually consisted of three layers. Up to two inches thick, the base coat was made from clay, straw, and dung. A second finer textured finishing coat and a third coat of active lime, which was whitened with washing blue or milk, were then applied over the logs. The surfaces of round logs were sufficiently uneven to hold this plaster, but with squared logs, diagonal strips of lath, often made from thin poles, were attached to the wall to afford purchase for the plaster. In the earliest years of settlement, the exterior plaster was decorated with painted geometric designs. This tradition disappeared quickly, but distinctive colour preferences for exterior wood work remained: Galicians preferred a sky blue while Bukowinians preferred green.[64] Maintenance of mud plaster finish was labour intensive because it had to be whitewashed frequently and a number of Ukrainian pioneers seem to have adopted milled lumber or shingles as siding.[65]

The first roof on many of these houses was sod, later to be replaced with thatch. While rye straw was traditionally used for thatching, slough grass was the comparable material available in Alberta. Thatching was a skilled art not known by all pioneers and that done on the prairies varied from the "proficient to the slapdash."[66] Thatched roofs demanded a steep pitch to ensure proper drainage, and when thatch was replaced with shingles in later years, the pitch was sometimes modified. Indeed, many settlers found steeply pitched roofs to be unnecessary since the rainfall in the prairies was so low. Towards the end of World War I, low rainfall had an unexpected influence on the use of thatch roofs. Feed shortages caused by drought conditions led many people in east central Alberta to tear down their thatch roofs, replace the thatch with shingles, and sell or use the thatch for feed.[67] Whatever the reason for changes in the pitch of roofs and in the use of roofing materials, it resulted in a "radical change of house profile and the elimination of the bucolic spirit and picturesque flavour of the vernacular style."[68]

Most of the houses built by Ukrainian settlers were relatively small, ranging in size from 26 to 30 feet across the front and approximately 12 to 17 feet in depth. Lehr believes these size preferences

◆ The first Russo-Greek
baptism in Alberta took
place outside this small
sod-roofed Ukrainian
house at Wostok in 1898.
PAA B2879.

◆ A traditional Ukrainian
house but with wooden
shingled roof, ca. 1930.
PAA 11863.

were a direct transplantation of Ukrainian traditional house sizes.[69] However, this size is roughly the same as other log houses in the province, where size seems to have been largely determined by limitation of materials. Of Ukrainian families surveyed in east central Alberta in 1917, 10 percent lived in one roomed houses while 56 percent lived in two roomed houses.[70] The interior of these early Ukrainian houses was based purely upon old country models. The houses almost always consisted of an entrance hall, a living-kitchen room, and the *velyka khata,* or formal room. The layout of these rooms conformed to one of four general patterns; two rooms only with no entrance hall, two rooms with an entrance hall on the west side of the house, two rooms separated by the entrance hall, and two rooms with the entrance hall taking the form of an exterior porch on the south side of the house.[71] The function of these rooms seems to have been rigidly defined by tradition. The main room was used for formal events, the accommodation of guests and, seemingly, for business purposes since postmasters in east central Alberta used this room as the local post office.[72] On its east wall hung icons, religious calendars, and photos. In contrast, the living-kitchen area was used for daily routines such as washing, cooking, sleeping, and family life. In the early years of settlement, the central focus of this room was a large willow-framed, mud-plaster stove. These stoves were huge, taking up almost half of the room, and were soon replaced with commercial iron stoves.[73] Nevertheless, the clay stoves continued in use, built outside in the yard as a supplement to the indoor stove. When thatch roofs were used, the chimney extended only to the attic and the smoke was allowed to seep out through the roof, which probably served as a natural insecticide and also minimized fire danger. With the adoption of shingle roofing, the chimney was extended out through the roof. The floors of the houses were usually packed earth, treated with a water-cow dung solution to give them a hard finish.[74]

The central European building traditions practiced in Alberta were rarely extended as a coherent whole to settlers of other origins. Nonetheless, settlers were pragmatic and often used methods if they proved effective. One example of cross-cultural exchange of building practices appeared in the *Farm and Ranch Review* in 1912, where an adapted version of central European log-plaster building methods was described. A frame was constructed by sinking upright posts into the ground and fastening them at the top with a plate. One inch poles were nailed on both sides of these posts to form a lathed wall. The lath was then covered with a stiff mud-straw plaster and smoothed with the back of a spade. Once the first coat was dry, a finishing coat of sand and clay was applied. The roof was shingled or covered with sod. It was suggested that the space between the walls be filled with straw as insulation. Indeed, the *Farm and Ranch Review* correspondent observed that "we know of one house made in this way where geraniums, petunias and other flowers were kept all winter" without any night protection. The floors of these houses could be either mud plaster covered with linoleum or wooden planking. The interior walls could be left in their original plaster state or kalsomined, although "one house we saw had an imitation wainscotting in light green and the upper part in white with a border... between the two to represent moulding."[75]

While the interior decoration described was reminiscent of the finished rooms of contemporary permanent homes, the building system represented an adaptation and modification of a central European building tradition. It was close to a wattle and daub method of building used by Ukrainians who had settled in areas of poor timber in Saskatchewan, although Ukrainians apparently did not use it in Alberta where better timber was available.[76] It was also close to the pole system of construction described by Frank Gilbert Roe and it made use of one of the dominant traits of Ukrainian building methods in Alberta: the use of mud plaster. Although the origin of the system described in the *Farm and Ranch Review* is unknown, the story was credited to a correspondent from east central Alberta, where various forms of central European building technology were widely practiced and known.

EARTHEN HOUSES

In farm and rural areas, other forms of temporary shelter were also common. The dug-out or pit house was one such form and was most commonly used by Ukrainians, although some Russian-German settlers at Stony Plain and some English-speaking settlers also constructed them.[77] It has been contended that their use by Ukrainian settlers was a revival of an obsolete form of shelter, triggered by the exigencies of the frontier,[78] but it is evident that the form was in current use among the poor and dispossessed in the Ukraine until the beginning of the twentieth century and was employed in western Canada when thousands of Ukrainian immigrants "found themselves unsettled, poor and isolated."[79]

◆◆ Exterior and interior
views of Tom Qually's
dug-out house, Groton
area. The house was built
in 1910 and was occupied
until 1922. GAI NA 2616-
17 and GAI NA 2616-18.

◆ A Barr colonist's sod
house near Lloydmin-
ster, ca. 1903. PAA P453.

The Marshall family's
sod house near Corona-
tion, 1907–8. The house
was used for one winter.
◆ GAI NA 474-3.

A great variety of dug-out houses was built in Alberta.[80] Most consisted of a relatively shallow pit, approximately 10 by 14 feet, covered by a roof of poles, mud plaster, and sod. To facilitate construction, they were often built on an embankment. Preferably, dug-out houses were used for only one winter, although they frequently served for the first two or three years in the new land.[81] More elaborate versions used machined lumber, tar paper, and manufactured windows, and, in at least one case, such a house was used for over a decade.

Another form of temporary shelter in rural areas in the plains regions of the province was the sod house. Since these areas were not settled until the close of the nineteenth century, sod houses were largely confined to this period. Although they were appropriate in the treeless parts of Alberta, they were also occasionally built in treed areas. Some of the Barr colonists at Lloydminster, and the Roes, who settled near Blackfalds, built sod houses. Perhaps building and living in a sod house, a symbol of independence and adaptability, had become part of the mythology of pioneering on the prairies. The Roes's sod house was constructed in 1894 under the direction of the family's eldest son who had "heard of the Mennonite sod houses" in Manitoba.[82]

The techniques used to build sod houses in Alberta seem to be almost identical to those used in prairie areas of the United States. Ideally, a breaking plough was used to cut a fibrous sod into a slab four inches thick, which was then cut into a rectangle 16 inches wide and 32 inches long. The grass was left on the sods which were sometimes dried slightly to make them denser. The sods were then laid without mortar, grass side down, to produce a wall between two and three feet thick. Generally, the building site was levelled but little attention was given to a foundation. If a cellar was to be included, it was dug before the walls were put up and sometimes the soil was banked up around the house. In such a case, the house became a variant on the dug-out house because the living area was below ground level.

As the walls rose, spaces were left for windows and a door. These openings were framed with sawn lumber or poplar poles once the sod had reached the top of the opening. Such framing prevented the sods from shifting sideways and carried them across the top of the opening. Once they were up, the walls were trimmed with an axe or a spade to make them neat, and any spaces were filled with soil or pieces of turf. Presumably, the walls were finished with a top plate to carry the weight of the roof evenly, and the roof was then put on.

The roof was also of sod and it was laid, grass side out, over a slab roof or over rafters first covered with tar paper. The roof was the weak link in the system because it deteriorated rapidly and leaked. A sawn lumber roof, weighted with rocks since it could not be securely fastened to the walls, was usually added when possible.

While only a few sod houses were finished with a mud plaster on the outside, interior walls were often covered with mud plaster, which was whitewashed or sometimes even wallpapered or hung with cheesecloth. In other cases, newspaper or cardboard was tacked onto the sod walls to give the interior a finished look. Such interior finishing was not just decorative; whitewash acted as an insecticide and lining the walls with heavy paper helped to keep insects from moving from the sod into the warm interior of the house. To keep debris from falling onto the occupants, cheesecloth or other fabric was strung up to form a ceiling. Wooden floors laid over 2×4 joists were sometimes used, but often the floor was simply packed earth.[83]

The design of sod houses was limited by their thick, squat walls. Some were gabled, but many seem to have been shanty-type buildings. Most had a porch and one or two rooms, the rooms being formed either by sod walls or with cloth hangings. A few were more elaborate. The sod house built by Evelyn Slater McLeod's parents near Consort in 1909, while typical in methods of construction and finish, measured an exceptional 44-by-16 feet, had a cellar that was entered through a trap door, and was divided by cloth hangings into six "rooms": a kitchen-dining area, a pantry, a parlour, and three bedrooms. Such extravagance was possible because the McLeods had moved to Alberta from North Dakota and were able to bring with them windows, doors, lumber, and other building materials. Moreover, they looked upon their sod house as a more permanent dwelling than did many other settlers. It continued in use as a dwelling for 12 years, during which time other improvements were added.[84] In general, sod houses were intended only as temporary shelter, and, as Frank Gilbert Roe recalled, he "never heard of anyone build[ing] one for a permanent choice where other materials were at all readily to be had." Even so, sod houses provided good shelter. They were warm in winter, cool in summer, and were easy and cheap to construct. Moreover, the squat elemental structures related directly to the prairie landscape, and they provided a sense of security and coziness for some. Frank Gilbert Roe recalled the comfort of hearing rain on a sod roof, which sounded like a "low rumble, not unlike a long freight crossing a trestle."[85]

Sod houses, like dug-out houses and log structures, relied upon building techniques that can be described as premodern. Based upon building traditions founded upon centuries of practical experience, they minimized the use of machined lumber and other commercially produced materials. Such techniques were not, however, uniformly employed or even typical of settlement housing. Commercially manufactured building products were commonly used for temporary housing and found greatest expression in tents and shacks. In both rural and urban areas throughout the settlement period, many people lived in tents while a temporary dwelling, or sometimes a permanent house, was being built.[86]

TENTS

Tents in urban areas were most often concentrated in enclaves throughout the city and were used when there was no affordable rental housing or when hotels and boarding houses were too expensive for a long stay. Despite frequent demands, there was little effort by government to build dormitories or to expand existing "immigrant sheds" for newly arrived settlers in the larger urban areas.[87] Dealing with this problem was difficult, however, because urban areas not only served as reception centres for people moving on to rural destinations but were also experiencing massive expansion. The population of Calgary proper almost tripled to 11,967 between 1901 and 1906 and reached 43,704 by 1911. Edmonton experienced similar growth, as did many towns. Red Deer's population grew from 323 in 1901 to 2,422 in 1911 and Medicine Hat's population increased fourfold to 5,608 in the same period.[88]

Such population increases forced many people in urban areas to live in tents until they could find better housing. In 1911, advertisements run by the Western Tent and Mattress Company of Calgary trumpeted that since houses were scarce, "Why not get a Tent and Camp Out?"[89] Following the arrival of the Canadian Northern in 1905, Edmonton experienced a housing shortage due to the population increase. In the fall of 1906 it was claimed that "fully 1,000 have been living in tents during the summer" and many would likely "remain under canvas all winter."[90] Indeed, tents were a permanent feature of the urban landscape in Alberta before World War I and in 1912 it appeared that 2,500 people were living in tents in Edmonton alone.[91] There was little regulation of these urban tent areas. In 1907,

◆ Living in a tent until the first house was built was a common practice. PAA A2537.

◆ Cities served as the reception centres for settlers but, lacking accommodation, many lived in tents over the winter. The Phillips family lived in a tent in Calgary in 1904 until homesteading in Crossfield. GAI NA 3458-2.

◆ Guy McCumsey building a shack at Munson in 1913. GAI NA 2543-10.

for example, Calgary rarely enforced its bylaw prohibiting tents in the central business district and requiring that in other areas they have access to pure water and sanitary facilities.[92]

While many of the tenters in urban areas were single men, a good number of families also lived in the tent communities. Although it was common practice for families from Ontario to join the father in the West only after he had found a house, other immigrant families did not have this choice. Charges that some people lived in tent communities out of frugality and not necessity were sometimes made. These were probably unfair—most people would likely have had no choice and life in a tent must have been hard. Cooking and cleaning were difficult and the areas where tents were pitched soon became foul with garbage and sewage. To keep out the cold, the tents were banked with snow, earth, or boards.[93]

SHACKS

Like tents and log houses, shacks were a quick and easy response to the need for immediate housing on the homestead or in towns and cities. Indeed, other than tents, they were generally the most common form of temporary housing to appear in urban areas, and they continued to be used by the poor as permanent housing. As the product of a modern commercial culture, the shack had no building traditions and instead relied on a crude functionalism. It was probably more widespread than any other form of temporary housing, and it, rather than log or sod houses, should properly be the symbol of the pioneering era. It most precisely expressed the spirit of the time for, despite its shoddy appearance, it had an aggressive spirit that was lacking in other forms of settlement housing. It not only defied its environment with its angularity, its ugliness, and its refusal to use indigenous nonmachined materials, it also rejected out of hand any tradition other than that of North American commercial culture. While no one wanted to live in a shack for longer than was necessary, many people preferred them to sod or log houses which were "not good enough," even though they were probably much better dwellings for prairie conditions.[94]

Essentially, shacks could take any shape within the limitations imposed by tar and building paper, 2 × 4s, shingles, and machined lumber. Materials were either purchased at the nearest urban centre or brought along by the settler. If necessary, the nearest lumber yard

◆ Charles Bishop built a pioneer home consisting of a frame shack and a sod lean-to at Cereal about 1912. GAI NA 2053-1.

◆ Shacks were brutally cold, but insulating with sod helped to keep out the winter, Nanton, ca. 1910-18. GAI NA 3535-110.

◆◆ Exterior and interior views of the Macpherson's shack at Nanton. The interior view is dated November, 1903. The shack cost $75.71 to build and $26.20 to furnish. GAI 3535-109 and GAI 3535-115.

would give instructions on how to build a shack. It took almost no skill to build such a dwelling, and the builder needed to have only the most rudimentary carpentry and building skills. Most shacks were small square or rectangular structures employing a variety of roof types ranging from the most commonly used shanty roofs to bowed roofs to shallow gable roofs. Many had porches and sometimes a lean-to was even added to provide more room. In a few cases at least, these lean-tos were made of sod. Typically, the shack was framed with 2×4s, covered with boards, and then sided with tar paper held down with strips of lath.[95] The roof was shingled or covered with asphalt roofing material.

The interior of these shacks was finished with building paper or, after the turn of the century, with a commercial wallboard product such as Beaver Board. Although the first sight of these houses sometimes brought their future occupants to tears,[96] attempts were sometimes made to decorate the interior in an attractive fashion. This took a fair amount of labour and ingenuity, especially when wallpaper was used. Nonetheless, wallpaper was a "boon" for shacks that had been sheeted with building paper. Building paper was easily broken, but holes could be patched by nailing a piece of wood onto the stud behind the break, gluing the torn paper onto this wood, and then covering the whole thing with wallpaper. Ceilings also presented problems because building paper on ceilings tended to droop and crack. One remedy was to hang wallpaper over the area after it had been reinforced with pasted newspaper.[97] This inventiveness also extended to the wallpaper itself—some settlers used newspaper while others covered the walls with magazine illustrations, calendars, photos and whatever was handy.

Despite their drawbacks, shacks were useful in both the urban and rural settlement process. For many, they were the easiest and most realistic housing option available. They were inexpensive, they could be torn down and the material recycled, and they were mobile since they could be dragged about on skids by a team of horses. Shacks were brutally cold, and settlers unfortunate enough to spend a winter in one banked it with earth and then with snow to provide some insulation. Gladys Rowell, who pioneered near High River at the turn of the century, recalled that their shack remained cold despite their attempts to seal the walls by nailing everything "we could get our hands on" over the interior walls.[98] Other people even veneered their shacks with sod to keep them warm. If at all possible, farm families moved to better housing in a nearby town or city for the winter and then returned to the shack in the spring.

As with other forms of temporary housing, shacks sometimes remained in use for a considerable time. In rural areas the bachelor and his shack passed into folklore, but shack housing in urban areas was rarely considered quaint or eccentric. In 1917 it was observed that because of high rents in prairie cities, many individuals bought a cheap lot and put up a shack until something better could be afforded, but "as time went on he got accustomed to his little kennel and oft times let it stop at that." In addition, speculators often built shacks on urban land and rented them out at high rents. Such buildings cost so little that "in two or three years" the costs of construction and taxes had been paid.[99] In Edmonton in 1914 there were many tents and shacks scattered in the outlying parts of the city. Many of these were temporary structures, but others were the permanent dwellings of the poor.[100]

◆

Alberta's early settlers demonstrated a strong pragmatism and a remarkable inventiveness in response to their need for shelter. While records exist of the forms of houses built, it is now difficult to determine their distribution throughout the province. The treed northern, parkbelt, and foothills areas of the province probably saw the greatest concentration of log houses. Experience in other plains environments in North America suggests that if logs were available, even within 12 miles of the building site, they were used for pioneer housing.[101] This would also seem to be the case in Alberta, although no one form of housing was relied upon exclusively in any single area. For example, while most houses in the Blackfalds area were log, frame houses were also built as part of the settlement process. The Roes built a sod house in this area as their first temporary house and then replaced it with one built of log, a pattern rare enough to cause puzzlement among their neighbours. It is logical to assume that sod houses were found in the treeless eastern parts of the province, such as the Consort district where Evelyn Slater McLeod's parents settled, but it seems that they were never a dominant form anywhere in the province.[102] Shacks, however, had no geographical limit and were built everywhere. Studies of American plains housing focus on necessity rather than tradition as the formative influence on frontier housing,[103] but no firm rules explain the distribution of pioneer house forms in Alberta. Necessity and pragmatism, conditioned by supply of materials and capital, were the most powerful forces.[104]

Tradition also played a part in the choice of houses that were built. The houses of Ukrainians in east central Alberta demonstrate the impact of tradition in pioneer housing. Yet certain traditions were rejected almost entirely. Ontario's timber-framed building tradition never took hold in Alberta; in part because it was being replaced with milled frame construction in Ontario by the late nineteenth century, but also because it was too complicated and labour intensive for early housing on the Alberta frontier.[105] Further, the small size of Alberta's timber made it unsuitable for timber framing; another example that if local circumstances did not allow one particular building tradition to be used, settlers turned to other parts of their inheritance for solutions. The Ukrainian builders of Manitoba used Ukrainian-derived post on sill and stockade techniques because they lacked timber to use other Ukrainian-derived methods. Fashion also determined choice. The recollections of pioneers often suggest, perhaps with hindsight, that log houses and pioneering went together and were evidence of the self-reliance and independence of their owners. Men demonstrated their masculinity in building them, while women's endurance and adaptability were proven by living in them. As the *Farm and Ranch Review* reported in 1907, "one can hardly imagine a more pleasing sight" than a little log house surrounded with flowers and a garden for it demonstrated "the use of resources that were near at hand."[106]

While much of this myth making drew upon American rhetoric about log houses, few people in Alberta seem to have accepted the American rhetoric depicting the log house and the frontier as democratic and egalitarian symbols of society.[107] Instead, language used to describe pioneer houses in Alberta stressed their role as forces of social stability. As the *Calgary Herald* wrote in 1897, mention was often made of foreign homes: the "indolent homes" of the tropics, the "refined" homes of England, and the "voluptuous" homes of France, but never of the "simple, happy and contented homes to be found right here in Alberta." Such an emphasis on stability implied predictable gender roles as well. The *Herald* went on to describe the log house with its contented "master," its busy mother, its "merry child" playing on the floor, and its "clean and bright" whitewashed walls decorated with the "handiwork of the lady of the house." Everywhere was "cleanliness and neatness," everywhere contentedness, including the animals in the farmyard, and the "ripple" of the nearby brook completed the pastoral scene.[108]

This extraordinary presentation of pioneer life owed its imagery of rural life to Canadian, American, and British popular culture. The emphasis upon stability and contentment could also have come directly from immigration advertisements or from the mouths of local boosters. Such images of pioneer life and housing were closely connected with popular conceptions about progress, economic growth, and the nature of man. In 1905, the pioneer in northern Alberta was portrayed as sighting his homestead with a "satisfactory sense of possession," which awakened in him the "homebuilding instinct." Soon, "from the silent woods comes the sound of the ringing axe," and shortly afterwards a log cabin was built. After another short interval, this was gone and a "commodious dwelling" stood in its place. If pioneer deprivation was good for a man's spirit, the simple cabin, "albeit a place of peace and contentment, was yet barren of the luxuries, and many of the comforts of life" possible in a modern house.[109] Thus, the lasting image of pioneer housing was not its security and its contentedness, but its impermanence. Its place in myth enshrined it as only a transition towards a more materially prosperous time when houses would be stylish, larger, more technically sophisticated, more comfortable, and permanent.

THE
MODERN
HOUSE

1883 – 1918

The Context of Designing the Modern House

At the close of the nineteenth century the preference for the detached home was a widely accepted cultural ideal in Alberta. As well, contemporary theories about house design were widely discussed and understood. Although they found expression mainly in the houses of the wealthy, by the time of World War I the urban middle class and some farmers could also afford to implement the basic tenets of what was called modern house design. Nonetheless, all social and economic groups were affected by these principles; a significant measure of their power and attraction. The models developed in the late nineteenth and early twentieth centuries, whether immediately achievable for the majority of the population, were powerful precedents and created a framework within which housing was designed for the next 75 years. In Alberta before 1918, a full fledged building industry also developed, with standard building practices, labour organization, and methods of financing.

While Alberta was being settled, North American housing design was responding to an emerging scientific and public consensus about sanitation and health. This influenced the layout of houses and helped to define the qualities of a modern house. Equally influential ideas grew out of social and political theories about the family and the place of property in social organization. While the house was the most tangible and realizable expression of private ownership of land, it also sheltered the family, the central unit in social organization. By 1900, these various currents of social, political, and scientific thought had coalesced in a composite definition of modernity in housing.

PRIVATE HOME OWNERSHIP

Private home ownership was considered a legitimate goal for all Albertans. It was a prevailing ideology which Alberta shared with the rest of Canada and was not modified until the late 1960s when subsidized public housing became part of provincial life. On a larger scale, the private ownership of land was a crucial determinant of political and social power. In Alberta, land ownership signalled wealth and status.[1] Speculation in urban and rural land was common, simultaneously shaping the province's social hierarchy and reinforcing the mythology that the frontier promised social mobility. Henry Klassen suggests that through land speculation "the first moneyed class" developed in late nineteenth century Calgary, and this sudden wealth "widened the gap" between prosperous and low income people.[2] City and town councils were largely dominated by real estate and business interests and their decisions often reflected these concerns. Moreover, their understanding of the objectives and meaning of civic life encouraged a "booster" mentality that judged any criticism of a town, its land policies, or its housing and sanitation conditions as a threat to the community's economic future.[3] While there was sometimes criticism of land speculation, this was rarely aimed at the principle of private land ownership, especially home ownership. Most Albertans, regardless of occupation or social place, endorsed private ownership as a value. It was a "right" guaranteed by the frontier and had motivated many to come to Alberta, where they owned their own home or aspired to do so. Such attitudes were assiduously cultivated by civic leaders and local newspapers. So authoritative were these views that they remained social ideals even when not personally achievable.

Since land ownership was central in the power structure of provincial society, private home ownership became inextricably linked with respectability. Paying rent was likened to pouring money down a drain, and the virtues of owning one's home were commonly described in social terms. While landlords generally escaped criticism, it was contended that renters were careless about the appearance and upkeep of their residences. Ownership engendered pride and concern about the welfare of one's community, created a better credit rating, and gave the owner a "standing in the city on account of his permanent residence there."[4] By linking ownership with respectability, it served to personalize the principle of private ownership, while its promise of social advancement confirmed popular arguments about the virtues of self-help, independence, thrift, and foresight, all of which overtly rejected collective solutions to social problems.[5] In 1910 the *Calgary Herald* defended the "little lot man," the individual with only a small residential lot, as a person "whose modest efforts at home making" were truly laudable.[6] A promotion for a "workers" subdivision in Calgary in 1911 endorsed these views in its warning to workers about their dismal future without personal home ownership. It suggested that when a man's skills were made obsolete by old age, he would be fired since "capital demands its 'pound of flesh' and you must pay the toll." With earnings gone and landlords refusing to rent houses for nothing, the aged worker would be forced to depend upon resentful children for shelter and, with this loss of independence, self-respect too would disappear. How did one avoid such a fate? The worker had to "try, try, economize, save, deprive yourself of luxuries and pleasures and rich garments in order to obtain this home, because the joy, comfort and feeling of independence you will realize later in life will repay you well for all your sacrifice."[7]

Such appeals implied a criticism of the working poor; but "luxuries" and "rich garments" were not the reason many could not afford to house themselves decently. However, the society's commitment to private property, speculative potential, and self-help was extended to all of its members, irrespective of their means, and reinforced the ideal that home ownership was a universal goal. In such a context, home ownership was inevitably associated with social order. The public was continually warned of the dire social consequences of a society without personal home ownership. Renting was said to encourage transiency, and a mobile society was seen as socially and economically unstable.[8] The solution to this problem was crude but effective; the ongoing costs of mortgages, taxes, and upkeep helped to stabilize society.[9] Moreover, home ownership was seen as a force that could mitigate class distinctions. N.C. Pitcher, the general manager of North American Collieries Ltd., argued in 1919 that privately owned permanent housing in mining towns would rid the mines of "drifters" and encourage miners to settle down in one location.[10]

Family life was also represented as being at its best within the sheltering arms of home ownership. A need for privacy was portrayed as a natural part of human nature that could be satisfied through home ownership. "A mated man and woman yearn for the seclusion of their own fire-side and their own home" said the *Calgary Herald* in 1908. Living with parents or renting a house was "all right when it is preparatory to getting one's new home," but "no matter how humble, no matter how small, there is a fascination about ownership."[11] But home ownership was not just about privacy. There was also a difference between a house and a home. While an owner-occupied house was sometimes automatically defined as a home, a home had certain social and ethical attributes, usually expressed through a standard range of cliches. In 1907 the *Farm and Ranch Review* reprinted the findings of an English survey which showed that most Englishmen saw the home as a "world of strife shut out, a world of love shut in," a place of charity, equality, and "the father's Kingdom, the Mother's world and the child's paradise."[12] In Alberta, the home was similarly characterized as a personal anchor and a source of security for its occupants and for society at large. The Alberta Department of the Attorney General, calling the home "the Gibraltar of Society," noted that "where there is a breakdown in home conditions, there are sure to be irregularities in neighbourhood life."[13]

In all of this, the physical attributes of a house were central. The house should be designed to be inviting yet intimate, protective, comforting, and suitable for informal group and family activities. One of the slogans in 1915 of Prairie Builders, a company selling prefabricated houses in Alberta, was "A House Not Properly Arranged Never Makes a Home and Never Gives Satisfaction." As Dean Paget of Calgary argued in 1910, since character was moulded in the home, the quality of the house itself was an important determinant of the sort of people a society produced.[14]

Implicit in definitions of the home were certain attitudes about women's role in society. Women's demands for political and social equality in the late nineteenth century had developed into an important public debate by 1910 when it "had reached a new peak of intensity" in North America and Britain.[15] Many men and women in Canada supported a higher social status for housekeeping.[16] At their meeting in Vancouver in 1907, the National Council of Women lamented the national shortage of domestic help which, they resolved, threatened "to entirely annihilate our home." One solution lay in raising "home-making to the acknowledged standing of a profession."[17] The year before, the same idea had been stressed at a cooking school in Medicine Hat where women were advised that "housework is woman's first and most legitimate task." It was "not a haphazard jumble of duties," but should be "regularly defined, clearly understood and systematically performed."[18] The obligations of the professional housekeeper were clear: to look after men and protect and cherish children and guide them towards productive citizenship. This implied a common role in the home for all women, regardless of social strata, and women, in meeting these responsibilities, needed to apply scientific management, efficient homemaking and, among others, sanitary standards to the home.[19]

HEALTH, PUBLIC SANITATION, AND HOUSE DESIGN

Maintaining sanitary standards was a particularly important task, which not only relied upon women's labour but required a properly designed house. By the turn of the century, house design in North America was beginning to reflect a new understanding about the importance of sanitation, fresh air, and sunlight for health. Orthodox medical theory at mid nineteenth century was divided into various camps, each holding often contradictory views about the cause of disease. Also popular was "a broad self-help oriented health reform movement" which stressed such factors in health as diet, physical exercise, and hygiene. This movement was sufficiently popular to challenge medical orthodoxy, and by the 1890s these health reform ideas "had become a standard part of the vocabulary of the medical doctor. Within newly emerging ideas of sanitation, for example, lay traditional self-help notions of personal hygiene, bathing and ventilation."[20] Equally important were Pasteur's experiments on contagious diseases, which in 1882 proved that many diseases were directly related to germs.

While the idea that the house should provide a healthy environment had received scientific sanction in the United States by the early nineteenth century, it had not become widely accepted until about 1860.[21] The integration of popular health reform ideas into orthodox medical theory in the last quarter of the century gave such ideas status, currency, and scientific authority that they had formerly lacked, permitting, indeed encouraging, their integration into contemporary house design theory. Dr. J.T. Reid of Montreal told Calgarians in 1911 that sunshine and fresh air promoted health and that "the ultraviolet rays of light are nature's germicides."[22] Some also contended that humans became sickly without sunlight because it helped to "accelerate tissue change" in the body in a way similar to photosynthesis in plants. Moreover, sunlight was important for "moral and spiritual" health since dark rooms were depressing and decreased "energy and vigor."[23] Similarly, fresh air was said to have value as a germicide. As the *Calgary Herald* editorialized in 1910, the "fear of what was called catching a cold has been exploded. What was called a cold . . . has turned out to be an infectious disease and is caught nowhere more readily than in close compartments."[24]

The combination of theories about sunlight, fresh air, and sanitation into an overall approach for preserving health was important for house design. It was rational because it was justified by scientific theory and credible because endorsed by professional medical practitioners. In addition, the argument that the complexity of industrial society made efficient planning essential for daily living made it imperative that design should produce living spaces that would best satisfy occupants' needs for health, happiness, and efficient completion of daily tasks.[25] After the turn of the century, this approach was widely accepted as basic in defining modern housing, with the result that the services contained in a house became an important component in its design, cost, and fashionableness.

In towns and cities, the need for sanitary standards in each household necessitated the development of public standards of sanitation to govern the relationship of the house with its environment. By the end of the 1880s, such community responsibility was being adopted, in theory at least, by governments throughout Canada. Prior to this time, the regulation of health in the North West Territories, as in much of Canada, had been *ad hoc*; boards of health were established only from time to time to deal with epidemics. In the early 1880s, Ontario was the first to create permanent boards of health in Canada and they became the model for the rest of the country.[26] While local government in the North West Territories was a complicated web of governments at different stages of development, nominal jurisdiction over health matters was assumed by local governments as they were created. Unincorporated urban areas were subject to the *Unincorporated Towns Ordinance* of 1888.[27] The ordinance was fatally flawed, however, as it relied upon voluntary reporting of unsanitary conditions; few risked the enmity of their neighbours by reporting their unsanitary houses and yards to the authorities.[28] Thus, in spite of the law, streets throughout the 1890s were awash with the manure from horses and other livestock, and pigs roamed freely in most towns.[29] In 1890, sanitation in towns in southern Alberta was "truly deplorable." The streets of towns such as Fort Macleod, Lethbridge, and Medicine Hat were filthy, while "every back yard and cesspool affords fruitful soil for the cultivation of disease germs. Wells are placed injudiciously, the water supply becomes tainted and typhoid appears on the scene."[30]

Even had they wanted to, individuals could not effectively deal with most of these problems because there were no sewers, piped water, or garbage disposal. In 1893 Edmonton did not have a "nuisance ground" and Fort Macleod, like most other towns in Alberta, lacked garbage pick-up until 1898. Even in towns with such service, it was often sporadic and careless.[31] Lacking sewers, people used outdoor privies or indoor chemical toilets which they emptied into back lane cesspools. Without piped water, most townspeople got their water from a local river or spring, a community stand-pipe, or a backyard or neighbourhood well. Ensuring pure water in such conditions was difficult. By the late 1890s, local officials regularly checked water sources, but they could do little about a distribution system that often caused contamination. In 1898, impure water caused an outbreak of typhoid at Fort Macleod. While the Health Officer found the river water pure, he could not speak for the many private wells in the town or for the distribution system by which water from the river was "carted around in tanks and emptied into barrels, tubs and other receptacles, the cleanliness of which would be very hard to vouch for."[32] Such conditions were common. Cholera periodically showed up in various towns, and typhoid, due to impure water supplies, was almost always present somewhere in the province before World War I. In 1910, because Lethbridge pumped raw sewage into the Belly River, typhoid was "general in the towns" downstream.[33] In the same year, a serious outbreak of typhoid occurred in the poorer sections of Calgary where, lacking connection to the water and sewer mains, people got their water from back yard wells polluted with seepage from outdoor privies and cesspools.[34]

Such conditions, and a growing understanding of their implications for health, stimulated support for better public sanitation. A by-law was introduced in Calgary in 1890 for a water and sewer system to free the town of "wells, the cess pits and the present dangerously unhealthy closets," but by 1893 the system was connected only to the business district and a few houses.[35] When Edmonton began installing a sewer system in 1901, the largest towns in the province were also taking similar steps, although most medium-sized towns did not have such services, or had only water service but not sewage, until World War I.[36] Small towns often did not have any services at all. In Hanna, in 1916, water was scarce because there was no municipal water system or consistent private delivery of water. People used well water in the summer and melted snow in the winter; drinking water was "proffered and received with the ceremony generally given Champagne."[37]

The need for an infrastructure for local sanitation was increasingly recognized as the first step towards better and healthier living conditions, and in 1897 towns were required by a territorial law to appoint health officers.[38] While this implied the recognition of objective criteria with which to judge sanitation, it often stimulated uninformed or exaggerated commentary. In 1910, the Calgary City Commissioner argued that typhoid was not to be unexpected "with flies, microbes, colon bacilli and such like flying about and into people's mouths."[39] Such views were a rejection of the arguments for better water and sewage treatment. Nonetheless, public sanitation was increasingly recognized as a legitimate extension of government authority that was justified by scientific knowledge. The *Calgary Herald* expressed this view in 1910 when it editorialized that while the view that

> an Englishman's home—or any other white man's for that matter—is his castle has passed into a truism but in these days neither drawbridge nor portcullis could bar the path of the sanitary inspector. The prevention and treatment of disease is a matter of public concern. The growth of a corporate consciousness is accepted as one of the signs of a sympathetic age. Cleanliness, fresh air, pure food and prevention from infection are the keynotes of modern medicine.[40]

Even so, local governments sometimes found that they lacked jurisdiction for such comprehensive control. Edmonton's solicitor argued in 1903 that the city's bylaws against keeping pigs in the town went "as far as they legally can," even though it was clear that they were unsatisfactory. The next year, residents in a downtown residential area complained about a neighbour who kept a large number of pigs which he fed with "swill" collected from hotels.[41] Eventually, technological change in the form of the internal combustion engine freed urban areas of their livestock population, especially horses, but the adoption of the car in urban areas was a gradual process.

More serious than ignorance and limited jurisdiction was a lack of political will to enforce, even to the extent possible, better community sanitation. In 1918, health regulations in small towns were "very seldom if ever properly observed." The health officer was often a local businessman or doctor who was loathe to antagonize his customers or his patients by enforcing sanitary regulations.[42] When Edmonton first installed water and sewer systems, the city passed a bylaw compelling houses on serviced streets to be connected to the mains. For owners unable to afford the connection, the city did the work and charged its cost against the property as an improvement. This was not always done, however, since "some Aldermen thought it would work a hardship on some owners who had only small houses or shacks." By 1910, this leniency was becoming more difficult to justify, and both Calgary and Edmonton city councils expressed a commitment to enforce their bylaws compelling owners to connect with the water and sewage mains.[43] This sort of prevarication was in sharp contrast with the commonly adopted civic policy of servicing vacant urban land. Until the economic collapse in 1912–13, urban expansion was rapid, and a great number of vacant lots were serviced at city expense. It was a practice that would later create significant difficulties for urban governments in Alberta.

TOWN PLANNING

By World War I, a communal responsibility for sanitation was only the beginning of public regulation for the common good. Critical reasoning about social issues also led to demands for town planning, which, Albertans were told in 1910, was "the art of arranging houses and public buildings in the most beautiful and commodious manner."[44] Another stimulus for planning was the hope that settlement in the province truly would be a new start, resulting in personal and social benefits. Planning could prevent the development of slums and incompatible land use adjacent to housing, issues directly related to public health, national efficiency, and social betterment. As a group of Edmonton citizens noted in 1916, it would be shameful if the haphazard cities of "older lands. . . . should be repeated in this new country, where we can build from the ground up."[45] Cities in Alberta, like others in Canada, were growing without attention to land use controls, aesthetic concerns, or sanitary or building standards. As Thomas Adams, the town planner for the Commission of Conservation, noted in 1916, urban land in Canada had been developed "in any haphazard way that suits each individual operator in real estate" and was "speculated in and boosted in value to the detriment of the user and without real gain to anybody. The first necessity of good housing is to control all land development by town planning schemes."[46]

Adam's critique was justified in Alberta where there was little regulation of land use in most urban areas. The 1906 *Land Titles Act* required only a minimum width for streets and lanes, and accessibility of each lot from the rear.[47] Local governments exercised even less control in this regard. Calgary required civic approval of subdivisions only in 1910, and even then, most were approved without question. The only regulation that the city imposed was the numbering and spacing of streets.[48] The main concern of Calgary's first building by-law in 1904 was fire protection in the central business district, and it was not until 1911 that it was amended to divide the city into residential and commercial areas, control the size of front yards and require that all lots be a minimum size.[49] Similarly, Edmonton did not have a comprehensive building bylaw for houses until 1912, when limits on site coverage, minimum space between buildings, and side and rear yard requirements were made mandatory.[50] In such an environment it is not surprising that there was no consideration of regional planning. Well before World War I, the high price of urban residential land had stimulated the development of fringe communities where the "mechanic, the clerk and others" could afford land on which to build either shacks or small houses. These fringe areas developed unsystematically and without reference either to their own sanitary or fire protection needs or those of the larger urban area upon which they relied.[51] Although the province had introduced a *Town Planning Act* in 1913 allowing local governments to regulate land subdivision and to carry out town planning, it was never effectively implemented, partly because the war stymied the little interest there was in the subject.[52]

The lack of rigour with which Calgary enforced its land use regulations provides a good example of the fate of prewar planning. In 1911, in response to public complaints about mixed land use, the city appointed a planning commission consisting of 50 members, mainly men with real estate and construction interests. The commission had little coherence or focus. Calgary's building bylaw was not applied consistently throughout the city and was called into play only when the city or property owners found it useful "to obtain some public good or to protect property values." Such planning followed development and did not precede it, making poor conditions almost irreversible.[53] This was especially telling with regard to lot size and the overall survey of the city. Alberta urban areas were laid out, as in most of North America, on a rigid plan of rectangular blocks, or a gridiron. Edmonton's "unkind fate" was to be surveyed on this plan, one characterized as "tainted with the greed of the speculator and the soulless complicity of the surveyor too glad to find a system so saving of thought."[54] The gridiron created very long streets and static residential areas, limitations that were sharpened because lots were small. In Calgary most residential lots had a 25 foot frontage. When laid out in the 1890s, such small lots had not created congestion since not all were built upon. As the city's population grew after 1900, however, the lots filled in with the result that houses were so close together that their eaves almost touched.[55]

In contrast, various planning solutions involving curved streets and varied street widths were proposed to reduce dust, admit more light and air, and create an imaginative integration of houses and other buildings in the urban landscape.[56] Such ideas, however, were deemed too radical and too interventionist before World War I. More often than not, planning held genuine appeal for city officials only when it enabled or enhanced the projection of an image of the city as a progressive, enlightened, and up-to-date place where investors and immigrants could find satisfaction. While this theoretically included the improvement of working class housing,[57] in practice it meant plans such as those prepared by Thomas Mawson, an English town planner, hired by Calgary in 1912 to prepare a plan for the city. Mawson produced a grandiose plan which would have transformed Calgary into a city with grand vistas, monumental buildings, parks, rational traffic routes, and residential segregation. But urban planning on such a scale was too costly to implement, especially after 1912–13, and Mawson's visions found little support among planning advocates. His ideas had been bypassed by "the mainstream of contemporary thought in town planning," which had shifted away from civic grandeur towards more practical issues about housing, sanitation, and urban efficiency.[58]

Zoning to prevent incompatible use was only beginning to be applied in Alberta cities by World War I. The broader forces affecting residential segregation were usually the product of market forces. Private developers determined the type of residential areas that were built through the size of the lots they subdivided or the sort of houses they built.[59] But most neighbourhoods were not uniform. In 1909 it

◆ This group of four small homestead houses built on a single lot in Edmonton, 1914, shows lack of suitable siting and separation of houses. GAI NA 1328-2569.

◆ A residential street in Sedgewick, 1910. Even in this residential area with probably the best houses in the town, the houses were placed with little planned relationship to each other and with sheds, barns and privies scattered throughout. PAA A7115.

was said that the situation in Calgary was like that in Victoria, British Columbia, where "one man will put up a fine residence on his lot and the next man will build a row of shacks."[60] There was, however, informal segregation by class and income, and therefore by ethnicity, in Alberta's towns and cities, but its particulars are unclear.[61] The residential and business segregation of Chinese in Calgary was achieved through community hostility, but the mechanics of segregation of other ethnic and racial groups is uncharted.[62] In general, however, land use, including residential development, responded to "market dynamics, individual decisions of the numerous different actors rather than the result of any collective decision making process."[63] One of these influences on individual choice was proximity to work. Public transit only began in Calgary in 1909, for example, and before then most people walked to work. Thus, housing tended to cluster around the downtown, or industrial sites, such as the Eau Claire lumber mill, or, later, the CPR shops. Even within these communities there were significant variations in housing, reflecting different incomes and occupations.[64] At the turn of the century, businessmen and professionals in Edmonton and Calgary often lived relatively close to the downtown where they worked, although exclusive suburban neighbourhoods had begun to develop for the very rich.[65] Overall, market determined segregation was the rule, although in the very wealthiest areas in Edmonton and Calgary, it was enforced through caveats which required owners to build houses of minimum value. In Calgary, Mount Royal had building restrictions to "ensure the erection of very handsome houses," although this was all but ensured by the cost of the lots, between $2,000 and $3,700 in 1911.[66]

Thus, despite numerous proposals and evident need, urban land use planning, including that of residential areas, continued to be largely unregulated by the end of World War I and the regulations that existed were poorly enforced. In defence of local governments, they had only a small bureaucracy to administer such undertakings and provide continuity between new and old councils. Further, their jurisdiction was often unclear and rapid urban growth forced them to focus their energy on servicing land rather than on the contentious enforcement or implementation of long range planning.[67] However, planning was often construed as an unwarranted interference with the rights of property. Land control proponents could not buttress their arguments with clinical scientific evidence as could those who advocated public sanitation. Arguments about the ugliness, unhappiness, and social chaos created by uncontrolled urban development were not persuasive to those guiding urban governments in Alberta. The power of the land development groups and the public appeal of the idea that land should be developed through an unrestrained free market were so deeply a part of urban life in Alberta before World War I that few arguments could counter them.

THREE

Designing the Modern House

Towards the end of the nineteenth century in North America, an increased need for housing, along with a newly achieved consensus about the cause of disease and methods of ensuring better health, were linked with views about the home's social role to shape the design of houses. For Canadians, American designs were highly influential, although British design was always important as well. Because these changes in house design roughly coincided with mass European settlement in Alberta, settlers could immediately build their first permanent houses using contemporary designs. For those willing to accept and able to afford new ideas, the frontier offered the opportunity to live in a house that was truly modern, progressive, and fashionable.

In Alberta before 1918, the three most widely used house forms can be classified as the bungalow, the foursquare, and the homestead. These forms evolved from North American popular housing, and the North American context is crucial in understanding the influences on house design in Alberta. It has been argued that the design of houses in North America was highly homogeneous after 1918 because house fashions were spread through the operation of a mass commercial culture,[1] but this process was in full swing well before World War I.

While ethnic traditions exerted powerful influence in the design of some houses in Alberta and provided a degree of resistance to the homogenization of domestic architecture, such resistance did not extend beyond the ethnic group in question, whose members were often attracted by the models of domestic architecture portrayed in widely circulated magazines, newspapers, and house pattern books. These designs had the authority of being new, fashionable, and accepted by the dominant cultural group in the society.

Before 1918, many Alberta newspapers subscribed to syndicated services or reprinted articles and floor plans from major American house magazines, such as *Keith's* and *House Beautiful*. After 1912, the *Calgary Herald* regularly printed house plans distributed through syndicated services. Many of these plans were drawn by American architects, but some were drawn by the local architectural firm of Holman and Gotch and by local builders such as William Emery. The *Farm and Ranch Review*, which had wide distribution in rural Alberta, also published house plans reprinted from syndicated services or drawn by Alberta architects and builders. Rural readers could occasionally find syndicated plans and design advice in local newspapers. Most newspapers and magazines providing plans usually supplied blueprints and an instruction sheet at a cost ranging between $5 and $10. Pattern books were widely available in Alberta and while some of the classic American plan books, such as those of Andrew Jackson Downing, were used in the late nineteenth century in Alberta,[2] plans and construction advice carried in magazines or plan books sold by lumber yards and through mail order services were more popular by the early twentieth century.[3]

The availability and attractiveness of published plans ensured that Alberta's domestic architecture developed as part of mainstream North American house design and construction techniques. In this sense, the frontier was obliterated by the spell of the current metropolitan fashions. For example, *Keith's Magazine* popularized the bungalow in the United States during the first decade of the twentieth century,[4] and the bungalow form was immediately picked up by the syndicated services and spread via subscribing newspapers throughout the continent. Local builders, like Samuel Shaw, attempted to meet the public's expectations with designs in the newest fashion. Shaw, an enterprising Calgary builder active just before the first war, designed and built houses throughout southern Alberta. He produced a pattern book called *Shaw's Dominion Bungalow Book* that was marketed in Alberta by some realtors and Crown Lumber Company yards. Plans were sold individually at $20 per sheet or in lots of twenty at $10 per sheet, with the seller receiving a 20 percent commission on the sale. Marketing the bungalow book through realtors was not successful, however, because it was found that house plans were usually "furnished by the contractor who will do the building."[5]

Before World War I, contractors such as D.A. Sinclair in Blairmore and H. Rowe and Company in Claresholm furnished plans and estimates for clients.[6] L. Pollard, an Edmonton carpenter, routinely prepared sketches of houses for presentation to prospective clients and, if hired for the job, charged $15 for drawing up the blueprints.[7] Many builders also purchased and sometimes reworked plans sold by lumber yards; this service was so important for attracting customers that the Western Retail Lumbermen's Association established a central building department in 1916 to draft plans and prepare estimates for lumber yard customers. While the building department drew plans to "any special individualistic ideas" customers might propose, it appears that most plans were stock designs. The overall service was highly popular, and by 1944 the building department had distributed about 10,000 plans in western Canada.[8] While there was a degree of disdain in some circles for houses designed in this way,[9] the lumber yard plans were professionally drawn, while those prepared by builders provided their clients with sketches and plans which, perhaps not of the technical quality of those drawn by most architects, adequately conveyed what the house would look like. In both cases, the plans provided designs that responded directly with recognized house forms that conformed to contemporary taste.

While there were a number of architects practicing in the province, their direct involvement with house building was limited and largely restricted to designing houses for the wealthy, almost all of whom were located in the largest urban centres. Local firms, such as Magoon and MacDonald in Edmonton and Hodgson and Bates in Calgary, designed a number of the largest houses in these cities. By 1908, the latter had designed about 30 houses in Calgary and a few outside the city including the residence of the manager of the Bank of Montreal in Medicine Hat.[10] These houses were often constructed from expensive materials, such as stone and brick, and usually imitated the styles then current with the central Canadian elite. Because of their size and their owners' ability to hire domestic help, they had a number of single purpose rooms such as separate dining and living

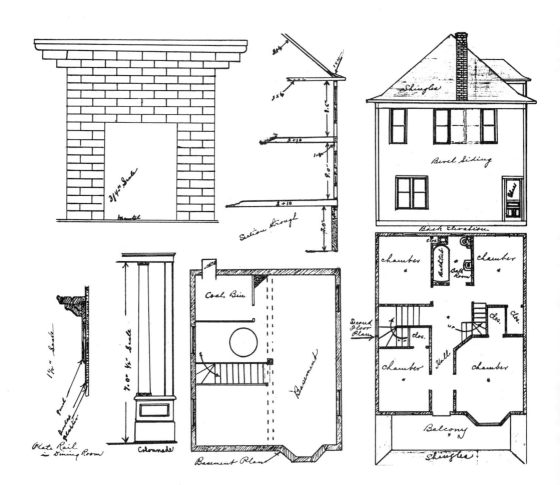

3/4" Scale

Mantel

Section through

Shingles

Bevel Siding

Back Elevation

Plate Rail
in Dining Room

1½" Scale

Rail

Brackets

7.0" ½" Scale

Colonnade

Coal Bin

Basement

Basement Plan

chamber

Bath
Room

chamber

Second
Floor
Plan

clos.

clos. clos.

chamber

Hall

chamber

Balcony

Shingles

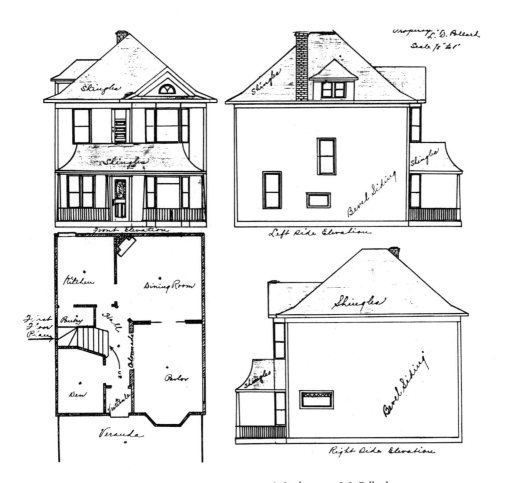

Property L. D. Pollard.
Scale 1/8" to 1'

Shingles

Front Elevation

Left Side Elevation

Shingles

Bevel Siding

Shingles

Kitchen

Dining Room

First Floor Plan

Pantry

Hall

Den

Parlor

Vestibule in Veranda

Veranda

Shingles

Bevel Siding

Shingles

Right Side Elevation

◆ In about 1918, L. Pollard,
an Edmonton carpenter,
drew this plan for a
foursquare inspired
house with a relatively
open plan but he retained
some closed plan features
such as a separate
vestibule. CEA MS 3,
FILE 53, manuscript
source.

rooms, a games room, a library, and a nursery. The houses of the Calgary elite were perhaps the grandest in the province and have been described by Bryan Melnyk as "pretentious, romantically styled mansions" built from sandstone, brick, or, sometimes, wood. Local architects were fully versed in the application of styles popular in such housing elsewhere in the country. Various English revival styles were especially popular in Calgary.[11] The houses of the rich in Edmonton expressed much the same taste, except that brick was used extensively.

It was sometimes suggested that architects should be involved further in house design to encourage the production of ordinary houses incorporating modern sanitary systems and "professional ideas and good taste and style,"[12] but architects in Alberta could not make a living specializing in designing houses. Few people could afford the product or believed that it was needed, given the easy availability of inexpensive mass produced plans whose popularity ensured that one's peers would see them as good and tasteful designs. Thus, the impact of local architects on the designs adopted by house builders was minor compared with the popular print media.

Changes that took place in the layout of houses towards the close of the nineteenth century were an indication that both taste and social habits in North America were changing. Before the turn of the century, most large houses were laid out so that the rooms were self-contained and accessible only through hallways or a foyer. This can be termed a closed plan layout. These plans featured highly differentiated and private spaces, and in two-storey houses this often led to the central placement of the stairwell to divide the interior into two large units which were then further divided into smaller rooms. The resulting layout was both symbolically and functionally restricting and private. It was believed that the rooms and windows of a house should be arranged to provide the family with maximum privacy since "the house is for the use of the family, not for the public or even the near neighbours." Privacy was also served by the reception area where visitors could be received away from the rest of the house or turned away without having caught sight of the living rooms. This spoke, superficially at least, of a degree of restraint and formality which extended even to the family group, as reflected in the rigid separation of rooms according to function. Such plans, with their formal reception area, also served to create an imposing first impression of the house and, by extension, its owners. The function was not only to

IN THE RESIDENTIAL DISTRICTS. EDMONTON 1912

◆ The homes of the wealthy in Edmonton in 1912 featured elements of Tudor and Queen Anne styles. The role of apartments in elite housing is suggested by the inclusion of the Arlington Apartments in the photograph. PAA A4679.

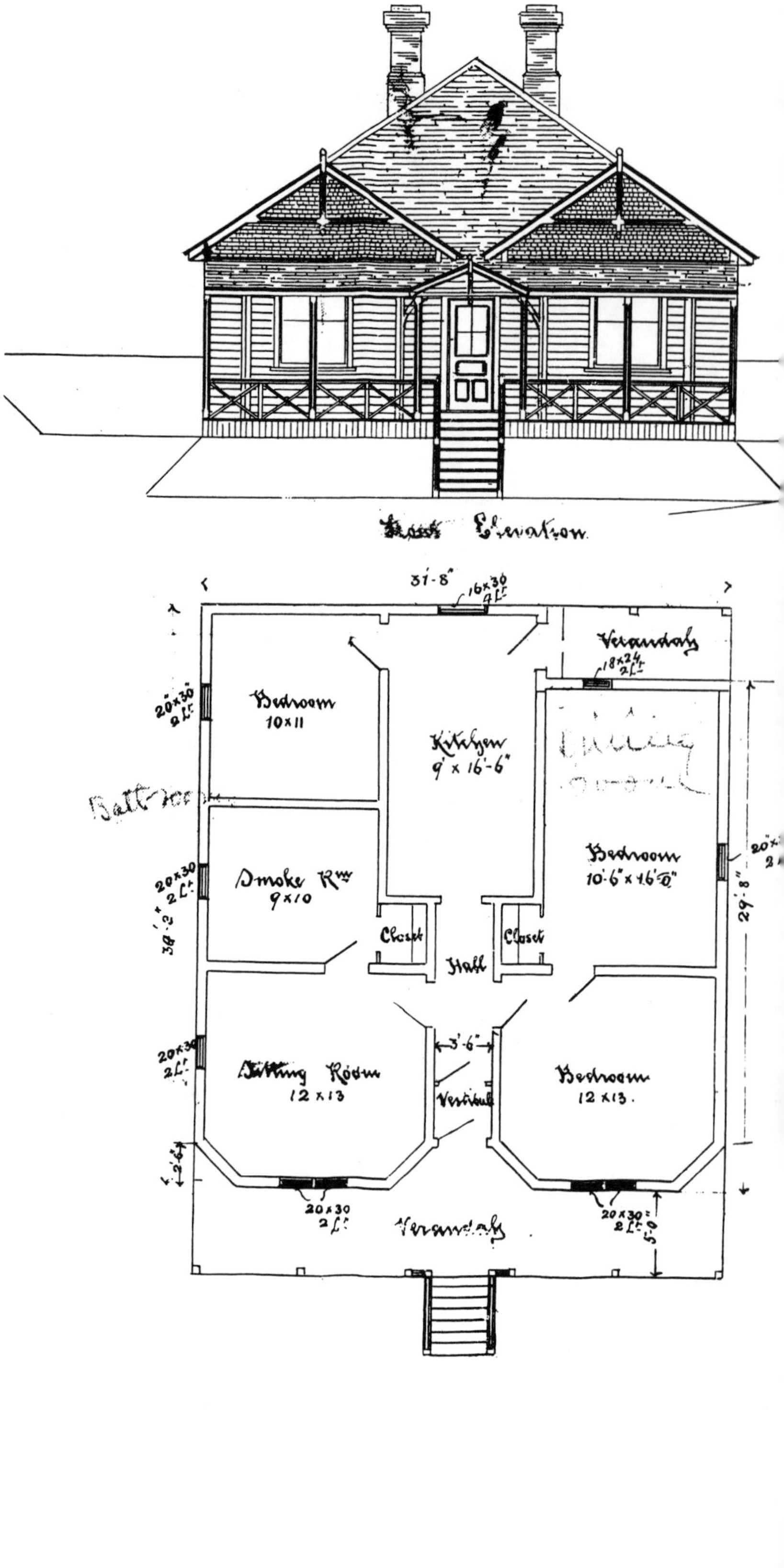

◆ This large 900 square foot closed plan cottage was built at Cochrane in the 1880s. GAI M421 manuscript source.

East Elevation.

31'-8"   16×30
          9 L

Verandah
          18×24
          2 L

20×30   Bedroom
9 L   10×11

          Kitchen
          9' × 16'-6"

Batt ⟶

20×30   Smoke R m
2 L   9×10

          Bedroom
          10'-6" × 16'-0"

          Closet   Closet

          Hall

20×30   Sitting Room   Bedroom
2 L   12×13   12×13.

          ⟵3'-6"⟶

          Vestibule

20×30   20×30
2 L   2 L.

          Verandah.

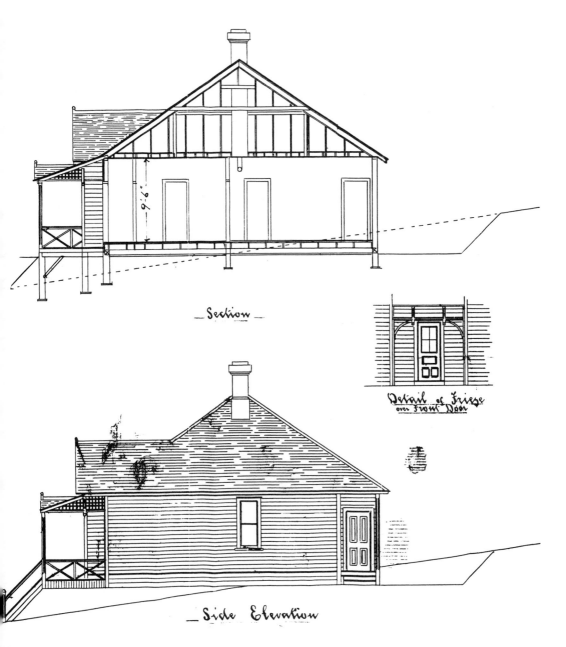

Section

Detail of Frieze
over Front Door

Side Elevation

Scale ⅛" = 1 foot.

impress visitors and restrict access; it was also to extend hospitality to invited guests. A "wide, inviting and prominent entrance augers a hospitable reception to the approaching guest" and provided comfort and shelter upon arrival.[13] There were more pragmatic benefits as well. Large entrance spaces made furniture moving easier, an important consideration in an age of heavy furniture, and helped to keep the house warm by preventing cold air from rushing directly into the living areas through the open door.[14] Smaller and single storey nineteenth century houses could not, of course, utilize such layouts to their utmost, but they tended, when possible, to separate space and make rooms autonomous.

OPEN PLAN HOUSES

By the 1880s in the United States, the interiors of many upper class suburban houses were becoming more open. They featured interconnected living spaces, in which rooms were "defined but not enclosed," and the placement of "walls, windows and columns produced some of the vistas of modern open planning."[15] By the early twentieth century, the layout of smaller houses, especially one-storey houses, began to change radically as well. With the exception of the kitchen and bedrooms, formal rooms with specific uses were replaced with open plans in which the living room, dining room, and reception area were interconnected to make a relatively continuous space that could be used for family gatherings, entertainment, and the routines of daily life. This amalgamation of the reception area with the living room meant that anyone standing in the entrance area could glimpse most of the main floor of the house. Yet the distinctions among living spaces were not abolished entirely; rooms were separated by large archways or square openings that provided some functional definition. Commonly, sliding or glass doors were installed in these openings to permit the rooms to be closed off if desired. Although sliding doors were expensive and took up space since they required thick walls, they were reassuring to skeptics of the open plan. They proved to be a transitional device and by 1912 their installation was discouraged because so few people used them.[16]

The open plan layout was the most influential concept of the age for small house design. It was particularly suited to small houses and a boon to the growing number of people who demanded modern, well designed houses but could afford only modest dwellings. Open plans were not restricted to very small houses. They were widely used in middle class housing by the turn of the century, and closed plans appeared mainly in very large houses. By 1909, nineteenth century closed plans, as well as styles such as Queen Anne and Second Empire, were described by one critic as "weird fancies" that rejected domesticity and reflected a time when "our habitation was more an abode than a home, built without consideration of its environments, poorly planned and unsanitary." All that was gone, for society had passed to a "higher plane." Progress was thus expressed in the modern house which was "more *en suite*, more livable" than the old system of box-like rooms and "more like what the name of 'home' implies."[17] Such notions had special attraction in Alberta because of its recent settlement and rapid growth. In 1910 it was argued that "we are just beginning to build homes in Edmonton; up to the present we have just been making houses." A "home," which was associated with companionship, memories, leisure, and refuge, was difficult to achieve in so "mercenary" a city, although "in time out here we will shake down to loving the land, not its market price."[18] In such an environment, a house layout that promised an instant "home-like" environment and a sense of permanency was immediately attractive. As early as 1890, such houses were held to be peculiar to North America where fewer servants and less concentrated wealth demanded more "careful and scientific planning" than was required elsewhere, for example, as in Britain where house plans tended to be "careless and diffuse" because of cheap domestic labour.[19] The open plan concept was said to derive much of its virtue from North American pragmatism, and it was categorically stated in 1915 that "no dwelling can be termed successful unless it is built according to need rather than precedent."[20] Thus, modernity in housing expressed progress and a gradual evolution towards greater mastery of the environment.

PRINCIPLES OF DESIGN

It was the nineteenth century English architectural critic, John Ruskin, who was often cited as the inspiration for this change. Canadian housebuilders were told in 1909 that the basic principles of design for small houses should be Ruskin's ideas of "truth, simplicity in. . . . lines and construction," "harmony in proportion," and a "sense of space in interior arrangements."[21] Such design meant "simplicity," "truthfulness," "honesty," and "purposefulness" rather than the mere absence of decoration; an idea close to much of the Craftsman style which stressed naturalness in materials and construction.[22] The itch to decorate so common in the late nineteenth century had also found expression in Alberta where decorations derived from Gothic style, such as fretworked bargeboards, and Queen Anne style features, such as cupolas and turrets, had been added to otherwise plain houses. In the United States after 1900, there was a trend away from such decoration and towards what Gwendolyn Smith in her history of American housing has termed the "minimal" house—a functional and efficient house without frills or unpractical decoration.[23] By 1910 such ideas had become orthodox in Alberta and "useless" house decoration such as fretworked bargeboards and turrets were downplayed because they obscured the line and workmanship of the house. Such architectural "honesty" appealed to many people in Alberta, coinciding with their political and social attitudes that held frugality and pragmatism to be virtues and pretension a sin. Many would have agreed with the Albertan who, in 1912, advised people to reject gingerbread bargeboards which represented "money worse than wasted." They looked bad when installed and "worse when the pieces break or the paint wears off." Similarly, turret rooms were "unbearably cold in winter and insufferably hot in summer." The best rule was that "the prettiest house is always the house of simplest lines." Indeed, gingerbread and other useless features were merely a plot by carpenters to make money from a gullible public.[24] Such warnings suggest that simplicity was justified as a cost saving measure, an especially important consideration at the turn of the century when lumber costs were rising rapidly.[25] Nonetheless, the power of fashion to change aesthetic judgements was also important. As was noted in 1910, "all the best houses now-a-days" in Alberta had no decoration even though "a few years ago we thought a house looked bare and plain without 'turned' ornaments." Now, "all things are as straight and simple as can be made."[26] While highly decorated houses continued to be built in Alberta until the end of the war, fashionable small houses by then usually featured simple exteriors.

Simple lines did not mean a total absence of decoration, especially in the interior. Some decoration was permissible as long as it was honest and related to function. As one Calgary architect phrased it in 1912, "decorate construction rather than construct decoration."[27] However, exposed beams, which usually served no structural pur-

◆ This otherwise simple
frame cottage in Ed-
monton used a complex
roof as a decorative fea-
ture. Undated but from
sometime before 1904.
PAA B4608.

◆ A modified homestead
house with cupola, Bow-
den, early 1900s.
PAA H795.

◆ This homestead house at the Shapka farm in east central Alberta was photographed in 1918. Such Gothic decorations were by this time un-fashionable. PAA UV558.

◆ This 1913 Edmonton bungalow with its simple, clean lines reflected a trend away from highly decorated exteriors. PAA B4676.

pose, were not seen as violating the principle of simplicity and honesty because they symbolized the strength and protection afforded by the family home. Fireplaces were also considered essential. The availability of stoves and furnaces made a fireplace unnecessary as a primary source of heat, but it was vital for projecting a sense of cosiness and as a focus for family life by radiating "warmth and cheer to those who sit around it on a winter's night."[28] It was an appeal to a popular domestic symbol of the past when the family had supposedly gathered around "great fireplaces" and life had been simple and direct.[29] Thus, the popularity of fireplaces, beamed ceilings, and the open plan demonstrated a belief that the house should facilitate family interaction. The living room was characterized as the centre of "home life" and the "workshop where brain and body are built up and renewed."[30] Living rooms were designed to be the "most. . . . livable room in the house,"[31] and house designs that promised cosiness, happy family life, and stability were highly popular.

BUNGALOWS

Before World War I, the bungalow was seen to fit these needs best and it became, for a time, the most popular small house form. Having evolved from Bengali prototypes, bungalows have a complicated pedigree but owe much to the arts and crafts movement. In North America they were simple houses that seemed to confirm the rejection of nineteenth century domestic architecture and the triumph of pragmatism and social purpose. Bungalows became popular in California at the turn of the century and by 1910 had become common in British Columbia and as far east as Edmonton. Their popularity continued to increase in the next decade, and in 1917 it was reported that in Grande Prairie, then a frontier village, "bungalows and cottages are springing up all over town," showing that people there were "rapidly acquiring a taste for beautiful well kept homes."[32] By 1920, bungalows had gained acceptance throughout western Canada. They were relatively small houses, in the range of 800 to 1,000 square feet. They employed a wide variety of low-slung roofs and borrowed decorations from a widely varied range of styles, including Spanish colonial, Craftsman, Swiss, and Tudor. Accordingly, the bungalow form was defined not by specific stylistic characteristics but by functional qualities such as "artful simplicity, efficient interior plan, adaptability and harmony with the surrounding landscape." In California, this produced a low-slung single storey house of horizontal lines with wide projecting eaves, large porches, plenty of windows, no basement, and use of "natural" materials.[33] As their popularity spread elsewhere, however, their design and construction evolved to meet the "weather stresses" of places such as Canada.[34] These adaptations included glassed porches, basements, steeper pitched roofs, shallower, overhanging eaves, and sometimes a half storey was added to make what was popularly called a semi bungalow. In many cases, these changes continued to draw inspiration from popular interpretation of arts and crafts ideas about the use of natural materials and concepts of design. Thus, due to their low profile, their use of warm materials such as brick, wood shingle, or stucco, and their integration with the landscape through their horizontal lines, bungalows retained their reputation as the embodiment of cosiness and domesticity.[35] If a house stressed these features, it popularly was called a "bungalow"; often any small house was so described.

While there was no standard interior plan for bungalows, all were laid out on an open plan with the bedrooms grouped around a large living/dining area, which was either a single room or two rooms divided minimally with arches or built-in features such as low shelves. The kitchens were small and located at the rear of the house. Some "more pretentious" bungalows had totally separate dining rooms, although this was unusual.[36] The bungalow avoided using vestibules, parlours, and pantries and applied efficient design and extensive use of built-in furniture and cupboards in an effort to increase livable interior space.[37] Bungalows were important in popularizing the open plan throughout North America and confirming its reputation as a modern and fashionable layout that brought the benefits of efficient planning even to small homes.

Due to their simplicity, bungalows were said to be inexpensive to build. Framing and installation of services such as heating and plumbing were straight forward in a one-storey house, and, since services were increasingly important, the cost advantage of installing them in bungalows was used as a selling point. Builders were also advised that the open plan appealed to women since it was "the very embodiment of cosiness, an attribute that appeals forcefully to the average woman." Reportedly, women were also attracted by the ease with which an open plan bungalow could be cleaned.[38] The reality of bungalow life was often quite different than promised by these promotional claims. Their small size meant that noise could be a problem, and

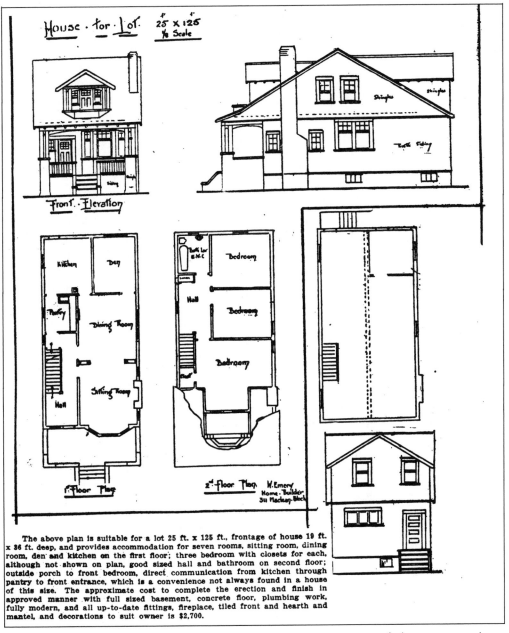

Front Elevation

House for lot 25 × 125 ⅛ Scale

1ˢᵗ Floor Plan

2ⁿᵈ Floor Plan

W. Emery
Home Builder
311 Mackeop Block

The above plan is suitable for a lot 25 ft. x 125 ft., frontage of house 19 ft. x 36 ft. deep, and provides accommodation for seven rooms, sitting room, dining room, den and kitchen on the first floor; three bedroom with closets for each, although not shown on plan, good sized hall and bathroom on second floor; outside porch to front bedroom, direct communication from kitchen through pantry to front entrance, which is a convenience not always found in a house of this size. The approximate cost to complete the erection and finish in approved manner with full sized basement, concrete floor, plumbing work, fully modern, and all up-to-date fittings, fireplace, tiled front and hearth and mantel, and decorations to suit owner is $2,700.

◆ A seven-room semi bungalow designed for a narrow lot in 1912 by W. Emery, a Calgary builder. The house was estimated to cost $2,700, excluding land. *Calgary Herald*, May 20, 1912.

they were not always as easy to keep clean and tidy as was said. It was soon discovered that small open plan living areas, especially for families with children, required constant tidying. Moreover, by World War I, the claim that bungalows were inexpensive to construct was being challenged in the United States where it was found that they were more costly to build on a square foot basis than two-storey houses.[39]

The disadvantages of the one-storey bungalow were sometimes overcome through the addition of a half storey, producing a hybrid called the semi bungalow. The addition of the extra floor meant a partial reworking of the definition of the bungalow form, but its essential characteristics of coziness, simplicity, efficiency, and integration with the landscape were retained. Semi bungalows had become popular by 1914 and featured wide projecting eaves, a shallow, sweeping gable roof and a horizontal appearance. Second floor windows were situated in the gable end and dormers were often built to admit further light. This design was seen to offer some important advantages over single storey bungalows as well as other kinds of houses. It was believed to be cost effective because all or most of the attic space was used for bedrooms. While the slant of the roof reduced the living space on the second floor, the useable area was expanded through dormers and by using the low areas around the perimeter as closet and storage space. The low roof line of the semi bungalow was attractive to those who feared cyclones which, according to one commentator, were "the 'bogey-man' of all new settlers" on the prairies.[40]

HOMESTEAD AND FOURSQUARE HOUSES

Bungalows and semi bungalows were not the only or even the dominant house form in Alberta before 1918. Even commoner were the homestead house and the foursquare house, which, in John Warkentin's opinion, were the characteristic permanent house forms on the prairies before 1920.[41] Homestead houses, also called temple homestead houses in the United States, were simple rectangular houses ranging from one- to two-and-half and sometimes even three-storeys in height. They had a gable roof, usually running back to front, and sometimes side gables were also included, especially on one-and-a-half storey versions. Normally, they also had a verandah or a large porch on the front. All were narrow houses suitable for small urban lots, which before 1918 in Alberta were often 25

◆ An example of the popularity of two-storey homestead houses and semi bungalows, Red Deer, 1920. PAA A6249.

◆ L. Pollard, Edmonton, drew this plan for a homestead house on an open plan sometime between 1914 and 1918. CEA MS3, FILE 32, manuscript source.

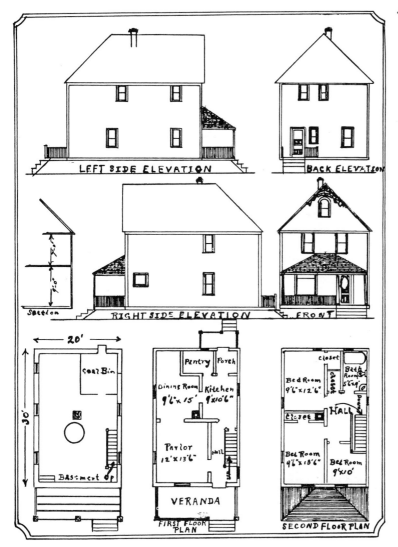

LEFT SIDE ELEVATION

BACK ELEVATION

RIGHT SIDE ELEVATION

FRONT

Section

Coal Bin

Basement op

Pantry   Porch

Dining Room   Kitchen
9'6"x 15'   9'x10'6"

Parlor
12'x13'6"

Hall

VERANDA

FIRST FLOOR
PLAN

closet

Bed Room
9'6"x12'6"

Bath
Room
5'x4'

closet   HALL

Closet

Bed Room
9'6"x13'6"

Bed Room
9'x10'

SECOND FLOOR PLAN

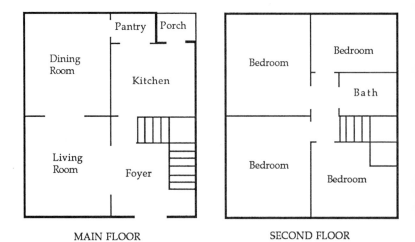

◆ Plan of a foursquare house, 85 Avenue, Edmonton, built in 1912.

MAIN FLOOR   SECOND FLOOR

◆ A small foursquare cottage with a back porch, Edmonton, 1910.
PAA A4744.

◆ A large foursquare house built of stone or cement block, Carstairs. Photographed in 1918.
PAA P3460.

feet wide. Even when land was not a consideration, such as on farms or larger lots, the form was usually unchanged, although the house was often enlarged with an addition at the end or at the side to produce a T or L shape. On narrow urban lots, enlargement of the house usually consisted of a lean-to at the back. By 1910, the layout of a typical two-storey homestead house reflected the influence of the open plan. Because such houses were usually laid out from front to back along the narrowest side, there was usually a small reception area which was relatively closed off from the rest of the house and linked by a narrow side hallway to the kitchen. The stairs to the second storey ran up from the reception area, usually along the wall. In some cases, the reception area was completely isolated and became a rather cramped entrance foyer. The living room and dining room opened into each other on a simple open plan, an arrangement that represented a transitional layout between the closed room layout of the nineteenth century and the open plan popularized by the bungalow. In very small versions, such layouts were impractical and the kitchen and the dining area were often combined into a single room, with the living room a totally separate room.[42]

The other dominant form of house was the one- or two-storey foursquare, so called because of its square shape, usually with a hip roof. It became a popular form in North America during the 1890s and was built widely in Alberta before World War I. Like the homestead house, the foursquare was suitable for small urban lots, but its shape also permitted its use for large and grand houses. Foursquares were solid looking houses, projecting a sort of modest dignity. In the common two-storey versions, the interiors typically consisted of three to four equal sized rooms on the main floor with the bathroom and bedrooms on the second floor. As in homestead houses, the stairs to the second storey and to the basement were located on the side, although in larger versions, a central stairwell was often featured. Because of the square shape, open plans were easy to apply in two-storey foursquare houses, and they often featured a more open plan than that found in homestead houses. Typically, the reception area of a two-storey foursquare was clearly linked by means of arches or glass or sliding doors to the living and the dining room areas which opened into each other. In small single storey versions (often called cottages), the same limitations of space found in one-storey homestead houses often resulted in a combined kitchen and dining room and separate living room.[43]

Elements of various styles were applied to the exteriors of both the homestead and foursquare forms. By 1910, when the traditional accoutrements of bargeboards and ridge decorations had disappeared, exterior decoration of homestead houses had become unusual, although subtle stylistic influences were apparent. Elements of Georgian styles with fluted or plain boxed columns supporting the verandahs, Craftsman influences with bracketed eaves, and, among others, Dutch colonial influences, which most often meant a gambrel roof, were also commonly applied. When the longest side of the house was turned to the street, elements of colonial styles were sometimes applied. All of these embellishments went in and out of fashion and were justified by contemporary trends in design, but the homestead form was sufficiently flexible to accommodate various stylistic influences so that its owners maintained a sense of being stylish and contemporary. The decorative potential of the foursquare form was even greater than that of homestead forms. There were a plethora of colonial revival styles that were appropriate to foursquare houses, especially various Georgian influences with symetrical facades. Tudor influences were also popularly applied to foursquare houses, which meant the use of half timbered effects, and windows with small panes, giving what was thought to be a homey look. In Alberta, peaking in about 1912, Craftsman influences were also applied to two-and-a-half-storey square houses.[44]

Many of these houses were adaptations, on a modest level, of those favoured by the upper classes. Michael Doucet and John Weaver have commented that in North America until about 1900,

> plans for inexpensive houses seem to have been scaled-down versions of more grandiose inventions. The cheapest dwellings had the outward form of abridged rectangular gothic cottages stripped of decoration. Somewhat larger dwellings were tall and angular, some looking like transplanted farm houses and others like scaled down versions of the Queen Anne style.[45]

After 1900, however, small two-storey houses tended to become less imitative, although the elements of formal styles continued to be used. Yet this rarely influenced interior layout, and one commonly found houses of identical layout but totally different exterior stylistic influences. Indeed, an architect's skill was supposedly shown if he could take a foursquare or homestead form, and without altering the layout, create a distinctively different exterior appearance by changing the roof type and exterior decoration and finish.

CHOOSING A HOUSE FORM

The reasons why people chose one house over another were varied and are now difficult to determine. Small one-storey bungalows or small cottages based on a homestead or foursquare form could meet a wide range of needs. Bungalows in particular also had the sanction of being new, fashionable, and progressive. Their size made effective use of small urban lots, a benefit commonly stressed in their promotion in Alberta. Although their cost per square foot was higher than for two-storey houses, their total cost was less simply because of their size, appealing to people with lower or average incomes. Full two-storey houses were, however, consistently popular before the end of World War I. Familiarity, both by carpenters and owners, probably played an important part in their popularity, and they were attractive to settlers who yearned for a familiar, traditional, and yet contemporary home. On both farms and in the city, two-storey houses were large enough for family needs and provided good separation between living and sleeping areas not always possible with bungalows. In the city, these benefits were reinforced because they suited relatively small lots. Further, they were said to be inexpensive to build on a square foot basis because they provided efficient use of space, and their cost advantage was said to be even greater after the turn of the century when important changes had taken place in the methods of installing services. They were reputed to be easy to heat and were thought to have good ventilation in the second storey bedrooms.[46]

With the exception of good ventilation on the second floor, most of the advantages of full two-storey houses were also thought to apply to all one-and-a-half storey houses. In 1913, the reputed wind resistance of a one-and-a-half storey house was an important advantage for one Alberta correspondent in the *Farm and Ranch Review* who argued that it was the ideal Alberta farm house. His general principle was to "build according to climate and country." He advised that the number of windows on the west and north of the house should be minimized because "our coldest winds are from those quarters during the winter." He also preferred sleeping rooms to be well separated from the living/dining area since this was "more sanitary than having all on one floor as in a cottage." Especially during winter, "we cannot have all the fresh air in our homes as we would like," but with bedrooms on a second floor, "one can air, sweep and clean without disturbing the lower part of the house." He further recommended an open living/dining area measuring about 18-by-16 feet, which would be suitable for farm life and for those times when "eight or ten drop in on us for meals when least expected." His final suggestion was for an unpretentious house. "We do not need elaborate homes out here," he argued, "a house finished off in pine is good enough for the average farmer" and, if well painted, it looked very "neat and clean."[47]

The belief that the rigours of the climate, social needs, and the demands of day to day living would be served by a one-and-a-half storey house, and at an affordable price, was shared by many other Albertans who aspired to own one. Further, the concern that house design encourage efficiency and sanitation represented an important issue for many, although not all would have agreed that a one-and-a-half storey house was the only route to satisfying such needs.

APPLYING MODERNITY: PLUMBING AND SANITATION

At the same time that sewer and water systems were beginning to be installed in Alberta towns and cities, plumbing methods were undergoing radical changes. Before the 1890s, each fixture had a separate vent and separate drainage pipes.[48] Even in the simplest installation, this created a snarl of pipes and vents which was hidden behind woodwork. By the turn of the century this approach had been replaced with a single stack system which, in terms of efficiency and cost, was revolutionary because all traps were vented to the roof and all fixtures were "located directly at the line. . . . or within very few feet" of it. The single stack provided good flushing action and was inexpensive to install and maintain. Plumbers were said to oppose it, supposedly because it was cheaper to install and maintain than the old system of separate vents. At the same time, galvanized iron was beginning to be used instead of lead piping. Traditionally, plumbers had worked in lead, even owing their name to the metal, but North Americans began rejecting lead piping in houses by the late 1890s. This was based on a fear of poisoning, which was dismissed by plumbers and other experts as groundless. Nevertheless, the public had its way, and while lead continued to be used in some plumbing applications because it was relatively inert, it was no longer commonly used for pipes carrying water. By 1903, the city of Edmonton stipulated that sewer piping inside buildings be made of cast iron with leaded and caulked joints.[49] Since the greatest number of prewar houses in Alberta were built after 1900, it is probable that Alberta plumbers mainly worked with cast iron and single venting.

The single stack system significantly affected the layout of houses. In single storey houses it became customary to place the kitchen and the bathroom adjacent to one another so that plumbing fixtures could be grouped around the main drainage stack. In houses with a second floor, the bathroom was placed directly above the kitchen for the same reason. Although such rules tended to make layout static, the system's simplicity and the savings it represented in installation, maintenance, and repair fully justified its use. Fears about sewer gas, a widespread phobia in the late nineteenth century, also influenced plumbing and the location of bathrooms.[50] It was held that bathroom fixtures should never be located in bedrooms, and some experts argued that the toilet should be located away from other bathroom fixtures, in a ventilated room by itself, but the popularity of this approach was short lived since it was awkward and took up space. By the turn of the century, it was customary in small houses to locate all bathroom fixtures in one room with a window for ventilation. At the same time, it was believed that all pipes should be exposed to allow air to circulate freely around them to kill germs and facilitate repair and detection of breaks that might release sewer gas.[51] Thus, the convention of enclosing all piping with woodwork was abandoned, and by 1915 the installation of cupboards beneath the bathroom sink was discouraged because they only became "receptacles of all kinds of rubbish which collect dirt and dust." Indeed, it was held that dirt around concealed pipes and under enclosed fixtures was as dangerous as sewer gas.[52] Cleanliness was further ensured by the design of bathroom fixtures. Tubs and sinks were available in metal that could be painted, or in enameled cast iron, or, most expensive, in porcelain. Of these products, enamelled cast iron fixtures were typically installed in "modern houses" in Alberta by 1912.[53]

While sanitation and bathroom design were widely discussed in Alberta, it is apparent that mainly middle and upper class urban houses built before 1914 had fully equipped bathrooms. Poorer dwellings had less sophisticated facilities. In the 1890s, one half of Calgary residents had no piped-in water in their houses and used outdoor privies and cesspools.[54] Conditions had changed little by 1903, when it was recommended that the city build public baths because people were "compelled either to resort to all kinds of secret ablutionary devices, or else refrain altogether from washing themselves."[55] By World War I, many houses in Edmonton and Calgary were still not connected to water and sewer systems. This situation also existed in other towns fortunate enough to have a water or sewer system at all.[56] Many medium-sized towns were only then installing water and sewer systems, and, at the end of the war, such systems were still absent in many small towns.[57]

Farm houses rarely had modern sanitation systems, which led some to accuse farmers of being slovenly and ignorant. In 1917, the *Calgary Herald* claimed that "there is no good reason. . . . why in the shack of the western settler the ordinary means of sanitation should not be observed." The high incidence of tuberculosis in rural areas was therefore considered to be the farmers' fault. Thomas Adams of the Commission of Conservation was more balanced in his conclusion in 1918 that health standards could not be maintained in rural Alberta because medical care and "other necessaries of life" were so disorganized.[58] In any case, low population density lessened the health threat from sewage on farms in comparison to that in urban areas. Moreover, some people thought that poor farm sanitation was mitigated by the amount of time farmers spent outdoors in the fresh air and sunlight, enabling them to ward off disease better than their urban fellows who spent too much time indoors.[59]

In the early twentieth century, water for domestic purposes on farms was secured in the same way as in many towns: it was carried from ponds, rivers and wells, rainwater was caught in barrels, and snow was melted in the winter. Water was "one of the hardships of life in the west" since it was often alkaline and "scarce and bad in many places."[60] Further, shallow hand-dug wells often became polluted with surface run-off. Most farms had only outdoor privies or indoor chemical toilets because, it was commonly charged, farmers willingly spent money for labour saving devices for the farm itself but not for household sanitary improvements.[61] Farmers were advised to connect eavestroughs to a cistern in the basement to collect pure water and to install a septic tank system drained by gravity into a tile field. Few farms in Alberta had such conveniences; many farm houses did not have basements, let alone cisterns, and septic tanks were labour intensive since they had to be cleaned. Moreover, it was argued that tile fields were unworkable since they had to be broken up and relocated every two or three years because of the heavy soils in most of the province. Thus, most farm houses continued to use outdoor privies or indoor chemical toilets and, in two-storey farm houses of contemporary design, the bathroom was often relocated to the main floor to eliminate carrying water upstairs and reduce the effort of emptying the chemical toilet.[62]

KITCHENS

In the late nineteenth century, it was believed that the kitchen should be well separated from the living and sleeping areas of the house to keep cooking smells and the heat from the stove from carrying throughout the house. On farms, the kitchen was often abandoned altogether during the summer and the stove was moved out to a "summer kitchen" located on the porch or in a separate building. Late nineteenth century kitchens tended to be large rooms in which at least one daily meal was eaten. In 1897, a kitchen, of about the same measurements as would be popular a decade later, was believed to be so small that it would irritate anyone who had to work in it. [63]

By 1910, the trend was rapidly shifting towards much smaller and, theoretically, more efficient kitchens. In keeping with the view that housekeeping should be a profession, the new compact kitchen replicated in its design the ethos of the factory. The stove, sink, and work surface should be placed close together to speed up the work and minimize the worker's movements. All activities unrelated to cooking and food preparation should be excluded from the room. Indeed, little other activity was possible since a kitchen measuring about 10-by-12 feet overall plus a pantry was considered "plenty large enough." [64] These changes were predicated upon a modern technological infrastructure. In 1910, it was said that the "modern" kitchen should have electricity, running hot and cold water and a sink and drain that were useable "even in winter." The kitchen should be a small room in order to save steps and make cleaning easy and efficient. In a larger house, food should be stored in a pantry with plenty of shelves, cupboards, and a work surface. [65] The pantry should have a window that could admit fresh air and cool the room, and both the pantry and kitchen required as many shelves and cupboards as could be fitted in. In keeping with the image of the factory, the cupboards should be highly specialized; for example, a spice cupboard should be shallow, "so nothing was behind anything else." The cupboards should run "from floor to ceiling" so that dust could not get "either under them or on top of them." They should be fitted with glass doors so "the housewife could see each article in its place and lay her hand on it without hunting and hunting." [66] In 1915, the kitchen cupboard was called, admittedly by a man, the "delight of womankind." [67] Since mechanical refrigeration was impractical, it was advised that a cold room be built in the basement and, if possible, connected to the kitchen by a dumb-waiter. Alternately, space should be allowed in the kitchen for an ice-box.[68]

The new small kitchens saved "miles and miles" of steps and conserved the housewife's strength for her other tasks. The family was banned from eating any meals in the kitchen, which, as the Lethbridge Women's Congress was told in 1912, allowed the woman to have a small efficient kitchen in which to accomplish her work.[69] Socializing in the kitchen was "out" and efficiency was "in," a fact that made a separate dining area desirable. G.R. Major, a Calgary architect, observed in 1912 that the dining room and the kitchen should be close together and "not separated by long passages as is the custom in countries where domestic help is not quite so difficult to obtain."[70] Further efficiencies could be had by use of a serving window, placed between the kitchen and the dining room, through which food and dishes could be passed.

The room in which food was prepared obviously called for the highest standards of cleanliness. Linoleum or tile floors were ideal because they could be cleaned easily.[71] All plumbing should be open, as in the bathroom, so dirt could not accumulate around the pipes. Sinks should be of porcelain or enamelled cast iron, which were easy to clean, and boiling water and washing soda should be poured down the drain at least once a week to keep them clean and free running.[72] Atmosphere was also important, and since the housewife spent so much time washing dishes, there should be a window above the sink so she could look "into the sunshine" and her garden. It was suggested that the kitchen be painted in pastel colours and "dark and fussy wallpapers" be avoided because "color affects the nerves, the nerves affect the digestion, and that's where health lies."[73]

Kitchen design was a frequent topic of discussion at women's congresses, meetings of organizations like the Women's Institutes, and in the educational programmes run by the Alberta Department of Agriculture. Much of this discussion was little more than fantasy, and perhaps a plea by women that their role in the home be taken seriously, although most middle and upper class urban homes of the period would have had many of the modern features. Other people, however, could not afford such kitchens, and renovating to meet modern standards and introduce services was expensive. For a farm, a light plant for electricity, a water system and a gasoline motor would have cost about $1,000 in 1912, and to this had to be added the cost of renovation and maintenance.[74] Such capital expenditures exceeded many annual incomes at the time, and, for the majority of people who lived in small houses, it was unrealistic and even foolish to talk about glass-doored ceiling to floor cupboards, running water, and other conveniences. Since many city houses were not connected to water and sewage systems by 1913, modern efficiencies were automatically excluded. Capital costs and house size further limited modern kitchen design because many small single storey houses combined the kitchen and dining room into a single room. In many homes lacking a pantry or a finished basement, food was stored wherever it would fit, often in a dug-out cellar, "devoid of light or ventilation."[75] Without connections to a sewage system, kitchen scraps were fed to the animals in the back yard or dumped in the yard or lane. Although electricity was available in some places in Alberta as early as 1890, it only became typical in urban houses by World War I and in rural houses after World War II. While the homes of the wealthier in the large urban centres had electricity by 1910, it was used primarily for lighting, despite its great potential for other applications in the home.

FLOOR AND WALL FINISHES

Traditionally, floors were of unfinished planking or tongue and groove wood, frequently covered with carpets tacked down around the edges and at seams. Frequent cleaning of carpets was necessary, and although it was a major task to lift and clean them and to wash the floor beneath, "sanitation requires that it be done."[76] By the 1890s, preferences in floor treatment were shifting towards finished floors that were easier to clean. Especially popular was flooring made of maple, and during the 1890s a greatly increased number of mills in Canada produced it.[77] These hardwood floors were highly waxed, creating a smooth finish that would not hold dust and germs, and were covered with area carpets that could be taken outside for airing and cleaning. This was more sanitary and also "decidedly better looking" than plain boards covered with carpet.[78] As one Alberta woman proudly reported in 1910, there "is nothing so easy to take care of as hardwood floors with a few light rugs which can be easily taken up and shaken. Nowhere, unless it were on the stairs, where one is apt to slip, would I have a yard of carpet."[79]

For those who could not afford hardwood floors covered with area rugs, floor boards were stained and waxed, painted with enamel, or covered with linoleum, which was available and inexpensive by 1910. Some suggested that linoleum be waxed or varnished to make it easier

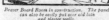

◆◆ Wallboard was easy to install and was reputed to be a hygienic wall finish. *Farm and Ranch Review,* Nov. 5, 1913 and Oct. 20, 1911.

to clean, but it did not need scrubbing as did plank floors since a "simple wipe" would do.[80] Linoleum was especially useful in the bathroom and kitchen where floors needed to be waterproof to prevent germs and dampness from building up. At the turn of the century, bathroom floors were sometimes covered with carpeting, although by 1912 this "fortunately. . . . is a thing of the past." Also dangerous were plain wood floors which became a breeding ground for germs.[81] While linoleum or paint provided sanitary and sound bathroom floor finishes, for those who could afford it, ceramic tile was best because it was durable, easy to clean, and "germ proof."[82]

Wall finishes also began to change in response to concerns about sanitation. Lath and plaster walls were often papered, but such a finish presented problems for people concerned with cleanliness. Warnings were given that the rough surface of the paper as well as the wallpaper paste harboured millions of germs. There were many folk remedies for cleaning wallpaper, but all were labour intensive and often risky. Washing with an antiseptic or fumigation with sulfur were two methods, but these practices often bleached the colour from the paper. Wallpaper was sometimes varnished to make it easier to clean, but, more often, dirty paper was simply covered with a clean layer—a common task given the grime produced by burning coal, wood, and petroleum for heating and lighting.[83] While some believed it to be unsanitary, given the alternatives, covering old paper with new remained a common choice.

The commonest alternatives to wallpaper were paint and wallboard. Lath and plaster walls could be painted if the workmanship was good, or flock paper could be glued onto the plaster and painted. Paint was often used in bathrooms and kitchens, but not in other rooms because it came only in high gloss finishes or in enamel.[84] A washable matte finish could be produced by applying three layers of paint, each successively diluted with turpentine, but a commoner approach was to use water soluble "wall powders" like kalsomine or alabastine. These were inexpensive enough that they could "be renewed very often," which, in practical terms, was necessary because they flaked off and were unwashable.[85] The other option was various wallboard products that were manufactured in large standard size sheets. Some were laminated wood and plaster with a fibre board finish, others, like Beaver Board, were fibre board that could be painted, while still others, like "Neponset," came ready-finished in various finishes. Wallboard provided a sturdy, smooth wall, and when the seams were covered with strips of wood, it presented a well-finished appearance. It also provided some insulation and was believed to be sanitary because it had a smooth continuous surface and the bonding agent used in its production was a "germicide." In addition to its decorative and sanitary potential, wallboard could be put up easily by anyone, unlike lath and plaster which was a highly skilled craft that almost always called for hired workers.[86]

VENTILATION, SUNLIGHT, AND HEATING

Sunlight and ventilation were essential throughout the house and features enhancing them were commonly advertised in the early twentieth century. It was thought that living rooms should be placed to gain the greatest amount of sunlight, although the convention that the living room face the street was almost never varied in urban housing. Since a verandah was useable less than half the year on the prairies, a sun room was said to be a better alternative.[87] Another suggestion for light, as well as ventilation, was the use of French doors opening onto a verandah. This was said to be practical "in the warmer parts of Alberta," although fixed windows were needed for colder areas.[88] In Alberta, sash windows opening from the bottom were usually used, even though the best windows were thought to be those that prevented draughts by opening at the top.[89]

It was often argued that Canadians kept their houses much too warm for good health, but there was no consensus on optimum temperatures. Some contended that a room should be as cold as could be endured while others said that it should be comfortably warm. There was general agreement that fresh air was essential, with stale air defined as that which had been "vitiated by the respiration of men and animals, by the waste products of combustion, or when it is loaded with dust particles bearing disease germs."[90] Illustrating the persistence of mid nineteenth century medical theory, Albertans were warned in 1908 that the body was like a furnace, which discharged "excretions which represent the ashes and foul gases which are produced from keeping the fires [of the body] burning. These excretions are poisonous."[91] Good ventilation was therefore necessary to rid a room of these and other pollutants. Such concerns were especially relevant for bedrooms since it was calculated that people spent one-third of their lives sleeping.[92] The effects of poor bedroom ventilation and "breathing over and over again the same air in small bedrooms" were a loss of appetite in the morning, "anemia and worse diseases."

People were advised to use plenty of blankets on the bed, put on a nightcap, and open the windows.[93] Another popular solution was to convert a second-storey porch into a sleeping area by lining it with screen; an idea which, while popular before 1918, gained its greatest currency in Alberta during the early 1920s in the wake of the influenza epidemics.[94]

The theory that houses filled with fresh air provided a healthy environment was predicated on the presence of a furnace that could keep the house warm, even with the windows open. While a good number of modern houses in urban Alberta had furnaces by 1914, many urban and most farm houses did not. In these cases, warmth, so laboriously gained in the cold Alberta winter, would hardly have been sacrificed, even for fresh air. Fireplaces were one of the earliest sources of home heating in Alberta. In 1881, fireplaces with a "coal grate" were becoming "fashionable" in Edmonton, the same year that the first brick yard started up in the town.[95] In the late nineteenth century, most houses were heated with stoves, although costly houses, such as the Pearce House in Calgary, had either steam or hot air gravity furnaces. In 1894 the installation of hot air furnaces in two houses in Medicine Hat merited notice in the local paper, suggesting their uniqueness.[96] By World War I, however, most middle class urban houses had central heating, either from steam or hot air gravity furnaces. Many others continued to use cook stoves and space heaters because furnaces were expensive to install and burned coal and not firewood, which was plentiful and inexpensive in rural areas before 1920. This was especially the case in farm homes, and people with two-storey houses commonly installed a stove on the upper floor because "one cannot always have furnaces. . . . if one lives away off in the country."[97]

While stoves were fueled either with wood or coal, coal was commonly used by people living in Edmonton, Lethbridge, Camrose and other communities located near coal mines. There was never a shortage of coal production in Alberta, but distribution was sometimes limited because of transportation problems and labour unrest; problems that led to public demands for better distribution and control of what had become an essential commodity. To minimize problems from interrupted supply, people with some capital stockpiled coal, and because a cook stove and furnace used about four tons of coal per month in winter, even many moderate-sized houses in Alberta had coal bins that could hold up to forty tons of coal.[98] Natural gas was an alternative to coal and wood. It was used widely for domestic lighting and heating purposes in Medicine Hat by 1905 and had been introduced in other southern Alberta towns such as Claresholm by 1911.[99] In stark contrast to the dirt and bother of coal and wood, gas was clean, reliable, and instant. The Gas Company, which held the franchise in Calgary, relied heavily on these benefits in its advertising, and its slogans, "Let Us Shovel Your Coal" and "Let Us Cart Your Ashes," must have had tremendous appeal. While gas was advertised primarily for cooking and heating water, it was also claimed that "with a Gas Grate to heat your sitting room, a few small [gas] radiators for the bedroom, your home is complete and comfort assured."[100] Despite such claims, gas was not adopted for household use outside some parts of southern Alberta to any great extent before World War I because the distribution system was limited and coal was competitively priced, giving people little incentive, other than convenience, to install gas in their homes.[101]

Hot air gravity furnaces were commonly available in Canada after 1880 but had a reputation for inefficiency which endured until World War I.[102] Although the general principle of drawing cold air from the rooms to create proper circulation was well understood by the turn of the century, gravity furnaces were often installed improperly. People who owned them complained about cold floors and walls, hot basements, and red hot furnaces, all of which could be prevented by siting the vents properly and installing the correct size of furnace and ducts. Despite their problems, gravity systems were used because they were less expensive to install and maintain than steam systems, which were used mainly in large houses and in "the better class of moderate sized houses."[103] In the late nineteenth century, steam systems required two separate sets of pipes, one to take the steam to the radiators and another to take condensation back to the boiler. By 1908, this approach had been replaced with a single pipe system in which steam and condensation were accommodated in the same pipe, making the installation of steam heat easier and less expensive.[104]

The adoption of central heating was a major factor in safety since it reduced the overall use of stoves which had often been vented by a simple metal pipe, without lining or insulation, run carelessly through walls and ceilings, a highly dangerous practice that resulted in many fires.[105] In addition, because small rooms no longer had to be heated individually or closed off in winter, the adoption of central heating probably affected the layout of houses by making open plans more practical in northern climates. Gravity furnaces in particular had a more direct impact on layout since they had to be placed in the centre of the basement, causing the chimney to be centrally located as well. Imitating the economies of single stack plumbing, a single stack chimney, to which the furnace, kitchen stove and fireplace were connected, was safer, cheaper to construct, and easier to maintain.[106] This affected the placement of the fireplace, relegating it to a corner of the dining room or living room against the chimney. The result was an awkward room layout because the fireplace was unable, in practical terms, to satisfy its major function as the centre of family gatherings. While not affecting layout, the installation of steam furnaces led to the construction of high basements because they required about seven feet of height to provide the proper incline for pipes.[107]

LANDSCAPING

An extension of the task of creating family centred modern homes was the planning and landscaping of urban areas and farm yards. In keeping with the notion that people's surroundings influenced their behaviour, cities and towns were urged to build parks, control land use and urban growth, and generally beautify the urban landscape. Before 1918, urban beautification rested upon individual effort rather than corporate or government action. While town planners discussed the relationship between the individual house and its wider urban environment, the landscaping of private residences depended upon the owner's initiative. Private gardens were said to be important because they expressed the individual's most immediate connection with urban beauty, although, more directly, gardens were linked with the common preoccupations about family life and a healthy home environment.

Gardening was held up as a moral pastime which could reform drunkards, correct other social evils, and increase the efficiency of workers.[108] These rehabilitative effects were thought to derive partly from fresh air and sunlight, but, as Reverend Pratt of the Calgary Unitarian Church observed, plants revealed the hand of God in their growth and beauty "just as surely as we are told that God spoke to Moses out of a burning bush."[109] While gardening was considered a moral pursuit, in a frontier environment, particularly in treeless areas, it also came to symbolize the process of settlement itself. Fruitful and beautiful gardens proved the fertility of the region and the suitability of the climate for European settlement. Moreover, beautiful cities and gardens impressed visitors who would later speak approvingly about what they had seen.[110]

The objective of garden design was to integrate the house with its surroundings and provide a restful and beautiful environment for home life. It was recommended that the house be surrounded with shade and fruit trees and that vines be trained over porches. Tree planting also provided shelter from snow and wind, thus conserving moisture and creating a microclimate in which tender vegetables and flowers could be grown successfully.[111] On farms, this objective meant surrounding the yard with trees and fronting the house with lawns. In keeping with "modern lines of landscape art," a curved driveway should bisect lawns bordered with "irregular groups of shrubs," and the house should be sited so that it would be immediately visible when coming into the yard.[112] The landscaping should also effectively separate the house from livestock barns, pens, and grazing areas. In urban areas, gardens were considered to be even more important than on farms because trees acted as air purifiers, countering urban pollution and dust.[113] Tree-lined streets, houses fronted with lawns, and yards filled with shrubs and flowers confirmed the home as a retreat from the world and a shelter for family life. In 1909, the President of the Calgary Horticultural Society recommended that people purchase large lots and site their houses to surround them with lawns, shrubs, and gardens to create a "quiet, restful and yet important look."[114]

Although the size and configuration of most urban lots restricted ingenuity in landscaping, a lawn was seen as the essential "canvas" upon which "you paint with flowers and shrubs the picture that your fancy desires."[115] Lawns were always described as "verdant," "lush," and "velvety"; the attraction of these images cannot be underestimated. The Calgary Horticultural Society petitioned against the installation of water meters from a belief that limitless and inexpensive water was essential for the average person to garden successfully on the prairies.[116] The lawn facilitated the use of the yard as a playground for children and kept them off dirty and dangerous streets. Playing in the garden convinced the child "to call the place home" and reinforced the virtues of family life and taught a sense of belonging at an early age. Moreover, yards with lawns, flowers, shrubs, and vegetables were considered an inducement to cleanliness: one would surely hesitate to throw garbage onto such a well-crafted landscape.[117]

It was frequently recommended that a lawn be framed with informal plantings to break the angularity of the lot. Annual and perennial

◆ This verandah on George Goodall's house in Edmonton created a bridge between the house and its community. No date, possibly about 1920. PAA B4647.

flowers should be planted either in imitation of the English mixed border or in more modest flower beds. A vegetable plot should be part of any garden plan to create a degree of self-sufficiency for the family. A good garden layout was expected to lead the eye from one feature to another, while background plantings framed the garden and integrated it and the house into a pleasing unity. Indeed, in 1896 it was argued that a well-planted garden could compensate for poor architecture since houses of "commonplace and inartistic design" could be "so beautified" through landscaping that they would "attract and delight the eye of all beholders."[118] Nonetheless, it was theoretically better to co-ordinate the architecture of the house with the garden and to place windows so that they, in effect, brought the garden into the house. Verandahs and open porches were one way to lower the profile of a house and integrate it with the landscape, and when plants were trained over these structures and over fences and walls, it was believed that the house was truly a part of its environment. While prairie gardeners were limited in the varieties of climbing plants that they could grow, hardy clematis, virginia creeper, scarlet runner beans, and hops were all possibilities.[119] A further limitation for foundation plantings was that the perimeter of the house often needed to be kept clear to allow banking of snow for insulation.

Verandahs and open porches were otherwise useful because they shaded the main floor of the house and permitted doors to be left open for ventilation. They also provided an outdoor space from which the garden could be enjoyed, a gathering place for family and neighbours in the evening, and, when fitted up as an "outdoor living room" with a table, some chairs and perhaps an awning, a place where one could spend hot summer days.[120] Such emphasis on the yard as an extension of the family home was not intended, however, to close the house off from its community. Low hedges, picket fences, or lattice were intended as boundaries and not as physical barriers. It was a convention that assumed a sympathy and unity of sentiment among neighbours. While the rear garden was a private space, verandahs fronting the street functioned as transitional elements, bringing the life and interests of the family in contact with those of its community.

◆

Before World War I, theories of house design underwent major changes. Advances in scientific and technical knowledge affected design, and the modern house became identified with progress. Modernity was not a style in domestic architecture but a concept that posited a healthier, more rational future through design and technological innovation. The arrangement and design of rooms that stimulated efficiency and sanitation, open plans that enhanced family life, and developments in plumbing and heating and the rest of the technological infrastructure of a house together formed a definition of modernity and served as the attributes of the modern house.

These modern innovations were embraced because they were both reasonable and fashionable. They posed no challenge to private property or customary social and economic relationships; indeed they helped to confirm them through their apparent support for the family, a patriarchal culture, and social order. Moreover, their gradual introduction, viewed as part of the steady unfolding of progress, permitted them to broaden the economy significantly by expanding existing trades and businesses and, in some cases, by creating wholly new ones. Nevertheless, people were reluctant to abandon all customs and precedents. For many, the house represented an anchor in a world of rapid technological and social change, and they attempted to incorporate the symbols of what they perceived to be the old fashioned home into the modern scientific house; a measure of the broader social change that was taking place. Thus, the house could at once be innovative and traditional by reconciling the potentially conflicting demands of technological and scientific change with personal needs for stability and a sense of belonging.[121]

In Alberta, such a reaction was intensified because of the newness of European settlement and the longing that many immigrants felt for more familiar and comforting places. In 1909, the *Farm and Ranch Review* demonstrated this reconciliation: by encouraging its readers to embrace the new ways, it extolled the symbols of past houses. It advised its readers that

> The closed parlor must be replaced by the cosy sitting-room, the heavy blinds by muslin curtains, and the carpets by rugs and varnished floors. There should be no closed, unused room in the house, and even the cellar must be lighted and aired. And, old-fashioned as it may seem, there is nothing that makes a room more livable than an open grate. It should be for use, and not for ornament, simple in design and fixture, for a home without a hearth is not complete.[122]

It was in urban areas that such modern ideas could best be applied, partly because they were wealthier and partly because towns and cities supplied infrastructures such as sanitary and electrical services for their application. In rural areas, modernity could not be so easily achieved, but its attraction was no less than in the cities, and in the twentieth century the lure of the city for farm people was in no small measure the dream of living in a modern house.

FOUR

Permanent Housing
Cost, Supply, and Building

The supply of materials and the cost and methods of construction had an important impact on the nature of permanent housing in Alberta. Despite frequent problems stemming from the cost of land and the availability of financing, the single-family detached house remained the most popular type of housing in the province. This had a profound influence on the shape of towns and cities and, given the explosive growth of the province's population after 1900, played an important role in the building, supply, and cost of housing.

The years between 1883 and the end of World War I were characterized by cyclical economic growth and depression. The most dramatic swing occurred in 1912–13 when the economy collapsed, following five years of increasingly frantic growth in western Canada. The cause of this downturn is little understood but it would seem that "a decline in British investment in Canada, a drop in wheat prices and rising freight rates made the vulnerabilities of the Canadian economy apparent."[1] The most telling consequence in Alberta was a rapid drop in the price of land, which had been driven to extremely high levels by the speculation engendered by the optimism and greed of the previous half decade. Although there was a brief revival of speculative activity in Calgary in 1914 after the discovery of oil at Turner Valley,[2] speculative fever was over for a time. The war years that followed were a unique period. Although war-related industrial production was minimal on the prairies, unemployment was low because of the enlistment of employable men and a boom in agricultural and resource industries. Most of the resulting gains disappeared in wartime inflation and, in terms of industrialization, the war probably had a negative impact on the prairies.[3]

Before 1918, the cyclical nature of the Alberta economy, when combined with rapid population growth, high demand for new houses, land speculation, and a lack of building regulations and planning, created poor quality building and either a shortage or oversupply of houses. John Saywell observed that, historically, "the immobility, durability and high initial cost of housing have meant that the problem has been one not simply of the aggregate amount of housing stock in existence, but its location and kind in relation to the movement, growth and composition of the population, levels of income, household formation and family size."[4] These factors were especially critical in Alberta in the settlement years before World War I.

NATURE OF DWELLINGS

In the 1901 census it was reported that Alberta had just over 73,000 people living in 14,842 dwellings. A decade later, the 1911 census reported that Alberta's population stood at 374,295, housed in 87,672 dwellings.[5] Thus, in ten years, 300,000 additional people were being housed in a further 72,830 dwellings. Since both censuses used the term dwelling to mean individual apartments or living areas within a house or apartment building, as well as houses occupied only by one family, these statistics cannot justify an assertion that a total of 72,830 new houses were built in the period from 1901 to 1911. Nonetheless, it is clear that a great deal of housing was constructed in a short time. So important was this construction period in the history of the province that, 35 years later, the 1946 census reported that about 17 percent of existing dwellings in Alberta had been built before 1911.[6]

While little information exists with respect to the nature of these dwellings, the 1911 census recorded the number of rooms per dwelling, which can be utilized as a rough indication of the overall quality of prewar housing. Table 4–1 shows that 25 percent of dwellings in the province in 1911 consisted of only one room. This was matched in Canada only by Saskatchewan, where one room dwellings comprised almost 28 percent of the total. Further, 57 percent of all dwellings in Alberta contained three or fewer rooms.[7] Although many of these dwellings were probably temporary, it is evident that the province's population was housed in small and crowded quarters since the average number of persons per dwelling in Alberta was 4.27, down from 4.9 in 1901.[8] Typical of small houses at this time was the "cottage" built by the Norman family in Calgary in 1908. It had a dug-out cellar, a combined kitchen/living room and two bedrooms, and later the same year, an addition was added to the back to serve as a separate kitchen. Four people lived in the house.[9]

The small size of most dwellings in Alberta in 1911 was most likely the result of affordability and not preference. Although there was a reluctance to challenge the pioneering myth that, as the Alberta Department of the Attorney General phrased it in 1912, "many healthy, robust families have been raised in one-roomed shacks," small houses were nevertheless thought to affect both sanitation and morals. "For whole families to eat, sleep and dress and perform all the functions of life in one room naturally tends to the break-down of those delicacies which are so necessary to the maintenance of a high moral standard."[10] This did not mean that huge houses were necessary. Even for those with greater means, it was suggested in 1910 that a six or seven room bungalow was perfectly fine, because large houses required too much cleaning and heating. Separate bedrooms were required, as well as a bathroom, a "big 'homey' living room, a cheerful dining room and a small kitchen with pantry." A "reception room" and a "den" were useless for "ordinary families" in Alberta.[11]

While a six or seven room house may have been considered ideal for "ordinary families," Table 4–1 indicates that most did not live in such conditions. Of the minority who did, such as the urban middle class, most were able to obtain good housing a relatively short time after arrival in Alberta. Many of these people came with some capital and, given the incomes they were able to command, were able to obtain financing relatively quickly. But housing conditions for urban labourers and semi-skilled workers, who relied almost exclusively on seasonal or low wages, were poor and showed little improvement up to the end of World War I. Many farm people also lived in poor quality small houses, continuing to make do by renovating their tempo-

TABLE 4-1 Size of Dwellings, Alberta, 1911*

	Number	Percentage of Total
1 room	21,929	25.01
2 rooms	16,995	19.38
3 rooms	11,070	12.63
4 rooms	10,214	11.65
5 rooms	7,588	8.66
6–10 rooms	18,491	21.09
11+ rooms	1,385	1.58
	87,672	100.00

Source: *Census of Canada, 1921*, Vol. III, Table 12, p. 40.
*See note on *Census of Canada* statistics, p. 303.

rary dwellings or by building inexpensive houses. People on the frontier tended to put capital into "productive enterprises" rather than "the amenities of life," and this "dominance of the pecuniary motive and the optimistic acceptance of a philosophy of expansion" were sharply reflected in housing standards.[12]

Many small businessmen who came to Alberta with some capital first used it to establish their businesses. Commonly, one's place of business was combined with one's home. In 1912 the hamlet of Delburne was made up of 30 buildings, of which 18 combined business and residence and included the butcher shop, harness shop, painter and decorator, two general stores, pool room, barber shop, furniture shop, real estate office, and the local "dealer in prize poultry."[13] Such practices were probably less common in larger towns and cities than in villages where it remained typical well into the twentieth century. While living above one's shop was acceptable at first, small merchants moved into a detached house as soon as possible, and rented out their former living quarters above their shops as office space or, more commonly, as housing. In Rimbey, Jack Beatty, one of the town's most successful merchants, lived above his store for several years before building in 1924 a 1,200 square foot semi bungalow, one of the finest houses in the town.[14] Similarly, in 1893 Edmonton businessman Johnston Walker moved from his attached residence and store, which he had built in 1886, into a detached house, a step that confirmed his success as a businessman and community leader.[15]

ALTERNATIVES TO ONE FAMILY, ONE HOUSE

In 1921, of a total of 136,125 dwellings in the province, the census reported that just over 97 per cent were single detached houses, the social ideal in Alberta.[16] Although comparable statistics are lacking for earlier years, newspaper reports and other evidence do not suggest that the 1921 figures represented a drastic change from prewar conditions. This does not mean that single detached houses were occupied by only one family. Light housekeeping suites and boarding houses, many of them located in single-family detached houses, were the commonest form of high density housing during this period. Since they were included in the overall definition of "dwelling" in the 1901 and 1911 censuses, it is difficult to determine their number or how many people lived in them. Nonetheless, they appear to have been quite common. By World War I, low paid single workers often lived in overcrowded boarding houses in the larger centres and in mining towns such as Coleman and Blairmore. In 1910 it was charged that Calgary rooming houses were so unsanitary and crowded that they posed a threat to public health. Yet the city had no regulations for enforcing sanitary conditions in such places.[17] Two years later, the provincial Department of the Attorney General reported the existence of similar conditions in an unnamed Alberta city where "fifty-nine roomers occupied a nine-roomed house." Of these rooms, the owner's family, consisting of "a man and wife and four children, occupied one room with two female boarders."[18]

Other types of higher density housing included duplexes, row houses, and apartments, but none of these were very common. In 1907, 130 of 478 houses built "across the Elbow" in Calgary were "double houses." Row houses, popular in late nineteenth century Ontario, were unusual in Alberta.[19] In contrast, apartment living, while not common in eastern Canada before World War I, was more popular in the west. In 1911, Montreal had a population of almost half a million and yet had only twelve to fifteen apartment houses, Toronto had nine or ten, and Ottawa had only four or five. In contrast, western cities had far more apartments, where their popularity was ascribed to a shortage of domestic servants, a reluctance to live in a detached house because of the winters, and a shortage of affordable good housing. In 1911, Winnipeg had 100 apartment houses, almost all occupied by people from the professional and commercial classes.

◆ An apartment under con-
struction during the
apartment building boom
in Calgary in 1912.
GAI NA 3882-4.

In 1911, Calgary had 25 apartment houses, or a number approximately equal to that of Toronto, Ottawa, and Montreal combined. Obviously, different forces were at work in western Canada, where recentness of settlement, housing shortages, and perhaps a certain transiency, even among those with good incomes, encouraged apartment living.[20]

Initially, apartments in Alberta cities, like those in Winnipeg, tended to be rented by the well-to-do. The buildings were generally located close to the downtown, had relatively few suites, and were modern in their services and design. The Arlington in Edmonton contained 40 suites, all "equipped with the most approved sanitary appliances and heating and ventilation apparatus."[21] Other apartments, such as the Devenish and the Connaught in Calgary, which had 57 and 12 suites respectively, were more extravagant with fine wood paneling and elegant design and decoration. The rent for these apartments was high. Although luxury apartments, such as the LeMarchand Apartments and the Gibbard Block in Edmonton and the Anderson Apartments in Calgary, continued to be built, apartment living ceased to be the monopoly of the wealthy after about 1912.

In response to the land boom and huge population increases, more modest apartments were rapidly constructed. By 1913, there were 81 apartment blocks in Calgary, many located near industrial sites. As the number of apartment buildings increased and filled with low income earners, civic spokesmen increasingly characterized them as socially undesirable housing that needed to be controlled for the public good. In 1912, while admitting that apartments might be required in a growing city, the Calgary building inspector believed that they should be abolished or, at the very least, regulated. They were criticized, as were rented houses, for becoming dilapidated and eventually turning into slums. Tenants were also said to receive all the benefits of city life without paying taxes, which justified the charge that an apartment was a "municipal parasite." In keeping with such attitudes, Calgary's building bylaws were amended in the midst of the apartment building boom in 1912 to require approval by two-thirds of the land owners in the block where construction of an apartment was proposed.[22]

While apartment blocks were becoming prominent types of rental housing in Alberta cities by 1912, they seem to have remained a minor part of the overall housing supply. Although there are no available statistics on house ownership for the period before World War I, it is apparent that in the late nineteenth century there were relatively few rental units in Alberta, leaving people little choice but to build. In 1890, rents in Calgary were at least double those in Ontario, forcing most people, even those "of moderate means," to buy or build a house. In 1910, it was still the case in Calgary that most houses under construction were for owners, "not so much as a matter of speculation," but to meet the need for better accommodation.[23] This seems partly to confirm the findings of a recent study of housing tenure in Canada, in which Richard Harris questions the accepted view that between 1900 and 1913 there was a large increase in the number of people living in rented accommodation in Ontario. Instead, he argues that there was a boom in home ownership in the early twentieth century.[24] The limitations of the available statistics make it impossible to test this view for Alberta. After about 1911, however, an increasing number of people began renting accommodation in urban Alberta, as suggested by the boom in apartment construction in Calgary between 1911 and 1913. Although almost 70 percent of families in Alberta owned their own dwellings in 1921, the first year that ownership figures are available, this conceals a significant difference between rural and urban areas. While almost 82 percent of families in rural areas owned their dwellings, only about 50 percent of those in urban areas were in a similar situation.[25] Seemingly, this high level of rental accommodation in urban areas was partly the product of wartime dislocation, but it also grew from prewar trends as well. Since just over 60 percent of the population was rural in 1921, the dream of home ownership was realized by a majority of Albertans, although its achievement was considerably more difficult for many urban dwellers.

THE HOUSING MARKET

Before 1918, Albertans faced a variety of housing problems. Periods of oversupply followed by shortages created unevenness in the market alternatively for purchasers, renters, and the housing industry. These problems were not uniform across the province. Shortages in one part of Alberta did not necessarily characterize conditions elsewhere since the province's housing market was the product of a range of economic forces and social conditions. Factors such as uneven economic conditions, inconsistent supply of capital, the seasonal nature of building, land speculation, and the organization, structure, and financing of small builders could at times collectively contribute to a cycle of housing shortages or oversupply that created immediate housing crises or sowed the seeds of future crises.

During the 1880s and 1890s, housing varied from expensive and scarce to cheap and plentiful. In 1890, a scarcity of housing in Lethbridge stimulated house construction, but "dull times" arrived three years later and "left many empty dwellings." Rents were so low that they did not cover taxes, insurance, and upkeep. By 1897, the boom was on again, and by 1899 a house could not be found for "love or money anywhere in the town."[26] Calgary and Edmonton experienced similar cycles. Edmonton went through a frantic boom in 1882, partly as a spill-over from the Winnipeg land frenzy and partly because of the expectation that the CPR would be routed through the town. Land prices in Edmonton rose to extraordinary heights, only to collapse a year later. The city did not again experience similar conditions until 1911, although there were mini booms and collapses in 1906 and 1909. Calgary's economy was even more volatile. Houses were scarce in the town in 1890 and yet stood empty by 1894. Oversupply remained a problem in 1897, when the town had "scores" of empty houses and shops and "people are leaving here by the hundreds for the Kootenay." By 1906–7, demand for rental housing outstripped supply by a ratio of ten to one. In 1908 houses were again empty and "went begging for tenants," although conditions had improved by 1909.[27] By 1911, the city was booming once again. This upswing, due in part to local causes, was also related to a nation-wide building boom. House construction in Canada from 1912 to 1914 reached an all time high of 48 percent of total construction, although Alberta's boom was shorter and had collapsed by 1913. While this boom affected the whole province, its effect was most clearly evident in Edmonton and Calgary. Edmonton, perhaps making up for lost chances, went into a speculative and building frenzy, and the value of building permits issued in the city in 1912 was not exceeded until 1946.[28]

In such an environment, land in and around urban areas was often subject to intense speculative activity leading to escalating costs and a proliferation of real estate schemes in which worthless or remote land was sold to out-of-province investors at high prices. Land speculation was big business and large blocks of land were traded on speculation.[29] To this was added the large tracts of land owned by the Hudson's Bay Company in Edmonton and the CPR in Calgary and other cities. The former tended to sell land "from time to time." The subdivision and sale of a block of its prime Edmonton land in 1912 at the height of a speculative boom proved to be uncannily lucky.[30] In the case of the CPR, the company sometimes provided a 25 percent rebate to purchasers who built a house on their lot in the first year,[31] a policy designed to encourage population growth in areas served by its railway. Thus, both agricultural and urban land was valuable, not only for the cash it yielded, but as a stimulus to the population growth that the CPR needed for its own economic health.

In the speculative fervour that so often gripped Alberta before 1913, looking at lots and thinking about land became both a collective obsession and public recreation. In 1911, Calgary held a "land show" that opened with a parade through the downtown. An extravaganza of realtors' booths and land hype, a special feature was an auction at which individuals could buy and sell land without commission.[32] The event indicated how widely the speculative mentality had been accepted by the city's population. There were also many other techniques employed to sell land: it was sold on installment, and land owners would often build and sell one house in an empty subdivision, hoping to convince potential purchasers of the area's promise. As well, a house was sometimes raffled to purchasers of lots in a subdivision, an exercise that reinforced the gambling mentality that periodically governed land transactions.[33]

Servicing of raw land also made it more marketable. Basic services such as water and sewer were provided by the city, and land speculators often subdivided raw unserviced land and then demanded that the city annex and service it. Population soon spread over far-flung subdivisions and in many of the closer-in subdivisions which were not fully built up, lots were fully serviced, causing the debt of the urban areas to escalate. Street car lines were also put in by the city. This inevitably affected the location of residential areas, for those owning land accessible to the city centre by public transit had guaranteed sales at increased prices. Before 1910, most people walked to work and therefore had to live close to their place of employment, usually the centre of the city. Construction of the first street railway in Edmonton began in 1908 and, in anticipation, property values in areas to be served by the line skyrocketed.[34] The same process was repeated in Calgary the next year, and it was said that property close to the downtown no longer had a "monopoly of the market" as it had when "the working man was compelled to walk to work."[35] Thus, the construction of public transit was a vital matter to speculators and was often the subject of charges of corruption at city hall.

The war years that followed the collapse of 1913 were ones of economic depression for the building industry in Alberta. Although some farmers were able by the end of World War I to build new houses with the profits made from high wartime agricultural prices,[36] construction in general came almost to a stand still. The number of building permits issued in the province in 1915 dropped to the lowest level since 1910.[37] Rents also fell. In 1917 there were many vacant houses in Edmonton, and one landlord, with some exaggeration, claimed that "houses that were renting for $100 per month are now let for $12.00." Property values had fallen correspondingly, and one would "almost have to give it [a house] away if [one] wanted to get rid of it."[38] This was a bonus for renters, although the long-term consequence was a postwar housing crisis marked by shortages and high rents.

HOUSING COSTS

In such a volatile economy, the supply and cost of housing was erratic, but lacking a statistical base for prewar housing costs, it is only possible to provide a subjective impression. For farm housing, it is almost impossible to generalize costs, except on a local level, and even then farm housing differed in fundamental respects from urban housing. It is, for example, illogical to discuss a farm "housing market" in the same terms as for urban areas since farm housing costs and supply were independent of land, usually included different types and levels of servicing, and were not subject to the stresses directly related to speculation and demand. Location and stage of development were crucial in farm housing; areas of recent settlement were distinctly different from those of longer settlement. In some areas, farm housing was commonly constructed piecemeal, while in others, temporary settlement houses were renovated and enlarged into permanent ones.

In the urban housing market between the 1880s and World War I, location, servicing, and economic conditions were crucial in determining cost. Land costs were volatile and standards of housing changed quickly. In 1881, for example, a frame house in Edmonton cost about $600 to $800 to build. Lots could be purchased for about $30 to $60, adding no more than 10 percent to the total cost of building a house.[39] These frame houses, then the finest in Edmonton, soon lost this status. In 1887, John Cameron had completed an $8,000 brick house which was said to be one of the best in the North West

Territories, and equally grand houses were being built elsewhere in the province. In 1891, J.D. Higginbotham built a house in Lethbridge that cost $4,200 and was designed by the Toronto architectural firm of Darling and Curry.[40] At the same time, the great mansions of the Calgary elite vied in cost and extravagance with those built elsewhere in Canada by the upper classes.

Nonetheless, most houses were still very modest. In 1890, a boom year, a "nice cottage" in Calgary cost $700 to $800 to build, plus about $100 for the land,[41] which meant that the proportion of land costs to the total was only slightly higher than in Edmonton a decade earlier. In 1899, the "more expensive" houses being built in Edmonton ranged from $1,000 to $3,500, with most at the lower end of this range, and the cost of a good but modest cottage in any urban area would probably have been somewhere around $800. In Calgary, approximately 63 percent of dwellings built in 1899 and 1900 were cottages costing $1,000 or less, with the average around $800. Of the rest, approximately 21 percent cost between $1,100 to $2,000, 13 percent cost from $2,100 to $4,000, and 3 percent cost $4,000 or more. The Baptist parsonage, the Church of England rectory, and a doctor's residence were among the dwellings costing between $2,100 to $4,000. The three percent over $4,000 included Pat Burns's house, said to cost about $20,000.[42]

While rental and purchase costs in urban areas from the early 1900s until 1913 were volatile, seeing some sharp rises and declines, generally speaking housing costs rose overall. Looking at the city of Calgary, housing close in to the city centre was most expensive and servicing added appreciably to costs, regardless of location. In 1905 a "nice 5 room house" near the CPR shops was for sale at $1,350 and was advertised as suiting "Men With Small Incomes," while an "all modern" eight-room house with barn and carriage house for $3,500 was advertised as ideal for "a doctor or prominent business man." By 1907, prices had increased substantially and $950 could buy a "very neat shack" on a lot close in to the city centre, while a five-room cottage close to the CPR roundhouse was advertised at $1,800, and an "excellent house suitable for [a] CPR employee" was advertised for $2,625. A seven- to nine-room house close in with electric light, furnace, and plumbing installed (but not connected) cost in the range of $4,000 to $5,000. After a downturn in 1908, prices again climbed. Street car service became a factor after 1909, and the suburbs stretched in all directions from the built-up portions of the city by 1911. One result was that both expensive and inexpensive houses were being built a considerable distance from the city centre. In 1910, a shack on a large lot east of the Elbow River was for sale at $775 while a "good" shack in the Mills subdivision was for sale at $1,155. A house with five to seven rooms, either new or preowned, in the relatively close-in northern areas of Sunnyside or Hillhurst with proximity to street car service, electric light, and probably only a stove rather than a furnace, ranged from $1,500 to $2,500. A similar house with a furnace, and connected to or at least fully equipped for water and possibly sewage, cost between $3,000 and $4,000. Equivalent fully modern housing closer to the city centre cost more, indicating that property in such a location still commanded a premium, especially in high status neighbourhoods. In Mount Royal, a "most up-to-date" five-bedroom house would cost about $6,500. Prices rose further in 1911 and 1912, with most houses reaching the upper end of the price ranges in 1910.[43]

While these costs reflected increasing lumber prices and the new costs of the infrastructure required by the presence of services in the house, they also reflected the rising cost of land. By 1911, lots in south Calgary in proximity to street car service were selling for $300 to $650, while similar ones in the northern suburbs of Sunnyside and Hillhurst were a minimum of about $250. Lots in Mount Royal ranged from $2,000 up to $3,700. The cheapest lots were those beyond the city's perimeter, and lots in Chesterfield, a proposed new subdivision one mile from the city limits, were offered at $75 to $140 each. Five $1,000 bungalows were to be given away as a promotion for the subdivision. These had no services and were very small, likely in the range of 500 square feet, which indicates the sort of housing anticipated for the area.[44] For those with low incomes, it was obvious that if one wanted to maintain the nineteenth century pattern in which land costs represented about 10 percent of overall house costs, one had to build in the furthest areas of the city on unserviced land.

The rental housing market showed much the same overall increases as did the purchase market. In Calgary in 1905, shacks rented on the average for $8 per month, a modest three- to four-room house with a well for water rented for $12, and six- to seven-room houses rented for about $20. By 1907, shacks were still about $8 per month, but three- and four-room houses had increased by about 20 percent to around $15, and larger houses were up by as much as 75 percent to about $35. Prices had risen yet higher by 1910 and were approaching their peak in 1911–12. The lowest increases in rent were for the smallest and poorest houses, while increases in the upper end of the market were dramatic. While a shack could still be rented for $8 or $10 in 1911, a three- to five-room house now ranged from $15 to $30, although the highest priced of these had at least electric light, and possibly a furnace and water connection. Fully equipped, serviced, and often furnished seven room and larger houses rented for $60 to $70.[45] In small towns, rents were generally cheaper. In Claresholm in 1911, for example, a house with good outbuildings on four lots just outside the town could be rented for $20 per month. With enough land on which to "produce the bulk of your household stuff," it was a bargain unimaginable for most city renters.[46]

RENT AND AFFORDABILITY

The rental market mainly served those who could not afford to purchase or who rejected ownership for various occupational or social reasons. For unskilled, low-paid, and many seasonal urban and industrial workers, there was always a housing crisis. Either they were without work during times of inexpensive housing, or their incomes were too low during times of high employment and housing shortages to afford good housing. Skilled workers were better off. Before World War I, the general assumption was that only about 20 percent of one's income could reasonably be spent on shelter. In 1905, it was estimated that the "average" working man in Calgary earned no more than $50 to $75 per month. At this level of income, the "margin required" for rent or house payments of 20 percent meant their total outlay for rent or payments could not reasonably exceed $10 to $15 per month, inclusive of taxes, insurance and interest.[47] This would have enabled them to rent a modest three- to four-room house costing about $12 per month, while a six- to seven-room house at about $20 was out of the question. Table 4–2 sets out the 1911–12 average earning of heads of working class families and illustrates that skilled workers had about $15 per month to spend on shelter. This would have enabled them to rent the most modest three- to five-room houses available at $15 to $30 per month. Only the trainman, the most highly paid, would have $23 per month for shelter and could rent a better serviced house of the same size. Larger and fully equipped houses renting at $60 to $70 were entirely out of reach and would have been almost exclusively middle and upper class. Labourers, with an average of $10 per month for shelter, could afford to rent little more than a shack.

TABLE 4-2 Average Earnings of Heads of Families in Calgary in
Specified Occupations, June 1911–June 1912

	Yearly	Monthly	20% for housing
Bakers	871.33	72.61	14.52
Bricklayers, masons & stonecutters	892.81	74.40	14.88
Carpenters	938.04	78.17	15.63
Domestic and personal	820.78	68.40	13.68
Electricians	969.48	80.79	16.16
Labourers	616.14	51.35	10.27
Painters & Decorators	948.29	79.02	15.80
Plumbers & Gas fitters	978.78	81.57	16.31
Trainmen	1,374.96	114.58	22.92
Street railway employees	879.13	73.26	14.65

SOURCE: *Census of Canada, 1921*, Vol. III, Table XI, p. xx.
Average earnings are based on census returns. The figures reflect
total earnings, including payment for overtime, deductions for
periods of unemployment, and income from employment of any kind.

FINANCING AND AFFORDABILITY OF HOME OWNERSHIP

Inadequate income was the basic contributor to poor quality housing, but the nature of the mortgage market intensified the housing problems of prewar Alberta. By the turn of the century, capital for housing in Alberta was raised from local and regional sources as well as from eastern Canadian and foreign lenders. The importance of nonprovincial sources of capital meant that the provincial economy was subject to international fluctuations. Building cycles, when occurring in conjunction with the speculative and developing character of the Alberta economy, exerted a disproportionate impact upon the province.[48] When British capital began to withdraw from Canada in anticipation of World War I, Alberta plunged into a depression.

Although there are no accessible statistics indicating the relative proportion of foreign and domestic investment, British, French, and Dutch capital were important in the west, with the four western provinces the target for the majority of British investment in Canada between 1904 and 1910.[49] Most of these funds were handled by brokers representing European banks. The Canada Agency Ltd. was linked to the British banking firm, Chapman, Milne, Grenfell and Co. Ltd. and had branches in England, Germany, France, New York, Montreal, Winnipeg, Edmonton, Calgary, and Saskatoon. While the company was involved mainly in purchasing Canadian bonds for sale in Britain, it also provided mortgage financing in Canada. This financing was handled in Alberta by two subsidiary companies, the Western Canada Mortgage Company, which advanced mortgage money for houses, and Western Homebuilders Ltd., a vertically integrated concern, which purchased land, made loans, and built houses. The latter also owned a lumber company, a sash and door factory, and other "subsidiary enterprises."[50] More indirectly, foreign capitalization was also facilitated by individual realtors, who sometimes acted as agents for British as well as Canadian insurance companies. Many trust companies, such as Canada Permanent, also lent money which it had raised both abroad and domestically. Even so, the amount of mortgage capital raised in this way was relatively small in comparison to that available from Canadian life insurance companies, which had aggressively entered the mortgage market by 1900.[51]

Local sources also played a part in providing mortgage capital. In 1894, money was "awful scarce" and people were forced to rely on local sources for mortgage money.[52] Although it was common to lament that Albertans were not interested in lending money, funds were often advanced through a local lawyer who arranged the mortgage, and in most towns, a lawyer, realtor, or insurance agent acted as an "investment broker" for local as well as other capital.[53] Local money was also available from larger provincial concerns. Building and Loans Ltd., a Calgary firm capitalized at $1 million financed and built houses for its customers. The firm was made up of local "capitalists" and businessmen. A.B. Cushing, president of a large Calgary lumber yard, was one of the directors and a number of local builders and tradesmen sat on the "Advisory Board." It was a cautious company, lending and building only for people who already owned their land.[54] Instead of integrated lending and building, the more usual practice was for an individual to have the necessary money in place and then approach a builder to put up the building and handle the required subtrades.[55] Few builders were sufficiently well capitalized to lend money to their customers, although many effectively financed the building of houses indirectly by taking their payment over a period of time.[56]

Before 1914, mortgage interest rates varied from 5 to 8 percent per year. Typical house mortgages did not have blended payments, in which payments on principal and interest were made on a regular basis throughout the term of the loan.[57] Most were "simply short term loans," requiring the borrower to pay interest through the term of the loan, usually for five years, and pay off the principal at the end of the term. Such mortgages in western Canada could be obtained from a trust company for 40 to 50 percent of the total value of a house.[58]

Given housing costs in Calgary in 1911–12, the workers typified in Table 4–2, most of whom earned under $1000 per year, would have had to save for a good number of years to accumulate a 40 to 50 percent down payment for a fully modern house on a lot close to a street car line. While many houses were offered for sale by the owners or builders on easier terms, varying from 20 to 50 percent down with the balance arranged as rent, many workers would not have been able to meet even these terms. Most of those set out in Table 4–2 had around $15 per month for housing, and even if they could save 20 percent as a down payment, the monthly payments on the balance were often greater than $15. One typical offer advertised in the *Calgary Herald* in 1911 was a six-room bungalow in the suburb of Sunnyside for $1750, with $350 in cash and the balance at $25 per month. Another fully modern six-room house with bath and furnace in the suburb of Hillhurst was for sale at $3000, available for $800 in cash with the balance at $35 per month.[59] While the down payments may have been manageable, the monthly payments on even the lowest of these arrangements would have excluded most working class people. This meant that most working class people would have been able to purchase or build only the simplest, largely unserviced, houses such as a one-storey homestead house or a foursquare cottage.[60] As one moved up the social scale, the housing improved. People of the lower middle class, such as small merchants, many civil servants, and especially successful skilled tradesmen could probably afford at least a partially serviced two-storey homestead house or a medium-sized semi bungalow. Fully modern larger foursquare houses and semi bungalows in the range of 1,400 square feet would have been affordable mainly by the upper middle class such as lawyers, successful businessmen, and the executive ranks of the civil service.

Since financing limited the housing options of many ordinary people, when better terms were offered, they were highly popular. About 1910, Western Homebuilders Ltd., the subsidiary of the British owned Canada Agency Ltd., bought the lot desired by a purchaser and custom built a house on it. The company demanded only 10 percent of the total cost as a down payment, with the balance paid on monthly installments over ten years. While the company brought this scheme into operation only "in a very small way," within a year it was unable to keep up with the demand.[61] A similar repayment approach was used in 1912 by the People's Home Company Ltd., an Edmonton based mortgage company. The company charged 5 percent for a $1,000 loan, and the borrower paid monthly installments of $10 which included the interest and about 5 percent yearly on the unpaid principal balance. The company pledged to give borrowers "six months grace on your payments in case of sickness or loss of position."[62]

Despite generally high costs, credit was still the lifeblood of the housing industry. In good times at least, it was said that mortgages were taken out and houses purchased without much thought about the total cost, "so long as the terms are reasonable at the start,"[63] an intriguing hint about the need for credit and popular attitudes towards it at the beginning of the century. But when credit was unavailable, alternative solutions to the problem of affordability were required. A greater percentage of income could be diverted to housing, or family income could be increased through employment of both adult family members and possibly the children as well. Another approach was to build a home oneself to save labour costs, possibly 25 percent of the total cost of a custom built house. While this was practical for some, the high percentage of people renting dwellings suggests that it was not always a feasible route to affordable housing.[64]

BUILDING PRACTICES AND HOUSING SUPPLY

While financing and its difficulties limited affordability, building practices restricted the supply of housing. Building in Alberta was largely a seasonal activity. Lumber mills closed during the winter, and, with the exception of inside finishing work, construction stopped completely by January unless the weather was unusually mild. Building with brick was impracticable during the winter because of the types of mortar used. Before 1918, most houses were constructed by builders who ran operations consisting of one carpenter and a few seasonal employees. Their progress was slow because they usually custom built houses one at a time, hiring subtrades as necessary. Indicative of the scale of operation, many of these builders combined house building with other work. A typical combination was that of builder and lumberyard operator, but other builders were more versatile. D.C. Gourlay of Lacombe, for example, sold both lumber and farm equipment, in addition to owning town lots and building on them. The Dobson Brothers of Innisfail combined undertaking, carpentry, and contracting in a single business.[65] While some small builders built houses, either for sale on speculation or to rent, most had too little capital for such projects on an ongoing basis or on a larger scale. In addition, such activity by small builders was limited because they were so vulnerable to the rapid inflation and deflation of land prices caused by speculation.[66]

In the cities, however, there were some larger builders, and at least some of them engaged in speculative building. In 1899 and 1900 approximately half of the small "cottages" built in Calgary were built by a few people, presumably on speculation or for rent. For example, T.S.C. Lee, a real estate agent, built eight cottages on Stephen Avenue East for a total of $6,000 and a Mr. Hatfield built 24 houses for $25,000.[67] While information about such large builders is scanty, this fragmentary data suggests a relatively high level of organization and capitalization of at least a few builders from an early date. A.J. McGuire, the most prominent builder in Lethbridge, employed 14 men in 1899, and in 1910 there were 15 "leading" builders in Edmonton. These men presumably set the market for building in the city, although many would have been involved in industrial and commercial construction rather than house building. In Calgary, there were 19 major building concerns operating between 1907 and 1915,[68] some of which carried out some speculative house building during boom times. In 1912, J.A. Knoepfli, a Calgary builder, constructed "several" bungalows of the "latest design" in Sunalta, Elbow Park, and Mount Royal on speculation. Both his designs and his marketing techniques were in the newest fashion; he took prospective purchasers around by automobile to inspect the houses.[69]

The predominance of small builders, and the seasonal nature of the work, meant that the building trades involved in house construction were usually unorganized, although labour organization of the building trades in general began to occur around 1900. A strike by carpenters in Calgary in 1903 was the first major building trades strike in the province, and it was roundly condemned by business leaders in the city. According to the *Calgary Herald*, "in a place like Calgary, and where the city is growing, any man or body of men who do anything to affect that growth, in which all, capital, labor and residents, are interested, must be taken as the enemy of the city."[70] De-

◆ A carpenter crew work-
ing on a house in Ed-
monton, 1912.
PAA A4665.

spite such conflicts, the major labour problem was not strikes but a shortage of skilled workers. Construction labourers were never in short supply, but skilled workers were often scarce, creating delays in the completion of all buildings, including houses.[71]

If labour was making some tentative progress towards greater organization, so were builders. Towards the end of the first decade of the century, the expansion of the building industry was accompanied by an increasing level of organization. The Canadian National Association of Builders was organized in Toronto in 1907, followed by the establishment of a building exchange in Calgary in 1910. These organizations indicated the emergence of leading figures in the industry and demonstrated the level of building activity, but each organization denied that it was a "combine." Their goals were to promote the interests of the industry and, just as "labor organizations send men to parliament and legislation is enacted on their behalf," building exchanges voiced the interests of builders.[72] The creation of a group to represent builders in Alberta was taken one step further in 1911 when the building exchanges in Edmonton, Lethbridge, Medicine Hat, and Calgary were federated into a provincial body. It was hoped that this agency could better deal with issues such as "legislation, agreements with architects, uniform maximum scales of wages and similar matters" than could a national body, although building exchanges could not legally negotiate provincial wage scales with unions even though they could at a local level.[73]

PUBLIC SERVICING AND REGULATION

Although it was commonly believed that the supply and quality of housing would improve through the operation of the market place, certain public measures, with varying degrees of support and application, were undertaken to enhance this process. Of these, the servicing of land was one of the most important, simultaneously reinforcing the speculative mentality of the time and meeting the economic needs of many influential sectors in the community. By 1914, Calgary had "provided graded streets, sewer and water services, and often street car services to 26,000 undeveloped lots, more than twice as many as were built on at the time."[74] Some of these subdivisions were located relatively close to places of employment, an essential element when public transit was minimal and when a horse and carriage or, later, an automobile, was owned only by the well-to-do in the city. Improvements in public transit led to the growth of more distant suburbs and the beginning of daily commuting. Yet because this added to time spent away from home, suburbanization was not always welcome. Moreover, it was sometimes said that it weakened the economic strength of the central business district by fragmenting the consumer market into "different districts in place of centralizing it downtown."[75] Despite such sentiment, public transit was used to encourage suburban development. In 1911, the City of Calgary provided roads, a street railway, and tax concessions to the CPR for housing developed on its car repair property. In other cases, developers promised potential purchasers the certitude of coming street car service in their promotion of areas like Forest Lawn on the outskirts of Calgary where inexpensive lots could be purchased for $60 in 1910.[76]

Municipal tax systems also were used to encourage construction. In 1904, Edmonton led the way in adopting the single tax system, by which raw and improved land was taxed at the same rate, and this system was imposed by the province on other Alberta towns and cities in 1912. The increased taxation of vacant lands and the exemption of improvements from taxation were expected to discourage speculation and encourage construction of houses for sale or rent, thereby converting vacant but subdivided land holdings into productive property.[77] While the single tax system may have encouraged construction of shacks on vacant land, it produced little in the way of increased construction or stimulation of business in general. Moreover, some attributed ulterior motives for the adoption of the system. In 1912, it was said that since Edmonton residents "owned all the improvements in the city" and nonresidents so much vacant land, the local residents' "motive for exempting improvements was really a very selfish desire to saddle the nonresidents with the greater portion of the taxes."[78]

A less politically popular but ultimately sounder approach to improving housing standards was through regulation by local governments. The earliest building regulations dealt with fire prevention, and since the firefighting abilities of most urban areas were poor, most attempted to regulate only in designated high-risk fire zones, such as business districts where buildings abutted each other. Fire regulations thus governed houses only if they were located inside these zones. In 1909 the Calgary Building Inspector argued that all houses in Calgary should be subject to fire bylaws. Opinions varied, and in 1911 the *Calgary Herald* stated that the "fault is with the builders" and the sooner they began using stone, brick, and concrete

for houses, the sooner the problem would end.[79] In any event, fire
regulation of houses was not a priority for the city, and, despite continuing recommendations that fire regulations apply to all housing,
the consolidation of the city's bylaws in 1911 did not include such a
requirement.[80]

In many towns, fire regulations comprised the whole of the
building regulations. In 1897 Edmonton did not have a building code,
and although specific building regulations were passed in the next few
years, these probably had little overall impact on construction practices. While bylaws such as those limiting the height of buildings,
requiring set-backs, and establishing lot sizes were enforced, local
government was often reluctant to regulate the construction of buildings. Enforcement was lax throughout the province and by 1904 calls
were being made in places like Edmonton for stricter building standards.[81] Commonly, local councils granted exemptions from the bylaws to some builders, while others, presumably not so influential,
were forced to comply with the regulations.[82] In one case, the Calgary
Council overruled its building inspector's enforcement of the bylaw
regarding the strength of bearing walls, then directed him to oversee
the work and, presumably, take responsibility should the building
collapse.[83] Enforcement was also hindered by administrative factors.
In 1911, the Calgary building inspector was extremely short staffed
and had to carry out all inspections and reinspections personally. In
view of his work load and recurrent political interference, it is not
surprising that he finally resigned, following a council meeting at
which he struck an alderman who intimated that he was a "crook."[84]

The application and enforcement of building regulations
improved little, if at all, before and during the war years. Like many
cities in western Canada, Edmonton and Calgary brought in more
comprehensive building bylaws before World War I, but like other
places too, Calgary's bylaw was described as "imprecise, particularly
with respect to residential construction."[85] After the boom, some interest was expressed in creating provincial uniform building standards, both to improve quality and decrease the cost of construction.
The Calgary building inspector "started a movement" in 1913 to develop a uniform building code that would apply to all towns and cities
in western Canada.[86] This approach held little attraction for most local
councils, probably because they regarded it as a threat to their patronage and to municipal autonomy. Moreover, there was little demand
from builders for such a scheme. The idea of uniform standards did
not die, however, and at the end of World War I, N.A. McIvor, the

Edmonton building inspector, urged that fire and building standards be made a provincial rather than a local responsibility, arguing that a provincial statute would "command a respect and observance that is not possible to obtain for a local by-law." The nub of his argument was that a provincial building code would "remove the Construction, Sanitation and Ventilation of our houses, factories and warehouses from the patronage of local influences which sometimes seems unduly anxious to please the owner in saving a penny regardless." Indeed, he thought it was "nothing short of startling to watch the efforts. . . . in framing and enacting Health and Sanitation laws when in many instances any attempt at their enforcement is already defeated by the housing conditions as they exist."[87] It was a telling comment on how little had been achieved in implementing minimum building standards in the years since settlement.

HOUSING INADEQUACIES AND SOCIETY

The overall failure to improve the quality of housing was not, however, simply the result of a lack of political will. Nonregulated building was consistent with the widely held opinion, deriving in part from the doctrine of self-help, that the individual alone was responsible for his fate. The social attitudes and economic interests of the secure and the wealthy gave them few reasons to be concerned about building codes, planning, and other regulations that would protect all members of society. They commonly believed that good housing was available to those who were thrifty, lucky, or prepared to demonstrate initiative. The *Calgary Herald* noted in 1907 that "one pleasing characteristic" of Calgary was the large number of "smaller residences" put up by private individuals who had been "fortunate enough to buy a few lots when the price was low" and then sell when prices were high. Their capital gain provided them with the cash to put up "their little home and thus render themselves independent of the landlord."[88] The comment revealed much about the social attitudes prevalent in Alberta and how the opportunities of the "last best west" could be realized.

Although it was usually accepted that the market could provide adequate housing for low income workers, there was some belief that both government and private employers should provide affordable housing. Government was reluctant to shoulder such responsibilities, even though there were calls for state supported low-income housing, such as that made by the Town Planning Convention held in Edmonton in 1912.[89] Employers were also reluctant to provide housing, although some was built in the province; the Eau Claire Lumber Co. in Calgary built and rented small cottages to its employees, and the CPR often provided housing for some of its employees in small towns.[90] Company housing was most common in coal mining communities where mining companies owned all the surrounding land and the mines operated only for a few years before closing. While housing conditions in some coal towns were acceptable, in others they were appalling. As one of the commissioners of the Alberta Coal Mining Industry Commission stated in 1919, the "average miner lives in a shack." Single miners lived in dirty, flimsy, and crowded bunkhouses, while those with families lived in small, poorly constructed houses without services. Typically, the response to these conditions was to blame the victims. The companies contended that the miners wrecked the houses and stole the fixtures.[91] Others blamed the miners in a different way. In 1918, the *Calgary Herald* editorialized that wretched sanitary conditions in mining towns were due "to their large foreign population,"[92] an opinion repeated by one of the commissioners and a representative of the United Mine Workers of America during the provincial inquiry into the coal industry in the following year.[93]

Public reaction to the fact that many people could not afford good housing was varied, and only few believed that much could be done about it. The broad economic issues involved in housing shortages generally lay untouched, although it was recognized that high housing costs were detrimental to the long term interests of the province. As some Albertans argued in 1905, "cheap rent and cheap living is [sic] one of the things that has contributed more toward the building up of industrial centres in the American republic and eastern Canada than any other thing." Accordingly, affordable housing was seen as a precondition for a diversified and strong economy in Alberta.[94] Nevertheless, little was realized. High housing costs led to a vicious cycle in which those who could not afford to rent built poor houses, and those who rented faced rent increases or eviction in boom times because "one never knows when the roof may be sold from off your head."[95] A common rationalization was that the relatively low number of houses built as rental units showed the home loving and stable character of Albertans and the only solace available to those who could not afford to purchase lay in the cliche, "be content with what you have and know."[96] While some people in Alberta objected to land speculation on

◆ A residential street in
Bellevue, Crowsnest
Pass, 1915.
PAA A11.537.

moral grounds, believing that it led to dishonest land dealings, most believed it was a legitimate and acceptable form of activity. Even so, while always eager for economic growth, the same people were concerned that speculation held the seeds of collapse. In 1890, it was observed that "one of the worst things that could ever happen to Lethbridge would be to have a real estate boom worked up. It would be disastrous for her business men, to her prosperity and her fame." In the same breath, however, recent increases in land values were applauded as evidence of the town's growth and potential.[97] In 1882, the *Edmonton Bulletin* was somewhat more clear headed in its argument that land speculation, when price was tied only to the "future," and not productive value, meant that the town could never be built up through long-term investment.[98] This view appears to have maintained some popularity, and when the 1911 boom started in Edmonton, the board of trade unsuccessfully attempted to cap speculation and prevent corruption by requesting the provincial government to pass regulations controlling land dealings.[99]

Overall, Albertans were caught by their own definitions of progress and economic growth. In the minds of many town and city leaders, increased permanent population was, understandably, the key to the future. In 1890, a number of men working in Lethbridge were forced to leave their families elsewhere because of the shortage of houses in the town, and the money sent to support them was "lost to us." Moreover, a man would be more likely to stay permanently in the town if his family was with him.[100] But the concern that housing shortages would slow economic development was mitigated by the fact that they were only the result of growth. In 1901 it was admitted that the housing shortage in Calgary was "inconvenient" but was, nevertheless, a "healthy sign" of the city's development and future.[101] More importantly, housing shortages posed a fundamental challenge to the financing of urban government. In 1921, the *Edmonton Bulletin* observed that the city had too few homeowners in relation to its financial needs. This was a "real and imminent menace. Unless the number of people who are 'tied up' to the city by ownership of property can be increased, there must come a time when its credit will decline to the point of forbidding future borrowing." As Carl Betke in his study of Edmonton observed, the comment revealed the "whole strategy of urban development" in Edmonton.[102] Although the *Bulletin's* remark was made in 1921, it applied equally to attitudes before the war and neatly illustrated the degree to which private home ownership was seen to intersect with wider economic issues.

Although the linking of home ownership and population growth with economic expansion and wealth was obviously true, especially in a province that was in a developing stage, such a policy of economic growth without planning, and which continually created social chaos, was inherently wasteful. This was becoming evident by World War I when most Alberta towns and cities were beginning to experience financial difficulties. The emphasis on home ownership and population growth along with a mania for development had created basic economic problems. Local governments had provided continually expanding services and had been deprived of revenue by the single tax system and by offering tax incentives to attract industry.[103] Such policies soon served only to increase urban debt and forced homeowners to pay higher and higher property taxes. These problems grew worse during the war, and by 1918 much vacant land, both serviced and unserviced, was being forfeited for nonpayment of taxes, creating an ever greater burden on town and city coffers. In one attempt to gain control of its finances, Edmonton, for example, brought in a civic income tax from 1918 until 1920, but it was too late. The city and its ratepayers struggled for the next 25 years to overcome the difficulties resulting from shortsighted policies of the boom years, and the added problems of the 1930s.

◆

Many people lived in small, poorly constructed houses without adequate sanitation or heating because of difficulty in securing mortgages, high housing costs in relation to income, and the use, especially by farmers, of capital for production rather than housing. All these problems were intensified in Alberta, as in some other parts of the country, because of its recent settlement. As A.E. Grauer noted in 1939 in his survey of the history of housing in Canada, "the housing difficulties of low income groups common to all countries have been complicated by conditions peculiar to a young country—rapid growth, inflated real estate values, speculative activity, influx of poor immigrants and lack of planning."[104]

Before 1918 housing was not seen as an acceptable field for public policy in Canada. However, a basic reorientation was taking place. By 1918, it had become possible to define and measure "adequate" housing systematically in relation to local, national, and even international standards. This meant that in postwar Alberta it would be possible to judge housing more uniformly, which would prove to be significant in how society and government could grapple with its housing problems. The development of criteria of adequacy combined after 1918 with a view that society needed to be redirected in the wake of the war. A belief that the war had been caused by materialism, greed, and a lack of co-operation gave new vitality to demands for town planning, sanitation, and other improvements, all of which encouraged a greater role for the state.[105] Yet, governments in Canada provided assistance for industrial development and population growth while, in John Saywell's words, "implicitly assuming that private enterprise would provide the necessary housing." Although the state increasingly accepted responsibility for the safety and sanitation of housing, and thereby increased the costs of "legally adequate housing," it simultaneously refused to control land costs or interfere with market determined incomes. As Saywell concludes, the consequences were recurring housing crises in Canada.[106]

FIVE

Building Materials

In a milieu where a maximum number of new housing units were required at affordable prices, construction materials were of critical importance. Wood was the cheapest material to build with in terms of labour and material, and it is not surprising that the great majority of houses in Alberta were wood frame structures. Brick, stone, and cement were also used by the few who could afford them. Settlers regarded houses built of all these materials as measures of the province's economic growth, permanence, stability, cultural continuity, and integration with the rest of Canada and North America. A move into one of these houses from a temporary log structure therefore was an event of symbolic importance, a view clearly reflected in the Crown Lumber Company float in the 1909 Calgary Exhibition parade. Portraying the development of housing in the province with replicas of a tipi, a log house, and a wood frame bungalow, it sported the placard "Home Sweet Home."[1] In spite of the self-interest evident in this lumber company's display, its slogans and images concisely expressed the prevailing views about the place of the house in definitions of economic and social success.

Brick, stone, cement, and wood were the principal building materials in Alberta. Wood was the most common material and was used

TABLE 5-1 Materials of Construction, Alberta, 1901–1921*

Date	Total Dwellings	Wood	Brick†	Stone	Cement	Other
1901	14,842	10,587	97	17	0	4141
1911	87,672	84,345	1173	149	57	1948
1921	136,125	130,686	3023	95	251	2070

† includes brick veneer
SOURCE: *Census of Canada, 1921*, Vol III, Table 5, p. 12.
*See note regarding *Census of Canada* statistics, p. 303.

for 71 percent of all dwellings reported in the 1901 census and 96 percent of those in 1911 and 1921. Considerably less than one percent of all dwellings reported in 1901, 1911, and 1921 were made of stone or cement, and never more than 2.3 percent were of brick.

BRICK

Brick and stone were widely regarded as elite building materials, perhaps because they were labour intensive to work and because few houses were constructed of them. In south western Ontario in the late nineteenth century, brick was a high status building material,[2] and this association was transferred to Alberta where brick houses were constructed from locally manufactured brick made from local clay. While the first brick yard was established in Edmonton in 1881, and brick was being produced in Calgary in 1886 and at Redcliff in 1887, the brick industry in Alberta was relatively limited until the turn of the century and did not reach maximum production until the boom years between 1907 and 1912. By 1907 most settled parts of the province were producing brick or were close to brick works, although supply was inconsistent because many manufacturers were poorly capitalized and bricks were normally manufactured only during the summer. The brick industry was severely shaken by the collapse of the land boom in 1913, and it suffered further during World War I since it was deemed "nonessential to the war effort and [was] denied supplies and manpower." Many brick yards closed, and although some reopened after the war and new ones opened during the 1920s, most failed during the Depression. Thus, the great activity in brick construction and manufacturing that existed before World War I never revived in later years.[3]

Before 1907, Alberta brick plants utilized a "soft mud process" where clay was worked with water and was then put into moulds. After drying for up to ten days, it was fired for about a week. Such brick often had an uneven surface texture, an attractive softness in its line, and was easy for a bricklayer to shape. After 1907, the Alberta brick industry became more highly mechanized and produced harder bricks with a sharper contour.[4] Although most brick produced in Alberta was used for the construction of commercial and industrial buildings or for house chimneys, fireplaces and basement walls, a few houses had bearing walls made of brick finished inside with lath and plaster. Around 1905, brick veneered houses became increasingly popular in Alberta.[5] By 1906 brick and stone were replacing wood in house construction in Olds, and in 1909 brick houses were becoming more common in Edmonton, especially in wealthier neighbourhoods.[6] As brick became more widely used for house construction, fashions changed. While hard edged, uniform coloured machine extruded brick remained common, brick of a rougher finish and less uniform colouring grew in popularity, which may suggest that the public was not wholly satisfied with the look of the mechanized product.[7]

The use of clinker brick for exterior work was one example of this changing fashion. Clinker brick was always produced by early kilns because their heat was uneven. The bricks nearest the fire were exposed to too high heat, making them harder and darker. Often, the minerals in the clay formed a natural glaze in hues of green, red, yellow, and purple. As well, a number of bricks often fused together into a cluster, which ranged in size from a few bricks to several hundred. Clinker brick was usually thrown away, although bricks of normal shape were sold as seconds for use in rough brick work. In Edmonton, however, the use of clinker brick on the exterior of buildings became fashionable for a time. In 1913, Trinity Anglican church was built of clinker brick, perhaps due to the influence of the arts and crafts movement and its emphasis on natural and rustic materials. This experiment seems to have set a fashion in the city where over 150 such houses were built in the next few years. However, as Jack Manson has noted in his history of brick making in Alberta, "other centres in Alberta didn't take up the challenge to build with these discards. Calgary had only one clinker-built house and there were a few in the Medicine Hat area, Wetaskiwin, and Red Deer."[8]

The use of brick for important public buildings and large residences demonstrated its appropriateness for grand or monumental projects. It was an expensive building product because it was labour

◆ This frame house in Calgary was being veneered
with brick in 1912-13.
GAI NA 3766-22.

intensive and bricklayers were the highest paid building trade in the province. In 1911 bricklayers in Calgary and Edmonton were paid 67 and 60 cents per hour respectively, while stonemasons were paid 65 and 62 cents per hour and carpenters about 50 cents and 48 cents.[9] A brick house was therefore a public declaration of the wealth of its owner. The first brick house in Lethbridge was built in 1888, and by 1890 the local newspaper was congratulating the town on the increasing number of brick houses. While there were many fine frame houses in the town, the paper noted that nearly all the new houses and other buildings under construction were being built from locally manufactured brick. This change from lumber to brick may have seemed only a "trifling thing," but for local residents it was "a sign of increased prosperity."[10]

STONE

In the years before 1918 there was some use of stone as a building material, although almost entirely in Calgary and southern Alberta. The first sandstone quarry was established in Calgary in 1886 and additional quarries soon opened near the city. The local stone was of fine quality; when first quarried it was "very soft, of a buff color with a green tint," but soon hardened with exposure.[11] The quarries continued in use up to World War I, but by 1915 there were "no stone quarries operating on a large scale in or near Calgary." Although stone was used for public buildings throughout the province, few houses outside of Calgary, even of the most lavish sort, were built from stone. In Calgary, one of the first permanent houses was a bungalow built of sandstone. In the following years, a number of the most notable houses in Calgary were built of sandstone, including Senator Lougheed's mansion, built in 1892; Pat Burns's house, completed in 1901; and the "Bow Bend Shack," built in 1889 by William Pearce and described as "the finest house west of Winnipeg."[12] The extensive use of sandstone in Calgary for both public buildings and houses earned it the name "The Sandstone City."

Sandstone was an elite material and both the cost of building with it and its use for imposing and important public buildings and for the homes of the wealthy indicated its status. Even more than brick, its use in houses produced a solid, imposing building that attested to the importance and wealth of its owner. Most of the great sandstone mansions of Calgary were of solid stone construction, but a few, like the Skinner house built in 1911, used sandstone as a veneer over a wood frame.[13] Local building stone was also used extensively for the construction of basements in Red Deer and in Calgary where it was also used for window sills and trim on large houses.[14] The design of houses with stone basements was sometimes criticized, however, and as the Calgary architect, L.M. Gotch, observed in 1912, while local sandstone was of good quality, it was given too heavy a facing. He found it "absurd" to build an "enormously heavy looking basement of rockfaced masonry and then erect a light looking frame house upon it."[15]

Other types of stone saw more limited use in house construction in Alberta. Washed stones set in mortar were often used as a decorative component on verandah supports or for fireplaces in bungalows when a rustic look was desired. A few houses of field stone were built, usually in the far south of the province, but this was a specialized and immensely labour intensive building technique. In some cases, wood was used for the second storey of a house and stone for the first, which solved many of the difficulties inherent in working with stone.[16] In Alberta, stone was perhaps most often used for footings as it was believed that "footings of broad stones without concrete are sufficient to carry an ordinary building" on the prairies.[17]

CONCRETE

Cement, made from fired stone and clay ground to a powder, began to be used as a building material in Alberta about the turn of the century. Portland cement had been developed into a consistent and strong product by the turn of the century and was manufactured in Ontario, Quebec, and British Columbia. At this point, it had generally replaced all other cements in the building trades in Canada. In 1908 the Alberta Portland Cement Company established a plant in Calgary, and in 1910 the Western Canada Cement and Coal Co., with offices in Calgary, opened a Portland Cement plant at Exshaw.[18] By 1910 many basements in the province utilized cement, either in the form of poured concrete or concrete block. However, very few houses in Alberta were constructed from concrete; none was reported in the 1901 Census, and by 1911 there were only a handful, most built of hollow concrete blocks, which could be readily purchased by that time in many parts of the province.[19]

One of the first concrete houses was built for Dr. Mackay in Edmonton in 1904. It was a "cottage" whose heavy walls apparently made it warm in winter and cool in summer.[20] Hollow concrete blocks were manufactured at the building site and were moulded to look like natural stone. This practice of disguising concrete to look like stone was common in Canada. Shortly after 1900 a number of companies, especially in western Canada, began to manufacture concrete blocks, often in the form of "artificial stone." Faced to look as if they had been hand tooled, the blocks provided a quick and easy way to get a masonry house, since the "stone" was easy to lay and required no trimming or cutting.[21] Plain blocks could be covered with plaster, but concrete block was also available in a wide range of facings such as "brush hammered," "broken ashlar," and "corrugated." In other cases, the block surfaces were embedded with pebbles or were made to look like granite.[22] There was some criticism of such practices, since the integrity of the material should be respected and on "no account" should concrete "be required to masquerade as stone."[23]

WOOD

For most people, brick, stone and cement houses were not affordable. For those moving from temporary to permanent houses, wood frame houses could be constructed more quickly and inexpensively than other kinds. In the largest and fastest growing towns in the province, building supplies and lumber were available by the 1890s, resulting in the rapid supersession of log houses by wood frame structures. The first frame house in Edmonton was built in 1881 and by 1885 almost all of the houses in the town were of frame construction, with log remaining in use mainly for stables and barns.[24] During the early twentieth century, some settlers used portable saw mills to produce sawn lumber but production by stationary mills was more common. During the late nineteenth century, there were a number of mills operating in various parts of the province. In the Edmonton area, the Hudson's Bay Company as well as the Roman Catholic mission at St. Albert operated sawmills during the 1880s while others were established in the 1890s. A small portable mill was operating at Red Deer by 1883, and although other mills were set up later in the decade, the biggest development in sawmilling in Red Deer occurred in 1905 when the Great West Timber Company was established. The first sawmill began operation in Fort Macleod in 1888, and Colonel Walker initially supplied most of Calgary's re-

◆ A photograph of the first frame house in Edmonton which was built in 1881. By 1900 it had become a real estate office. GAI NA 1337-4.

◆ One of the leading citizens of Lethbridge, E.T. Galt, manager of the North West Coal and Navigation Company, lived in this frame house in 1885. PAA A8287.

◆ Lumber and supplies for the Barr colonists at Lloydminster were rafted from Edmonton on the North Saskatchewan River in about 1903. PAA B5606.

quirements from his mill established in 1882.[25] The Walker mill was too small to supply Calgary's rapidly expanding needs and sawn lumber was therefore scarce and expensive, forcing people to build with sandstone or continue living in "less substantial quarters." Sawn lumber became more readily available after 1887 when the Eau Claire Lumber Company was established. Because of the size of its timber holdings and its "special rights" to raft logs on the Bow River, it gained a near monopoly of the Calgary lumber market in the late nineteenth and early twentieth centuries.[26] The lumber from all of these mills was mostly consumed locally, although some of the largest sawmills provided lumber to a few areas beyond their immediate hinterland. By 1890 Edmonton lumber mills were exporting lumber to the Battleford market by rafting it down the North Saskatchewan River.[27] Similarly, lumber for the Barr colonists at Lloydminster was rafted from Edmonton in 1903. In many other parts of the province, however, sawmills were not set up until after World War I, and in these areas sawn lumber had to be imported by rail, often from British Columbia.[28]

It seems that a great deal of poor quality lumber was used in Alberta. In 1907, it was asserted that the lumber trade in Calgary was passing out "of the village stage" where only "mill refuse" had been used.[29] While it was an exaggeration to call Alberta lumber "mill refuse," most local sawmills could only supply spruce and tamarack which was used mainly for rough framing, sheathing, sub floors, and lath. Better quality lumber, especially fir and cedar, was imported from British Columbia. Many Alberta lumber yards mainly sold British Columbia lumber and by 1906 mills in Cranbrook were filling much of Calgary's demand.[30] British Columbia timber was able to penetrate the Alberta market because of its quality and because of railway transportation. "Building lumber was an early cargo" on the railway; indeed, "one of the first evidences of a nascent service centre was a lumber yard along a railway spur."[31] While British Columbia lumber had a natural advantage because of its quality, the British Columbia government also tried to stimulate consumption through advertising. Pamphlets called "British Columbia Timber for Prairie Farm Buildings" produced in 1915 contained floor plans and building hints for wood construction.[32]

While most of this imported lumber was used for finishing work, many houses were also framed with British Columbia lumber. In addition, large Alberta mills, such as D.R. Fraser and Co. of Edmonton, processed rough British Columbia lumber into finished building products. A number of similar manufacturing operations existed in the province, and in 1911 there were four sash and door companies operating in Edmonton alone.[33] One of the most successful of these in Alberta was the Cushing Company, established in Calgary during the mid 1880s. The company imported rough lumber from British Columbia and manufactured siding, moulding, and other milled products. In 1891 the Cushing Company boasted that it custom manufactured "every kind of builders' supplies" and was producing large quantities of "doors, window sashes and blinds, mouldings, scroll work, turnings, frames of all descriptions, store fronts and fittings, stairs, etc." By 1910, Cushing's product line and stock had expanded further and included mantels, light fixtures, and, among others, bevelled glass ovals for a "classy front door or vestibule door."[34] By the early twentieth century, many more companies were supplying or manufacturing building products in Alberta. The Edmonton Paint and Glass Company was a major supplier of screen doors, paint, and other products, and the Edmonton Metal Works Ltd. manufactured metal goods such as eavestroughing. By 1905, department stores such as Revillon Frères had hardware departments that sold building materials and tools, and building supplies could be ordered from mail-order suppliers such as Cordon Van Tine Co. in Davenport, Iowa. Eaton's was also a major supplier of building materials such as building paper, plasterboard, roofing material, and even lumber by the carload lot.[35]

SUPPLY OF BUILDING MATERIALS

The participation of companies such as Revillon and Eaton's indicated that the market for building materials in Alberta was significant. By the early twentieth century, changes in retailing, the expansion of the market, and the steady increase in the variety of building products meant that a single retailer carried a huge range of products. The department store model was increasingly copied by building product retailers, who stocked or could order lumber as well as all the products needed for building a house.[36] Many of these businesses were single outlets, but many others were operated as part of a chain of stores throughout the province and even the region. The Cushing Company opened a factory and store in Edmonton in 1894, following with a supply depot in Regina in 1905 and one in Saskatoon in 1911.[37] By 1908 the Staples Lumber Company, based in Calgary,

◆ Lumber yards, such as
the Globe Lumber Yard,
Holden, shown in 1915,
were important busi-
nesses in many early
towns. PAA A6686.

had established lumber yards throughout the province south of Red Deer and claimed that it had the largest retail building supply network in Alberta.[38] In later years, large national and international lumber companies such as Beaver Lumber and Crown Lumber Company confirmed the chain store trend.

By the early twentieth century, the supply and distribution system for lumber and building materials for those building in or near the major centres of the province was fully developed. Affordability was a different matter, especially after the turn of the century when lumber prices increased rapidly. Much of this was blamed on the actions of the Western Lumbermen's Association. In North America, building suppliers were commonly involved in cartels, a method of price fixing that was used in western Canada as well.[39] The Western Lumbermen's Association, which operated throughout western Canada, included most retail lumbermen in the west and almost all the "sawmillers from Lake Superior to the coast." It was alleged that the association established trading territories to limit competition and that members dealt only with members, boycotting all others. From about 1900 to 1903 the price of lumber increased 20 percent, even though freight rates had fallen. Subsequently, supply was said to be restricted further by the lumber dealers and sawers, forcing prices even higher. This occasioned much violent language among consumers, and some thought the association should be renamed the "Lumbermen's Burglars Association," while others described it as a "villainous" organization that was slowing down building.[40] In 1906 there was a split in the Western Lumbermen's Association, and while it continued for a time to operate in Manitoba, Saskatchewan, and part of Alberta, most Alberta retailers joined another association called the Alberta Retail Lumber Dealers' Association. The two Associations were alleged to act in conjunction with sawmillers to fix lumber prices on the prairies.[41] In 1907 the Edmonton *Saturday News* warned, "let no one mention Standard Oil" because "the octopus of the mountain has got them faded into mere shadows."[42] At this point, the Alberta government stepped in, bringing charges of conspiracy to unduly prevent competition and to keep up prices against members of both the Western Lumbermen's Association and the Alberta Retail Lumber Dealers' Association. The Crown proceeded with a test case against W.H. Clarke, the president of the Alberta Retail Lumber Dealers' Association, which was defended by R.B. Bennett before Chief Justice Sifton. In his judgement, Sifton held that the charges against the Western Lumbermen's Association could not be sustained because it had already ceased to operate in Alberta. In respect to the charges against Clarke, he held that although there was insufficient evidence to show a conspiracy to fix prices, Clarke was guilty of conspiring to unduly prevent competition in the sale or purchase of lumber in Alberta.[43] In mid 1908, Chief Justice Sifton's judgement was upheld by the Alberta Supreme Court and within days the price of lumber began to fall.[44]

WORKING WITH WOOD: CONSTRUCTION PRACTICES

Before 1918, milled frame construction consisted of two variants, balloon framing and platform framing. These two systems existed coterminously up to 1930, although balloon framing was probably the earliest to be developed. By the last quarter of the nineteenth century in North America, milled framed construction had replaced the older timber frame methods of house construction. These timber framing methods were labour intensive since a timber skeleton, fastened together with mortise and tenon joints, was constructed. In contrast, balloon framing used studs running the full height of the building. The floor joists sat on a sill and were nailed to the studs.[45] This skeleton was given lateral strength through sheathing consisting of milled boards nailed to the frame and covered with siding. In a balloon framed house each stud was a load bearing element. The resulting frame was rigid, requiring a good foundation that would not let it shift and fracture.[46] Such framing was in use in British Columbia and in Winnipeg in the latter part of the nineteenth century, having been brought north from Chicago where it had been perfected during the 1830s.[47] In 1886 a balloon frame house was built for the Peace Hills Indian Agency near Edmonton.[48] Balloon framing relied upon the mechanized production of standardized sawn lumber and plenty of nails to hold it together. Once a costly item, nails had become so inexpensive by the 1880s that they could be used in huge quantities and even wasted on a job site. As Thomas Ritchie noted, it was "cheaper for a carpenter who dropped a nail to let it lie rather than take the time to pick it up."[49]

One disadvantage of balloon framing was its use of expensive long lengths of wood. The other form of milled frame construction, platform framing, avoided this problem. After the first floor joists were laid in place, single-storey-height studs were erected and the second floor joists were then laid to provide the working platform for erection of the second storey studs.[50] This permitted rapid construction and produced a sound structure with less expensive material. With the existing information on early Alberta building techniques, it is impossible to determine the proportion of balloon framed buildings to those using platform framing before 1918 but it was probably similar to Manitoba, where inventories of provincial buildings suggest that after 1890 platform framing was in common use.[51]

The primary advantage of milled frame construction, whether platform or balloon framed, was its low labour requirements. The skills needed for such construction could be mastered easily and a few men could build a house quickly, an advantage in places where experienced workers were scarce and where quick construction was necessary to meet the housing needs of a rapidly growing population. Like all frame methods of construction, such houses could be enlarged easily. People with limited capital could build a basic, affordable house and renovate and enlarge it later as the family grew and money became available.

Milled frame construction was an efficient approach to building, but further economies could be realized through its use in prefabricated systems promising increased housing supply through factory organization and marketing. One form of prefabrication consisted of manufactured modular, knock-down units which were then shipped by train and assembled on the site. The British Columbia Mills Timber and Trading Company of Vancouver manufactured houses, schools, banks, and other buildings. The company patented a system in 1904 which consisted of "a panel incorporating a series of layers of wood and tarpaper separated by an air space." These panels were finished on the outside with siding and the interior was either lath, which could be plastered, or tongue-and-groove cedar. These laminated panels were linked together by a weather-proof moulded joint that ran along the sides of each panel. Once the panels were linked together by coupling the mouldings, they were reinforced with bolts, and further stability was achieved with mortised sills. Similar systems had been developed at an earlier date in the United States, but the American buildings were found to be unsuitable for western Canada as they were draughty and cold, a defect the B.C. Mills system corrected by use of its weather-proof strip.[52]

Such prefabricated systems of building had advantages in frontier environments and "met an urgent need for instant houses in labour and timber scarce areas" which were linked by railway to manufacturing centres. Moreover, they were relatively inexpensive, ranging

◆ The use of balloon framing is shown in this photograph taken at Edmonton in 1904.
CEA 10-566.

An important benefit of milled framed construction was that buildings could be easily enlarged as this photograph of the construction of an addition to a homestead house in Carlstadt shows (no date, pre 1915).
◆ GAI NA 2083-24.

◆◆ Advertisements for ready-cut houses. *Farm and Ranch Review*, Dec. 5, 1917 and Jan. 5, 1918.

from $100 to $200 for a small temporary house to $400 to $785 for larger, permanent structures. Prefabricated systems were also flexible because their modular design could be varied according to site and individual need.[53] While it is unclear how many B.C. Mills houses were built in Alberta, they appear not to have been in widespread use. They were manufactured only from 1904 until 1910, and, in her study of housing in Alberta, Thelma Dennis found only a handful of surviving examples.[54] Although it is unknown why these houses were not more popular, one factor seems to have been a stigma associated with "instant" houses; a bias the B.C. Mills houses tried to overcome by sometimes using a shingle cladding which disguised their tell-tale panels.[55] Moreover, the ready-cut manufacturers, whose products were the main competition to the B.C. Mills houses, advertised their houses as being permanent structures, implying that modular buildings were temporary. Indeed, the ready-cut house seems to have been a more popular system of prefabrication. The manufacturers provided pre-cut mitred and notched materials including joists, studding, sub-floors, and siding. They supplied windows, glass, doors, stairs, verandahs, and mouldings, as well as building paper, nails, screws, other hardware, and, in some cases, even paint. The pieces were numbered and were assembled by reference to an instruction manual. This was said to be a cost efficient system because it conserved materials by eliminating waste and, more importantly, it saved labour by eliminating the "IMMENSE amount of measuring, cutting and sawing required in construction work."[56]

Ready-cut houses were available in the United States by about 1904 and were marketed by Sears, although the best known U.S. manufacturer was the Aladdin Company.[57] While Aladdin marketed its houses widely in western Canada, Canadian manufacturers were more active in the western market than were American ones. In 1911, and especially by the end of World War I, there were a number of companies, such as the Western Construction Company, Regina, and Prairie Builders, Calgary, marketing pre-cut houses in Alberta. These manufacturers provided a wide variety of one-, one-and-a-half, and two-storey houses in the currently popular designs. Many of these were given names, usually of local significance, with the "Regina," the "Edmonton," and the "Lethbridge" all marketed on the prairies. The popularity of these houses is difficult to measure but judging by the number of companies serving the prairie market and the wide array of available designs, it can be assumed that they were popular. They were relatively inexpensive; Eaton's eight-room gable house sold for $945 in 1910 and other smaller models were available for about $700,[58] which was said (and appears to have been) about one-third the cost of a comparable custom-built house. In their advertisements, the ready-cut house manufacturers played to the popular virtues of self-help and independence by telling purchasers that if they could "use a hammer," they could build their own home and "do all the work like an Expert." Another commonly stressed quality of ready-cut houses was that they were "not portable, but up to stay," and thus were "real homes."[59] They were not identifiably prefabricated, as were the B.C. Mills houses, which may have been an important consideration for those who wanted their house to look custom-built.

INSULATION

Despite their reputation as modern, permanent, and fashionable, buildings utilizing milled frame construction had thin, hollow walls which permitted cold draughts to penetrate the house easily and travel along the floors. Balloon framed houses were not only cold, but the continuous wall studs from sill to top plate meant that, unless blocks were inserted at the second storey floor level, there was also a continuous passage up the wall through which fire could spread.[60] Consequently, the insulation and heating of these houses became a matter of the greatest importance. Although interiors often were finished with lath covered with plaster, this provided only minimal insulation for the hollow wood walls. Indeed, in many cases, lack of money or time meant that houses were not lathed and plastered until a later day, leaving the unfortunate inhabitants shivering behind the thin walls.[61]

There were various methods used to insulate milled frame houses. Spaces between the wall studs and the ceiling joists were filled with sawdust, shavings, and even peat moss in order to keep out the cold. Storm windows and doors were also used on permanent houses from the beginning of settlement.[62] Lath and plaster was initially considered to be part of the insulation of a house, but its effectiveness was being questioned by the end of World War I when energy prices had increased substantially. Various products, some of which had been around for a number of years, began to be promoted as the answer to energy conservation. Beaver Board was claimed to have insulating properties, as was Linofelt, a treated fibre product

◆ Phil Broder and Jim
Campbell did plastering
over lath in Castor in
1910. GAI NA 3876-4.

that came in rolls and could be laid easily beneath roofs and floors and inside walls. Another product that enjoyed a revival because of war time shortages of manufactured products was raw flax straw stitched between heavy paper. This came in bats that fitted between the wall studs.[63]

More complicated and expensive approaches to insulation included recommendations that all flooring be double; that double floors have a layer of plaster in between; that lath and plaster be applied to the inside of the roof in the attic; and that the space between wall studs be filled with plaster, concrete, or brick up to three feet from the plate. The latter was meant primarily to prevent floor draughts, but it also helped to keep vermin out of the house.[64] This was a system favoured by George Brown, a Winnipeg architect, who in 1894 recommended that prairie builders ensure air tight construction through tight joints. He also suggested filling the walls with plaster to create an "air tight jacket of plaster for the building." Such practices were unusual in Alberta, although one house built in the late nineteenth century in Calgary used it, much to the consternation of its owners many years later when they attempted to move it to a different lot.[65]

The commonest method of insulation was to lay building paper, as well as tar paper, between the wall sheathing and the siding, under the shingles, and between the interior lath and the studs.[66] As well, double floors, but without any plaster, lath and plaster on the inside of the house, and shavings between the wall studs were commonly used. Often, however, wall insulation was neglected entirely. While good quality, fully modern houses would have been insulated, usually with wood shavings, many houses had no insulation other than generous amounts of building paper. In a desperate attempt to keep out the cold, many houses were banked with straw, snow, and even dirt. Even then, since most houses relied upon stoves rather than furnaces for heat, many were cold, miserable places in the depth of the prairie winter.

◆

Rapid population growth, labour shortages, material costs, and the prairie climate all affected the construction and the price of houses in Alberta. Yet, a massive amount of housing was constructed in the province in the first two decades of the twentieth century. This level of construction was possible in part because of modern methods of construction and processing and distribution of materials. Milled framed construction made an important contribution to quickening the pace of house building, and the skills it demanded were easier to master than those of the older timber framed systems. All of these advantages were further enhanced through prefabricated building systems. Given the standardization of house design in North America and the extent of the transportation network in Alberta by the late nineteenth century, these building systems found ready acceptance because they were affordable and produced houses that met conventional taste. In this context, the need for rapid and affordable construction served to reconfirm the higher status of brick and especially stone as building materials. Materials and methods of construction thus may have been founded upon pragmatic considerations of efficiency and technical development, but they inevitably became tied to social assumptions and interpretations about status.

INTERWAR AND WARTIME HOUSING

1919 – 1945

SIX

Housing Conditions 1919–1945

The Alberta economy slumped immediately after World War I, turned upwards in the mid 1920s, and by mid 1928 began the decline leading to the Great Depression. The slow down of construction during the Depression, combined with low wages, created housing shortages and poor living conditions. These problems were becoming acute by 1939, and the outbreak of World War II intensified them, especially in urban areas. Agriculture remained the most important sector of Alberta's economy between the end of World War I and World War II. In 1927–28 it made up almost 70 percent of Alberta's net value of production, with the balance in manufacturing, construction, mining, and other sectors. While better weather and a minimally diversified economy resulted in a less severe depression in Alberta than in Saskatchewan, Albertans too had their share of misery and dispossession.[1]

The near collapse of the house construction industry in Alberta during World War I, and its continuing problems during the 1920s and 1930s, fuelled arguments that public housing was needed because private enterprise could not supply housing inexpensively or efficiently. These arguments, although rarely reflected in government policy, continued to be made until the end of World War II. Although the first national housing plan was created in 1919, it proved to be shortlived, and national housing programmes did not become a permanent reality in Canada until the 1930s. Alberta did not effectively participate in these programmes until 1944, by which time a housing crisis of unprecedented proportions existed in the province.

Despite Alberta's nonparticipation, the national programmes established before 1944 did have an indirect impact on housing in the province. The development of formal housing standards in connection with these programmes heightened public consciousness about design. These standards were largely extensions and elaborations of pre 1918 ideas on open plans, on the connection between light, sanitation, ventilation and human health, and on the relationship between urban planning and the quality of housing. On the whole, houses continued to be built by small builders. Milled frame construction continued to dominate, while techniques of installing and locating services showed little significant change, although electricity became increasingly important.

In the interwar years, home ownership continued to be associated with family life and social stability, and it remained an indicator of community development and individual economic and social standing. The Alberta press frequently advised that home ownership was the route to self-respect and independence, that it was a good investment, and that it was the cornerstone of public morality and community vitality. Good homes were thought to make great leaders, and in 1922 it was said of Premier Herbert Greenfield that, "behind him, in his Premier's Office, was the strength of the home life in Edmonton that had always been on the farm near Westlock."[2] Rental housing continued to be characterized as a waste of money, a source of social chaos, and a sign of individual irresponsibility. This attitude was clearly indicated by one Edmonton Alderman when, in 1929, he termed apartments "nothing better than slums."[3] The identification of material well-being with social responsibility was clear, but the home was also an example of the progress of civilization and the superiority of twentieth century life over all previous times, peoples, and achievements. Moreover, it was contended in 1920 that "if you can make the people love their home, you have saved that people from the blight of Bolshevism." Thus, the home measured progress for, "of all our civilizing influences, it is homes that shall longest and strongest endure."[4]

While the virtues of home life were promoted by the press, by lumber companies, and by other beneficiaries of house building, a good number of people in Alberta needed little convincing. Home ownership, or living in a detached house, remained a deeply rooted preference. Although statistics were imprecisely gathered, the census reported that over 94 percent of all dwellings in 1921 and 1931, and about 90 percent in 1941, were located in single detached houses.[5] This did not mean that these homes were occupied solely by their owners. While most people in Alberta lived in a detached house, many, especially in urban areas, were renting either a room, a flat, or the entire building. Approximately 50 percent of urban dwellings from 1921 to 1941 were rental accommodation of some sort, roughly the same proportion as in other urban areas in English Canada. The number of rented dwellings was much lower in rural Alberta, where they made up approximately 18 percent between 1921 and 1931, increasing to 23 percent by 1941. Thus, while between 66 and 70 percent of all dwellings in Alberta between 1921 and 1941 were owner occupied, home ownership was unevenly spread between rural and urban areas.[6]

POSTWAR ADJUSTMENT AND HOUSING

The slow down of construction during World War I had created serious housing shortages by the end of the war. Some believed that slow building conditions were the fault of people putting money into automobiles rather than houses,[7] but it was soon obvious that the problem lay in affordability. Housing was widely recognized as a priority for postwar adjustment. Both Britain and the United States had developed housing programmes as part of the war effort and these precedents were important for Canada. As Thomas Adams of the Commission of Conservation observed in 1918, "if there is a shortage now, what will be the conditions when several thousand men return from Europe?"[8] Adams's question pointed to the dual housing problem that postwar adjustment faced: taking care of returned soldiers and meeting the already pressing housing needs of the civilian population.

In 1917, the federal government passed the *Soldier Settlement Act*, which enabled soldiers to obtain loans on a 20-year term to homestead or purchase land for farming. The loans could be used for a variety of purposes, including building a house. In Alberta, most of this settlement took place in the Peace River country and in the areas north and east of Edmonton. By the end of 1920, almost 20,000 soldier settlers had taken up land in Canada, 5,785 of them in Alberta.[9] By 1919 the federal Soldier Settlement Board had issued architectural drawings for outbuildings and four different kinds of modest houses which could be built easily and quickly by soldier settlers. The plans were drawn with prairie conditions in mind and included double floors, storm windows, "liberal use of building paper," and an exterior wall finish of an asphalt "flint coated ready roofing," all of which would "make a wind-tight job." The interior was finished with wall board. The houses ranged from a two-room gable roof shack of 238 square feet to a small six-room two-storey homestead house. All were designed to be enlarged easily in the future. Soldier settlers could buy building materials at reduced prices, and complete packages of the materials required could be purchased from Eaton's as well as from many lumber yards.[10]

Another postwar adjustment programme, introduced in 1919, aimed to create employment and stimulate the economy by meeting the demand for affordable housing by low income urban people. Under this housing scheme, the federal government lent $25 million at 5 percent to the provinces, distributed according to population. The provinces in turn lent this to municipalities where jurisdiction in the housing field lay.[11] Loans were made to prospective owners at 5 percent, as opposed to the current rate of 8 percent, amortized over 20 years. The plan did not apply to farm housing; it aimed to provide industrial housing for people with incomes of less than $3,000 per year. Local governments were required to provide land at cost, by expropriation if necessary, in order to eliminate speculation. As well, each province was required to develop a housing plan according to which the houses would be built, ideally on a single serviced site close to amenities and employment. The federal government drew up recommendations for design and construction, which, while not mandatory, were considered the "minimum standards for health and comfort, and not as ideals that are difficult to attain." The cost of the houses to be built under the scheme could not exceed $3,500 for a seven-room wood-frame house.[12]

The houses built under this plan were to be of "modern character." This meant that each house had to be part of a general plan in which it faced onto a street or a large courtyard and was accessible to playgrounds, parks, and other public services. It could not occupy more than 50 percent of the lot, and the land was expected to represent about 10 percent of the total cost of the house exclusive of local improvements. Houses were expected to have proper sewage disposal systems and ample clean water. The bathroom was to be located on the second floor of a two-storey house and each room, including the bathroom, was to have a window placed to provide good cross-ventilation. Basements were not to be used as living space. Minimum sizes were established for rooms, and all ceilings on the second floor were to be at least eight feet high and were to cover no less than two-thirds of the floor area.[13] These standards were promoted not only by the federal government but also, with some slight modifications, by the Ontario Housing Committee whose recommendations received wide coverage in Alberta newspapers and in Canadian building journals.[14] Clearly, what had been the elements of modern design before World War I had become standards that applied universally across the country. This was one of the most important effects of the scheme, and, as was observed in 1919, "by this legislation, Canada has lifted the study of the homes of her people from a local. . . . interest to a national status."[15] Surprisingly, there were few objections to the entry of the state into a field that had so far been wholly in the hands of private enterprise, but the importance of the scheme as a model and the need for affordable housing for workers outweighed its challenge to "the virtues of free competition."[16]

The federal housing scheme was introduced in Alberta against a background of troubled local governments, housing shortages, rising costs, and high urban unemployment. During the massive expansion of urban areas in the province before 1913, local governments had serviced great amounts of vacant land. When the boom collapsed, the prospects for rapid development of this and other subdivided but unserviced land disappeared, and much of it was forfeited for nonpayment of taxes. Between 1918 and 1920, Edmonton took possession of 70,000 building lots in the city, almost all for tax arrears, and by 1919 Calgary owned two-thirds of the land within its boundaries for the same reason.[17] Yet, despite this land glut, and illustrating that the causes of housing shortages varied over time, there was a housing shortage that pushed up costs. In 1919, rent in Edmonton and Calgary was up 25 percent, and even as high as 50 percent over the year.[18] Most of these increases were due to a shortage of capital for housing and the cost of materials and labour which, by 1920, had risen by between 70 and 80 percent over 1914. Thus, a house that had cost between $4,000 and $6,000 in 1914, now cost between $6,500 and $9,500. The only saving grace was that land was cheap and lots that had cost $2,000 in 1912 could be had after the war for $500.[19] The increase in labour costs was a result of inflation, and calls for cheaper labour were unrealistic in light of increased consumer costs.[20] At the same time, unemployment was high, and in 1919 carpenters in Edmonton lobbied the city and the provincial government to initiate building projects to create employment. As the *Calgary Herald* editorialized, most of those who "went to the front were connected... with building and construction work," and given the need for housing and for employment, house construction would solve a number of postwar social problems.[21]

Thus, the provincial government was initially enthusiastic about the federal government housing scheme. Premier Charles Stewart estimated that Alberta would be eligible for about $1.6 million in loans, or enough to build 530 houses at $3,000 each. This new construction would promote urban renewal and forestall the development of "slum conditions" in downtown Edmonton and Calgary. Further, it would help to improve housing conditions in mining communities such as Drumheller, where housing was extremely poor.[22] Critics of the plan observed that payments on a $3,000 house, even at 5 percent, would be about $33 per month including upkeep and taxes, which was more than the "average workingman" could afford.[23] The provincial government also began to reconsider its support, with the provincial treasurer arguing that Alberta would benefit more from a programme directed at encouraging renovation and repair of houses in industrial areas than one directed at new house construction. The province also contended that it wanted the money as a grant, not as a loan, and further argued that if it had control of its natural resources, which were controlled by the federal government, it would be able to fund its own programmes. While the province showed some concern about enforced minimum standards, its main fear was that local governments would never repay provincial loans. Thus, despite a number of calls for Alberta's participation in the programme, the premier informed a delegation of mayors in 1920 that Alberta had decided not to participate, and, "as to borrowing money from the Dominion government on municipal securities, he was inclined to think that every municipality in the province was already pretty well up to, or past, its borrowing powers."[24]

Local governments supported the provincial government's refusal to participate in the programme. Calgary was concerned that the programme would add to its civic debt and refused to assume responsibility for loan repayment by issuing debentures. Alberta cities also resisted development of a uniform provincial plan. Edmonton, for example, argued that the money should be available for renovating, repairing, and moving houses onto serviced lots, while Medicine

Hat wanted to make loans to anyone, including landlords, to build what and how they wanted. Moreover, urban governments refused to provide land from their rapidly growing holdings, and all promised to charge borrowers full administrative and land costs. In practical terms, this would put the houses built under the scheme out of reach of the intended market.[25] Of course, had local governments participated in the programme, their land holdings would have been reduced, needed houses would have been built on vacant serviced land, and some revenue would have been produced for the cities. However, no urban government took a long view, which, along with the provincial government's justifiable reluctance to take any risk in the circumstances, scuttled the programme in Alberta.

By 1921 when it was repealed, every province except Alberta had passed housing legislation under the scheme, and all except Alberta and Saskatchewan had received advances under the programme.[26] Despite charges by the provincial opposition that Alberta's failure to participate in the scheme lay solely with a "faint-hearted" provincial government, the programme had a number of drawbacks.[27] It was not particularly successful anywhere except Winnipeg. One basic problem was its reliance upon local governments, which were too inefficient and uncaring to make it work. Because it made no provision for assisting rural home owners, provinces with large rural populations, like Alberta and Saskatchewan, were also disadvantaged. In addition, Alberta's major urban problems were not slums, as they were in many other parts of Canada, but a large number of small, poor quality prewar houses scattered throughout urban areas. In this light, the province's concern for renovation was understandable. The urban housing problems in Alberta immediately after World War I and during the rest of the interwar period were the legacy of prewar land speculation and overexpansion. The federal housing scheme did nothing to solve these problems and it, in certain respects, promised only further trouble by overextending already burdened civic governments. In any event, because the scheme was undertaken at a time of high prices, the houses built under it proved uneconomic in relation to those built after costs had fallen.[28]

HOUSING STANDARDS

Although the failure of the 1919 housing programme helped "to discredit the idea of government assisted home construction" for over a decade,[29] the scheme did establish the first universal housing standards in Canada. While health and public safety standards had become formalized before World War I, the 1919 housing programme expanded such criteria to include those of comfort and enjoyment, which was an important precedent that became apparent in the 1930s. In 1934, the National Construction Council, a lobby group and clearing house for the Canadian construction industry, drew up minimum standards of housing in terms of two broad criteria, health and amenities. Substandard houses were defined as those dangerous to the occupants' health or "incompatible with decency," while amenities set out those things necessary to "provide satisfactory environmental conditions which Canadian customs and standards demand." As in 1919, health standards in 1934 demanded that the house be dry, that it be designed to take best advantage of natural light and fresh air, that all rooms have windows that opened, and that the house have piped-in cold water, an inside toilet, a separate room for cooking, and adequate storage space for food. Structurally, the house need not have a basement to conform to minimum health standards, but it had to have at least a two foot crawl space. In houses with cellars, the cellar was to be dry and well-ventilated and, ideally, should have a cement floor. No living rooms were to be located in basements, except in "specially planned" apartments where the floor was not more than four feet below grade. Central heating was not required for minimum standards of health, although it was necessary to meet minimum amenity standards, as were electric light and complete inside plumbing.[30]

These 1934 standards applied to the whole country, and it is apparent that they were acceptable in Alberta as well.[31] Although they did not specify minimum house size, this concern was implicitly addressed by the insistence upon "satisfactory environmental conditions." In this respect, many houses in Alberta were too small. In 1918 it was observed that the predominance of bungalows and small houses in Calgary demonstrated an "increased and desirable thrift,"[32] but this was simply the talk of local promoters trying to justify that many people could not afford to build or rent adequately sized houses. While dwellings containing four or fewer rooms had dropped from 69 percent in 1911 to 58 percent in 1921, this still represented a significant number of small dwellings. The balance consisted of almost 14 percent with five rooms, just over 26 percent with six to ten rooms, and just over 1 percent with eleven or more rooms.[33] Such gains were not, however, improved upon further in the next two decades. In 1931, just over 58 percent of all households were still

housed in four rooms or less and there was a significant difference between those in urban and rural areas. In Alberta's submission to the
Rowell Sirois Commission, it was observed that in 1931 just under 69
percent of rural households occupied one to four rooms, while only
43 percent of urban households were similarly housed. Even so, conditions in Edmonton and Calgary were still below the national average. Nearly 25 percent of the households in the two cities lived in
three rooms or less, as opposed to the national average of about 16
percent in similar accommodations in cities of 30,000 people and
over.[34] Provincial averages tended to obscure further variations due to
tenure. Overall, housing conditions in Alberta tended to be worse for
renters than for owners. In 1931, of all households in the province
consisting of a family with two or more persons, just under 60 percent of renting households while just under 52 percent of owning
households lived in four rooms or less.[35] As shown in Table 6–1, in
smaller urban centres of less than 30,000 people, just under 29 percent of owning households lived in four rooms or less in comparison
to just over 50 percent of renting ones. In larger urban centres of
more than 30,000 people, the discrepancy was greater: about 22 percent of owning households lived in four rooms or less while just over
55 percent of renting ones were in similar circumstances. While renters were clearly worse off than owners, especially in the larger centres, the greater poverty of smaller towns is suggested by their
greater percentage of owning households living in four rooms or less.
Further, some conclusions on the nature of the rental market can ten-
tatively be suggested, especially in the larger cities where about 55
percent of renting households lived in four rooms or less. Although
apartments, light housekeeping suites and other room rentals are included in these statistics, they still suggest that houses rented in their
entirety by one household or family also tended to be small, indicating perhaps a relatively low capitalization of the rental house market,
and perhaps also that a proportionately greater return could be realized from small houses.

The existing data makes it impossible to discover the difference in
the overall quality of accommodation between rural and urban areas.
While large towns and cities had public water and sewage systems,
many small towns and most farms had neither. Other than this important difference, the standard of city housing, both owned and
rented, should not be overestimated. In 1931, Calgary had 15,047 detached houses, and in 1936 the tax assessor reported that 4,142
houses had dirt basements, the majority with a plank or dirt floor,

TABLE 6-1 Number of Rooms Occupied by Renting and Owning
Households of One Family of Two or More Persons, by
Percentage in each Category, 1931

| | Centres of 30,000 or more | | Centres of 1,000 to 30,000 | |
	Rented	Owned	Rented	Owned
1 room	6.9	0.3	3.6	0.8
2 rooms	15.5	1.6	12.9	3.7
3 rooms	16.3	4.9	14.1	6.9
4 rooms	16.9	15.2	19.8	17.4
5 rooms	17.9	26.4	18.1	21.1
6 rooms	13.7	24.1	16.5	22.7
7 rooms	6.5	13.3	8.0	13.4
8 rooms	3.3	8.1	3.9	7.9
9+ rooms	2.0	5.8	2.7	5.9
not stated	0.7	0.0	0.4	0.1

Calculated from *Census of Canada, 1931*, Vol. 5, Table 65, p. 1030

3,697 were heated with stoves rather than with central heating, 2,151 had less than three plumbing fixtures, 712 were without sewer service, 233 were without water, 856 had basement rooms and 2,529 were reported to be in "poor condition."[36] In other words, most houses in Calgary in 1936 met minimum standards of health, but, in some respects, notably heating, basements, and structural repair, a substantial percentage were below accepted amenity standards.

BUILDING BYLAWS AND TOWN PLANNING

The formulation of health and amenity standards were important preconditions for improving housing conditions, but their implementation often rested upon the presence and enforcement of local building bylaws. After World War I there was growing support for the idea that building bylaws could contribute to, rather than impede, economic growth and stability. In 1919 the *Edmonton Journal* editorialized that while the prospects for postwar growth were good, "there was a danger that at this point must be guarded against. It has happened in Edmonton before that houses have been built for quick selling without particular regard to quality, and some of the derelicts in the city at the present are the result of such half-done work."[37] As before the war, local bylaws did little to stimulate better housing standards. In 1925, Alexander Ross, Minister of Public Works, observed that while the typical building bylaws in Alberta promoted fire protection, "methods of construction and appearance of buildings is not now generally considered because the cities are usually very glad to see buildings erected on vacant lots even if they are not nice to look at. . . . I feel that the same thing would apply to towns and villages."[38]

Nevertheless, some attempts to improve local bylaws were made. Edmonton passed a new building bylaw in 1923, although by 1929 it was admitted to be "singularly deficient" because it was "very sketchy."[39] Accordingly, a new building bylaw was produced in 1935. By this point, building bylaws had also been passed in a number of smaller centres such as Wainwright, Tofield, Drumheller, and Grande Prairie, while other towns such as Brooks and Bassano used combined building and zoning bylaws.[40] In 1929 Calgary began revising its building bylaws, which "were so obsolete as to necessitate new ones," but this meant little without the will to enforce them, and as the mayor of Calgary was pointedly told, "it is very evident that a more rigid inspection is necessary in order that houses and other small buildings may be constructed sanely and safely."[41] In lieu of such willingness, and lacking any compulsory provincial standards for construction, the regulation of building standards remained much as it always had, prey to local political and economic priorities. In this context, the province established in 1932 the Provincial Engineering and Planning Bureau to encourage better servicing in small towns. The bureau provided advice on municipal concerns such as building and zoning bylaws and gas, water, and sewer installation. However, it was not until 1938 that the provincial department of health appointed an inspector to issue permits and inspect plumbing installations in places without "adequate supervision."[42]

Town planning was another means of promoting health and amenity standards, one which the federal government had incorporated into its 1919 housing scheme. The 1913 town planning legislation in Alberta had never been effective, and by 1929 the province had redrafted and consolidated its town planning legislation. A Town Planning and Rural Planning Advisory Board was established, and local governments were empowered to appoint local town planning commissions and pass comprehensive zoning ordinances and master plans. The advisory board provided advice to local communities, developed model plans and building bylaws, carried out educational work, and heard appeals from local planning commission rulings. However, after only three years of work the provincial planning staff was fired in 1932 as part of government retrenchment during the Depression.[43] The central planning board continued to operate but at a reduced level, and in most parts of Alberta before 1945 town planning meant little more than resurveying and zoning.[44] Nevertheless, the 1929 legislation represented an important effort to fix the house within an officially ordered environment that would express a rational relationship between the house and its wider context.

Many urban problems stemmed from the fact that towns and cities often encompassed far too much land in relation to their population, making it expensive to provide services to a dispersed population. Many residential areas in towns and cities were not built up completely, with the result that new house construction in the interwar years was largely infill housing.[45] Many local governments encouraged and even subsidized the moving of houses from outer to inner locations in order to create more compact urban areas, and throughout the 1920s, house moving was a continual spectacle in Alberta towns and cities.[46] Another remedy for overextended urban areas was to resurvey subdivided vacant land; plans of subdivision were cancelled and the land was designated for other uses, usually agriculture. In 1922, Red Deer cancelled 39 plans of subdivision, Camrose cancelled 22 and the same process was repeated throughout the province. Even so, urban areas in Alberta remained huge in relation to their population. In 1925, Edmonton and Calgary, with a combined population of about 100,000, had a combined area as great as Toronto with a population of 500,000.[47]

Zoning, or the regulation of land use, was undertaken by many Alberta communities during the interwar years. Early attempts at zoning included Edmonton's adoption, in 1923 and 1925, of "zoning type restrictions" which specified land use, density, and space around buildings, and defined some areas as strictly residential. Calgary's zoning bylaw, passed in 1934 after several years of debate and opposition from some business groups, was similar and created three types of residential districts: single family, two family, and multiple dwelling.[48] In 1929 the province brought in new subdivision regulations which stipulated that streets had to be a minimum width, all lots had to be at least 50 feet wide and 100 feet deep, and that side, rear, and front yards had to be of a minimum size. In conjunction with the au-

◆ A homestead house on the move in Edmonton, 1935. CEA 160-961.

◆ The collapse of the economy after 1913 left many Alberta towns and cities with dispersed housing. One solution to the problems this posed was to move houses into more built-up areas. This large foursquare house was moved across the Elbow river at Calgary in 1929. GAI NA 2186-6.

thority granted to local governments to prepare comprehensive plans under the new *Town Planning Act,* 26 communities adopted zoning bylaws in the decade after 1929. None of these zoning bylaws were part of comprehensive planning, however, but were "simply pragmatic documents aimed at protecting land values by separating land uses from one another."[49]

Local political dynamics continued to be important in the application of planning legislation, and exemptions from zoning were easily gained through political influence or because local governments believed they would stimulate economic growth. Thus, in practice, while zoning provided some safeguards for urban residential areas, such protection was usually only sporadic.[50] These small gains, however, were frequently lost during World War II. In 1942, the federal government, attempting to alleviate housing shortages, overrode all municipal zoning bylaws. This measure remained in effect until 1951 and, as a result, "garages were partitioned and pressed into living accommodation by the hundreds, basements and second floors were made into suites and large dwellings converted into apartment houses and rooming houses with little or no regard to Zoning or Building Regulations." This created much additional living space, but it was often of wretched quality and established a pattern of development that cities later found difficult to reverse. In 1951, it was recalled that while some owners participated in this wholesale conversion "from a strong sense of patriotism. . . . the majority of these developments were carried out for purely monetary reasons," and it was difficult, after the wartime emergency had passed, to force owners to lose income by readopting the prewar zoning requirements.[51]

Development and planning controls and provincial health regulations had little effect on farms. Although rural planning had been part of Premier Brownlee's original objective in the 1929 town planning legislation, rural development and planning controls were never practicable. A dispersed farm population ensured that the occasional proposals for various forms of rural planning, usually in the form of nucleated settlement, were never viable.[52] Development regulation through local governments proved difficult, and the only pragmatic approach to the improvement of farm life seemed to be through educational and service programmes. For example, the province provided lists of appropriate flowers, trees, and shrubs, and the names of suppliers, in the hope that farmsteads would be improved through horticulture. It also attempted to encourage farmstead planning through the Town Planning and Rural Planning Advisory Board which drew up model and custom plans for farmers. By 1931, 169 requests for custom plans had been received and plans had been drawn up for 73 applicants.[53] Conforming to prewar theories, these plans emphasized the need to separate the farm house from other farmyard buildings, livestock pens, and pastures by planting trees and siting buildings appropriately. The province also provided recommendations for farm water and sanitation systems. Horace Seymour, Director of Town Planning, told the United Farmers of Alberta convention in 1929 that farmstead planning was essential to reinforce and sustain the family farm, and the first improvement for "happy living" was running water and sanitary facilities in the farm home. These services made "for self respect, for the respect of others, and on this respect the happiness of the home is based."[54] Doubtless, the subtleties of such remarks were not lost on his audience, but the official recommendation that "chemical closets" be used only when the subsoil prevented the use of a septic tank was rarely followed.

OIL AND MINING COMPANY TOWNS

Planning in rural areas was focused on the family farm and nonurban development and planning controls were implemented only in the oil producing area around Turner Valley. Exploration and extraction were underway around Turner Valley on the eve of World War I, but development began in earnest around 1924 and was in full swing by 1928.[55] In 1929 the province designated an area of about 30 square miles around Turner Valley as oil producing. Permanent housing was to be concentrated in the town of Turner Valley where no further drilling was anticipated. This ruling attempted to protect public safety and simultaneously promote natural resource development since the oil companies wanted complete freedom to drill throughout the area. Outside the town of Turner Valley, but within the designated area, employees of the oil companies could obtain yearly permits to live in temporary housing, usually shacks and houses on skids. In the province's view, this controlled development and ensured public safety, while the oil companies were satisfied that permanent housing developments would not interfere with future exploration and extraction.[56]

The concentration of development in the townsite of Turner Valley was Alberta's first attempt to control housing as part of a regional plan and to deal with housing within the context of natural resource development.[57] In large part, the attempt was successful, although some problems did occur. For example, because they wanted to drill at the settlement of Bamford, the oil companies resisted the registration of a subdivision there, even though it was not within the designated oil producing area. Most buildings in the settlement were subsequently moved or burned, but about 20 families who were unable to move continued to live in the midst of the exploration work going on around them.[58] Overall, however, the provincial policy of controlled housing in oil producing areas succeeded in encouraging compact settlement, a policy that was to reach its zenith after World War II, especially in places such as Drayton Valley and Devon.

Turner Valley represented only one aspect of Alberta's highly varied nonurban housing which ranged from desperately poor conditions in many coal mining towns and for Metis in northern Alberta to somewhat better conditions for those on many farms and in small towns. Although the housing crises created by World War I had stimulated discussion in Canada about the need for better quality subsidized housing for industrial workers, this debate had little practical effect on Alberta coal miners. Much of the housing in many remote and single industry mining communities was provided by mining companies, which the province was reluctant to regulate. In the early 1920s, all housing in the settlements in the Coal Branch, near Edson, was company owned and most of the houses were either simple bungalows or two-storey frame houses of one to four rooms. In some communities, such as Cadomin, the class structure of the community was reinforced by the site plan, which separated supervisory staff houses from those of miners with woodlands and a road. Rents varied among settlements, but a house at Mountain Park rented for $9 to $11 per month, plus utilities; not excessive by provincial standards.[59]

In other cases, miners received poor return for their rent payments. Housing conditions in some communities were poor; sanitation, water, heating, and garbage disposal were either lacking or haphazard. In 1925, the Alberta Coal Commission, a provincial board of inquiry into the coal industry, noted that in coal mining areas, "on the average, the conditions found cannot be described as satisfactory." In the Crowsnest Pass, conditions at towns such as Blairmore were "fair to good," although "even here. . . . slums have been allowed to spring up in the various 'Bush towns,' 'Slav Towns,' [and] 'Shack Towns.'" The Commission described housing conditions at Lethbridge as fair, although since it reported that water and sanitation were a problem, as they had been before World War I, this description was not entirely justified. The poorest conditions were near Drumheller, where "some of the worst living and housing conditions" in the province were found. Conditions in Drumheller itself were fair, but there were many mining communities scattered throughout the valley, few of which were planned or had services. Poor housing was aggravated because "short periods of employment seem to have precluded the workmen from building themselves anything more than the barest of shelters." Of all the mining communities, the best conditions were found at Nordegg, where the company had developed a planned town in which the houses were built in rows permitting installation of some services. By 1925, many of these houses had water and sewer connections, while others had water piped to the outside of the house, a level of sanitary services considered acceptable at the time. The main problem at Nordegg lay in housing shortages during periods of peak production, when many workers lived in tents.[60]

The commissioners contended that responsibility for improving housing conditions in coal mining communities lay with both mine owners and government. They concluded that owners of new mines in remote areas should be compelled to provide good housing for workers, initially in the form of boarding houses, and later in a properly planned compact townsite where building regulations could be applied and where up-to-date electrical, sewage, and water services could be provided. The commissioners also noted the miners' objections to closed camps, where only the company owned land. Although it described these objections as "both sentimental and real," it recommended that there be both company supplied housing and building lots for private dwellings. In either case, the commissioners stressed that proper town and regional planning was the key to improving housing and such requirements should be enforced in new and old coal mining communities. They unequivocally rejected the argument that "pioneering conditions" justified poor housing, and they stressed that it was "time that minimum requirements of health, decency and comfort should be enforced on all without discrimination."[61]

These clear recommendations produced no results, and in 1935 another inquiry into the Alberta coal industry found conditions unchanged. Housing conditions in the Drumheller area remained "thoroughly unsatisfactory" and again it was recommended that "a determined effort" be made to improve housing and living conditions in the mining areas through state enforcement of health regulations

◆ A group of small cottages
for miners at Nordegg,
photographed in 1964.
PAA A8277.

◆ Metis dwellings near St.
Albert, early 1930s. Re-
produced with permis-
sion from *The Metis in
the Canadian West* (Ed-
monton: University of
Alberta Press, 1986).

and town planning. In the view of the commissioners, such requirements were reasonable since the industry was "well established and (certainly in the case of the bituminous mines) profits have been realized for a considerable period."[62] Nevertheless, corporate profits at least meant regular employment for miners, a luxury for many in the 1930s, and in 1939 it was remarked that seven years of fairly steady employment in the mines at Coleman had led to the construction of new houses in the town. Almost all building lots were occupied, and as the editor of the *Coleman Journal* noted, "Coleman had indeed been fortunate compared with many places in Alberta."[63] In contrast, in mining communities with less robust economies than in the Crowsnest Pass, and where mine owners were responsible for providing housing or community services, improvement in housing conditions was difficult to bring about. Miners, in comparison with mine owners, had little political influence and often stood outside of the mainstream of provincial life because of their ethnicity and their political views.[64] In such a context, poor housing conditions in some mining towns became institutionalized within a framework of owner exploitation and hostility between miners and mine owners.

METIS HOUSING

The Metis, who possessed neither land nor control over their lives, experienced some of the worst overall conditions found in rural Alberta. In 1935, a provincial inquiry into the conditions of the Metis revealed extremely poor standards of housing. The Bishop of Grouard, the Right Reverend Guy, O.M.I., declared that less than 50 percent of the Metis in his parish lived in "decent houses" and he observed that, given such conditions, the people "become indifferent to their conditions after a while" and built shacks along the road allowances. At Lac La Biche, it was estimated that 90 percent of the Metis lived in tents in the summer. In the winter two or three families lived "in a small shack plastered with mud from which they are driven out in the spring by innumerable insects."[65] Comparable conditions could also be found on some Indian reserves, but Indians were often better off than the Metis, particularly on the reserves in southern Alberta where houses were built by the federal government. Differences in the land rights of the two groups affected their housing. While the Indians did not technically own any land, they at least had security of tenure, whereas the Metis had neither. While Mr. Chris tianson, the federal Inspector of Indian Agencies, observed that most Metis knew how to build with logs and were "fair carpenters," Felix Calihoo of the Half Breed Association told the commissioners that the problem was not a lack of skill. Many Metis lived in temporary shacks here and there on public land because "they don't own any land."[66]

Demoralization among the Metis and high incidence of diseases such as tuberculosis were certainly aggravated by poor housing. The official response to such conditions was paternalistic. If the government provided education, the major problems, including those of housing, were expected to disappear.[67] The province refused to recognize Metis aboriginal claims, and the land question was later dealt with by the creation of "settlements," where the Metis lived but neither owned nor controlled the land. While this policy at least meant that they no longer had to squat on public lands, by the 1960s the Metis were still living in poor housing.

FARM HOUSING

While conditions on many farms were poor, they were never comparable to the desperate quality of most Metis housing or the worst conditions faced by coal miners. Because the settlement process continued to occur in Alberta during the interwar years, shacks, log houses, and other pioneer shelters continued to be built in the frontier areas. In the Lesser Slave Lake area, the Peace River country, and northeast Alberta, houses built in the 1920s and 1930s possessed all the characteristics of pre World War I pioneer housing.[68] In addition, permanent farm houses elsewhere in the province did not always mark an improvement over frontier conditions. In 1936, it was judged that "not one farm home in ten is fit for human habitation."[69] Although this was an exaggeration, it is evident that a great many farm houses were rudimentary, having little or no insulation and usually only the most elementary sewage and water services. In 1920, a typical farm house in the Stettler area was described as a series of "add-ons." The house started out as a small two storey, then possibly an addition made it into an L or T form, and later still, lean-tos were sometimes built at the back and on the side.[70] Farmers were continually urged by government agencies and by retailers to build modern houses with modern services, but this was unaffordable for many farmers, especially in the 1930s when farm incomes were extremely low. In 1936, for instance, net farm income in Alberta averaged $229 per farm.[71]

◆◆ Log houses continued to be built in frontier areas in the interwar years as shown in Harry Holmes's construction of a log house at St. Lina in 1922. PAA A2147 AND A2148.

◆ A farm house with a
lean-to, no date, ca. late
1920s. PAA 68.199/173.

◆ A semi bungalow for the
farm was featured in
Gordon's Lumber Supply
exhibit at the Vegreville
fair, 1928. PAA B2759.

Farm housing conditions varied immensely, even in the same area, but were usually worst in recently settled areas. In 1924, a survey of conditions in west central Alberta, around Sylvan Lake, Eckville, and Alhambra, showed that houses in this area included frame houses with electricity and fully plastered interiors as well as shacks and log houses. These variations were linked to length of settlement, land quality, and micro climate, and while the survey carefully noted the ethnic origin of the settlers, it drew no connection between ethnicity and housing conditions.[72] In 1936, in Alberta as a whole, only one farm in forty had electricity, running water, and sewage systems. In 1943, a comparative study of housing in the Bonnyville and the Red Deer-Wetaskiwin areas revealed the differences between areas of longer and more recent settlement. Of the farm houses near Bonnyville, an area of recent settlement, half were log, 70 percent had "dirt" basements, about 23 percent had "improved or full basements," only an average of 5 percent had electricity or central heating, 4 percent had cisterns, and none had bathrooms, running water, or septic tanks. In the longer settled Red Deer-Wetaskiwin area, the picture was somewhat brighter. Fully 15 percent of the farms had electricity, 30 percent had central heating, and an average of about 12 percent had bathrooms, running water, septic tanks, and cisterns.[73]

HOUSING IN URBAN CENTRES

A similar pattern of varied housing conditions existed in Alberta's small towns. Some towns in the 1920s were in a pioneering stage, while others had moved from this stage completely. For example, Okotoks had cement sidewalks, gravelled streets, and natural gas by the 1920s, while the town of Fahler in the Peace River area had only begun to develop and in 1930 was still facing all of the sanitary, water supply, and housing problems of a frontier town.[74] Post World War I inflation was as significant in towns as it was in cities and created the same problems. In 1920, housing shortages and high costs in Drumheller forced many to crowd into existing dwellings, while others built even though they could not afford to. The consequence was "that some of the one and two roomed shacks so thickly scattered throughout the town are housing such numbers that they can only be classed as a menace to the health of the community." Such housing shortages persisted in many towns, and in the mid 1930s housing was in short supply in Peace River and in

Cardston.[75] The *Cardston News* editorialized in 1936 that a federal-provincial programme was needed to stimulate house construction to help get people off relief and improve housing conditions in the town. Housing in Cardston suffered from the combined legacy of poor construction and low incomes. Many houses were so poor that renovation was pointless:

> What is the use of spending money on so many of these old fire traps called houses in Cardston when a good fire would wipe them off the earth. Scores of houses in this town are neither warm enough to live in, nor fit from a sanitary point of view to house human beings. A good Jersey cow would die in many of them. The value has gone out of them, and many of them are mortgaged to a point beyond all value, and most of them are taxed until the town year after year is acquiring more and more of them.[76]

Housing shortages in almost all urban centres were a recurrent problem throughout the interwar years. The worst hit segments of the population were immigrants and the poor. In 1927, the Canadian Pacific Railway and the Canadian National Railway continued to bring immigrant farm workers to Edmonton, even though there were few jobs, and then often at such low pay that the men refused the work. Nor was there adequate housing, and the men lived in appalling conditions, crowded into box cars, sheds, and basements in downtown Edmonton.[77] Others, however, were able to take advantage of falling prices and there were booms in house construction, especially in the late 1920s. The cost of living index showed an irregular but steady decline from 1920 to 1933 when it reached its lowest point since the end of World War I.[78] For those with steady incomes or some capital, this was a boon, and in many cases, a house could be purchased in Edmonton and Calgary in 1929 for the same amount as at the height of the boom in 1911–12. In Edmonton in 1929, the City Commissioner noted that "a good commodious house can be purchased or even a new residence built to a cost of anywhere from $3,500 to $6,000 according to size and finish and the location of the building."[79] It will be recalled that a fully modern five- to seven-room house in suburban Calgary in 1911–12 would have cost in the area of $4,000. Lower housing costs were partly a result of the lower cost of land throughout the interwar years and the decline in the cost of materials in the 1930s. As well, labour costs fell. Carpenters' wages

declined by as much as 20 percent between 1920 and 1922, not re-
gaining their postwar high until about 1926. By the early 1930s,
wages had begun to fall again, and by 1935 the building trades in the
province were earning desperately low wages; by 1939 their wages
were less than they had been in 1932.[80] As before World War I, a cycle
of low wages meant that the housing of lower income earners did not
improve; indeed, it probably became worse. The pre World War I
rule that housing should cost no more than 20 percent of gross income continued to be used. In 1930, another approach to defining affordability was that the cost of purchasing a house should not exceed
100 times the weekly wage, or in other words, an amount equivalent
to almost two year's wages.[81] Even for many skilled workers, such as
brick and stone masons and carpenters, who were employed 27 and 29
weeks on average respectively in the 12 months preceding June 1,
1931,[82] the possibility of owning a good house was a distant one.

Even though 1929 was the high point in the building cycle during
the interwar years in Alberta, the market was seriously unbalanced,
especially in Edmonton, Calgary, and Lethbridge, and in the next decade incomes continued to fall and house construction continued to
slow. When people built houses, they tended to build small inexpensive structures, thus augmenting the stock of poor quality buildings
in the province. Many people renovated, and by 1936 the amount
spent in Alberta on alteration, maintenance, and repair was nearly
equal to that spent on new construction. Much of this renovation
consisted of converting houses into flats or, as they were known at
the time, light housekeeping suites.[83] By 1929, a number of large
downtown Calgary houses, most of which were located in the area
south of the CPR tracks, had been made over into furnished light
housekeeping suites. These suites were not licensed by the city and
often were inadequate, many having limited toilet and washing facilities. Rooming houses continued to be common, serving mostly single
men, often railroad workers who moved to the city for the winter.
These rooming houses were licensed by the city, and the Calgary
Health Inspector claimed that overcrowding was not generally a problem. When it occurred, however, he claimed that it was mainly in
"those occupied by foreign people, mostly Southern Europeans." In
fact, he claimed that poor housing and overcrowding were "not found
to any great extent" in the city, except in some rooming houses and
light housekeeping suites. Low wage earners occupied a number of
small houses and shacks on the outskirts of the city, and there were
also many small houses in the city proper, but he believed that none

of these presented a civic problem even though a number of these houses were not connected to the sewage and water systems. While they were located on serviced streets, most were "occupied by the owners and in many cases they have not the means. . . . to install proper sanitary facilities and would have to vacate their property if forced to connect."[84]

Despite such claims, it is apparent that housing conditions for the urban poor were substandard by 1929 and became worse during the Depression. From 1930 to the late 1930s house building in the province stopped almost entirely. Fewer residential building permits were issued in Calgary for the entire decade than had been issued for the single year 1929. By 1938, the deterioration of old houses, population growth, and the lack of new construction had created a shortage of 2,000 houses in Edmonton.[85] Even for those with some income, moderately sized houses were hard to find and a "great many people" could not furnish them even when they were available. The number of rooming houses and light housekeeping suites mushroomed. Single family houses were converted into suites in both Edmonton and Calgary, and by the late 1930s these conversions were occurring at such a rate in Edmonton that some believed it was "creating slum conditions."[86] In Calgary, suites were filling with people who had "sold their household equipment in an effort to keep off relief only to find they were forced to go into housekeeping rooms." While light housekeeping suites were licensed in Calgary by this time, apartments were not. Hence, many owners, by putting a stove in a room "automatically switched (possibly overnight) their homes into apartments consisting of 6 or 7 suites," where small families of "three or four are found to be living and having their entire being in one room." Office buildings were also converted into apartments, but these buildings at least usually provided adequate space. While simple greed led some owners to rent their property in this manner, others coped with their own poverty by breaking up their houses into suites and renting them, enabling them to stay off relief and live "from day to day and get by" on the small rental payments they received.[87]

Even at low rents, light housekeeping suites were beyond the means of many people. In 1936, single men on relief received $1 per week for accommodation, enough to buy only a spot in a rooming house which was, "to say the least, very miserable." A number of these places were capable of accommodating fifty or more men "under the cubicle system." The beds were "ramshackle, the linen conspicuous by its absence, blankets are in a very poor state of repair, and there is ofttimes no adequate accommodation to take care of bathing and personal hygiene." Nevertheless, there was little that civic authorities could do in the circumstances. While people were living in places that should have been condemned, officials were reluctant to apply the law because there were no alternatives and "people cannot be turned into the street." The law was only enforced where basements were converted into suites, but even here the regulators felt constrained and "how far we will be able to continue stressing this is a matter of some debate."[88]

HOUSING AND WORLD WAR II

The ongoing housing crisis, intensified during the Depression, became even worse during World War II. By 1940 the shortage of housing in Edmonton and Calgary was even more desperate than it had been before the war, exacerbated in Calgary by population growth caused by expansion in the oil and gas industry. Light housekeeping suites were becoming a way of life in urban Alberta. Even more marginal housing was becoming common, and in 1940 it was no longer unusual to find people living "in more or less adapted garages" in many parts of the province. Lethbridge was said to need 100 houses to meet demand. Rents were high, and a "very humble bungalow" in Calgary rented for $45 per month, at a time when the average working person earned about $60 per month.[89]

Wartime restrictions and uncertainty inhibited house construction. In 1939 the City of Calgary estimated that although 500 new houses were needed just to meet demand, they had issued only 54 permits during the year. Even this limited activity had slowed by 1942 when shortages of manpower and materials had become more extreme.[90] Further demand was created by an influx of military personnel and their dependents into the province during the war. The establishment of an air base at Claresholm created unprecedented demand for housing in the town, and by early 1941 there were 250 men living in hotels or rooming in the town.[91] Crowding was especially bad in Edmonton where the RCAF set up an air training base and the United States army established its Northwest Service Command. While the military usually built barracks for its personnel, it did not usually do so for their dependents. Local facilities were nonetheless sometimes commandeered for personnel and in 1941 the RCAF took over the student residences at the University of Alberta, forcing 600

◆ Wartime Housing Incorporated built these houses in Edmonton in 1944 in response to wartime housing shortages. PAA BL720.

students to find accommodation elsewhere. As a consequence, they crowded into single family dwellings and as Cecil Burgess, professor of Architecture at the University of Alberta, observed, "though the students may appear to enjoy this, the crowding is probably far from desirable."[92] While cramped student accommodation was one thing, crowded family housing was quite another. In mid 1943 the Edmonton Emergency Accommodation Bureau had 1,350 names on its waiting list for houses, suites, and rooms, and most of these were "couples with one or two children." Despite such conditions, the Edmonton Chamber of Commerce protested Washington's order that dependents of U.S. servicemen return to the United States because of the housing crisis in Edmonton. The chamber succeeded in having the order cancelled by arguing that such a withdrawal would damage the city's economy. The population of Edmonton continued to increase at an alarming rate, and it was estimated that over 20,000 people arrived in the first half of 1943 alone. Even when the Americans moved their headquarters to Whitehorse in 1944, the departure of thousands of military personnel made little difference to the city's housing crisis which persisted for the balance of the war.[93]

Implementation of specific programmes in response to wartime housing shortages came only from the federal government. In 1941 it established a crown corporation, Wartime Housing Incorporated, to relieve wartime housing shortages and provide housing for war workers, recognizing that productivity could be increased if workers were decently housed.[94] Wartime Housing Incorporated built 438 houses in Alberta during the war and more afterwards to accommodate returned men and their families. After energetic lobbying by city officials, a number of these houses were built in Edmonton in 1943–44.[95] They were two- and three-bedroom permanent dwellings with basements. Although such houses were usually mounted on posts or blocks, Edmonton's climate made basements essential. The houses were located in the north end of the city near the airport, and while they were not built as a single community, they were grouped together as much as possible. They rented for about $30 per month, a low rent for the time, and it was anticipated there would be some future arrangement to sell them to the tenants. Despite the desperate need for housing, there was some grumbling from city council about the project. One alderman observed that the housing would all be "owned by the government and our people here will be just a bunch of renters," which, in addition to its callous ignorance, showed how remarkably tenacious were the ideals of private enterprise and individual home ownership. Nevertheless, the public was enthusiastic about the programme. There were 1,800 applications for the 244 houses, and those who managed to rent one of these homes were able to get inexpensive, good housing with reasonable security of tenure.[96]

In addition to Wartime Housing Incorporated, the federal government attempted to regulate the economy in order to increase housing supply and stabilize the market. The federal override of local zoning regulations was one aspect of this policy, and rent control was another. The federal government's promise to prevent war profiteering was appealed to by rent control advocates who alleged that landlords were gouging their tenants. The province refused to become involved on the grounds that rent control was a federal wartime responsibility,[97] and in late 1940 the Wartime Prices and Trade Board brought in rent control in Calgary, the first in Alberta. At the first hearing, 1,200 cases were heard and "in quite a number of cases" increases in rents were permitted.[98] Claresholm, Red Deer, Edmonton, Medicine Hat, Lethbridge, and other communities were placed under rent control in mid 1941, and later that year controls were established throughout the province. Wartime rent control was probably necessary, although it created some bitterness among landlords who contended that permissible rents were too low, that they were inconsistently applied, and that controls were a demeaning and unwarranted interference in property rights.[99] Yet, given postwar dislocation, federal rent control stayed in place for a considerable time after the war, and the province continued it, albeit reluctantly, in 1951.

SEVEN

Government Housing Programmes

The problems experienced during the Depression intensified arguments that affordable housing could not be found solely in free
market production. Public housing, in which construction and rent
were subsidized by the state, was said to be necessary. Such measures
had been used in Europe as part of postwar adjustment in the 1920s
and these programmes were cited as models by Canadians interested
in the problem of affordable housing. Instead of state constructed
housing on the European model, however, the Canadian solution was
to provide subsidies and guarantees for mortgaging; in effect, subsi-
dizing private housing built by the free market. This was effected not
by local and provincial governments, which had jurisdiction in the
field, but by the federal government which alone took any practical
steps in regard to housing in Canada during the 1930s. These federal
policies did not, however, develop from a political conviction that
people had a right to good housing. Rather, they were designed to
meet the crises of the Depression and to create employment; policies
developed against a backdrop of demands by the building industry for
housing programmes to stimulate the economy.[1] While these housing
schemes were designed primarily as economic stimulants, it was significant that they were focussed on private housing. By using hous-

ing for such purposes, the state became involved in one of the central aspects of everyday life and helped reinforce the primacy of the single family detached house as the Canadian ideal.

FEDERAL HOUSING LEGISLATION

Under pressure of a coming election, the government of R.B. Bennett appointed a special parliamentary committee to examine the development of a national policy on house building. In 1935, the committee recommended that a comprehensive programme for slum clearance, the construction and repair of houses, and the construction of public, or low rental housing, be initiated through the provision of low interest loans. It recommended that the first priority be the repair of existing structures as a supplement to other employment measures.[2] Later the same year, the government appropriated $10 million for a housing programme and passed the *Dominion Housing Act* (DHA). The DHA provided low interest loans for the construction of new houses, duplexes, and apartments, but not for the renovation or repair of existing dwellings. The money for these loans was provided jointly with private lending institutions, and this use of a joint lending approach endured in Canada until 1954. The owner provided a minimum 20 percent down payment, while the private lending institution lent the balance, made up of funds provided jointly by the federal government and the lending institution. The federal government "provided an interest subsidy and capital guarantee which virtually eliminated all risk of capital and interest loss on funds advanced by institutions." Consequently, the interest rates on DHA mortgages were lower than on conventional mortgages. The greatest innovation in the DHA was the use of blended payments where the mortgage was paid off in monthly installments consisting of interest and principal. In keeping with the economic objectives of the programme, it was administered by the Department of Finance.[3]

This legislation was designed almost purely as a remedy for unemployment. It was soon apparent that the DHA was doing little to stimulate house building or improve housing for low income people, and in 1938 it was repealed and replaced with the *National Housing Act* (NHA).[4] The NHA consisted of three parts. Some provisions of the DHA were re-enacted as Part I, under which low interest loans of up to 90 percent of the cost of a $2,500 house, or 80 percent of higher priced houses, were available for the construction of owner-occupied homes. Once again, funds were provided on a joint basis by the federal government and private lending institutions, with the lending institution making the loan and taking a mortgage on the property as security. The federal government also provided a collective guarantee of the loans. With almost no risk, private lenders, such as trust companies and insurance companies, thus became central instruments in Canadian state housing policy. To qualify for a loan, a house had to meet certain minimum standards of design and construction.[5]

Part III of the NHA (1938) was operative only to 1940 and assisted new home owners with property and school taxes. Part II of the Act allowed the federal government to provide money at very low interest rates for the construction of low-income rental housing, either through local housing authorities or local housing corporations acting on behalf of a local government. The local government was required to exempt partially such houses from taxation. This low-income housing was intended for those people who were paying more than 20 percent of their total income on rent. Part II of the NHA was never implemented, and its low-income housing provisions accomplished nothing except to raise the hopes of public housing proponents. While it was the first legislated provision for public housing in Canada, it was a testament not to political will but to the lobbying efforts of supporters of public housing. It did, however, establish the "principle of selected tenancy and of an economic ratio between income and rent," an innovation in Canada.[6] The failure of public housing in the 1930s has led some historians to argue that the housing legislation of the 1930s, as well as much of the subsequent legislation, was primarily designed to provide assistance to the middle class and to the private building industry. As John Bacher has shown in his study of Canadian housing policy, this was not an accidental result of the legislation but was "reflective of the marketplace ethos that. . . . shaped all federal housing efforts."[7]

In 1944 a new *National Housing Act* (NHA) was passed as part of postwar planning. The NHA (1944) grew from the recommendations of the Curtis report, which had studied the potential role of housing in postwar reconstruction. The NHA (1944) was designed to stimulate the construction, repair, and renovation of houses, improve living conditions, and increase employment after the war. It retained most of the basic features of the 1938 Act, but it permitted a greater number of initiatives in the housing field. In addition to loans to individuals, the act provided for loans to co-operative housing projects; loans to builders to build houses for sale to NHA borrowers or for rental;

loans to large-scale low-income rental housing projects put up by limited dividend housing corporations for which the profit could not exceed 5 percent; guarantees to life insurance companies to invest up to 5 percent of their assets in housing; and grants to municipalities for slum clearance. In addition, it allowed the federal government to undertake planning, research, and education about housing in Canada.[8] The act established the parameters for postwar housing policy in Canada, although, as will be seen in a later chapter, not all of its provisions were enacted immediately.

FEDERAL HOUSING SCHEMES AND ALBERTA

Neither of the two major federal housing programmes of the 1930s, the DHA (1935) or the NHA (1938), was operative in Alberta. The only federal housing measure that applied in Alberta before 1945 was the Home Improvement Plan (HIP), established in 1937. This programme was designed as a make-work project and allowed private lending institutions to make low interest personal loans to houseowners for repair, renovation, and, in some limited cases, for construction of houses. Loans to a maximum of $2,000 were available and the federal government guaranteed to each lending institution up to 15 percent of the total loans it made.[9] When the programme was abolished in 1940 in an effort to divert manpower to war-related construction and production, almost 10,000 loans, worth over $4.3 million, had been extended in Alberta. Under the programme, local governments exempted home improvements carried out under it from increased assessment. While the programme did nothing to increase the number of houses, its provisions were "liberally interpreted" to permit renovation of houses and other buildings into "suites or apartments."[10] In other words, landlords were receiving low interest loans to create more light housekeeping suites. In any event, the HIP was a relatively minor programme, and in 1940 the Edmonton city commissioner described it as a "palliative rather than a solution" to the city's housing crisis. Indeed, contending that what was needed was Part I NHA loans, he noted that "overcrowding has arrived at a point which cannot be described as other than menacing."[11] Nevertheless, the HIP was the only federal programme in which Albertans could participate because lenders agreed to make the loans based on the overall credit worthiness of the applicant.[12] In contrast, Part I NHA loans were secured by mortgages on land, and institutional lenders refused to provide such mortgages in Alberta because of the province's debt legislation. This meant that, almost until the end of the war, the Part I NHA provisions were only of academic interest to Albertans.

While legislation affecting the rights of lenders to recover debts had been passed in Alberta as early as 1920, increasingly contentious legislation was passed by the Social Credit government after its election in 1935. Some of this legislation aimed to protect borrowers against the loss of their land under foreclosure actions for nonpayment of mortgages. Even more contentious was the legislation allowing cancellation of debts and moratoriums on repayment of loans. As Lucien Maynard, the provincial Attorney General, recalled in 1945, the government believed that "a man's home was more sacred than his bond and that it would be most unfair and unjust to let people, families with small children, be thrown out in the road simply because they were not able at that time to meet their iniquitous obligations."[13] While most of this debt legislation was aimed to protect farmers, some of it was also designed to assist urban homeowners. For example, *An Act for the Security of Home Owners* passed in 1938 protected both. A lender holding a mortgage executed before 1938 could not foreclose on a farm home, and before it could initiate or continue a pending foreclosure on an urban home, a lender had to deposit $2,000 with the court, which was to be paid to the homeowner if the foreclosure action was successful.[14] In other words, lenders had to pay an urban mortgagor $2,000 on any foreclosure.

For critics of Social Credit, who had long railed against its economic policies, this was the last straw. In the same year, the Edmonton Chamber of Commerce, reflecting its members' economic and ideological interests, petitioned the federal government to disallow as unconstitutional this Act, along with other debt legislation passed in 1938. Arguing that the reputation of the whole country "will suffer if policies of confiscation and repudiation go unchecked in Alberta," the petitioners contended that, while "poverty is most unfortunate," "confiscation and repudiation [of debt] strike at the very foundation of civilized society." A month later, the governor general, acting on the advice of Ernest Lapointe, the Minister of Justice, disallowed the *Act for the Security of Home Owners* along with one other Alberta act.[15] This left much of the offending legislation untouched, however, and did nothing to persuade lenders that Alberta was a safe field for investment. Thus, challenges to the province's debt legislation continued. In 1942 the Supreme Court of Canada ruled that Alberta's debt adjustment legislation was unconstitutional and the Alberta legislature consequently repealed it the next year. Some restrictions on debt recovery remained, however,[16] and institutional lenders continued to refuse to loan money to Albertans under the NHA, in part to pressure Alberta to abandon all of its restrictive debt policies and in part because they feared for the security of their loans. Thus, the mortgage guarantees and other provisions of Part I of the NHA (1938) were a dead letter in Alberta. Since it was never enacted, Part II of the NHA (1938) could not alleviate the housing problems of low income earners in Alberta and served only to raise false hopes. In 1938, the Edmonton city charter was amended to give the city the power to undertake housing schemes under Part II of the NHA (1938), and it was amended yet again to allow the city to do likewise under the NHA (1944). Edmonton was obviously eager to participate in these programmes in an effort to improve its desperate housing conditions,[17] but it was ultimately unable to do so.

LOCAL GOVERNMENT HOUSING INITIATIVES

Both local and provincial governments were free to implement housing policies of their own since housing lay within their jurisdiction. In both cases, however, policies on housing tended to be sporadic responses to immediate crises and never developed with any consistency. Neither the province nor most local governments supported public housing if they had to pay for it or provide land at cost. Small towns were apathetic, too poor, and too absorbed in the problems of the Depression to take any initiative in the housing field, and only the two largest cites, Calgary and Edmonton, attempted to become involved in housing.

The earliest attempt by a local government in Alberta to establish a housing programme was in 1929, when the housing committee of the Calgary city council resolved that houses should be built by the city and rented or sold on advantageous terms to those who otherwise could not afford them. The city solicitor argued that Calgary would have to secure a charter amendment to proceed with the scheme,[18] and it was found that, even with a municipal subsidy, the cost of the houses would still be too high for many of Calgary's poor. Nevertheless, the housing committee recommended that the programme go ahead, but civic elections intervened and the new council abandoned the scheme because of its cost. Even so, the need for public housing

◆ The Sunset Cottages, the
first senior citizen's
housing project in Ed-
monton, were built in
1938. PAA KS23.

remained critical. In April 1930, the same council that had rejected the housing scheme permitted the erection of tents in one part of the city "for individuals who could not find suitable accommodation."[19]

In Edmonton, a willingness to enter the housing field came later than in Calgary, but Edmonton showed greater innovation. One attempt to bring in a general public housing scheme in Edmonton was rejected by the ratepayers in 1938.[20] However, limited public housing was developed in the form of a complex of houses for indigent senior citizens who were able to care for themselves. In 1937 city council resolved that Edmonton should construct "cottage homes for the aged who are the responsibility of the city" and who were being housed at city expense in rooming houses and light housekeeping suites. The local Lion's Club, eager to find a community project, joined the city in building houses for these elderly people. The city supplied the land and secured a grant from the federal government, while the Lion's Club raised further funds for construction, furnishing, and landscaping of the houses. The dwellings, called the Sunset Cottages, consisted of four duplex houses. Each unit had a bedroom, kitchen, living room, bathroom, and a garden area of about 400 square feet. The facility was only for couples, who paid $15 per month if both received the old age pension. If only one pension was coming in, no rent was charged. It was the first such project in Canada and its success led the Lion's Club to build additional cottages in later years.[21] This was the beginning of what would later become a major area of government involvement in the housing field in Alberta.

Another housing project undertaken in Edmonton was a self-liquidating housing plan. The city started the project in 1937 as part of a work-for-welfare scheme. It received a grant of $32,000 from the federal government and added $42,000, with which it built sixteen houses by 1938. A further $19,000, left over from the initial fund and supplemented by purchasers' annual payments on the first group of houses, was used to build five more houses in 1939. Another two houses were built in 1940 and three were slated for construction in 1941. These houses were not a form of public housing because they were not subsidized, but they did provide a few houses for a crowded city.[22]

ALBERTA GOVERNMENT POLICIES AND HOUSING

Although Edmonton's senior citizens' housing and self-liquidating housing plan had demonstrated what could be accomplished with some initiative and imagination, they were not major projects and did little to lessen public demand that Albertans be enabled to receive NHA loans. However, if the province had any housing policy at all during the late 1930s, it was framed solely by its commitment to debt legislation. Beginning in 1936, frequent demands were made for the repeal of this legislation in order to bring DHA, and later, NHA, lenders into the province. Among others, the Calgary Local Council of Women, The Union of Alberta Municipalities, various individuals, and, of course, building organizations, petitioned for repeal of what the *Coleman Journal* called Alberta's "freak legislation."[23] These demands became even stronger after the beginning of the war, and Albertans' bitterness increased with the realization that they had received nothing while $52 million in loans had been extended to other Canadians under the programme by 1940. In 1941, the Edmonton Real Estate Association claimed that about 1,000 new homes were needed in the city, where many people had enough money for a $1,000 down payment but were unable to finance the balance.[24]

The demands that Alberta dismantle its debt legislation in order to bring NHA lenders into the province became increasingly harsh. Richard Needham, a staff writer with the *Calgary Herald*, typified these views in a series of seven articles which appeared just before the 1940 provincial election. Calling it "Mr. Aberhart's Building Blackout," Needham described provincial debt legislation as the reason for Alberta's housing crisis and high rents. Not only did the legislation have to be changed, he argued, the government and its belief that "all financial institutions are beasts prey" had to go. "If they are defeated at the polls," wrote Needham, "and a stable, sensible government takes over at Edmonton, the whole [housing] picture will change" because NHA loans would then become available in Alberta.[25] Social Credit was not defeated, nor did it soften its determination "to protect the people from exploitation." While much of the offending legislation was repealed after it was ruled unconstitutional by the Supreme Court of Canada in 1942, the government did not abandon the concept. It did, however, offer to exempt NHA loans from the remaining debt legislation, but the lenders refused this concession and insisted that all debt legislation be lifted.[26]

The logjam over the NHA in Alberta finally broke in late 1944. It was obvious to both the federal and provincial governments that relief for the housing crises had to be found. Moreover, Alberta had a new premier. Aberhart died in May 1943 and was succeeded by Ernest Manning, a less radical individual who seemingly did not share Aberhart's visceral dislike of the "money interests." By late 1944, the provincial government publicly signalled that it wanted discussions with the federal government and lenders about the application of the NHA to Alberta.[27] Although the province held firm on its long standing argument that "future debts had no relation whatsoever to past debts and should be considered in a category by themselves," there was a new spirit on all sides and in most respects the province had its way. It passed *The National Housing Loans Act (Alberta)* in 1945, which exempted NHA loans from existing debt legislation, and by 1945 loans under the NHA began to be extended to Albertans.[28]

The contests over Alberta's debt legislation illustrated the authority of rural interests in the province. Alberta's policies on debt coincided with Social Credit, and earlier United Farmers of Alberta, attitudes that lenders were little better than parasites feeding on the farm economy. Significantly, the refusal of lenders to loan money in the province under the national housing acts hurt the urban middle class more than rural people. Few rural people had sufficient income to obtain such mortgages, and their priority in the 1930s was to fend off lenders' attempts to seize their farms for nonpayment of loans. Overall, the government's position was that there was no justification for the lenders' attitude, and it had no qualms about restricting their rights.[29] It was clear that Social Credit's choice between the collective economic interests of farmers and those of the urban middle class lay squarely with the former, who were, after all, the backbone of the economy. Social Credit anti-banking and monetary theories predisposed the government to reject the commoditization of money and reinforced its paranoid and insular tendencies. Yet it must be stressed that the Depression had truly been a crisis; one that propelled Social Credit to power and gave ample proof of how brutal and callous some lenders were.

This animosity towards lenders, which became part of the ideology of Social Credit and part of Aberhart's personal crusade, had a significant negative effect on the provision of housing in Alberta because Social Credit was unwilling, or unable, to develop effective housing policies that would replace the free market NHA programmes. The crisis of the war did little to stimulate changes in provincial thinking. The province made only two attempts to formulate programmes to encourage housing; one was a very marginal success and the other was a failure. In 1940 legislation was passed allowing three or more private individuals to form a building association which could receive low interest provincial loans to build houses for resale. No associations were formed, but in the next year a somewhat more successful tack was taken when the programme was broadened to allow for the formation of co-operative building associations. These operated like a co-operative credit union or savings and loan association that made loans to members at 5 percent amortized for a 20-year term. Modeled on British and American precedents, the scheme allowed individuals to save for a house by purchasing shares in the association. When they had sufficient shares for a 25 percent down payment, the balance could be borrowed from the building association. The province provided a start-up grant and guaranteed the debentures of an association. The first association, and the first of its sort in western Canada, was established in Edmonton in 1942, and 75 houses had been built through it by 1946. Another building association was established in Calgary in 1944 and by 1955 had lent money for 19 homes.[30] The other provincial effort regarding housing was the introduction of *The Alberta Housing Association Act* (1945), which permitted the formation of a municipal association to facilitate the provision of affordable housing, but the act was not proclaimed.[31]

Despite the contention of many that Social Credit's debt legislation alone limited investment in Alberta, it remains that other factors were also important. For one, property taxation was a deterrent to investment in urban housing. Edmonton's abandonment of the single tax in 1918 did nothing to correct its financial woes, and the continued forfeiture of vacant lands for nonpayment of taxes meant that the total number of taxpayers in the city actually declined. In 1920, there were just over 32,000 persons paying taxes on unimproved property and just under 10,000 paying taxes on improved land. Fifteen years later, the total number of taxpayers had declined by about 62 percent to just over 16,000, out of a total population of over 85,000. At the same time, city debt was high because much of the forfeited vacant land was serviced and yet produced no revenue. Demands for welfare, partly covered by municipal governments, also increased dramatically in the 1930s. All of these factors led to higher and higher taxes for city ratepayers. In 1938, the Taxpayers Protective Association of Edmonton claimed that the feeling has grown that property in this city has become not only unprofitable but. . . . in many cases a liability rather than an asset, and people having money to invest are turning to other forms of investment, or leaving their money in the Bank. As a consequence, little building is being done. . . . [and] existing buildings are being allowed to depreciate and are generally in a run down condition.[32]

This situation was exacerbated because many taxpayers were in arrears on their taxes because of the Depression. Yet, urban governments could not, with any degree of conscience or political acumen, proceed with tax arrear seizures and sales. As Mayor Davison of Calgary phrased it, "the homes of some of our people [are] their life savings."[33]

Alberta thus had approached World War II, after a decade of low investment, with a housing crisis. The provincial government was unwilling to sacrifice its debt legislation for the national housing programmes, yet it had no coherent policy of its own. Instead of developing housing programmes, the provincial government indulged in wishful thinking and parochialism. The province commonly argued that Alberta's housing problems were only temporary. In a revealing comment, Aberhart informed a correspondent in 1942, "you know that when this war is over many of those who are living here now will suddenly move away, and leave plenty of room for our citizens."[34] This was the true foundation of Alberta's housing policy. Other than waiting for the Depression to be over, and then waiting for the war to end, there were few provincial initiatives to meet the province's housing problems; Alberta's housing policy before 1945 was a studious avoidance of having a policy at all.

EIGHT

Meanings of Modernity

House Design and Servicing

Theories about house design during the interwar years evolved out of pre World War I ideals. In 1930, Cecil Burgess, who taught architecture at the University of Alberta, observed in a radio talk that "the idea of the home is to serve the needs of the family so that they may be happy there together. This idea is crucial in life and design."[1] The President of the Edmonton Area Home Economics Association had also promoted the same ideals when she argued in 1925 that the home should be "economically sound, mechanically convenient, physically healthful, morally and mentally stimulating, artistically satisfying, socially responsible, spiritually inspiring, and most important of all, founded upon mutual love and respect." In 1933 the association repeated, word for word, its 1925 declaration about the ideal home.[2]

While such theories could mean different things to different people, they were not as vague as first appears. The design of the house was expected to be such that it would create a "home," a place that would serve family life by expressing continuity between past and present and creating a welcoming and comforting, yet reclusive, environment. It should incorporate the most advanced technology for services and amenities and its layout should encourage maximum efficiency and hygiene. These basic objectives were largely reformulations of pre World War I ideas about the necessity of compact areas for efficiency and sanitation and the importance of light and ventilation in ensuring health and contentedness. The house was conceptualized as more than an inanimate object: it had to be planned as a "living creature, a distinct organism" that functioned with its inhabitants in a dynamic relationship.[3]

MODERN VERSUS MODERNIST HOUSES

The concept of the "modern house" must be distinguished from the architectural concept of "modernism" as it was practiced in Europe in the 1920s and 1930s and represented by Le Corbusier and the architects of the German Bauhaus (founded in 1919). The modernists argued that the house should be like a machine whose essence was its functional quality and its relationship with a planned environment. This meant that architecture should make "full use of modern technology and its honest expression in design." It posited that architecture was "a scientific approach to human needs and uses in programming, planning, and design," and that housing schemes should be designed for "varied social uses: old people, single women, families and different income levels, and so on." For its proponents, who often rejected styles as useless, modernism was not a "style" of architecture, but a new philosophy of building in which housing, urban planning, and architecture were inseparable.[4] Planning was especially important. Modern industrial cities demanded high density housing which had to be planned and integrated into increasingly concentrated and complex areas. Given such objectives, the modernists often saw themselves as revolutionaries deliberately rejecting tradition.

The modernist house promoted hygiene through smooth undecorated surfaces, plenty of natural light, and efficient ventilation. However, as Cecil Burgess observed in 1932, a definition of the modernist house was difficult and could best be done by listing its attributes. A "thorough going modernist house," he argued, rejected old materials if something different was available, used reinforced concrete for the walls, had corner windows, a flat roof, rubber and/or tile flooring, smooth plaster or veneered plywood walls, and among other features, metal window and door casings.[5] The modernist house aimed to create a hygienic, efficient, and functional space, an aim shared by what

North Americans had long called the "modern" house. However, while both the modernists and the proponents of modern but traditionally designed twentieth century North American houses often shared the same aims, they attempted to fulfill them through different means and for different reasons. Each were political in their way: modernism's commitment to democracy and collective needs was expressed through revolutionary forms of materials, design, and urban planning; the proponents of the modern house expressed no less a political commitment to liberal individualism and personal acquisitiveness.

By the early 1930s, modernism had become a topic of discussion in Canada, but it had little direct impact on domestic architecture in Alberta before 1945. When discussed, it was usually treated as a stylistic development rather than a process of building and planning. In 1931, the Calgary architect, W.S. Bates, reported on the "new style of architecture" that had been developed "in Europe by a group of architects of which M. Le Corbusier is, perhaps, the greatest exponent." He believed the new "style" created houses with "a very strong resemblance to a small ocean liner."[6] When treated as a style, modernism lost most of its meaning as a process, and few people in Alberta built houses that even copied the designs of modernism. Although Part II of the NHA (1938) was aimed at housing for special groups, and the municipal government in Edmonton had been responsible for the Sunset Cottages for the elderly, neither arose directly from European modernist ideas. The NHA provisions stemmed from North American traditions of industrial housing and were never enacted, while the Sunset Cottages were a pragmatic response to a social problem that devolved from the middle class volunteer social reform tradition of the interwar years. And despite its rhetorical commitment to housing for the common man, modernism was impractical for ordinary houses. It was, as Cecil Burgess observed, "an expensive business" due to its devotion to new materials, many of which were not mass-produced and required special skills to work. Nevertheless, he was confident that many of the new materials would, before long, come into common use and become affordable through mass-production.[7]

If cost was not a sufficient deterrent, modernist house plans were not readily available in Alberta. As before World War I, most house builders refused to pay much, if anything, for plans which were easily obtained from newspapers, commercial plan books, magazines, and local lumber yards. In 1921 the Western Retail Lumbermen's As-

◆◆ The bungalow continued to be a popular house in the 1920s as this Revelstoke Sawmill Co. Limited calendar indicates. The calendar was produced in the United States. GAI M1491, manuscript source.

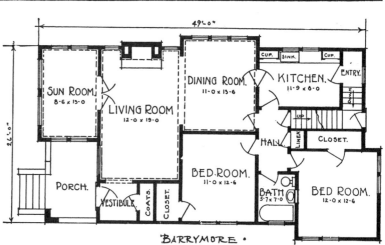

BARRYMORE •

◆ The Hudson's Bay Company built bungalows on speculation in the current fashion in Edmonton in 1920. GAI A688.

sociation, based in Winnipeg, distributed its house catalogue very widely on the prairies. It featured 18 houses, plus plans for barns and outbuildings.[8] Many of the other plan books, with titles such as "Kosy Homes" and "Kraft Houses," came from the United States and were designed for American conditions, but they also appealed to Canadians. Few of them, as indicated by the plan names, paid any attention to modernism but instead presented popular traditional twentieth century North American house plans. This emphasis on North American popular houses persisted, even in plans drawn by Canadian architects. When Maclean Building Reports, the largest Canadian syndicated service for building information, began in the late 1920s to use Canadian architects for many of the house plans it provided to newspapers, there was little apparent difference between them and those produced by American syndicated services.[9] Thus, most people were given no opportunity to adopt modernist principles, nor did they want to. Their tastes were conservative, rooted in what they perceived as traditional forms, which fit their needs and were sufficiently flexible to accommodate modern conveniences and meet contemporary needs without requiring radical changes in design. Progress could be had without modernism. In an observation that went to the heart of Albertan's rejection of modernism, Cecil Burgess noted in 1932 that people did not want to live in a "machine," for "we may make it a machine, but we cannot love it."[10]

Traditional North American twentieth century houses seemed the best anchor in a changing world. Smaller families, public leisure, greater mobility, and a consciousness of hygiene and the benefits of efficiency were all met by the traditional single family dwelling, which provided an efficient working and living unit and still sheltered and protected family life. It was believed that the social change brought about by mass entertainment could best be controlled and integrated into everyday life through the home. In 1930, Cecil Burgess expressed the commonly held view that the traditional home was a means of countering negative social tendencies, for if the home was made more attractive than were "modern outside attractions" such as movies, it could counter the feared disintegration of the family. This concern could be met by designing the house with a view to making it serve "human happiness and helpfulness."[11] It was this challenge, and not that of European modernism, to which people responded in choosing their homes.

Modernism did, however, have an indirect influence on housing in Alberta in the interwar years. The modernists confirmed the importance of hygiene and efficiency and formalized and reinforced the idea that the house should be part of a planned environment. Their exploration of new materials, while not immediately applicable, did have profound implications for housing after World War II. Their experiments with horizontal designs and their innovative use of large glass surfaces, new paints such as a high gloss enamel called Cellulose, rubber flooring, slab doors, and plywood also began to have important applications by the early 1930s. In Alberta, materials favoured by the modernists were usually incorporated only when readily available or feasible without any design changes.[12]

HOUSE SERVICES

There were few innovations in the servicing of houses during the interwar years in Alberta. Construction materials such as wood, brick, cement, and finishing materials were being produced and distributed in much the same way as they had been before World War I. The design and construction of bathrooms and the installation of plumbing remained roughly as they had before 1914. Although coloured fixtures and built-in bath tubs became available in the 1920s, they were rarely used in Alberta.

Heating technology also paralleled pre World War I developments, although there was a greater emphasis upon central gravity heat, rather than steam heat, for ordinary houses. One innovation, forced air heating, was introduced in North America in the early 1930s. In 1932 Burgess described it as a "most valuable improvement and a minor revolution," but such furnaces were not adopted to any extent in Alberta until after World War II.[13] As before World War I, the use of natural gas for heating houses continued to increase in southern Alberta. By 1929, gas furnaces were "in common use" in Calgary and in many small towns in the south where gas was inexpensive. Although Edmonton was connected by pipeline to the Viking gas field in 1923, gas was not used widely because it was more expensive than coal. While Northwestern Utilities, which held the franchise for distribution in Edmonton, admitted this higher cost, it argued that gas was clean, comfortable, and more convenient.[14] Nonetheless, the use of gas during the interwar years remained unusual outside southern Alberta.

As before World War I, there was a growing interest in the interwar years in the use of proper insulation to conserve heat. While the time-honoured prairie practice of banking the house with snow or straw continued to be widely employed, the use of good insulation in houses became more widespread and scientifically based. Experiments conducted at the University of Saskatchewan between 1921 and 1923 proved that wood shavings between the wall studs provided the best affordable insulation, findings that spurred interest in insulation and helped to change the common habit of relying only on building paper and tight construction.[15]

The greatest change during this period was an increased use of electricity in the home. Electricity had been installed in some urban houses in the late nineteenth century, but it was not until the 1920s that it became universal in towns and cities. By 1931, nearly every village and hamlet in the central and southern areas of Alberta also had electrical service.[16] Initially, electricity was used only for home lighting, but by the end of the 1920s it was powering many "modern conveniences," especially in the kitchen. Through "electrical demonstrations" sponsored by manufacturers and power companies, and an increasing number of newspaper and magazine articles, home owners were urged to purchase electrical equipment and rewire their homes to take full advantage of electricity. Outlets should be installed carefully to match the layout of the house and the family's activities, and by 1925 the outlet for the radio had begun to be especially important.[17] Electrical "conveniences" were important adjuncts to modern houses, giving force to the argument that the home was the primary place for the application of scientific change. Indeed, electricity added significantly to the realization of the ideal of the modern house, which reached its fullest expression after World War II when electrical equipment became indispensable in modern home services. By 1938, electricity was already called the "modern home's central nervous system,"[18] but it remained an exotic service in farm homes. Almost no farms were connected to power grids before World War II, and the few farmers who did have electricity used gas or wind-powered generators.[19]

LAYOUT OF HOUSES

Like servicing, there were few radical innovations in the layout of houses in the interwar years, although the concept of the open plan evolved. Influenced by the belief that the house should be efficient yet welcoming, open plans continued to be popular. At the same time, clear separation of certain space was an obvious necessity, and in one-storey houses it continued to be said that the bedrooms should never connect directly to the bathroom or the living room but should connect through a hall.[20] Open plans were preferred for reasons of hygiene and ventilation, and it was recommended that houses be designed so that sunlight and fresh air could penetrate throughout them. Sleeping porches gained in popularity, and as the Beaver Lumber Company warned Albertans in late 1918, if the epidemic of Spanish Influenza proved "of any value," it was to remind the public of the need for "sunny, well-built, well-ventilated and consequently healthy homes."[21] As well, materials that were difficult to clean were to be avoided and replaced with those that met the criteria of whiteness, smoothness, and impermeability. This favoured the use of plaster, painted or varnished wood, panelless doors, surfaces with a minimum number of projections, and hardwood or linoleum floors.[22] Thus, the pre World War I demand for hardwood and linoleum floors continued to grow, and the move away from dark colours, wallpaper, carpets, and other "unsanitary" features continued to gain ground.

The persistence of these concerns did not, however, prevent some changes in layout, especially in the kitchen and the living areas of the house. The openness that had come to define modern housing in the pre World War I years became even more pronounced. Under the pseudonym Buildicus, a Calgary architect, Robert Stacy-Judd, wrote a series of articles entitled "Chats on Practical Architecture" for the *Calgary Herald* in 1922. He pointed out that the "typical" new house of the previous decade had featured a moderately sized living room plus a dining room on an open plan. Any division between the rooms was becoming less and less important, however, and while the earliest means of division had been sliding doors, this had soon been abandoned, leaving just an opening between the rooms. The opening became larger over time until after 1918 "a farcical division of the two rooms was attempted with a make-believe division in the form of book cases and writing desks." He recommended that any division between the rooms be abandoned. Reflecting an evolving ideal of family life, the living room was now the centre of the house, the place where the family gathered for "the social hours." It was "in one, a reception room, a dining room, a general all-in-all room." He also recommended that the pantry be abolished and replaced with a dining nook in the kitchen where breakfast and lunch could be eaten. Even more radical were his recommendations for the basement. A den should be built as a supplementary family social centre or, if the grade of the lot permitted, the garage should be put in a portion of the basement. Otherwise, the garage should be attached to the house because it could then be heated and, more importantly, because "valuable machines are not given the consideration which is their due."[23]

Stacy-Judd's recommendations generally reflected current Canadian housing theories, although his idea that the basement be used as a den was unorthodox, as was his proposal to integrate the garage with the house.[24] It was a common apprehension, especially in the 1920s, that cars might explode while in the garage. Garages were therefore usually built separate from the house, but if they were attached, fire walls were recommended to protect the house.[25] Stacy-Judd's recommendations for opening up the living areas to an even greater extent anticipated the coming trend. The exaggeration of the living and dining area into a single large room reflected both an expansion of pre World War I notions about greater social informality and a hope that the family would have a satisfying social life at home which would bind it together and compete with public entertainment made possible by greater mobility. This desire to reinforce the family unit also accounted for the continuing popularity of fireplaces, beamed ceilings and other "homey" features.[26]

The greatest change in layout, however, took place in respect to the kitchen. The abolition of a separate dining room and the installation of an eating area in the kitchen, a heresy only a decade earlier, became a highly popular idea in the interwar years. First, it became acceptable to eat only the evening meal in the dining area of the living room and gradually it came to be used only on formal occasions. Eating in the kitchen necessitated design changes. The proposed solution was to construct extensive built-in kitchen cupboards and replace the pantry with a dining nook. Thus, the dining nook did not necessitate enlarging the space devoted to the kitchen. While originally designed as a high booth to shelter the diners from the smells and sights of the cooking area, this approach was not always followed in Alberta, and as in many farm kitchens, a table was often simply placed in the kitchen. In either case, the pantry was abolished to make way for a dining area in the kitchen, and by 1927 women who wanted a pantry were told that they were "painfully old fashioned."[27]

With the important exception of the dining nook, pre World War I concepts continued to be expressed in kitchen design. The overriding objective continued to be that of efficiency. As a profession, homemaking required a suitably designed kitchen, or as it was

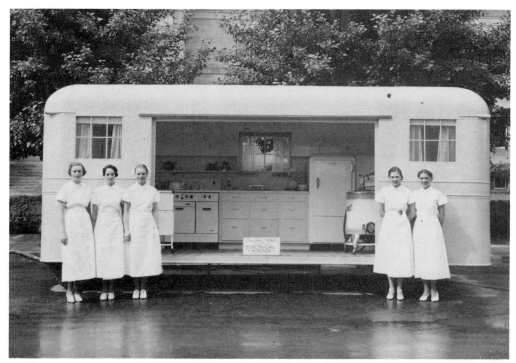

◆ Calgary Power encouraged use of electricity through its "Electrical Kitchen" in 1939. GAI NA 1846-28.

◆ Assuming that life would be made healthier through the application of new technology, the Alberta Department of Health promoted modern kitchen design using displays such as this one at the Edmonton Exhibition in 1931. PAA A10.764.

phrased in 1927, "Mother's Workshop and Laboratory."[28] By 1935, a new language was being used to describe this work space. The kitchen was to be designed according to "use sequence," that is, as a series of work centres, a concept that may have indicated a modernist influence.[29] Fixtures continued to be grouped for maximum efficiency, floors were covered with resilient, durable, and easy to clean materials, walls were painted in light colours, and windows were placed over the sink. Efficiency was further increased through the use of modern electrical conveniences. The use of this equipment and the adoption of "step saving principles" could contribute to a "successful home" and leave time for "true homemaking," in other words, the encouragement and support of the family.[30] A number of electrical companies and retailers mounted education programmes in the 1930s to convince women that they needed such appliances. Calgary Power used a demonstration kitchen mounted in a mobile trailer staffed by women in nurse-like uniforms, a reminder that housekeeping was a female, caring, and scientific profession. The provincial department of health also mounted displays at fairs and other events to explain the new kitchen and its appliances. This pursuit of efficiently designed and electrically equipped kitchens had a number of implications. Small functional kitchens reinforced the characterization of housekeeping as a profession and yet clearly confirmed maternalism by making more room available in the rest of the house for family life.[31] The lesson was clear: a woman who wanted a big kitchen was not only inefficient, she was rejecting her legitimate role by denying her family the space needed for family life.

Resistance to these design changes in kitchens and dining rooms seems to have been limited. In 1932, separate dining rooms were apparently still considered by some to be fashionable, but in the previous year the Calgary architect, W.S. Bates, had noted that in new houses in Calgary "the dining room had contracted, [and was] supplemented by the dining alcove off the kitchen."[32] By 1945 this idea was very widely accepted and only a minority of new house designs included a formal, separate dining room. Rather, the dining area was commonly connected to the living room in an L shape or was simply located at one end of the living room. Although these concepts were said to be valid for farm as well as urban houses, some farm women continued to favour a large pantry for storage and a large kitchen where family and social life could be centred. While pantries were just as old fashioned for them as for urban women, many farm women refused to turn their pantries into dining nooks. Farm families were too large for either a dining nook or a small kitchen to be practical and a large and convenient space for meals was needed. Nevertheless, some farm women eagerly took to the new ideas. When building a new house in 1920, Kathleen Strange insisted on a small kitchen since she "was determined that we would not 'live in the kitchen' as so many farm people seemed to do."[33]

THE DOMINANCE OF TRADITIONAL DESIGN

Trends in the layout and servicing of houses during the interwar years reflected the belief that the house should reinforce the family unit. These same objectives governed exterior appearance and led to the persistence of traditional styles and house forms. House exteriors continued to be influenced by what was socially acceptable and fashionable, and European modernism clearly had no part in Alberta or Canadian notions of fashion. Only a few houses in the late 1930s and early 1940s were built in Moderne style, which commonly employed modernist ideas, and the rejection of modernism was an act of social conformity. The exterior of a house was expected to reflect the virtues of financial stability, family life, and concurrence with the dominant fashions of the time. It was commonly held that "the individual's standing in the community is influenced by the exterior appearance of his home. . . . One is labelled as having good taste or bad; as being progressive or indifferent; as being worth while or the reverse through the appearance of his home."[34] The matter of "taste" presented problems for a society with a relatively open social structure and one that tended to be directed by commercial priorities. The observation that house style in the United States "was no more than a superficial coating, intended to please without any relation to [architectural] objectives," applied equally to Alberta.[35]

The influence of fashion was especially noticeable in the decline of "ethnic" influences on housing. While newly arrived settlers continued in the interwar years to build houses of log in the forms and with the techniques of their homelands, North American designs soon supplanted traditional houses for more established individuals. Although this was ultimately a matter of individual choice, there were pressures to conform. As was observed in 1928, the assimilation of non-English-speaking people into "Canadian standards" and "true Canadian citizenship" would be stimulated if they lived "in homes more comparable with those occupied by native born citizens."[36] In any event, non-English-speaking people, according to their financial ability and their increasing contacts outside of their communities, began to adopt North American house designs in the 1920s, and by World War II there were many examples of such new houses standing beside abandoned traditional dwellings or ones converted into farm out-buildings. This process often began with transitional houses, which combined traditional building techniques with "Canadian" exterior appearances, and a number of these houses could be found by the early 1920s among people of Ukrainian descent in east central Alberta. Changes also occurred in the interiors of these houses, which were renovated to install chimneys, cellars, wooden floors, and wood ceilings, all of which marked departures from traditional practices. Some English-speaking Canadians welcomed these changes and congratulated the Ukrainians on their "progress,"[37] but many of these houses retained an interior layout that owed more to Ukrainian tradition than to Canadian precedents.[38] There was a proud melancholy to many of these houses. Posing as "Canadian" on the outside, they signaled an eager acceptance of the new world and its ways; yet, they held to tradition in the interior and resisted, almost secretly, the encroaching culture.

Non-English-speaking peoples were not the only ones who felt the pressure to conform. Popular fashions constituted a pressure for everyone. The dominant trend in the 1920s, in both urban and rural areas, was towards a lower profile. In Edmonton, for example, there was a steady decline in the construction of two-storey houses in the 1920s and 1930s.[39] This, no doubt, was partly caused by the Depression, but the trend, even in more expensive housing, was towards one-and-a-half storey houses or the lowering of house profile through use of features such as a sweeping roof, dormers, and the extension of first floor verticals up to the eaves. Nevertheless, the majority of houses built during the interwar years were small, unpretentious structures. In 1928, the *Journal of the Royal Architectural Institute of Canada* commissioned a series of articles on recent domestic architecture in Canada. No article appeared about Alberta because as Edward Underwood, the president of the Alberta Association of Architects, noted, "there is practically nothing to write about." Houses built since the end of World War I in Alberta were "entirely unsuitable for. . . . publication and at any rate do not reflect very much credit upon the architects as they are nearly all of the cheapest possible type." Alberta clients had "champagne tastes and beer pock-

◆ Folk houses were replaced with "Canadian" ones during the interwar years as shown at Smoky Lake in this 1941 photograph. PAA A11878.

◆ Semi bungalows, such as this one on Bill Reid's farm at Rockyford, were a fashionable house for farm or city in the 1920s (no date, early 1920s). PAA P590.

The Demonstration Bungalow
In California Style, Adapted to Alberta Conditions

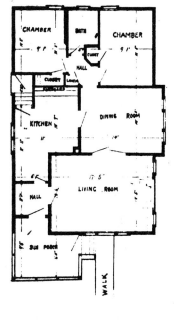

◆◆ A model house in Edmonton in 1927 was a California inspired bungalow. The design adaptations for Alberta conditions were minor, consisting of a glassed porch. *Edmonton Journal*, March 5, 1927.

ets" and wanted a $20,000 house for $10,000.[40] But beer pockets were all that most people had, stimulating the continued use of the bungalow form for small houses.

Interwar bungalows in Alberta, like those of before World War I, emphasized utility, efficiency, harmony and economy, and the application of these principles continued to be enough for any small house to be popularly referred to as a bungalow. Most, as elsewhere on the prairies, were modeled on current North American fashions. The only common local adaptation was a porch or a glassed sunroom so the outside door did not open directly into the living areas and let in the cold.[41] Most of these houses were small, one-storey structures that were the direct descendents of the small bungalows built before World War I, and it was still commonly argued in the early 1920s that a bungalow was the perfect design for Alberta. Its design was said to fit Alberta's climate because it was easy to heat, and its small size but efficient layout made it affordable even though the cost per square foot increased as the house got smaller.[42] In 1935 it was accepted in Canada that a two-bedroom house cost 28 cents per cubic foot, a three-bedroom house cost 25 cents per cubic foot, and a four-bedroom house cost 22.5 cents per cubic foot. The higher unit cost for small houses represented a higher proportionate cost for servicing,[43] but they, like the mobile homes of a later generation, were popular because of their lower overall cost. Their affordability made them the typical choice for low and moderate income people, but a bungalow was still a modern and stylish house that one need not be ashamed of owning. Indeed, readers of the *Edmonton Journal* were told in 1926 that a bungalow was "delightfully simple, homey and artistic" and "free from useless frills and decoration." It was like a "well tailored suit" which was "always in good style and perfect taste."[44]

Demonstrating current ideas, model houses built by contractors and building associations for promotional purposes serve as a useful tool to analyse what constituted the standards of design, construction and modernity. A two-bedroom gable-roofed bungalow was featured as the model house for the Building Exposition in Edmonton in 1922, and bungalows were featured once again in similar promotions in 1927 and 1928. The most advanced technology practical for ordinary housing was used, as were the currently popular designs. The 1927 model bungalow, designed by the contractor, Archie Randall, was a two-bedroom house with a relatively open plan and good isolation of the bedrooms. The house was finished inside with lath and plaster and all walls were wallpapered, except those in the kitchen and the bathroom which were painted. Floors were hardwood, and the house had a fireplace, where "one may sit snugly before the fire," plenty of built-in cupboards, and other features such as a built-in ironing board in the kitchen. It had a separate dining room connected to the living room on an open plan, but there was also room in the kitchen for a table or a breakfast nook. An enclosed sunroom and porch not only helped keep the house warm but also isolated the living areas of the house from the front door and the street. The basement was built of brick and the house was insulated with wood shavings in accordance with the tests at the University of Saskatchewan which demonstrated this as the best insulation for prairie conditions.[45]

Another model bungalow was designed and constructed in Edmonton in 1928, this time by the local architect William Blakey. Although the plan was less open than that of the previous year, the house had the same components; two bedrooms, an enclosed sun porch, kitchen with dining table, lath and plaster walls, and hardwood floors.[46] Since winter construction was still unusual in Alberta, both the 1927 and 1928 model houses were built during the winter to demonstrate that such construction was feasible. Since they emphasized open plans and adopted current theory about kitchen design, both indicate that contemporary theories about layout, servicing, and finishing of houses found practical expression in the houses built in the province. Neither of these model houses paid any attention to European modernism and illustrate how firmly house design in the province was rooted in North American popular culture.

Bungalows were not, of course, the only houses built in the province during the interwar years. Semi bungalows and two-storey foursquare and homestead houses had many supporters, including farmers immediately after World War I.[47] In urban areas, such houses were often the homes of middle and upper income people, and although their overall cost was higher than a bungalow, their unit cost was lower. Taste was, however, shifting away from the two-storey foursquare and homestead form. Readers of the *Calgary Herald* were advised in 1920 that while such houses were good designs for western Canada, the best was the semi bungalow which offered "some of the features of the bungalow, [but] places the sleeping accommodation on the second floor and facilitates the heating problem."[48] In such houses the habitable second floor area was not equal to that on the first floor. These houses were nearly square, and commonly had either a porch or a low-pitched gable roof with a gabled or a flat-roofed dormer in front. They owed much to current North American trends and were commonly finished on the outside with stucco, a fashionable and modern exterior cladding.[49] Like one-storey bungalows, they were clearly descended from pre World War I designs.

As in the rest of English Canada, English Colonial and Georgian style two-storey houses continued to be popular until after World War II and these houses usually had a design integrity that produced a pleasing and unified appearance. Tudor styles were also popular in large, upscale houses.[50] The elements of these and other styles were often applied, not only to upscale one-and-a-half and two-storey houses, but to bungalows as well. Tudor styles were reflected in the use of half timbered effects and small paned windows, while arched windows and iron work typified Italian and Spanish revival styles.[51] In an effort to express the often obsessive fascination of the 1920s with elegance, these stylistic influences were often combined in a single house in a puzzling mixture. By 1930, this eclecticism became more extreme and seemed to have linked an emotional fantasy about the past with contemporary dreams of upward mobility. Seemingly, if one lived in a house that resembled a baronial hall or the estate of an hidalgo, one had earned an equivalent status.

In 1929, E. Litchfield, an Edmonton contractor, and later the author of Alberta's housing submission to the Rowell Sirois Commission, began building in an exclusive Edmonton neighbourhood what he called "modest mansions." Most were six-room houses based on ideas "brought from Los Angeles and San Francisco where English and Spanish mansions abound." All the "modest mansions" contained "modern conveniences" that were "ordinarily found only in larger and much more costly residences," but otherwise they owed little to the twentieth century. They ruthlessly pillaged the designs of the past, including "circle head windows," "antique latches," and other features from the "old world," while living rooms had "either dome or studio ceilings with the necessary arches and niches."[52] The exterior featured an "English cottage" look with stucco cladding, leaded glass windows, and roof shingles laid to resemble thatch.[53]

In another instance, a fashionable new house in Edmonton in 1930 was California inspired, of "Spanish style" and based on "an Italian plan," which meant a two-storey rectangular house placed sideways on the lot. It had a stucco exterior, rounded arches, stained glass, and decorative iron work. In 1930 the contractor, J.P. Desrochers, took this eclecticism to its furthest point yet in Edmonton. He built a home in brick veneer and stucco that imitated a candy-cane house. Locally, the house was said to be of "Modesesque" style.[54]

◆ The eclecticism of house design at the beginning of the Depression was shown by this "Spanish style on an Italian plan" house in Edmonton. *Edmonton Journal*, May 31, 1930.

◆ The "Home Modesesque" built by the Edmonton contractor J.P. Desrocher in 1930 reflected a fantasy of retreat. *Edmonton Journal*, May 10, 1930.

Some Edmontonians found it somewhat startling, but this was part of its intended effect; it was advertised not as a model home but a "Dream Home." It was built according to customary practices, employing wood frame construction, asbestos roof shingles, plenty of built-in features, and hardwood floors in most rooms. But there were new touches. There was extensive use of "plastic" (probably cellulose) wall finishes, plenty of niches and alcoves in the living areas for objects such as statues and candlesticks, a beamed ceiling in the living room with indirect lighting, rubber tile flooring in the kitchen and den, and rubber treads on the stairs. These materials were those of European modernism, but the overall effect was startlingly different. Rather than creating a simple, functional environment, this "essentially modernistic" house created a "homelike atmosphere that is always prevalent in the old homes of the [European] continent."[55] It was graphic evidence of the way in which modernism was applied in Alberta. The new materials would be used, but in service of the North American aesthetic.

These eclectic designs remained popular until World War II, when they disappeared to all intents and purposes. It is interesting to speculate on their connection with the ethos of the interwar years. Perhaps they represented an escapism or a flaunting of wealth and security in the face of a general economic disaster. The 1930 Edmonton "Spanish style" house based on the "Italian plan" had, next to the front door, a false window which imitated a medieval alms door. Although such a feature may only have been promotional nonsense, it was significant that this was fashionable in an economy that was into its second year of the Depression. By the late 1930s, reality had reasserted itself, and although modernism was beginning to creep in, homeyness and protectiveness as expressed in traditional colonial styles were again favoured, perhaps in a sober reaction to the Depression and its challenges to traditional social and economic organization.[56] Indeed, this protectiveness was most noticeable in the abandonment of verandahs and street oriented private spaces. The houses of the late interwar years no longer welcomed the neighbourliness that the verandah had presumed; space had become private and lives had retreated indoors or to the back yard.

The popular houses of the interwar years shared certain characteristics. None of them were monumental, like the houses of the elite in Edmonton and Calgary at the turn of the century. A shift in taste had taken place, away from the awe inspiring and towards the privacy of retreat which sometimes found expression in medieval or renaissance fancies. The later popularity of colonial styles proved a simpler route to the creation of the traditional home and family retreat, a point illustrated by their adoption by Wartime Housing Incorporated. Although these houses were modest, functional, and inexpensive, they combined homeyness with a straightforwardness and a directness that demonstrated new tastes. Wartime Housing Incorporated houses imitated the Cape Cod style houses of colonial Massachusetts,[57] illustrating the fact that even official Canadian housing imitated foreign ideals and depended upon the United States for an understanding of domesticity and functionalism.

MODERNIZATION

Since there was so little new house construction in Alberta after 1929, it might be expected that changing ideas on house design would have had limited application. However, new ideas were applied both in newly constructed and in renovated homes, and they provided the essential planning framework for houses constructed after World War II. Significantly, renovation was called "modernization," and it became an obsession for many. At its most practical level, modernization meant the installation of water and sewage systems in urban houses. In other cases, dining rooms were torn out to create larger living areas, pantries were eliminated and replaced with dining nooks, open verandahs were enclosed to make sun rooms, sleeping porches and dormers were added, decorative shutters were tacked on, exteriors were stuccoed, additional windows were installed, and, in extreme cases, second storeys were altered to produce a more sweeping roof line.[58] Much attention also seems to have been given to redecorating interiors to accord with the current trends. There were plenty of articles in both the urban and rural papers on the current fashions and colours, and while these do not constitute direct evidence that the recommendations were followed, they do suggest the parameters of interwar taste.[59]

Lumber companies and other building interests found it profitable to encourage modernization. While modernization was a fad for much of the 1920s, interest picked up further in the early 1930s, stimulated by a major advertising campaign sponsored by the various lumber associations in western Canada. With the slogan "Don't Blunder, Use Lumber," people were urged to renovate. The campaign enlisted the support of local newspapers and prominent individuals

◆ The old could be made
fashionable again
through renovation as
shown in this advertise-
ment sponsored by the
Western Retail Lum-
bermen's Association.
Calgary Herald, April
26, 1930.

and organizations, and in Edmonton, the mayor, the Federation of Community Leagues, and the *Edmonton Journal* all urged people to modernize their homes. Although there was a frank admission that one of the main reasons for the campaign was to create employment and increase sales of building materials, such factors were viewed as inseparable from social improvement. As the President of the Edmonton Federation of Community Leagues declared in 1930, "modernization is the tonic that promotes progress in a community and it is essential that we have modern homes if we are to have a modern aggressive city."[60]

That the advertising campaign for modernization petered out in the mid 1930s could indicate many things. Although renovation was fairly extensively undertaken in Alberta, the extent and the motives of such renovation are unclear. It is likely that a number of urban homes were renovated in the 1930s in an effort to maintain equity in the property, and it also seems that a good number of farm homes were upgraded during the 1920s when agricultural prices permitted. The Home Improvement Programme also gave modernization a boost; 10,000 loans were made in Alberta up to 1940. Many of these loans would have been used to install services such as furnaces, hot water tanks, and upgraded wiring, although some of the loans were also used to convert single family dwellings into light housekeeping suites.

◆

The housing built between 1919 and 1945 illustrates a direct continuation of planning and design concepts from before World War I. The emphasis on the house as an incubator for family cohesiveness and stability was intensified, perhaps partly because broader technological change in transportation and entertainment was seen as a challenge to the family and maternalism. Yet, increased application of technology in house servicing, especially electricity, could serve as an antidote to this challenge, demonstrating the way in which cultural and social values were expressed in housing. Moreover, house servicing and design continued to be central to the definition of progress, which, in turn, was linked to commercial interests. While the social values attributed to the house were expressed through shifts in stylistic influences, all consistently reinforced the long held notion of a social structure based upon the nuclear family and private property.

P O S T W A R
H O U S I N G

1 9 4 6 – 1 9 6 7

NINE

Postwar Programmes and Approaches

The two decades following World War II were years of immense change in Alberta. Although the provincial government believed that the agrarian economy would revive after the war, 1945 marked the beginning of a fundamental shift towards an urban economy and society. Alberta's immediate problem was to meet the housing needs created by the war and growing urbanization. The postwar housing demand, experienced in Canada as a result of rising incomes and an increase in net family formation, was compounded in Alberta by the economic boom that followed the opening of the Leduc oil fields in 1947. Leduc, and other oil fields, created unprecedented economic growth in Alberta in the next three decades, redirecting the provincial economy away from a reliance upon agriculture. The population of the province had been almost 800,000 in 1941; by 1951 it was almost one million and by 1961 it was 1.3 million, 63 percent of which was urban.[1] From 1956 until 1963 there was a slow-down in the economy because of uncompetitive oil prices and relatively few new oil discoveries. These periods did not, however, represent a retraction in economic growth and from 1947 until the 1960s Alberta experienced among the highest rates of economic growth in Canada.[2] By 1960, agriculture's net value of production had been passed by mining, including oil and gas, and manufacturing.[3]

Within this economic framework, housing was a central postwar issue, but provincial housing policy was slow to respond. The accommodation by which Alberta had entered the NHA in 1945 meant little in terms of a provincial housing policy. The province was wedded to the idea that market forces alone would correct existing housing problems and that there was little that the government could, or should, do if this mechanism did not work. It seemed the provincial government believed that the increasingly urban Alberta of the postwar years was the same as the rural Alberta of before the war, and that the old approach could adequately meet new and increasingly complex problems. Accordingly, although housing was within provincial jurisdiction, the federal government remained the primary source of housing programmes. Under Premier Manning, the province, to an even greater extent than the federal government, was committed to a free enterprise policy that limited government involvement in the housing field, and it was not until the mid 1960s that Alberta began to exercise its jurisdiction with any sense of responsibility. This change in attitude marked the end of an era in the history of housing in the province. By the late 1960s, fundamental changes had taken place in planning, house design, construction, and use of materials, as well as in the type of housing in which Albertans lived. The emergence of high rise apartments, condominiums and mobile homes marked significant changes in housing types.

POSTWAR ADJUSTMENT IN ALBERTA

In 1945–46, as at the end of World War I, returned soldiers had to be reintegrated into the society, and housing became a vehicle for this reintegration as well as for the satisfaction of the population's expectations about postwar life. This task was complicated by the almost simultaneous economic boom in Alberta. When Alberta joined the NHA in 1945, it had been hoped that it would be like "a big charge of 'Dynamite' to help blow away some of the unemployment threatening to dam up our economic structure in Post War days."[4] Although house construction played an increasingly significant role in the postwar economy, the years immediately following the war did not see an easing of the housing crisis in Alberta. Housing problems were not only the inheritance of the extraordinary conditions of the Depression but of the equally extraordinary conditions of the war. E. Litchfield, the former Edmonton builder, observed in early 1945 that the housing problem had become serious "because it has been so long ignored; it has been considered an unpleasant task and left in the vain hope it would somehow disappear; it has been shunned by businessmen and used as a football by Politicians. Even today its prominence is due to its employment possibilities."[5] It was soon clear, however, that Alberta's reluctance to deal with housing problems could not continue. In the fall of 1945, Alfred Hooke, the provincial minister in charge of housing, told the premier that "the prevalent idea that a large number of persons who were attracted to the larger cities during the war will be returning to the rural districts thereby easing the housing situation can be dismissed."[6] However, the province had no plans with which to meet the postwar housing situation, and, before it could develop such policies, the opening of the Leduc and Redwater oil fields had started a massive economic boom in Alberta.

The existing housing crisis was aggravated by the high expectations for postwar life held by many people. Canadians, who had a tradition of viewing economic advantage as a central aspect of freedom and progress, identified material gains with the democracy for which the war had been fought. Also, the trauma that the war had brought to so many perhaps could be reconciled in personal terms through the stability that material betterment was believed to offer. Housing played an important role in these expectations because the house was seen as the focus for a reunited family, a family that would find contentment and purpose through its material possessions.[7] These growing expectations were revealed in surveys undertaken by Alberta's Post War Reconstruction Committee. In 1945 farmers and urban householders planned to spend as never before. There was, it was discovered, a potential demand for more than $650 million in goods and services. Many farmers anticipated that their expenditures would take place over a five year period, but most urban people were in a greater hurry. They planned to make their expenditures in "the first two post-war years" and fully 32 percent of them planned to build a new house. Those in Calgary and Edmonton had the highest hopes. They anticipated that their new house would cost $4,700, while people outside of these two cities planned for a new house costing $3,650. An equal number planned to buy new appliances, furniture, and cars. Much of this urge to spend was pent up demand from wartime shortages and was expected to be satisfied through the use of savings. Nonetheless, since savings amounted to only $140 million in Alberta, it was obvious that there was a great deal of planned borrowing in the offing as well.[8] The end of the war thus promised not only peace but material fulfillment, a fact that was to be of crucial importance for housing.

The most immediate problem lay in the needs of veterans, who demanded attention from both federal and provincial governments. The federal government had various programmes to help them, including financial assistance to attend university and low interest loans to buy land and build a house. The latter was an important programme, and it was used extensively in Alberta. In the Edmonton area a number of veterans used it to purchase three acre parcels of land just outside the city.[9] Nonetheless, once the men began returning to civilian life, the immediate demand for housing could not be met by existing programmes. The federal government therefore directed Wartime Housing Incorporated to build houses for veterans. These houses were built at the request of a municipality and were rented at low rates. From 1946 until 1948 alone, almost 1,700 such houses were built throughout Alberta. In all cases, the municipality provided a fully serviced lot but in return received a grant in lieu of taxes from Wartime Housing Incorporated and the right to purchase the houses for $1,000 at a later date. Most of these projects were undertaken as a series of large suburban developments. Those constructed in Lethbridge were typical—they were simple two- or three-bedroom one- or one-and-a-half storey structures in a New England saltbox style and, to lessen costs and construction time, did not have basements.[10]

Such projects went a considerable way towards meeting veterans' needs generally, but they did not address the needs of all who had been discharged. Exservicemen, many of whom had been led to believe that their efforts and sacrifices would be rewarded after the war, were not willing to settle for high priced and poor quality housing. Alfred Hooke, the minister responsible for housing, was told in early 1946 that "it would be impossible to exaggerate the depth of feeling which exists among veterans regarding housing conditions" and that a political price would be paid for ignoring their resentment.[11] Neither the province nor the municipalities had planned for this eventuality; as late as the fall of 1946, none of the four major cities in Alberta, Calgary, Edmonton, Medicine Hat and Lethbridge, could even make recommendations about the housing needs of the 22,500 veterans already in these communities or the approximately 2,000 who would be arriving shortly.[12]

◆ Elements of colonial
styles were popular in
wartime and postwar
housing as shown by this
display of model homes
at Eaton's in 1946.
PAA BL1107/1.

◆ Elements of colonial
styles were still impor-
tant in the 1948 Canada
Mortgage and Housing
Corporation model home
display at Eaton's, but
the new low profile
single-storey bungalow
had appeared.
PAA BL1441.

◆ One aspect of post World
War II readjustment was
housing under Veterans'
programmes such as this
house built in the late
1940s. Photograph made
available through
Alberta Culture and
Multiculturalism.

◆ Veterans attending the University of Alberta were often thankful for housing such as "Camp 109," the converted United States army buildings in Edmonton, shown in this 1949 photograph. [Wetherell/Kmet photograph.]

One of the main problems in providing houses for veterans was an inadequate supply of building materials. There were two ways to meet this problem, by salvage operations or through government production and control of building materials and the compulsory organization of labour. Building materials remained under federal wartime price controls for a time after the war, but this policy aimed to control inflation rather than increase the supply of materials. The province opposed all such controls and instead saw salvage as a way of obtaining building materials. When the American army base at Dawson Creek, British Columbia, was closed at the end of the war, the province offered up to $1 million in loans to Calgary and Edmonton to acquire and dismantle the buildings and use the salvaged material for veterans' housing. Ultimately, only Edmonton agreed to the programme and it built 261 housing units, mostly for veterans attending the University of Alberta.[13] Further salvage material was acquired in 1946 when the province, after lengthy negotiations with the federal government, purchased a number of army camps and air bases. In most cases, the buildings were torn down and the salvaged material was sold at 30 percent of cost to contractors and house builders. Veterans had priority in renting or buying houses built with this material, which was said to be "of the finest quality" and "included almost everything that goes into the building of a house." In a limited manner, the province also supplied materials that were in short supply when it began in 1946 to import plumbing fixtures directly from the United States.[14]

Another popular approach was to convert existing army buildings into emergency shelters for veterans and their families. In Red Deer, the old A-20 training centre was converted into twenty apartments which were turned over to returning servicemen, and the same approach was used in Calgary.[15] While housing for veterans in all western Canadian cities was a problem, Edmonton's shortages were the worst. The University of Alberta at Edmonton had a large number of married veteran students whose housing needs periodically reached crisis proportions. Former American army huts were renovated and rented to veterans at low rates, and while there were "continual complaints about the overcrowded and unsanitary conditions,"[16] they provided economical and welcome shelter for many families.

NATIONAL HOUSING ACT

Despite salvage operations and the conversion of military buildings to civilian needs, the core of Canada's and Alberta's housing policy after the war was the National Housing Act (NHA). In Alberta, the NHA was most important for its mortgage provisions, which permitted house mortgages at less than prevailing interest rates and with lower down payments and longer repayment periods. For upper and middle income people, housing was not an overriding problem. Through the NHA, they could comfortably afford to purchase a house. In 1950, it was observed that a man 45 years or younger with a "good salary" had "no difficulty whatever in solving his own housing problems under the NHA."[17] To meet this demand, there was an extremely high ratio of construction to existing units. In 1946, there were just over 53,000 dwelling units in the four major cities in Alberta, and 4,120 houses were under construction.[18] The oil boom after 1947 sustained this pace of construction, and by late 1948 contractors were "so full" that many refused additional work. Materials and labour were in such short supply that those who wanted to build were generally unable to obtain firm bids from contractors.[19] Nevertheless, a great number of houses were being built, and while they were often costly, the NHA made them accessible to young, middle class Albertans for most of the period before 1967. While the NHA did much to increase the supply of housing, to see this initiative solely in these terms ignores that it was also an integral part of federal economic policy. In such circumstances, housing inevitably was focussed on the most economically and politically powerful consumers of housing. In late 1945 the administration of the NHA was moved from the Department of Finance to a new crown corporation, Central Mortgage and Housing Corporation (CMHC). While this gave a better focus and greater coherence to Canadian housing policy, the new corporation carried on the tradition of combining housing with national economic policy.

By the early 1950s, the aim was still to stimulate housing supply although it was somewhat curtailed by attempts to control the inflation caused by the Korean war. Demand for mortgage funds was high, and in 1954 the NHA was amended in order to increase capital for housing. The joint loan system, whereby the federal government and a lending institution contributed funds for a loan, was dropped, as was the "pool guarantee fund" which had provided a collective guarantee for all loans rather than for each individual loan. These were replaced with a system of insured loans. The lending institution alone made the loan under the NHA and it was guaranteed by the federal government through a fund, to which all borrowers contributed in the form of an insurance levy assessed against each mortgage. While maximum interest rates were still set for NHA loans, these and other changes brought the chartered banks into the NHA mortgage lending field, from which they had previously been excluded.[20]

These amendments increased capital for housing for a short time only. With rising interest rates, the banks soon left the NHA mortgage market. In 1957 housing starts in Canada fell, and, in response, the government eased NHA lending restrictions, raised the interest rate on NHA loans, and injected funds into CMHC so it could lend directly to the public.[21] Prior to this point, CMHC had been restricted in its direct lending activities to a number of specific cases, but after 1957 there was a dramatic increase in direct lending by the corporation. In 1956, it had contributed only 2 percent of all mortgage loans for new houses in Canada; in 1957 this had risen to 25 percent, and from 1960 until 1965, CMHC contributed 45 percent, with the balance coming from life insurance and trust companies. The banks contributed about 1 percent.[22]

None of the amendments to the NHA in the 1950s and early 1960s concerning individual loans changed the Act's basic orientation towards middle and upper income groups. As in conventional loans, the amount of money that an individual could borrow was tied to income, and although the ratio increased over time, in 1956 no more than 23 percent of an individual's annual income could be used for payment of principal, interest, and taxes. This meant that "generally speaking it is impossible for a person with an income of less than $3,000 annually to qualify for a mortgage under the NHA."[23] Nor, of course, could low income earners acquire houses through other forms of bank financing. Despite such restrictions, NHA loans were important for house construction in Alberta. From 1945 to 1967 the incomes of Albertans rose steadily, and so the number of people who could afford to finance their houses through the NHA increased. By 1967, it was argued that "Alberta and Calgary in particular" had "consistently used a higher percentage of NHA financing rather than conventional financing."[24]

The orientation of the NHA to the single-family detached dwelling was central in Canadian housing policy. Government policy to 1968 assumed that by providing single detached houses for the middle class, the housing problems of those with less income would be "solved through filtering. That is, the middle income groups moving to the suburbs would vacate smaller, older, and cheaper housing, making it available for lower income groups."[25] Thus, as Albert Rose, a prominent analyst of Canadian housing policy, observed in 1968, the federal government's policy (one that was also endorsed by Alberta) essentially aimed at "the attainment of home ownership by every family." It was a policy expressed in political speeches on housing and through the policies of CMHC which, before 1967, generally stressed the production of new single-family dwellings. As Rose noted, the "heart" of federal housing policy was to

> provide adequate supplies of mortgage money, to manipulate the interest rate, and to set forth appropriate terms to encourage individual home ownership. Not only was mortgage money made available through the National Housing Act at rates lower than those prevailing in the money markets, but down payments were successively reduced as loan amounts were increased. The period of amortization increased from 15 years in 1946 to 20, 25, and now 30 years or more to enable lower-income families to acquire a home of their own.[26]

Thus, housing would be increased through personal debt guaranteed by the state. But despite government-backed mortgages, filtering, and increased amortization periods to make houses affordable, lower income people were increasingly squeezed by rising house costs. In 1955, noting that about 80 percent of new residential construction in Calgary was financed under NHA provisions, the Calgary House Builders' Association argued that it was "practically impossible" for the average wage earner, who it defined as earning about $3,100 per year, to purchase a house.[27] This situation became worse in the 1960s. By 1966 the average income of borrowers in Alberta for new houses under the NHA was about 40 percent above the national average, which meant that "average" wage earners, those earning $5,000 to $7,000 per year, were finding housing too expensive.[28] These problems were largely the result of rising land costs in the 1950s and 1960s, partly due to market forces but also the consequence of a new approach to servicing land. Before 1953, all local improvements in Calgary were installed by the city and recovered through local improvement charges. After 1953, however, all services, including water and sewer mains, curbs, and sidewalks adjacent to the property, became the responsibility of the land owner.[29] This added an estimated average of $1,100 to the cost of each new house. Although CMHC increased the loan amount in such cases, this did not equal the total increase in the price of the house, and so, larger down payments were required.[30] Another element in rising house costs was the entrenchment of the view that one's house was a speculative commodity. As people began to move to new houses in the suburbs, they now expected to sell their former house for more than its original cost. One individual wrote to Premier Manning in 1957 that this was "surely inflation of the worst kind, for here is one manufactured product— and one which is a necessity, not a luxury," which increased in value "as it sells at second or third hand." This was "absurd" but "no one seems much concerned about it."[31] Such circumstances showed the limitations of "filtering" as a solution to housing shortages.

LOW-INCOME HOUSING

The NHA of 1944, while heavily oriented to providing mortgage funds for new single-family dwellings, in theory also recognized the need for construction of housing for those low income earners who could not qualify for an NHA mortgage or afford the housing freed up by new house buyers. There had been much discussion in Canada in the interwar years about the need for such housing, and during and after the war this discussion intensified. In 1944, E. Litchfield observed that "we certainly face no easy task in providing homes for the lower brackets, we have never yet been able to get down to this class."[32] Of course, no government had seriously attempted to "get down to this class," and the provisions of the NHA (1944) which provided for public housing projects to be built by limited dividend corporations were largely ineffective. Instead, the federal government decided that the newly created family allowance programme, in conjunction with NHA mortgages for individuals, constituted an adequate postwar housing programme.[33] In such circumstances, it was not hyperbole for one commentator to claim in 1946 that the NHA's promises of innovative and alternative housing programmes to deal with low-income housing "have all gone 'phut'."[34] It was not, however, only the federal government that neglected low-income housing projects. Premier Manning applied Social Credit economic theory to justify Alberta's refusal to support them. He observed in 1945 that such housing projects "tend to only temporarily relieve rather than cure the general financial situation of a large group of Canadian citizens," whose problems originated with the "monetary system" which denied them sufficient "purchasing power to obtain reasonable housing accommodation."[35]

In 1949, federal resolve on low-income housing seemed suddenly to strengthen. The NHA was amended to give greater scope to low-income housing projects, establishing the framework for a "federal-provincial partnership" in respect to this funding. The federal and provincial governments would respectively pay 75 and 25 percent and the local government would provide services to the building site as well as some financial support for the project. A clear local initiative was also necessary before a federal-provincial programme could be implemented. The Manning government disliked this scheme, claiming that the federal government was committing provincial revenues to projects over which the province had no control.[36] This argument, while having theoretical merit, was essentially only a reiteration of the government's hostility towards public housing.

The federal-provincial partnership outlined in the NHA required provincial enabling legislation, which Alberta passed three years later. However, by transferring the 25 percent financial burden from itself to the initiating local government, the province all but ensured that there would be no low-income housing projects in Alberta. Local governments had to take funds for such projects from the unconditional provincial grants already paid to municipalities or had to raise money for them by issuing debentures following a two-thirds favourable majority vote by the ratepayers. Other conditions were also imposed. The capital cost of any such housing project could not exceed four times the funds raised by the local government, and, to ensure that these funds were indeed available, they were to be deposited in a provincially administered trust fund.[37]

The "federal-provincial partnership" approach lasted until 1964. It contributed virtually nothing to low-income housing in Alberta and little elsewhere in Canada.[38] Initiative rested almost totally with the federal government, which did little. Because most provinces, like Alberta, were hostile to public housing, they found this state of inertia acceptable. Thus, in the two decades after the war, Alberta refused to expend either effort or money on public housing. In such circumstances, local governments remained trapped, not only by the financial burdens that such low-income housing projects would bring, but also by a measure of public hostility towards them. There was concern that public housing would create ghettos and devalue adjacent property.[39] While such views had some legitimacy, property devaluation did not have to accompany public housing. By 1957, a growing consciousness of the need for urban renewal gave impetus to arguments for public housing. Alberta, however, remained unresponsive. The first urban renewal project in the province came only in 1966 when a number of older buildings in downtown Calgary were demolished and replaced with a civic centre and other new buildings, including a senior citizens' high rise.[40]

During this period, neither the province nor local governments developed the administrative machinery necessary to deal effectively with the construction, management, and planning of public housing projects under the NHA. Alberta, like the other provinces, continued to insist that housing should be controlled provincially, although it was unwilling to make any financial contribution to exercise its jurisdiction. In such conditions, CMHC developed administrative procedures to regulate its expenditures on low-income housing projects, which, when coupled with the corporation's "desire for excellence," created an administrative system "in which a local initiative might bog down completely."[41] This ensured that "only where the political demands were strongest would any public housing be constructed."[42] Since such support did not exist in Alberta, no public housing was built under the "federal-provincial" partnership provisions of the NHA.

The only low-income housing built in the province was that provided by three limited dividend housing projects. Under the NHA (1944), loans could be made to limited dividend corporations to build low rental housing. The local government was required to co-operate in providing area planning, zoning, and servicing. By 1956, there were 344 rental units in Calgary, spread over two projects, and 236 rental units in a single development in Edmonton, "all of them under private enterprise." In these housing projects, rent was not determined as a percentage of income, but there were ceilings on the rent that could be charged. Nevertheless, by 1968 rental of such units was still too expensive for the lower third of income earners.[43]

THE RENTAL MARKET

Because there was little low-income housing available in the province before 1966, and because low income earners could not obtain a NHA mortgage, let alone a conventional loan, most had to seek other solutions to their housing needs. Many of them rented.

While 37 percent of all dwellings in urban areas were rented in 1951, a drop from the all time high of 51 percent in 1941, this nevertheless represented almost 47,000 dwellings.[44] For a period of time, rental housing in Alberta had been under rent control. Despite the province's dislike of government intervention in the market place, federal rent controls brought in during World War II remained in place until 1951, when the national government finally vacated the field. Over time, these controls had steadily decreased in scope. First, newly constructed buildings were exempted in 1947 and then controls were lifted on rental property that was untenanted as of 1948. This meant that if one lived in a rent controlled dwelling in 1948, it continued to be regulated; if one rented after that date, rent was not controlled. Rent control was the last wartime economic measure to be removed by the federal government, revealing the scale of postwar housing shortages across Canada and the inability of postwar construction to meet the shortfall.

When the federal government abandoned rent control in early 1951, the housing market in Alberta was so strained that the province was forced to assume the role. In spite of its dislike of such policies, removal of controls would have been too socially and politically disruptive. Landlords argued that rent control was an unwarranted interference in property rights and inhibited construction of rental housing,[45] although the fact that new construction had not been subject to these controls since 1947 undermined their argument. In any event, it was clear that rents were much higher than necessary. The former president of the Edmonton Real Estate Association noted in 1949 that tenants had been, and continued to be, "greatly exploited." The only way to achieve "a fair and equitable rent would be to have all rented premises appraised by competent men or appraisers."[46] Similarly, there was a loud outcry from tenants, the provincial CCF, the Canadian Legion, labour unions, and other organizations that rent control was necessary if people were to make ends meet.[47] With this encouragement, the province assumed responsibility for rent control in 1951, but it was able to resist other forms of control such as those affecting the price and supply of building materials. Although politically unable to abandon rent control, the province argued that it would be in place for only a short time, until some other way could be found to assist low and middle income people without challenging the free market.[48] What this meant was unclear, given the province's position on public housing. In any event, by 1951 federal rent control had become so limited that the province could accept it, at first maintaining and then expanding the exemptions. Even so, the fact that it undertook rent control at all was a measure of the existing housing crisis.

Under the stimulus of the oil boom, the province's population was increasing dramatically, and in 1952 it was reported that rents had risen to "extortionate levels" in many parts of the province. This was obviously so in the cities, but other centres were also affected, especially Wainwright, Penhold, Claresholm, Peace River, Cold Lake, and Jasper, "where service personnel and construction crews on large projects have created an extremely grave [housing] problem."[49] Rents increased under the pressure of these shortages and the influence of the boom mentality. In Wainwright there was a serious shortage of housing for military personnel. Prior to the construction of sufficient quarters for the servicemen and their families, many lived in the town. Rents rose to extreme levels and the Alberta Rental Control Board found that while some landlords in Wainwright dealt fairly with their tenants, many others were motivated by the basest greed. Garages, shacks, and even shacks connected to a tent to provide an additional room were commonly let for high rents. Not unexpectedly, there was often deep hostility between landlords and tenants in the town. The board argued that the local government did nothing to control the situation and at times abetted it. Although water mains and sewers had been installed, the majority of rental houses were not connected and the town council appeared not "to realize its responsibilities in these matters, claiming that the onus is on the provincial authorities." Indeed, two of the town councillors "stated quite openly that as there was always the possibility of the army camp 'folding up,' landlords were expecting to get any expenditure made to accommodate tenants back in three months, a policy these two elected officials thought just and proper."[50]

In 1951 there were a total of about 47,000 dwelling units being rented in the province and in 1952 the Rental Control Board received an extraordinary 20,183 inquiries, about half from people who were not eligible for rent control. "The great majority of grievances," the board reported, came from "tenants with regard to extremely high rates of rent and abuses by certain numbers of landlords."[51] Such abuses occurred throughout the province, and in 1952 "it was painfully apparent that many owners of decontrolled property" were setting rents solely on "what the traffic will bear," without regard to decency or value for money "in the knowledge that desperate tenants have no alternative to paying whatever they demanded."[52] Many of these renters appealed to the Rental Control Board, telling stories of avarice, greed, meanness, and deception by landlords.[53] The rental board, being powerless over decontrolled property, could only express its shock at the "outrageous" rents that were being charged and consoled one supplicant with the observation that "you may yet live to see the day when such a landlord will be begging for tenants at whatever rate they are willing to pay."[54]

In light of these problems, the Alberta Rental Control Board argued in 1952 that "it may yet be necessary to tighten up rental controls if the present exploitation of freedom under decontrolled conditions continues to exist."[55] The government refused to support such a position, even though existing rental control had become increasingly meaningless. By this time, many rental units had become ineligible for control and those which were eligible consisted mainly of "the old-type apartment blocks, old business blocks and old homes located in the downtown districts of the cities." Controls now applied largely to pensioners and low income people who, either because of poverty or old age, had not moved since 1948.[56] In early 1955, the province decontrolled all property, with Premier Manning arguing that controls were unjustifiable in a market economy. Landlords' associations had kept unrelenting pressure on the government to get rid of the programme, presumably because they disliked the precedent that it set.[57] In any event, the great majority of rental accommodation was no longer controlled and the programme had been serving only the least influential groups in the society.

FRINGE COMMUNITY HOUSING

In lieu of any effective government programmes to assist low income earners to purchase housing, those who could not or did not want to rent found other alternatives. In the late 1940s and throughout the 1950s they often took the time honoured option of the urban poor in Alberta and moved to a fringe community. This happened in towns as well as cities. Even though in 1952 the main residential area in Brooks was characterized as "discontinuous and sprawling," the town's fringe area was growing because of the need for residential land where "very small dwellings can be built quickly and cheaply and then gradually improved." In Brooks, as in many towns, houses also were towed into the fringe area from elsewhere, and the owners enlarged or renovated them to make them habitable.[58]

But it was near Edmonton and Calgary that this development was most prevalent. The fringe areas of these two major cities experienced rapid growth immediately after World War II. Many communities, such as Bowness and Forest Lawn near Calgary, which had been the objects of pre World War I speculative land subdivision, were only settled to any extent forty years later. From 1946 to 1955 Bowness grew from 650 to 5,881 persons. Forest Lawn's population nearly doubled in 1952 and had tripled by 1954. Another fringe community near Calgary was the hamlet of Montgomery. In 1947 it had 60 houses, but by 1956 this had increased to 1,069. The same process was occurring in Edmonton where two communities were the focus for most fringe development; the town of Beverly, which had been established in 1913 as a coal mining community, and Jasper Place. Although the coal mines at Beverly had closed in 1952, the town's 1946 population of 1,171 expanded to 3,600 by 1954.[59]

All fringe communities were similar in that they provided an option for low income earners. Families tended to be larger than in the city and incomes were almost always lower. In the early 1950s, 50 families moved from Drumheller to Forest Lawn. The depressed coal industry had forced them to leave Drumheller and, as was noted by the Royal Commission on the Metropolitan Development of Calgary and Edmonton in 1956, this was "a useful reminder that the growth of the oil and gas industries, like all economic change, has not been without its debit side." Housing in these communities was generally below city standards, consisting of small single detached houses without basements, running water, or sewage connections. Many residents used chemical toilets or outdoor privies and obtained water from wells. Many of the houses were built by the owners and there was, with the exception of Beverly, little rental accommodation. Most of the residents worked in the city, and each fringe community, as was said of Beverly, was "a low income dormitory suburb for workers in the city."[60]

These communities existed because they permitted the opportunity for affordable housing. Although land was still available in both Edmonton and Calgary, people in the fringe communities could build on unserviced land, which they could not do in the cities, and unserviced houses were cheaper to build and maintain. In Jasper Place, more than half the residents were found to have moved there "not because it was their first preference, but because there was no practical city alternatives [sic] within their means." Most were relatively recent migrants to the cities who could not afford city rents, or city landlords often refused to rent to families with children. They also could not buy a house in the city because they could not obtain a mortgage through conventional means or under the NHA. The Calgary Real Estate Board argued in 1955 that the lack of adequate financing for people with incomes below "the minimum required by the NHA is one of the chief reasons for fringe communities growing so rapidly in recent years." NHA mortgages were not available for houses built on unserviced land and devices such as the 1954 amendments to the NHA to increase capital for housing did not help "the fringe residents who live without city services, and the low income groups who can only afford small down payments and who are more uncertain risks." In these circumstances, they moved to the fringe communities where they built a house themselves or had one built by a builder with only a low down payment. In the latter case, the balance owing was paid under a lease option or an agreement for sale, which the builder in turn often sold at a discount. While such discounts ran as high as 40 percent, they were commonly about 22 percent. The "end result is that the builder receives his capital quickly and so can employ it again to build still more houses; the person who buys the Agreement or Lease Option takes the risk; and a home is provided." Nevertheless, the new home owner had paid a high price for his house. The houses in the fringe areas were small, inferior, and substandard. For the same cost, he "could almost certainly purchase a better dwelling in the city if the financing could be arranged."[61]

ALBERTA'S NEW ROLE IN HOUSING

Such conditions pointed to the fact that the ideal of owning a single-family home in Alberta was becoming more and more difficult to realize. By the early 1960s, conditions were approaching the point where even many middle income earners were either impoverishing themselves to own a single-family detached house or finding it unattainable. The NHA had been able to assist only a limited sector of the society, and demands for social equality were becoming more insistent, with inadequate housing cited as proof of government's failure to set policy and regulate the economy. In such a climate, government policies changed. In 1964 the federal government brought in amendments to the NHA which "proved to be a turning point in Canadian housing history." The existing NHA provisions for federal-provincial arrangements for public housing had not worked and it was clear that they never would. The changes to the Act were substantial and provided for, among other things, greater funding for urban renewal programmes and direct loans to the province of up to 90 percent of capital costs and 50 percent of operating costs for public housing. Even though the federal government continued to provide the bulk of the funding, the 1964 amendments slanted the NHA "in the direction of new forms of initiative by local or provincial governments." By decentralizing housing policy, the social questions of low-income housing and urban renewal "were put squarely in the lap" of the provinces, which were now forced to grapple directly with the housing question.[62]

The 1964 amendments marked the end of Alberta's lethargy on the housing front. In the next year, *The Alberta Housing Act* was passed, and subsequent amendments allowed the province to enter into joint programmes for urban renewal, land assembly, and development of housing. It also provided for a crown corporation to administer the act and to implement programmes for low cost and specialized housing. While a crown corporation was not created immediately, in 1965 the province established the Alberta Housing Committee to provide housing for low income people, and in 1967 the Committee became a crown corporation, The Alberta Housing and Urban Renewal Corporation. The new entity marked a watershed in the province's housing history. It was empowered to deal with low-income housing on a number of fronts, including co-operative housing, public housing, and senior citizen housing.[63]

The inexperienced corporation got off to a slow start because few planning studies, forecasts, or analyses of provincial housing had been done, but it was forced to learn quickly. Up to 1968, CMHC, through direct lending, had provided about 55 percent of the total residential mortgages in Alberta, but in 1968 it reduced residential mortgage funds to 5 percent, redirecting the balance to housing in remote areas and to public, student, and senior citizen housing. In 1968 the Edmonton office of CMHC had a quota of 20 loans per month for direct lending, the majority of which was lent in towns and villages in northern Alberta where prospective owners had difficulty securing conventional mortgages.[64] During this period, further changes were initiated to stimulate the availability of capital for housing. Maximum interest rates on NHA mortgages were removed, minimum NHA mortgage terms were reduced from twenty-five to five years, and, via amendments to the *Bank Act*, chartered banks were allowed to make conventional loans and the ceiling on interest rates on bank loans were removed.[65]

Although it now should have been advantageous to all private lenders to provide mortgages for detached housing, this did not happen. Instead, private lenders concentrated on lending for the construction of high rise apartments and, as the Alberta Housing and Urban Renewal Corporation noted in 1968, it appeared that the withdrawal of federal funds and increased interest rates had not fulfilled their purpose. Indeed, it had intensified Alberta's housing problems, especially in small towns which were "now faced with the probability of receiving little or no mortgage money from any source."[66] Although CMHC consistently urged private lenders to finance housing under the NHA, lenders ignored this advice and continued to make loans for apartment construction, denying "speculative loans" for the construction of single-family houses.[67] All of this helped to confirm the province's involvement in housing, but it had already begun to think about housing in a way that it had never before. By 1967, the minister responsible for housing, E.H. Gerhart, had defined provincial housing policy primarily in terms of the housing needs of two groups. The first was the working poor who required public housing in which rents would be pegged to income. The second, and larger, group had incomes too high for public housing and too low for CMHC loans. This group especially needed programmes that would complement their "initiative of. . . . wanting to own their own home." The province was careful to point out that public housing was not for people on welfare, who, presumably, were a social welfare and not a housing problem.[68] Attempts to assist the working poor and average income earners remained the core concerns of provincial housing policy in the following decade when boom conditions in the province drove the price of housing even further beyond the means of moderate and even middle income people. The year 1964 thus saw the beginning of a new era of provincial involvement in the housing field. From this point, the provincial government was committed to a number of housing programmes and implemented a number of projects and studies dealing with the whole field of housing.

One area that received attention was that of public housing. The first public housing programme in Alberta after the 1964 watershed was in Peace River, a town that had grown rapidly and had a large number of substandard houses. In 1966, a low-income housing project was built there, consisting of 30 two-storey semi detached houses sited on a cul-de-sac. Another was built in Fort McMurray at about the same time.[69] Still, the province often remained willing to leave the initiative in federal hands, and these projects were funded on a 15–75–10 percent split among the provincial, federal, and municipal governments respectively. In 1968 a joint prairie royal commission on consumer problems argued that the Alberta Housing and Urban Renewal Corporation, like its Manitoba counterpart, had concerned itself "mainly with the financial arrangements for projects initiated by others" which was "much too narrow a view to take of the responsibility of a provincial agency in the field of housing."[70] Perhaps such a judgement was prematurely harsh, given the newness of the corporation and the province's lack of experience in framing housing policy.

HOUSING IN NONFARM RURAL COMMUNITIES

Many people living in villages and towns faced similar problems to those in the large urban centres. At the end of the war, housing was scarce and of poor quality in many towns, although houses in more prosperous places were being renovated and improved.[71] One prevalent problem was the difficulty of obtaining mortgages in such centres; when a mortgage was granted, the lender often demanded a larger down payment than it did from city dwellers. Lenders were concerned both with the viability of many small towns and by the fact that incomes in most towns and villages were too low. In areas distant from Calgary and Edmonton, from 50 to 70 percent of all nonfarm families in 1961 had incomes below $4,000 per year. Such incomes were insufficient for NHA loans, and, consequently, by 1961 new residential construction in nonfarm areas of the prairies was taking place at a rate of only 1 percent per year of the existing building stock. This was said to be such a low rate that it would barely replace houses lost through physical deterioration. Indeed, more housing was being provided by moving houses from farms into towns than through new construction.[72]

Another problem in many villages and some towns was the lack of infrastructures for services. While electricity was common in most towns and villages, water and sewage systems were not. In 1945, all cities in Alberta had water and sewage systems, but only 23 out of 51 towns and only 3 out of 144 villages had a water system. The Alberta Post War Reconstruction Committee had recommended that all communities with a population of over 300 should have public systems to deliver such services.[73] Sanitation and water services were gradually installed in the decade after the war, and this was one area of priority for the provincial government, which provided funding to local authorities. By the late 1950s most towns had such services, although about one-half of the villages (centres of less than 1,000 people) did not.[74] As late as 1962, many hamlets still lacked running water, sewage, or septic tank systems. At Beaumont, a village south of Edmonton, most people relied on wells for water, while 16 of the 50 households had no water supply at all. Water shortages were worst in winter and in 1961 the school was closed for a short time because of a lack of water.[75] In 1961 CMHC created a lending programme under which municipalities could borrow funds to install sewage treatment plants, and 33 such loans were extended in Alberta in 1961 and 1962. Since housing was scarce, and that which existed was often little better than on farms, it was hoped that these loans would stimulate new house construction by increasing the number of serviced lots in these communities.[76]

There was, of course, great variation in housing conditions in nonfarm rural communities. The worst were in Indian and Metis settlements, where living conditions were extremely poor and community services were often totally lacking. In the years immediately after World War II, housing for Indian and Metis was of no official concern. Poverty led to severe crowding and dismal standards; in 1965, 70 percent of all Indian homes in Alberta had three rooms or less and less than 1 percent had water or any form of indoor sewage system. This compared to 57 percent of housing with three rooms or less for Indians nationally and 11 percent for the general population in Canada.[77] The conditions for the Metis were just as bad. It was estimated in 1968 that 83 percent of Metis housing was substandard and overcrowded. In 1960, the Alberta Metis Rehabilitation Branch began constructing frame houses in the Metis settlements and by 1968 it had built 248 houses,[78] but this was only a minor contribution in terms of the need. Extremely crowded shack housing, without any water or sanitary services, remained typical.[79] After his return from an inspection of Metis housing in Fort Chipewyan in 1968, A.O. Fimrite, the minister in charge of the Northern Alberta Development Council, informed the premier that

> it is understandable that the Metis people feel they are second class citizens when they compare their living conditions with their relatives who qualify for assistance under the Federal Indian Affairs Department. The Metis people that I talked to do not want the government to build homes for them that they cannot afford to maintain and pay for. They want the government to implement a program so that they can build their own homes.[80]

In other words, the Metis wanted a housing programme that would meet their needs, not those of urban Canada.

FARM HOUSING

In 1945 the Alberta Post War Reconstruction Committee confirmed that poor farm housing was general throughout the province. A majority of farm houses had no plumbing and 69 percent consisted of one to four rooms. Since adequate housing was the "right of every rural family," the committee concluded that the province should actively assist in improving farm housing. Implying an obligation on the part of the government to preserve Alberta's rural society, the committee argued that the province should help farmers acquire better amenities, better services, and a higher standard of living. It was assumed that farm life had some special virtue and the committee, sustaining the visions of 40 years earlier, observed that "if safeguarded and appreciated," farm homes "will once again act as a fountain-head, sending to town and city alike, a stream of life giving men and women and sending food and clothing materials to aid in their perpetuation. Let us plan for better rural homes, attractive and modernly equipped."[81]

Before 1967, government attempts to encourage better farm conditions consisted of a number of educational, loan, and electrification programmes. Rural electrification was a major undertaking and was handled on a "co-operative basis" by the province, rural electrification co-operative associations made up of farmers, and two private corporations, Calgary Power and Canadian Utilities. The co-operative associations borrowed money for installing local distribution lines and the province guaranteed the loans and subsidized the interest rates. The power companies were responsible for planning, engineering, providing the electricity, and constructing and operating the main transmission system as well as the local lines owned by the co-operatives. Rural electrification was thus a product of local, corporate, and provincial government co-operation, but, in keeping with Alberta's commitment to the free market, it was the private corporations that were the most significant players. This did not please everyone, and in 1946 the United Farmers of Alberta resolved at its annual convention that rural electrification should be handled by a crown corporation, as had been done in Ontario and would be done in Manitoba and Saskatchewan.[82] Nevertheless, under Alberta's co-operative system, 14,350 farms in Alberta had been connected by 1951 to power grids. There had also been a dramatic increase in private lighting plants. Almost 17 percent of farms were connected to the power grid, while almost 12 percent had a home generated source of electricity.[83]

Despite the generally poor standards of farm dwellings, electricity created a revolution in farm standards of living and farmers could now have some of the amenities and services that many urban people had taken for granted since the early twentieth century. Otherwise, governments offered few solutions for improvement of farm housing. Before 1959, the provincial government relied upon educational programmes to stimulate farm home improvement. One result of this approach was the creation of the Prairie Rural Housing Committee in 1948 by the three prairie provinces and CMHC. The committee conducted research and produced house designs which it hoped would encourage the construction of new rural housing or the renovation of existing dwellings.[84] Its association with CMHC gave it the opportunity to promote efficiency in housing by popularizing contemporary house designs. It also promoted research and publications about farm planning and on services such as heating and sewage. Further, in conjunction with the University of Alberta, it undertook research on the use of septic tanks in clay soils and on farm water supply.[85]

Despite the production of numerous pamphlets and educational sessions, farm housing showed little improvement in the 1950s. In 1961 the census reported that in Alberta just over 62 percent of farm dwellings did not have running water, and, while 27 percent had a flush toilet and just over 5 percent had chemical toilets, the balance used other facilities, presumably an outdoor privy.[86] Many farm houses were of such poor construction or in such bad repair that it was not worthwhile to install electricity or plumbing. Because of low incomes, and because income was directed towards production as well as improving living standards, many farm houses were patched together or unfinished structures built from poor materials. This applied equally to newly constructed farm houses, and in 1966 it was observed that commonly "the exterior has not been completed, front stairs are temporary or missing. . . . and plumbing facilities have been allotted for in the design but not completed." These conditions were common throughout the province, but were most prevalent in the northern areas.[87] Such uneven standards had typified farm housing throughout the century. Jean Burnet, in her study of the Hanna district, commented in 1946 that as one drove east from Calgary, one

◆ Many farm and small
town houses lacked run-
ning water in the 1940s.
Baths were taken beside
the warmth of the kit-
chen stove, as shown in
this photograph from
Mannville, 1949.
GAI NA 4171-4.

initially encountered large, well maintained and landscaped farm houses and yards, but by the time one arrived near Hanna, the houses had deteriorated and the "dominant type of building changes to an unpainted grey shack" without services or amenities.[88] Farm housing was still a problem in 1967, especially in the north central and northern parts of the province, where it compared unfavourably with urban housing.[89]

The idea that educational programmes could correct poor standards of farm housing was naive. No one ever seriously suggested that postwar urban problems could be solved in such a way, nor should it have been expected to work for farm housing. The problem was money, not ignorance. The federal government provided loans for housing under the *Farm Improvement Loans Act*, but these could only be obtained if the farmer had clear title to his land. As a consequence, between 1951 and 1962 relatively few loans for new houses or renovation of existing dwellings were granted.[90] The other federal source of funds was, of course, the NHA, but many farmers could not meet the age or income qualifications for loans.[91] In theory, the province met these difficulties with the passage of *The Farm Home Improvements Act* in 1959, but this legislation was little used. Under its provisions, farmers could obtain a loan to a maximum of $2,000 but only for renovations. Additions to houses, except for a bathroom, were not allowed. The government guaranteed 50 percent of this loan, which the banks considered insufficient. The programme was hopelessly obsolete by 1969, but it had never been of much assistance, making only 304 loans between 1959 and 1968.[92]

The *Farm Home Improvements Act*, like the NHA and the federal farm improvement lending programme, revealed the inadequacy of existing loan mechanisms for farm housing. Because of the low capitalization of many farms, dispersed settlement, and the poor standard of much farm housing, these problems were difficult to address. Many farmers were poor, too old, or did not have clear title to their land, and, when debt was taken on, it was directed to improving production and, hopefully, future income.[93] These conditions illustrated how complex an area housing was. Government programmes could be created, but if they did not grapple directly with the social and economic causes of poor housing, the problems would remain. Thus, the urban model of assistance for housing did not work in rural areas and government farm programmes must be counted to have been failures before 1967.

SENIOR CITIZEN HOUSING

A more successful housing programme was that for senior citizens. Here, success was the result of government commitment and the ease of identifying a target group with relatively similar needs and a common financial profile everywhere in the province. Traditionally, the only special provision for senior citizens was privately run nursing homes. There was no housing for active senior citizens, with the exception of projects such as the Sunset Cottages in Edmonton which were built in 1937 by the city and the Lion's Club for indigent, active elderly persons. This effort was expanded after the war, and by 1954, 14 cottages had been built and the Lions were planning and raising funds for a low rent apartment complex for seniors, a building that opened in 1959. A similar project was carried out in Red Deer by the Kiwanis Club.[94] By this point the province had actively entered the field since it was clear that the level of services needed throughout the province could not be met through volunteer or local efforts. In 1945 the province had passed legislation permitting municipalities to construct homes for the aged, but this legislation was unproductive. Accordingly, further legislation was passed in 1954 authorizing financial assistance to municipalities for senior citizens' housing. Initially, the emphasis remained on nursing homes,[95] but by 1958 it began to shift towards facilities for active senior citizens. Interest in establishing such facilities was growing throughout the province, and the provincial government responded by increasing grants, by promoting a design competition for senior citizens' housing, and by constructing the buildings. This programme was wholly financed by Alberta, and in 1967 it became the responsibility of the Alberta Housing and Urban Renewal Corporation.

In 1960 there was still a need for nursing and medical care facilities for elderly people, but there was a growing trend towards providing varied types of housing within a single complex, including both self-contained housing units and nursing care facilities. This kind of structure indicated a new way of thinking about the aged in society. The extended family had broken down and could no longer give the elderly a social context. The "modern engineered bungalow" had no room for grandparents and, as Premier Manning argued in 1958, there was a clear need for special housing to give senior citizens dignity and "opportunities to form new social ties to replace those which family dispersal and death have broken."[96] The construction of such homes presented a peculiar difficulty because they were needed everywhere in the province. While housing for seniors was not a distinctly urban or rural problem, in 1956 rural areas had a greater number of people over 70 years of age than did the two largest cities. The province determined that 50 homes were needed, and by 1960 31 homes comprising 1,550 units had been built, consisting of self-contained units and "lodge" type facilities. These complexes met differing levels of health and social needs and attempts were made to locate them to serve all areas of the province. While it was believed that these facilities should, if possible, be self-sustaining to reduce costs for the province and save the elderly from the "stigma" of social assistance, subsidized rents pegged to income were required since 40 percent of people over 70 had no income other than pensions, mainly the federal old age allowance.[97]

The senior citizens' housing scheme was a direct public expenditure for housing and demonstrated the potential of public housing programmes. Many people who would otherwise have spent their old age in substandard boarding houses were provided with decent accommodation. The province was proud of this programme, but it did not see it as enhancing arguments for other public housing programmes. The calculation of average income of seniors and the setting of rent in relation to their income was properly justified as conferring dignity upon the old. Yet, when such an approach was recommended for low income younger people, it was stigmatized as a policy of degradation. Senior citizens' housing never became a precedent for public housing and the distinctions between the two were easily sustained through an appeal to history. The generation for whom public complexes were built had pioneered the province and embodied in Alberta the cult of the individual, and a collectivist response to their needs did not challenge the ideal of private home ownership or the free market in housing. Indeed, it confirmed them by implicitly rewarding sacrifice and deprivation.

◆

The ideology of private home ownership remained powerful and was supported by all classes in the society, reinforced by the often wretched conditions and high prices of rental housing. As E. Litchfield observed in 1949, housing schemes modeled on European public housing projects, which he thought "unquestionably impressive," simply did not fit North American thinking where the single-family home was not only "an accepted order of things" but whose attainment was

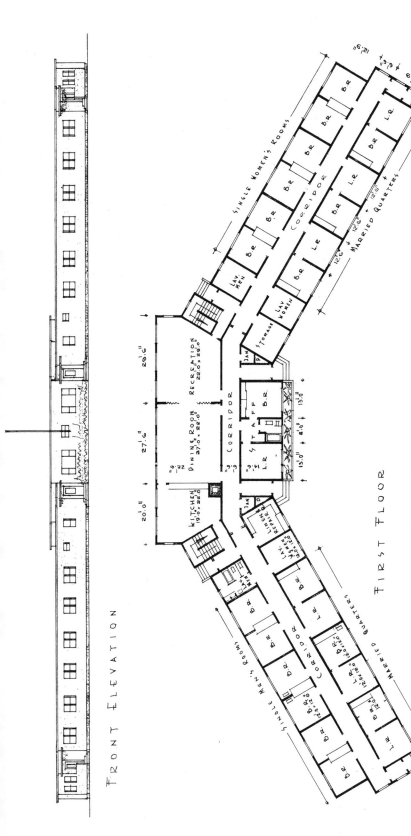

PRELIMINARY SKETCH OLD PEOPLE HOME — 1/16" = 1'-0"

◆ Senior citizen housing emerged as an important part of Alberta government housing policy in 1954. "Lodge" type facilities were designed for a varied group of seniors who needed some level of care. CEA RG 11/53/3.

one of the principle driving impulses of individual and national life. Land is owned here in individual lots and plots by people in all walks of life, our working population owns no small section of it. . . . This is a condition peculiar to this North American continent. Certainly, a like condition does not now, nor has it ever existed in Europe. I think most students and admirers of European Planning and Housing miss or ignore this quite important difference, but they soon find out.[98]

Litchfield exaggerated the uniqueness of North America, and he also ignored that such views about property and the home were not mere accidents of time, place, and history. They were the fruit of a long commitment to the free market system, which made the privately owned detached house an integral part of the economic and social order. These views had been encouraged and assisted by governments, the official organs of opinion such as newspapers, and through popular social theory. The house was popularly said to be an expression of individuality, and in some ways it was. While most of these attempts at individuality had been merely the aping of current fashions, involving no individualized expression, it remained a popular belief that one could not express oneself as an individual through a rented house or an apartment, let alone through a state subsidized housing unit.

Almost all of the housing built in Alberta between 1945 and 1967 was provided through the private construction of new houses for private ownership. For those who wanted to purchase an older house, there were simply not enough to meet the demand. Despite grumbling about high prices, few in the middle class seemed to object to this, and there were few laments that Albertans could not live in older houses. The belief that new buildings signalled the taming of the frontier had been transformed into a belief that newness demonstrated personal success and upward social mobility. The deprivation experienced during the Depression and then during World War II reinforced the commitment to newness, as did the postwar fixation with material rewards. And the recipients of these rewards were easily recognizable through the houses they built, which looked different and were often sited in a different way than were houses of earlier times.

TEN

Redesigning the
Residential Landscape

The design of the urban residential landscape in Alberta underwent radical change after World War II. Planning became not
only accepted, but more complex, more professionalized, and, most
importantly, more integral to all forms of development as never before. It was now applied not just to the planning of cities, but to the
regions in which cities were located. As the ideal of the single-family
detached house on its own plot of land led to almost inexorable
growth of suburbs tied to the urban environment through private
transportation, the emphasis on planning on a larger and larger scale
became imperative. The foundation for this emphasis had been laid
during the interwar years, and while planning at Turner Valley had
been one early expression, its full realization came after World War
II. By 1950, large cities such as Edmonton had appointed town planners and regional planning commissions were beginning to appear.
The provincial planning legislation was under almost yearly amendment in the late 1940s, and a new town planning act was passed in
1950 and again in 1953.[1] By the early 1950s, the major urban centres
were adopting general plans, and for housing, postwar planning had
two broad applications; the development of new towns in resource
areas and the layout of residential areas in large urban centres.

NEW TOWNS

One immediate result of the oil boom was the movement of people into areas that had little or no housing. Of course, this was nothing new in Alberta where boom towns were an integral part of provincial history, but whereas such towns in the past had been chaotic, unplanned environments, attempts were made after World War II to control and eliminate unsystematic growth.

Two towns illustrate this attempt at planning: Drayton Valley and Devon, both of which were part of the development of the Leduc and Pembina oilfields. The most dramatic development occurred in Devon. By the end of 1948, the town had a population of 500 and 123 houses had been built on land which a year before had been a barley field. Imperial Oil purchased the land for the townsite, handled real estate sales, and, in conjunction with CMHC, provided some financing at low interest rates. It was not, however, a company town, but a permanent community with privately owned houses. The town was laid out by J.H. Holloway, Director of Surveying and Town Planning for Alberta. It had a full range of amenities and houses were sited on 60 and 68 foot wide lots. Built in Calgary and transported north by trucks, the first houses were prefabricated structures built to minimum structural and design standards.[2]

While the circumstances of Drayton Valley's development were similar, the planning was not as controlled, nor was it as successful. In 1953, oil was discovered near the hamlet, which had a population of about 75. It became a centre for exploration and within a year hundreds of workers had arrived.[3] In the next three years, $3.5 million in building permits were issued in Drayton Valley, but, even with such levels of construction, accommodation was scarce and workers lived in bunkhouses, trailers, and "skid shacks." The latter were

> simply frame structures, small enough to load on a two-wheel trailer or on the back of a truck. Dimensions range from 8 × 10 feet up. They are usually meant to house no more than a man and wife. In Drayton Valley, where roofs were so scarce at the height of the excitement that men were sleeping in road culverts, a "skid shack" is still a mansion. As many as 16 men slept in a single shack this past winter.[4]

In spite of the pressures of expansion, the province regulated land sales and drew up a town plan. The population growth of Drayton Valley was rapid and by 1951 had reached 3,000; much of it transient. Planning was difficult, and by 1956 the town still faced many problems. Trailers and skid shacks were placed "helter skelter on industrial, commercial and residential lots throughout the town," which not only made the town unattractive but created sanitary and fire hazards as well. By 1967 the town was showing a better appearance, although some problems with separation of land use and some poor quality housing remained.[5]

DISTRICT PLANNING

Planned towns could prevent this type of chaos, and it is revealing that postwar Alberta no longer accepted that such conditions should simply be endured. After 1950, district planning was implemented in an attempt to control development in areas adjacent to large urban centres. Bedroom communities and "acreages" were relatively limited until the 1960s, and fringe areas continued to be the focus for development adjacent to cities. Nevertheless, it was clear that planning for a rational urban future required district planning, and such planning was being implemented by 1955 at Edmonton, Calgary, Medicine Hat, and, among others, Red Deer.[6] Red Deer's approach to planning was innovative. Development outside the city limits was controlled through the creation of a corridor around the city in which subdivision was restricted. In 1954, Dennis Cole, the City Engineer and Town Planner, observed that "the main idea is to sterilize that land against development so that it will be available should the city continue to expand."[7] Red Deer was innovative in another important way. In 1958 the city began land banking and thereafter operated "almost wholly. . . . under a system of public land ownership, and public financing and installation of services." No other city in Alberta or in Canada was as farsighted or fortunate. Land speculation in Red Deer was almost eliminated, improved amenities like parks were provided, and a cost efficient and successful approach to land development and house construction meant that population growth was easily accommodated.[8] In contrast, the areas outside Calgary and Edmonton showed fragmented development by the mid 1950s and both cities tried to alleviate the problem, at least partly, through continued annexation of outlying areas. This satisfied the cities' needs for land, planned growth, and, of course, revenue, but additional pressure for annexation came from residents of these outlying areas because they wanted city amenities. In Calgary, these annexations proceeded relatively smoothly, but in Edmonton the process was often difficult because some areas adjacent to the city were richer, more independent, and more politically powerful than was the case around Calgary.[9]

Before 1960, peripheral development near Edmonton was focused mainly to the east of the city. As late as 1958, most of the counties around Edmonton refused to permit subdivision except under controlled arrangements.[10] The one exception was the County of Strathcona on the eastern boundary of the city. Although this area had been under a regional planning commission since 1950, in 1951 the county began encouraging residential subdivision and the establishment of a satellite community. Despite substantial opposition within the Edmonton District Planning Commission to such development, the county went ahead. In 1954 it withdrew from the Edmonton District Planning Commission and continued to promote development, especially in an urban area called Campelltown, later renamed Sherwood Park. Plans for this community varied. In 1951 a city of 30,000 was envisioned but by 1954 this had been reduced to 5,000. Nevertheless, it was clear that the county had "definite plans for the creation of a very large urban community within close distance of Edmonton's crowded east boundary." It was noted in 1956 that should the plans for a population of 30,000 be fulfilled, there would be erected just outside Edmonton a new city that was larger than Medicine Hat, which then was the third largest city in the province. By 1956, the development of Campelltown was proceeding under a private developer who was creating a residential community with local shopping, educational, and service facilities. Model homes had been built and one inducement held out to purchasers was lower property taxes than in the city.[11] While the County of Strathcona remained the major focus of subdivision activity in the Edmonton area until the early 1970s, there was some other activity around the city. In the 1950s and 1960s, however, there was more subdivided land in the counties around Edmonton than there was demand, and it was only later that subdivision and the development of "acreages" became popular in these areas.[12]

NEIGHBOURHOOD PLANNING

Of greater immediate importance than development adjacent to cities was the way in which planning affected new urban residential districts. While many districts continued to be laid out on a traditional, but limited, gridiron plan, a different concept was also applied. It was based on the notion that planning should aim to create "neighbourhoods," an approach referred to as Neighbourhood Unit Concept. According to this theory, the city would be planned as a series of neighbourhoods, each with a population of about 15,000 which would be integrated into the general urban environment through an efficient transportation system and, of course, a common political focus. Each "neighbourhood" would have residential areas of mixed density, a safe internal street system with no through traffic, park space, and services such as shops. Its boundaries would be well defined by parks and roads. A centrally located school would provide a focus for the local population. Some theorists held that the school would become what the town hall had been in colonial New England, a notion hardly relevant to prairie Canada with no such tradition. Curved streets and irregular shaped blocks would help to break the monotony of the gridiron plan, and higher density housing, such as duplexes and apartments, would be included in the neighbourhood.

Neighbourhood planning was not new. It developed from garden city planning of which the most famous North American example was the 1929 plan for Radburn, New Jersey.[13] After World War II it became highly popular and was applied in varying degrees in a number of housing developments in Alberta. Noel Dant, the newly appointed town planner in Edmonton, liked the concept, which was then being discussed in planning schools, and he applied it to Edmonton.[14] The first planned "neighbourhood" in Alberta was Parkallen in Edmonton, which was approved in 1951. Such plans were later created for other areas in Edmonton and elsewhere. Calgary began neighbourhood planning in a partial fashion after 1948, but the first fully developed neighbourhood was not developed there until 1954.[15] Although these plans were subsequently modified or changed according to practical experience, the general principles of neighbourhood planning continued to be applied.[16]

The justifications for the use of neighbourhood planning are good indices of the attitudes and conditions that affected postwar housing development. The gridiron was thought to have created sterile and often unattractive environments. It was also accused, as town planners had argued for decades, of being a wasteful system, unable to take advantage of differing topography because of its rigid adherence to uniform lot and street widths. Thus, when earlier subdivisions were replotted to incorporate neighbourhood planning, large land owners presented no opposition. Under the new system, density per acre could sometimes be increased without sacrificing a sense of spaciousness, and the new planning could be applied without challenging the

◆ Planning new postwar
suburbs reflected a new
vision of urban life as the
resurvey of Parkallen in
Edmonton in 1951 dem-
onstrated. SOURCE:
Robert Graden, "The
Planning of New Resi-
dential Districts in Ed-
monton, 1950–1976,"
M.A. thesis, 1979, p. 28,
Bruce Peel Special Col-
lection Library, Univer-
sity of Alberta.

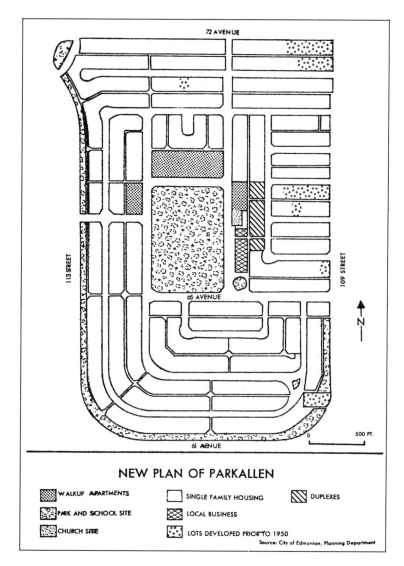

NEW PLAN OF PARKALLEN

WALKUP APARTMENTS   SINGLE FAMILY HOUSING   DUPLEXES

PARK AND SCHOOL SITE   LOCAL BUSINESS

CHURCH SITE   LOTS DEVELOPED PRIOR TO 1950

Source: City of Edmonton, Planning Department

◆ An aerial view of a new
suburb using open plan-
ning concepts in Leth-
bridge, 1951. The suburb
was developed by Engi-
neered Homes, Ltd.
GAI NA 5327-293.

preeminence of the single-family detached dwelling.[17] The NHA also aided the implementation of the neighbourhood planning concept by favouring it through its lending policies. In an area "adequately protected by community planning and zoning restrictions," loans would be amortized over a 30 year period for owned units or a 25 year period for rental housing, in contrast to the 20 years allowed for housing in nonplanned areas.[18] This was a powerful incentive indeed, and although CMHC never officially endorsed neighbourhood planning, its informal support was clear. Consequently, cities began to apply neighbourhood planning concepts to ensure that potential house purchasers would be eligible for NHA mortgages.[19] In the 1950s, Calgary included CMHC in its approval process for development proposals, and proposed plans were sometimes changed to comply with CMHC's wishes.[20]

Neighbourhood unit plans were adopted not simply because of the needs of developers and because CMHC favoured them. They were also a sign of modernity and were different from existing neighbourhoods in Alberta cities, except for a handful of elite residential districts. Neighbourhood planning also appeared to be a way to reinforce family life by providing a yard and safe environment for children in the new suburbs where the majority of people would soon live. This aspect of the concept tied nicely with the continuing idealization of the role of the home in family life. Cecil Burgess felt the spell of neighbourhood planning when he wrote in 1947 that, in planning housing for the future, "it will be well to do whatever we can to recapture some of the neighbourliness of the old fashioned village along with whatever spiritual and material elements can be added to it and with freedom from its serious drawbacks."[21] That such villages had never formed a real part of twentieth century Alberta life seemed irrelevant in the heady days of postwar optimism, an optimism that was expressed in a yearning for stability and order and in an almost relentless acquisitiveness, at least partially appeased by a house in the suburbs and by its necessary adjunct, the car. In 1945, the Royal Bank of Canada argued that the planning, construction, and siting of housing should promote "neighbourliness, civic sense, architectural pleasantness and a feeling of stability." It could "advance industrial efficiency, better citizenship, higher standards of family life, comfort and contentment," and "help to eliminate class hatred, social unrest and revolutionary propaganda, which are the accompaniments of crowded housing."[22] Clearly, the expectations for neighbourhood planning were high. Of course, housing had always been recognized in Alberta as a symbol of permanency and as a source of social and political stability, and, in this sense, postwar planning only represented a new approach to a long held ambition.

Neighbourhood planning also facilitated the need to make construction less expensive. Economy was essential, given the increased cost of building materials, labour, and land in the postwar years. In 1945 E. Litchfield observed that neighbourhood planning would help to encourage economy in house building because large blocks of land and large developments would make housing less expensive and might prevent the "speculative excesses" seen in subdivision and sale of land lot by lot. Further, services would be less costly when installed as part of a large scale development, and it would be possible to make use of mass-produced building components. Litchfield believed that good housing could only be produced by planning and building well in the first instance; "as soon as the neighbourhood unit has been accepted as the most effective method of planning, many old conceptions and habits will become quite meaningless."[23]

OUTLINE PLANNING

The neighbourhood plans represented a theoretical model for the solving of postwar social and economic problems. During the mid 1950s, however, planners began to shift their attention to larger geographical units. By 1960, outline or sector planning had become popular. This change of focus, according to Robert Graden in his study of post World War II planning in Alberta, was adopted "for the sake of order and economy in suburban development, and not necessarily for the purpose of creating more satisfactory living environments."[24] Outline planning coincided with a need for large tracts of land on which to build detached houses and meet the needs of the rapidly expanding populations of Alberta cities. The Edmonton House Builders' Association argued in 1961 that to promote "smooth development," Edmonton should annex outlying areas to make more residential land available, since the lack of good building sites in the city was "slowing the rate of industrial expansion and halting population growth."[25] Outline planning was intended by its advocates to make expansion controllable and "smooth development" possible by developing residential and service areas on an extremely large scale. According to this approach, the neighbourhood unit concept was enlarged. Instead of focusing upon a school or other public facility, a series of "neighbourhoods" were grouped around a town centre which included not only a school, but a shopping centre, medical facilities, and high density housing.[26] Thus, the "neighbourhood" became part of a larger entity which was termed a "community."

The important theorist of outline planning was Humphrey Carver, a Canadian who argued that it was possible to create a community with "a full range of age groups in the population, and a full roster of social and commercial institutions."[27] Carver believed that a "community" should be composed of three or four neighbourhoods with a total population of around 20,000. In Alberta, however, the size of the "communities" that were envisioned were much, much larger. Six "communities" were planned for Edmonton, the largest being Millwoods for which development began in 1972. It was 6,000 acres in size and was expected to house a population of 120,000.[28] All of these "communities" were to be linked to the urban whole by freeways. Suburbia, with its earlier promises of comfort, security, and a strong sense of locality, had become giganticism.

Informed by the optimism and buoyancy of the 1960s, outline planning was expected to produce rational urban development and, like neighbourhood planning, protect "property values through the creation of residential areas of lasting social and monetary value."[29] Further, massive economic and population growth was expected to be accommodated and socially neutralized. Without sacrificing the single-family detached house, density in outline planned communities could be higher than in neighbourhood unit plans, and because of the speed of postwar urban development in Alberta, this was an attractive feature of outline planning. Advocates believed that each "community" should be a microcosm of the society. It was hoped that suburban residential life would be made more "organic," more private, and yet more integrated at a local level. In physical terms, these suburbs looked different. Pedestrian walkways connected parts of the "community" and houses were sometimes "turned around to face walkways and open spaces rather than streets." They were to be equally innovative in social terms. There was to be a mix of housing types, including mobile homes in some plans, and a mix of social classes. In Edmonton, the general plan held that every citizen had a right to live and work in decent surroundings, and in 1971 the city council resolved that 5 percent of the population in all future subdivisions should be accommodated in public housing, sited to prevent public housing ghettos and to give its occupants access to public services and amenities like any other citizens. This "balanced community," with its mix of housing types and classes, was held to be necessary for mutual understanding and a democratic society. This was a laudable objective, but few local politicians probably stopped to think what a radical shift it represented from the traditional approach of houses located in enclaves based on class and ethnicity. The theory did not, however, address the underlying causes of social inequality. Rather, it was based on a naive belief that "understanding" would be sufficient to solve the problems created by social inequality and the unequal distribution of wealth.[30] The recognition that housing was one of the best visual proofs of social inequality had been combined with an assumption that the mere relocation of housing could correct this inequality.

ELEVEN

Postwar Housing
and Design

Between 1946 and 1967 there were important changes not only in the layout of residential urban areas but also in the design of houses. Both neighbourhood and outline planning provided some new opportunities in terms of siting, while new construction techniques and materials, when combined with the postwar demand for newness, often stimulated design changes. Although postwar designers, as well as many social theorists, congratulated themselves that theirs was a new world, such assertions were only partly true. Many prewar ideas about the layout, servicing, and purpose of housing continued to be important but were now often assumed rather than articulated as conscious design principles. The housing of the postwar years pared down design elements to produce a cleaner and simpler look, but an urge for economy, without an accompanying well thought out aesthetic of simplicity, often created a tightness in the feel of some of these houses. This was especially so in the wartime houses, although the result was understandable in view of the need for rapid, inexpensive construction.

POSTWAR HOUSE FORMS AND STYLES

The designs utilized in wartime houses were important because they inspired such a large proportion of housing constructed immediately after World War II. Typically, these were one-
or one-and-a-half storey houses, featuring fairly steep roofs and
"high Gothic porches rising over the entrance doorways, and for a
time it was very popular to eliminate eaves and to paint outside walls
in two-tone pastel colours."[1] Door and window casings were nar-
rowed and the use of large windows changed the look of houses completely from prewar designs. While wood cladding was common, the
exterior was often stuccoed. These houses were commonly called
"bungalows." Although they remained popular until the early 1950s,
single storey houses with a more pronounced horizontal profile than
had been usual before the war began to appear on the scene after the
mid 1940s. These too were called "bungalows," and while they took
their essence from the bungalows of the early twentieth century,
they could well be described as a new house form. For lack of a better
term, these bungalows, with a few modifications such as a higher
basement, had become dominant in Alberta within ten years. By
1958 eight out of ten houses built in Canada were single storied with
hip or gable roofs, and the same ratio would probably have applied to
Alberta. Eaves reappeared, and an almost obligatory feature was a
"picture window," which defined the front of the house and dominated the living room, and throughout the 1950s and 1960s these
windows became larger and larger. A majority of these bungalows
were three-bedroom structures of about 1,100 square feet, a size favoured because "lenders are hesitant about making loans on houses of
less than 1,000 square feet because of the difficulty of resale."[2] A significant change in the 1950s was the use of the basement as a "den"
or "rumpus room," which became fashionable and something of a
status symbol in new suburban housing. This room was portrayed as
a space for family and social life and conformed to the view of suburban life as comforting and meaningful. Only 30 years before, such
use of the basement had been a heresy and a sign of poverty, but the
practice was soon institutionalized in new postwar housing. Possibly
these multi-use living rooms in basements camouflaged a desire for
more privacy and a retreat from the obligatory open plan. About this
time, the term "ranch style" came to be applied to some of these bungalows, generally referring to the larger ones emphasizing strong
horizontal lines, overhanging eaves, and a hip or gable roof. Rectan-

◆ A street of typical postwar bungalows in Ed-
monton, 1945.
PAA BL935/5.

◆ Many houses built im-
mediately after World
War II, such as this Ed-
monton home photo-
graphed in 1951, all but
eliminated eaves and fea-
tured stucco and Gothic
porches. PAA KS798.

◆ Low profile houses such as these built in Lethbridge had become typical suburban homes by 1955. GAI ND 202-48.

Photographed in 1964, Dr. Hall's ranch style house in Edmonton demonstrated a fine proportion and sense of scale.

◆ PAA KS823.

gular shapes predominated but an L shape was also common. These ranch style bungalows were most often built by the upper middle class in the postwar years, and some of the best designed of these houses had an elegance and proportion that must surely rank them among the finest domestic architecture of the century in Alberta.

While both the smaller and the larger ranch style bungalows in Alberta were identical to those built in suburbs everywhere in North America after World War II, they were "remarkably well suited to the prairie landscape, where trees are low and these buildings can be more easily sheltered than the high rise structure of earlier years."[3] With these horizontal lines, changes in garden design followed. The early twentieth century prairie garden had tended towards formal plantings to frame the house and integrate it with the landscape. Given the narrowness of lots and the verticality of houses, plantings to accommodate such conditions had often tended to vertical shapes. For lower house profiles, however, gardens began to emphasize plantings that stressed the integration of horizontal rather than vertical elements. Accordingly, groundcovers and low trees and shrubs, that would reinforce the horizontal line of the house without blocking the view of the yard from the large windows, were used. The use of large windows, made possible in part because of more efficient heating systems, also led to attempts to make the garden private and to prevent passersby from seeing into the house, especially from the back alley. This stimulated an increased emphasis on fences and trees around the perimeter of the lot.[4] In later years the fences became higher and higher, especially when a demand for patios developed in the 1960s.

While these single-storied bungalows were dominant in the mid and late 1950s, a new form, the split level, began to emerge in the early 1960s. The novelty of the split level may have helped to account for its popularity, but it was also recommended for its efficient design. This reputation for efficiency was earned "because each floor level is only six or seven steps from the next; at the same time it provides a greater separation between sleeping and living areas."[5] Often it contained only a half basement, which somewhat lessened construction costs. What was significant about the split level, however, was that it was the first practical application in ordinary housing in Alberta of the ideas of the American architect, Frank Lloyd Wright, who, a half century before, had designed houses with interpenetrated space. In Wright's early twentieth century houses, the living areas "consisted of interlocked spaces separated not by doors but by care-

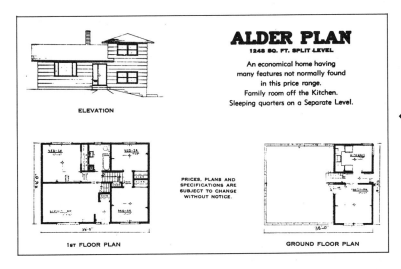

ALDER PLAN
1248 SQ. FT. SPLIT LEVEL

An economical home having
many features not normally found
in this price range.
Family room off the Kitchen.
Sleeping quarters on a Separate Level.

ELEVATION

PRICES, PLANS AND
SPECIFICATIONS ARE
SUBJECT TO CHANGE
WITHOUT NOTICE.

1st FLOOR PLAN

GROUND FLOOR PLAN

◆ The split level was a new
house form that had
emerged by 1960. This
one, featured by Art
Batty Construction Ltd.,
Lethbridge, was one of
the largest homes the
company featured in
1959. "1959 Homes You
Can Afford,"
PAA 71.225.

◆ A few Modern style
houses were built in Al-
berta, such as Howard
McBride's Edmonton
house, photographed in
1953. PAA KS402/1.

fully developed angles of vision." Using devices such as different ceiling heights, free standing walls and overlapping rooms, interior space had been given a new complexity.[6] The open plan houses that had been built in Alberta to this time had rarely used such devices since rooms simply opened into each other in a one dimensional and linear fashion. The split level was the first significant modification of this layout, and although this was to be taken much further in later years, in "bi-level" houses for example, the split level was its first modest application.

While the split level was immensely popular by the mid 1960s, upscale housing by this time began to tend to a two-storey house, often in a colonial style. These houses had a pleasing simplicity and good proportion but some had too much self-conscious sobriety to be comparable with the best of the ranch style bungalows. The period also saw the moderne style house with a flat roof, a stuccoed exterior, and frequently curved corners. A few such houses had been built in the early 1940s, and a few continued to be built until the mid 1950s, but they were a minor part of new housing.[7]

OTHER DESIGN TRENDS

In general, postwar houses in North America were "neither bizarre nor austere. They did not require a change in a way of life. . . . and they needed neither manifestos nor exhibitions to explain themselves."[8] Still, the old urge to decorate lurked in the background. In 1966, the seventh annual Edmonton "home parade," called "Honeymoon Village" in this year, featured eighteen houses in the currently popular designs. Most were conventional "colonial, ranch and split level" houses, but there were also two "Polynesian" houses. One of these featured a "long open outside gallery. . . . Space is excavated below for inclusion of a long patio. The decor alternates between brilliant and drab, taupe and black, broken with scarlet." The same tendencies, albeit to a lesser extent, were also exhibited in some of the other houses, one of which featured a window design that gave "an Elizabethan tone."[9]

Despite these occasional breaks with the dominant trends, there was a uniformity in design and environment in the huge postwar suburbs. Perhaps Polynesian influences and Tudor touches were small attempts to break the monotony of postwar suburban housing. The streets, curving in gigantic sweeps across the land, were lined with houses that were almost indistinguishable from one another or from houses anywhere else in North America. Of course, suburban developments at the beginning of the century had looked little different. They too were basically a repetition of the stock designs of the age, but beginning in the early 1950s criticism of the suburban world and its sameness began to mount. Noel Dant, the Edmonton planner, observed that contemporary suburbs contained row upon row of "almost identical houses spaced as closely together as the bylaws and regulations of the loan institutions will allow." Builders attempted "to disguise the essential similarity of the houses" by using different coloured brick, false gables, and the like, but this "attempt at disguise fools no one and the sameness and dullness of the residential areas in an average city is to be deplored."[10]

It is true that these seemingly endless rows of similar houses are a daunting sight, open to the criticism that better design rather than further planning was needed. Yet as landscaping matured, their sameness was minimized. Nonetheless, the criticism of suburban houses became so widespread that even those who had designed and built them tried to pin the blame elsewhere. In 1960, a past president of the Edmonton House Builders' Association lashed out against "City Hall which causes stereotyped mass produced housing and standardized layouts."[11] Yet, if blame was to be placed, it should not have been attached to standards of construction that specified minimum room sizes or the thickness of plywood subflooring. House design was hardly the inevitable outcome of building regulations.

While standardized building materials and techniques had produced suburban environments which many felt were too uniform, efforts in design were directed towards creating a truly functional interior. This emphasis applied to farm and urban housing alike. The Prairie Rural Housing Committee noted in 1949 that design principles for farm and urban housing were the same, although it was concerned that since "the farm house is the business center for farming operations as well as the centre for family life," planning needed to account for this difference. There was, however, no appreciable change in the layout of farm houses. Like urban house design, the principle of interior layout aimed to create an open plan "to ensure freedom of movement, more light, greater sense of spaciousness and less complicated structure."[12]

The Alberta Department of Agriculture advised farmers who were building new houses in 1952 that modern living conditions demanded a house "not for looks, but for living." It was an oddly am-

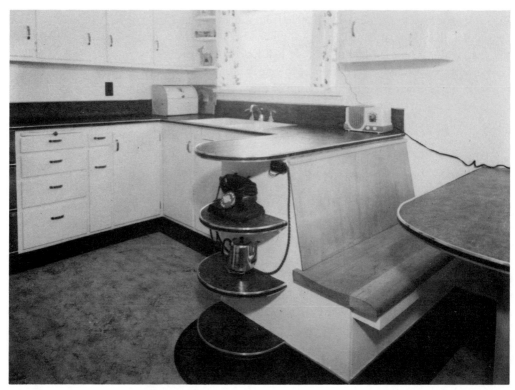

◆ The kitchen in a house
built in 1946 by
Armitage McBain, Ed-
monton, featured a
dining nook off the
kitchen. PAA BL730/2.

bivalent and almost apologetic phrase, but it was clear that the key-notes of modern design were "comfort, freedom from drudgery, practical usefulness and economy." In meeting these objectives, four principles governed house design. First, maximum use of natural light should be ensured. By properly designing "roof-eaves and over-hangs, sunlight is made to seek the farthest corners of the rooms in winter, and is excluded to a desired degree in summer." Second, "the lot is made part of the house," which could be accomplished by having large plate glass windows to bring the garden visually inside the house. "The old cramped and shut-in feelings are gone." Third, because houses were expensive, "economy of space" was essential. The living room and dining room should be combined into "one large area," and, to maximize useable space and save costs, "special purpose" rooms that were seldom used should be avoided. The "fewer partitions required in a house the cheaper the construction will be." Lastly, though not by any means least, the house should be efficient. "Dust catchers" should be rigourously eliminated, woodwork should be designed to save cleaning and maintenance, and utilities and appliances should be grouped to save work and promote efficiency.[13]

While these principles were indeed applied in much postwar housing, all essentially evolved from pre World War II design principles. As in the interwar years, kitchens often had a dining area, and although separate dining rooms continued to be built in some cases, it was more popular to have an L shaped living/dining room where the dining area was placed adjacent to the kitchen. Although some post-war houses adopted a closed plan, likely because the houses were small, open plans continued to be immensely popular. Exaggerated openess led one architect to comment in 1947 that "we will soon arrive at the Great Hall plan—the modern version being one living space, cleverly subdivided without actual walls so that the function of cooking, eating, relaxing and sleeping can be defined with minimum maintenance and waste space."[14]

Open plans were justified on the grounds of enhanced family life and informal lifestyles, just as they had been for half a century, and in keeping with this objective, fireplaces continued to be installed as a focus for family hospitality and cohesion. In this case, the principles of honesty of design and functionalism were dismissed in favour of tradition and family togetherness. Albertans were advised in 1946 that "there is something cheerying, something friendly and welcoming about the glow of an open fire," and if one could not have a genuine fire, a fake would serve nicely. A fireplace could "be easily simulated, for there are available fireplaces for electric fires complete with mantlepiece, which are invaluable on chilly nights or drizzly days."[15] By the late 1950s, the fireplace was being replaced by a television which slid effortlessly into the role that the fireplace had once held. Thus, television had little immediate impact on house layout. One study in the United States in the mid 1980s found that despite television's immense impact on home social activities, its influence on the use of space in the house was minor. The television was generally located in a specific room, and other spaces maintained their traditional and specific uses.[16] The emphasis on multi-use living areas since the beginning of the century had paved the way for the living room as an ideal setting for television.

In the postwar years, hygiene became an assumed objective of design and no longer needed much explanation or justification. It became more common to advocate many design qualities, such as the elimination of "dust catchers," because they lessened housework and promoted efficiency than because they enhanced sanitation. Hardwood and linoleum continued to be the favoured flooring material for ease of maintenance. The design of kitchens ceased to be the obsession that it had been previously because the standardization of equipment made kitchens homogeneous.[17] Bathrooms also came to be standardized, although there was a greater attempt to "decorate" them. This suggests again that hygiene had become an assumed objective. The need for efficiency became almost a slogan of postwar life: "Mrs. Canada expects to do her own housework and supervise the children. She naturally wants all rooms planned and arranged to make her household tasks easier and more pleasant, and to allow her as much free time as possible." Of course, the average "Mrs. Canada" had always done her own housework, but such concerns led to a continued emphasis on traffic patterns within the house. In selecting designs in 1947 for Canadian small houses, CMHC "carefully examined" plans to ensure that "communication from front entrances to the rest of the house. . . . avoided using the living room as a passage." A related criterion was the need for "ease of access from the kitchen, as the working centre of the house to all other parts" of the dwelling.[18]

Interior design that aimed to create an efficient environment for the home tasks of "Mrs. Canada" assumed that she would stay at home and be a housekeeper. This was an important part of the postwar suburban dream, and it had much the same attributes in 1945 as it had in 1910. Yet this assumption soon began to break down when married women began entering the paid workforce in greater numbers. In Alberta, 13.2 percent of married women were in the paid workforce in 1921, 11.5 percent were working outside the home in 1941, which then increased to 19.4 percent in 1946 and 33.7 percent in 1951.[19] It was uncertain at the time if this was a temporary phenomenon, but within a decade it was apparent that the nature of middle class family life had changed. There were miles of subdivisions, populated largely with school children in the day. The implications for suburban life were considerable but unresolvable, and when divorce rates began to increase in the late 1960s, it had become clear that the suburban ideal articulated at the end of World War II was facing major challenges.

APARTMENTS

Although the postwar suburban dream never included living in apartments, they became a common phenomenon. While the traditional hostility to apartment living remained after World War II, wartime shortages helped to diminish such feelings, and apartments were a preferable alternative to the light housekeeping suites of earlier years. In 1945 the Alberta Post War Reconstruction Committee observed that since the "keynote in housing today is efficiency together with convenience," apartments, flats, and duplexes provided "efficient housing and what they lack in space they often make up in modern conveniences. For many families they provide the right size of home."[20] The interior layout of postwar apartments relied on the same design principles as did houses, although the smaller space made efficiency even more important. CMHC provided apartment builders with suggested layouts that would promote efficiency in small apartments, which were almost always built in the form of low rise structures.[21] In the 1950s, apartments remained common only in the largest urban areas such as Edmonton, Calgary, Lethbridge, and Medicine Hat. In 1955, there were no apartments or multiple dwellings "as such" in Camrose, although there were plenty of light housekeeping suites and basement suites.[22]

By the late 1950s, many more walkup apartments began to appear in Alberta cities, of which Edmonton's experience was typical. Walkups were initially built in the central part of the city but soon pushed out and clustered at various points near business and institutional centres throughout the city.[23] Initially, they frequently imitated the pared-down designs in stucco that were common in houses of the

◆ Stucco walkup apart-
ments such as this one in
Edmonton in 1952 met
the needs of a growing
urban population.
CEA 64/64.

immediate postwar years, but by the mid 1950s these designs began to change. Among the important models for apartment design, both for exterior style and interior layout, were Scandinavian designs which often stressed the use of small balconies and efficient interior layouts.[24] The Danes did important work in creating integrated housing developments which were part of a general plan, much in the fashion of neighbourhood units. Such planning for apartments did not occur in Alberta until the 1960s, and, before then, apartments were generally built with little reference to an overall plan, although some were developed as part of a neighbourhood unit plan in Edmonton and Calgary.

With the increased construction of apartments by the early 1960s, public acceptance of apartment dwelling became commonplace. From 1961 to 1966, the stock of single- and two-family dwellings in Edmonton increased by 15.5 percent while apartments increased by 56.2 percent.[25] As was the case with suburban houses, a limited number of designs and layouts for walkup apartments led to some criticism about sameness and sterility. Again, however, they were a qualitative improvement in accommodation, certainly better than converted garages and most light housekeeping suites.

Other popular forms of rental housing in the postwar period were the duplex and fourplex. These were no different than single-family detached houses in terms of design, except that the floorplan was reversed on one side in order to give a central access to all the units. There was little objection raised to these buildings, although some argued that they led to the degradation of neighbourhoods. It would seem that this was the case in Edmonton when adequate setbacks and side and back yards were not enforced.[26] The duplex and the fourplex, along with low rise apartments, were largely the domain of the lower income levels and it was not until the advent of the high rise that apartments were, as they had been before World War I, again built deliberately to attract tenants from upper income levels. The first high rise in Calgary was built in 1952, but soon they were appearing in all the larger urban centres. These buildings usually offered different sizes of suites and a number of different floor plans. They tended to be located in central parts of the cities and were often promoted to attract tenants of similar age, family type, or occupation.[27] High rise apartment blocks were perhaps the most visible example of the change in postwar urban housing. They provided a housing option that was attractive to many people, and promotions illustrating their occupants' lifestyle as glamorous helped high rises escape the opprobrium that had attached to apartments in the past. Their size and technical sophistication relied upon the highly important and complex changes in steel framing and concrete technology in the twentieth century.[28] They were seen as progressive because of their location, their aura of fashion, and their use of technologically up-to-date equipment in the apartments and in the buildings as a whole. Increased demand for them illustrated the emergence of a younger and more mobile class, which wanted or needed centrally located and good quality rental housing, and they filled a growing but highly specialized housing need in a changing Alberta.

CONDOMINIUM AND ROW HOUSING

New arrangements for high rises and other buildings became possible with the passage in 1966 of *The Condominium Property Act*. While condominiums had a long tradition in Europe, they were a new development in Canada. The Alberta act, modeled on similar legislation in New South Wales, was among the first in the country, the others being in Ontario and British Columbia. The essence of the condominium concept was that units in a single property were individually owned while areas common to these units were collectively owned by the unit holders. An administrative framework was created to enable the owners to manage the property.[29] This was obviously a radical change, introducing a new dimension in housing to Alberta by permitting ownership on the basis of a "horizontal division" of a single property. It proved popular, not only because land owners and developers could now sell multiple units built on one piece of land, but because it allowed private ownership of property, with all that this entailed in social and economic terms, in high cost land areas.[30] The introduction of condominiums constituted a major change in housing, although their greatest application came after 1967.

Another high density option for individual ownership was row housing. It, however, had never been popular on the prairies and was relatively uncommon before 1967. Row housing was apparently thought of as monotonous and inconvenient and seems to have invoked in the prairie mind "the spectre of the interminable terraces" of English industrial cities.[31] In 1953, Noel Dant, the Edmonton Town Planner, prepared a cautiously supportive report on row housing in which he argued that the monotony of the new suburban developments meant that the "differences between the existing housing pattern and row housing is almost negligible." Yet, row houses involved less construction, took less land, were cheaper than detached houses, and could be made into highly attractive housing developments through imaginative and skillful planning.[32] Such reasoning did not calm the hostility to row housing. The Edmonton Trades and Labor Council protested against the proposal on the grounds that it would create an unattractive living environment for renters.[33] Since it did not express a similar concern about unattractive houses, it can be surmised that the council was also alarmed at the decrease in building that row housing might occasion. Row houses, renamed town houses, did not become commonplace until well into the 1970s, and a row house development planned for Calgary in 1967 was described by the developer as the "family accommodation of the future." Cognizant of the traditional dislike of such dwellings in Alberta, he took pains to note that "town housing. . . . can be new and exciting and should not have to bear the stigma usually attached to row housing."[34]

MOBILE HOMES

While the bias in Alberta against row houses prevented their widespread application until the mid 1970s, the mobile home saw increased use in Alberta as early as the late 1950s. Most mobile homes were 10 feet wide at this time, but 12 foot wide units had become typical by the late 1960s. Many of these units were imported from the United States, but by 1961 two plants in Alberta, one in Fort Macleod and another in Wetaskiwin, were manufacturing them. There was great variety in mobile home sizes, ranging from 10 feet wide and 34 feet long up to 12 feet wide and 60 feet long, and these homes were no longer the functional, temporary dwellings they had once been. The "Esta Villa," one of the models produced by Estevan Industries in Fort Macleod, used wood extensively in the interior finishing and its aluminum exterior came in a choice of four different colours.[35] The major innovation in the 1960s was the manufacture of "double wide" units which came in two sections and were joined together on the site. This produced a living area of up to 1,440 square feet.[36] While Estevan Industries built their models to "withstand the Western Canadian climate," mobile homes tended to be cold, a defect that owners tried to correct by adding porches and boxing in the open space between the ground and the floor of the unit.[37]

Mobile homes were never a fashionable form of ordinary housing. Like the prefabricated houses of earlier times, they were factory produced and therefore were at an immediate disadvantage in a culture which regarded houses as expressions of individuality. By definition, they could never express stability and permanence. Nor were they inexpensive. While their overall capital cost was lower than that of a house, they were expensive on a square foot basis and they depreciated at the same rate as a motor vehicle. Lot rental was often expensive as well. Before 1967 there were insufficient mobile home parks to meet demand, and financing for mobile homes was difficult to obtain because lenders demanded high down payments and high interest rates for such loans.[38] Mobile home parks were often unattractive and crowded, and most local governments, which were responsible for their regulation, treated them either with apathy or hostility. Mobile home owners did not represent a class that politicians needed to cultivate. While owners often had high incomes, they were frequently transient and only gained the municipal franchise in Alberta in 1968. Before 1967, Edmonton seemed to express a hostility to mobile homes while Calgary was more welcoming. In Edmonton, mobile home parks were regulated only for health standards and were restricted to highway commercial districts. Calgary passed regulations in the late 1950s governing mobile home parks and in 1969 allowed mobile homes in residential areas.[39]

In 1968 there were 8,239 mobile homes in Alberta. This high number was generated largely by the resource industries in the province. In 1968 over 50 percent of the people living in mobile homes on the prairies were employed in the construction or petroleum industry and about the same percentage of people reported that they lived in a mobile home because of their need for mobility. In Edmonton in 1967, the average mobile home stayed on one site for only 26 months. In keeping with these patterns, most mobile homes were located in the large cities or in small resource towns of less than 5,000 people. In 1961, there were no mobile homes located in towns of between 5,000 and 99,000 people, but there were 2,542 in cities with a population of over 100,000 and 1,059 in towns of less than 5,000. By 1966 this pattern was changing and mobile homes were appearing in all urban areas in the province. Indeed, by 1966 some towns in Alberta were little more than huge mobile home parks; in Swan Hills and Slave Lake, mobile homes accounted for almost 54 percent and 65 percent respectively of all housing in the towns, while Fort McMurray and Drayton Valley also had substantial numbers.[40] In the next decade, these patterns persisted, although use of mobile homes by low income earners in urban areas increasingly became a solution to high housing costs.

◆

Following the end of World War II, the public's growing interest in technological change was often focused and expressed in technical and structural changes in the home. Modernity in housing demanded the application of contemporary technology, whether it was electricity, plumbing, or televisions. While technological changes appeared to be unlimited, North American twentieth century domestic architecture was sufficiently flexible to incorporate these developments without necessitating revolutionary change in design. This process was not new. From the beginning of the twentieth century, modernity in housing had incorporated technological change without sacrificing familiar design principles. In the postwar period, houses adapted earlier design ideas and principles in a smooth accommodation with an overall process of technological change. While ranch style bungalows and split levels marked a fundamental change over earlier exterior designs, and housing like mobile homes and increased apartment living further represented the scale of change taking place, postwar design changes were not as radical as they first appeared. They continued to sustain particular views about family, personal status, social stability and organization that had been central for housing in Alberta since the beginning of the century. Postwar changes in housing conformed to a pattern in which newness and fashion supported traditional social objectives and structures.

TWELVE

Constructing
Affordable Housing

As in the first half of the century, a central concern in housing after World War II continued to be the reduction of building costs.
This ambition was framed by a continued emphasis on the single-
family detached house as the ideal, and given the level of new construction after World War II, the house building industry grew dramatically. In an effort to reduce costs, standardization of materials
increased and standard building codes became more significant for the
residential construction industry.

SEARCHING FOR AFFORDABLE CONSTRUCTION

In 1946 it was noted that in Edmonton a house that had cost
$3,000 in 1939 now cost $5,000 and "takes twice the time to
build," presumably because of labour shortages. In such circumstances, "the temptation to lower the standard is. . . . almost over-
whelming and is not being entirely resisted." Standards were being
lowered by shoddy construction, by decreasing the room size, by developing the basement as a bedroom, or by abandoning basements
altogether.[1] Houses resting on a concrete slab were frequently built in

Calgary, and Noel Dant remarked that they appeared "to contain all the faults of a basementless house." One problem lay in locating services and in providing adequate heating. As well, many of these houses were not large enough to compensate for the storage and working room lost because of the lack of a basement. Generally, housing critics and designers in Alberta were opposed to basementless houses and at times mortgage money was awkward to secure for them.[2] In any event, the elimination of basements as a means of decreasing costs was a fleeting phenomenon. The disadvantages appear to have outweighed small savings because in a well constructed house without a basement, footings to below frost level (five to six feet) were necessary in Canada.[3]

Rather than such approaches, technological change was widely regarded as the agent which would make housing affordable. During World War II, many people clung to the hope that enhanced technology, in the form of improved prefabrication methods, would provide the solution to postwar housing needs. Indeed, so great were the hopes about the future of prefabrication that, by the end of the war, individuals were postponing building a house in anticipation of the great changes and lower costs that prefabrication would bring. The Alberta Post War Reconstruction Committee recommended that a publicity campaign be mounted to offset "some of this propaganda" and "clarify the public mind as to the limits of prefabrication."[4] In 1944, E. Litchfield, also skeptical, noted that Americans were the great proponents of "factory fabrication whereby homes are alleged to be fabricated in 15 minutes." While he admitted that factory produced housing could be erected relatively quickly, he thought that this was only "probably suitable to the type of mind that can accept boogie-woogie music," and that it posed as many dangers as promises. Factory production of houses might make the task of building easier, and might even displace much of the labour component in building costs, but it would not create a better product, the main reason for adopting such an approach.[5] Nevertheless, for a time it appeared that prefabrication would be the wave of the future. Wartime Housing Incorporated used prefabrication for some of its houses in Alberta, including those in Edmonton. The first houses in Devon were prefabricated, built in Calgary by Engineered Buildings (Alberta) Ltd. and assembled on the site.[6] A number of companies, especially lumber yards, also produced "ready built" or "ready-to-move" houses. Like the catalogue houses of an earlier generation, these houses were designed to look like any other suburban house to com-

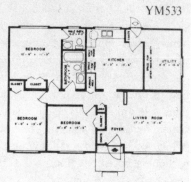

YM533

YOUNG MODERN

Three bedrooms, 1½ baths with built-in marble vanity, a Marlite mural on the shower wall (giving the impression of a custom feature), beautifully finished Canadian Maple kitchen cupboards, all emphasize the attention to detail which makes this home individually yours. The high bedroom windows, giving additional wall space as well as adding privacy to your home, is an added feature of the Young Modern.

YM502

YOUNG MODERN

The feeling of 'Easy Living' is obtained in this 'Modern as Today' home. Three bedrooms, ideally situated so as to minimize household disturbance, have plenty of high, wide closet area, complete with folding doors.

◆ Prefabrication had a long tradition in western Canada. ATCO built these ready to move houses in contemporary designs in 1966. *Art of Modern Living* catalogue, in PAA 75.530.22, manuscript collection. Used with permission of ATCO Enterprises, Ltd.

bat the stigma of being factory made. It seems that these houses were most often used in small towns and on farms.[7]

Prefabrication was attractive partly because of the widespread belief that labour was overwhelmingly responsible for high housing costs. In 1947, the *Edmonton Journal* editorialized that 80 percent of the overall cost of construction was labour, and it was commonly held that if labour could be reduced through mass production, the cost of housing would fall.[8] The fact remained, however, that the level of services in a house remained constant, no matter how the house was fabricated. In addition, the cost of land played a large part in pushing up housing costs after the war. Various studies have concluded that construction costs in Canada increased about 40 percent between the early 1950s and the late 1960s, while land costs increased 200 percent.[9] Prefabrication, therefore, was inherently limited as a means of reducing costs in the construction of ordinary housing, although it was evident that prefabrication of mobile structures would be a valuable aid to resource exploration. In 1951, Don and Ron Southern of Calgary constructed the first prefabricated structures for Shell Oil to house oil exploration workers in northern Alberta. This was the beginning of ATCO's success, which in later years became a major builder of prefabricated mobile dwelling units for individual use, as well as ready-to-move houses.[10]

NEW MATERIALS

Complementing the postwar interest in prefabrication was a growing interest in new materials and their application to house building. By 1942 the potential importance of plastics in house building had begun to be realized, and they were said to hold great promise for prefabricated houses.[11] By 1967, plastics had indeed become common in house construction, although not to the extent predicted two decades earlier. Despite initial problems with installation, the use of plastic pipe in plumbing in Alberta had begun by 1955 and proved in many ways to be a revolutionary development.[12] The other major development after the war was the use of standard mass-produced materials, including laminated panel boards, mainly plywood, for sheathing and for interior wood work.[13] The use of standardized mass-produced panel boards was, of course, not innovative, although its use for exterior sheathing was relatively new. By the late 1930s plywood was being used for exterior sheathing, an application which

◆ Plywood was becoming
a common method of
sheathing as shown in
the construction of the
Dewar house in Edmon-
ton in 1940. CEA 160-
957.

became typical after World War II. Other standardized materials included metal chimneys, which by the mid 1950s were replacing traditional brick or concrete block chimneys.[14] By 1950, plaster began to lose ground to dry wall construction for interior wall finishes, and this too promised cost savings.[15]

STANDARDIZATION AND BUILDING CODES

The use of standardized materials meant that house building was becoming more and more a process of assembly than on-site craftsmanship. Because these products were manufactured in standard sizes, studs had to be placed exactly. Traditionally, studs were spaced 16 inches centre to centre, but this seems to have been a rough guide only, being varied according to the demands of the particular structure, including changes to accommodate the placement of a window or a door. Now, however, consistent spacing was necessary, especially for insulation. In 1951 the Division of Building Research of the National Research Council surveyed stud placement in Canada and found that, in new construction, 34 percent of "the exterior wall area will be found to have studding so spaced as to be unsuited to the incorporation of factory-made building materials designed on a 16 inch module." This not only lessened the labour saving potential of the new materials but, more importantly, decreased the effectiveness of materials such as "the patented types of thermal insulation."[16] Along with these changes in materials and their consequent possibilities for decreasing construction costs, platform framing became the only system used in residential construction. It permitted rapid construction, produced a sound structure, and allowed greater prefabrication since the walls could "easily be prefabricated off the site or assembled on the subfloor and erected one story at a time."[17]

The move towards standardization stimulated a renewed interest in development of standard building codes. There had been a number of demands made before 1939 for better building codes, including ones of provincial and even national application. While there were existing general codes in use in Alberta, such as the American uniform building code,[18] it was not until 1941 that a national building code was produced by the National Research Council (NRC) and the Department of Finance, which then administered the NHA. The code drew on extensive research and dealt with all aspects of construction including materials, design, foundations, concrete, plumbing, electricity, and construction safety measures. It was a "model" code, and the federal government had neither the authority nor the wish to enforce it nationally. Nevertheless, the need for such standards, and the excellence of the code, ensured that it would be widely used. In 1947, a Division of Building Research was established by the NRC to carry out specific research on building materials and techniques and act as the research wing on technical aspects of residential construction for CMHC.[19] Informed by this research, as well as public input, a second edition of the National Building Code was brought out in 1953 and subsequent editions were issued on a regular basis after 1960.

It was frequently contended that the adoption of a national building code would lessen construction costs. Calgary house builders claimed in 1967 that a saving of $700 could be made on a house through the adoption of the National Building Code.[20] Application of the code was said to lead "to real economy in actual designs," but did not compromise standards of fire protection, public safety, and structural soundness.[21] By the mid 1950s, provincial regulations on plumbing and electricity, largely based on the National Building Code, applied to all buildings in Alberta, and many communities were looking at ways to implement the National Building Code, or at least some of its provisions, in their building bylaws.[22] By this point, many of these bylaws needed revision; Edmonton's building code, passed in 1935, had been amended only slightly before a new bylaw was passed in 1960.[23] Various enforcement problems also faced many communities. In Edmonton, there were too few building inspectors in 1953 to keep up with the high levels of construction, and the fines for infractions of the local building bylaw were so low that it was "quite often to a builder's advantage to commence building without a permit and pay the meager fine."[24] While many smaller cities and towns wished to make use of the National Building Code, it was observed in 1955 that because it was a "very technical document," many of the "smaller places" were unable to find inspectors who could enforce its provisions "with any degree of understanding."[25] While the National Building Code was therefore not a solution to all problems, it was frequently used as a guide for local building bylaws. By 1953, five centres in Alberta had adopted the National Building Code in whole; 18 communities had used its provisions in local bylaws; 21 had used it as a general reference in drafting bylaws; and a further 15 communities were studying the code for possible use.[26] By 1966, 93 percent of the population of towns and cities and 74 percent of the total population in Alberta were "voluntarily" using some form or editions of the National Building Code of Canada.[27]

THE BUILDING INDUSTRY

During the interwar years, the construction industry in Canada was dominated by builders who, as a rule, built only a small number of houses in the course of a year.[28] While builders in earlier years had themselves often done much of the work in all phases of construction, the trend in the interwar years was towards the general contractor who contracted with subtrades to complete various aspects, including plumbing, heating, electrical, and, among others, plastering.[29] In Alberta, these builders usually built houses for individual owners and did not undertake many large projects where a number of houses were built in a single area at one time. In discussing the housing crisis in Alberta in 1940, Cecil Burgess was critical of this process and noted that "present methods under which individuals build one house here and another a mile away, each house requiring everything specially made to meet what are, in many cases, individual and expensive notions, are extravagantly dear building methods and in most cases very inefficient in result." He believed that cost of construction would be reduced by "building many houses at one time as one contract and by keeping the main features somewhat standardized."[30]

Despite their intermittent appearance in Alberta and the rest of Canada before 1945, such large scale builders were slow to emerge.[31] In 1956, the construction industry in Canada was "neither cohesive nor homogeneous." It was a "dispersed, compartmentalized, and competitive industry." Entry into it was easy, and there were a great number of partnerships and proprietorships, many of which were "continually organizing in patterns appropriate to the technical and commercial requirements of each project." The industry had a lower level of equity financing than did, for example, manufacturing or the wholesale trade, relying instead on short term debt, usually bank loans.[32] Generally, the industry was made up of several types of builders. There were some large general contractors who were involved in all types of building, including residences. In Alberta, Bennett and White Construction, while not usually involved in residential construction, built over 800 houses in Calgary and Edmonton for returning soldiers after World War II.[33] Other types included "merchant builders," the name often given to those who planned, built, and developed whole neighbourhoods and had subsidiary companies to handle financing and sales. There were, additionally, contract builders and "a very large number of others who fall into none of even these ill defined categories."[34]

While there was a wide variety of builders, a trend towards larger residential builders, which was encouraged by CMHC, was emerging in the 1950s. Because of the possibilities offered by the use of heavy equipment and other mechanization in house building, large builders had a market advantage. While two-thirds of all builders in Canada produced less than 15 houses a year in 1955, "5 percent of the builders who built under the National Housing Act were responsible for 40 percent of that year's NHA programme." Many of these large builders also began to develop and plan whole residential areas.[35] They could bring the techniques of the assembly line to house construction:

> the earth moving machinery excavates for each house in a successive progressive manner; then prefabricated forms are placed, moving from one excavation to the next and concrete foundations are poured; the floor framing crews come next; then the wall framers and other specialists with particular crews moving across the project from house to house in an orderly, prearranged manner.[36]

One effect of this trend towards large scale builders was the stimulation of winter construction, which was encouraged by government by the mid 1950s to create year round employment. The building industry also supported winter building because its capitalization demanded continual activity. Typically, houses were roughed in by the fall and interior work was done in the winter.[37]

The rapidly expanding housing market after World War II brought many people into the building industry in Alberta, and many of these builders began to undertake larger projects. There were, however, recurring financing problems. In 1948 the Alberta branch of the National House Builders' Association wrote to the premier requesting a conference to discuss the licensing and bonding of builders. In support of their request, they noted that an increasing number of builders were building houses either for owners or on speculation even though they did not have a sure supply of materials nor sufficient "financial backing or credit" to complete the project. As a result, a number had "collected the difference between the amount of the mortgage and the selling price" before the house was completed but then ran out of credit or cash and were unable to fulfill their contracts with "the lender of the mortgage money or with the purchaser or owner of the house."[38] An example of this occurred in Calgary in 1948 when 40 houses, funded under the NHA, were not completed by the builder because of cash flow problems.[39] Such financing problems were ongoing, and many builders in Edmonton and Calgary in the mid 1950s were poorly capitalized and largely dependent on mortgage money to finance house construction. In 1955 in Calgary, "approximately 80 percent of the building industry. . . . is financed through mortgage money advanced by lending institutions under the National Housing Act." Two years later, builders in Edmonton had "practically given up" planning any fall or winter projects because of "the inability to obtain forward commitments of mortgages, and in truth, any commitment for mortgages."[40]

Even in this climate, a number of large scale developers were beginning to emerge, handling all aspects of residential construction from the assembly of land, servicing, house construction, and sales. One of the first such developers was Nu-West Group Limited, which began operations in 1957. It first operated mainly in Calgary and soon became the largest home builder in the city. In 1969 it entered the Edmonton market, where it rapidly became one of the largest developers in the city. Nu-West's success rested partly on its ability to control land. In the early 1950s in Calgary, the prime source of developed residential land was the city and it was customary for home builders to line up outside city hall to obtain lots. This changed in 1958 when Carma Developers was created by 45 Calgary developers, including Nu-West. Carma was a unique company. It acquired and assembled land for its members, which, while not competing for land, continued to "compete against each other for sales" of houses. This arrangement was highly successful; by 1981 Carma was producing nearly 30 percent of the available serviced residential lots in Calgary and 20 percent of all Calgarians were already living on Carma developed land.[41]

Between 1961 and 1972 housing was an extremely important component of the building industry in Alberta, making up about one-half of the total building construction in the province.[42] In spite of its highly variable nature, the house building industry did have some measure of organization. Local building associations were formed as early as the late 1940s, and the Edmonton House Builders' Association, for example, had 48 builder members and at least an equal number of supply and subtrade members in 1956.[43] The parent association, the National House Builders' Association (later HUDAC), provided a national focus and, among its other functions, lobbied government on behalf of the industry. This was a far higher level of organization than found among those employed in the construction industry generally. In 1974, labour organization in residential building trades was still much as it had been traditionally, with approximately 5 to 10 percent of workers unionized, a much lower rate than in other types of construction.[44]

Prefabrication, the use of new materials, and the standardization of materials and construction practices were all part of the implementation of technological change in the housing field. Much of this was in direct response to the higher postwar demand for single detached houses. Another result was the emergence of large developers and builders. This was encouraged by a government supported preference for such housing, and as the policy of encouraging this type of construction worked its way through the economy, "the house building industry came to represent a sizeable portion of Canada's annual capital investment."[45] The industry began to assume a disproportionate role in the economy, one that relied, despite the industry and governments' commitment to free enterprise, upon publicly guaranteed loans or direct government lending. In such circumstances, the claims of the previous half century that the privately owned home represented good citizenship, independence, and social worthiness were given official endorsation. Not unrelated was the fact that housing, between the end of World War II and 1967, became an increasingly important element in government social and economic policy.

CONCLUSION

THIRTEEN

Building, Trends, and Design in Alberta

In the twentieth century, the place of housing as a measure of social and economic success in Alberta was not only sanctioned by tradition but was reinforced by an increasingly complex marketplace and by burgeoning commercial, industrial, and other interests. North America, whether the United States or Canada, represented an opportunity for material and social betterment, and, for many, it provided a better political and social environment in which to live. Dreams of personal freedom and material wealth were integral to the economic and social structure of prairie life. Moving from a log house to a frame house, or to an even more prestigious house of brick, made these dreams real and justified the economic and political structures of the society. While such ambitions eluded many people, they were nonetheless believed to be realizable, if not for oneself, then for one's children.

Commercial forces and agencies helped to disseminate ideas about how a house should look and function. Lumber yards, builders, newspapers, magazines, radio programmes, and movies collectively and individually influenced the preferences of consumers. Given the prairie dream of upward mobility, it would be logical to see the styles of elite housing reflected in ordinary houses. While this did occur, it was not a general pattern. Bungalows, although pioneered in California by the upper class, had become totally divorced from such origins by the time of World War I. By 1914 as well, the essential elements of homestead, foursquare, and semi bungalow houses, whatever their historical origins, formed the basis for typical houses in Alberta. These remained the norm, although various revival styles copying elements of what were popularly thought to be elite housing appeared. This was carried to an extreme in the late 1920s and early 1930s when eclectic designs, such as the "modest mansions" of Edmonton, were portrayed as signs of upward social mobility. These fantasy designs of the interwar years were diffusions of style caused by mass communications; magazines, movies, and radio programmes promoted the imitation of the houses of Hollywood stars, renaissance princes, and the English gentry. For most Albertans, however, such houses were unattainable and these designs, in any event, did not last. The Colonial style houses of the late 1930s and 1940s, including those built by Wartime Housing Incorporated, signalled a retreat from fantasy, although their apparent imitation of colonial American domesticity was equally a fantasy for prairie Canada. The one-storey low profile bungalows that succeeded these colonial houses in the 1950s were evidence of a reassertion of sobriety. They owed almost nothing to ideas about an invented past or the wealthy, and perhaps it was their straightforwardness that stimulated some to claim that they were boring and monotonous.

Permanent house design in Alberta after World War I did not evolve within the particular environmental needs of the prairies nor did it express a particular sense of place. The house forms brought by the settlers reflected tradition and the practices of other places. In subsequent years, definitions of taste were left to the market place because people rarely thought that they had unique requirements that needed to be met by the design of their houses. The standard North American models were seen to accommodate nicely their social and cultural ambitions, and the origin of these designs outside the province, the region, and the country did not restrict the expression of these hopes. House design in Alberta, like the rest of the prairies, was largely North American, and because commercial forces and communications became increasingly important in the years after 1900, the possibility of a regional expression became even more remote. Technological change reinforced this pattern. Construction materials and methods were becoming fairly standardized in North America by 1900, and this increased in the next 75 years. Justified by scientific knowledge, servicing became a significant part of the definition of modernity, adequacy, and quality in housing, and it was an equally important factor in standardization. The application of uniform approaches for servicing reinforced the use of typical North American housing models which relied upon a standard technological infrastructure. Whether or not these services were immediately attainable for all Albertans, they nonetheless proved that life was being improved through technological change, or, in popular language, through progress. Progress was not static, however, and expectations were continually adjusted. Once basic needs for sanitation, heat, and light were satisfied, they were assumed as givens, at which point new needs were drawn from technological change. In such a context, workable houses could be designed with little specific reference to geography or environment, a possibility that limited and made unnecessary indigenous adaptations based on tradition, custom, and cultural preference. Thus a house could be designed by an architect in Toronto or Chicago, the plans could be sold through an Alberta newspaper or lumber yard, and neither a builder nor an owner building a house for himself needed to modify the design to any appreciable extent.

The impact of these forces was reflected not only in the look of houses and the way that they were designed and built. The economy was also profoundly affected as well. New businesses and whole new economic sectors emerged or developed to meet changing needs. As only one example, new businesses, such as utility companies, became significant forces in the economy. Albertans increasingly became dependent upon marketed commodities and services such as coal, gas, electricity, water, and sewage disposal. The corollary was that house maintenance increasingly depended upon regular cash expenditures. The technological revolution of the early twentieth century which promised improved services, convenience, and health also bound individuals more firmly to a cash based society. The attraction of the new services was so great, however, and their justification so persuasive, that no one seemed to mind the changed demands that they brought in terms of work, time, and money.

Increasingly better standards of living were an essential part of housing theory, which was deeply influenced by ideas about the relationship between social development and personal character. If the individual was to a large extent shaped by his environment, then the house had obvious implications for social well being, stability, and the quality of the civilization. Like the lessons of microbiology, this was formulated in scientific language, and it too had implications that ultimately involved the state. An increasing number of people argued not only that social misery and instability, crime, poverty, poor health, and ignorance were partly the result of poor living environments, but that the state was obligated to prevent such conditions. This manifested itself in several ways. In some cases, it meant the creation of standards to ensure that houses were sanitary and healthful and that they met certain minimum requirements of light, space, and amenities. The willingness of the state to be involved in such issues was not consistent. Enforced minimum standards and urban planning were not initially undertaken willingly, in part because the organization of government, especially at the local level, was inadequate, and in part because it did not accord with the objectives of those in power. In other respects, however, the state willingly became involved, especially in the installation of the technological infrastructure demanded by modern servicing and the linking of suburban houses to the urban whole through transportation systems.

In the years after World War I, state involvement in housing emerged in yet a different way. Affordable housing became the subject of increasing demands from a complex of economic and social interest groups. In response, the federal government brought in a series of housing programmes. While it proved ineffective, the first such programme was the 1919 housing scheme. The programmes of the 1930s to the early 1960s, beginning with the DHA (1935) and continued by the NHA after 1938, reflected the triumph of economic forces in shaping policy. Because of its high capital costs and its substantial labour component, housing was used to stimulate private sector growth. The main technique that permitted this was the guaranteeing of personal debt by the state. In this, the lending policies of the NHA fundamentally served only certain groups in society. Through lower down payments, increased amortization periods, and federal government guarantees of mortgages, housing could be provided to those with the security and income to afford it. And this approach supplied a great deal of housing to such people. Even so, an increasingly greater portion of income had to be devoted to housing. The ratio of income to loan increased and by the late 1970s it was accepted that annual payments could be 30 percent of gross annual income for a single-family detached house and 42 percent for a semi detached house.[1] This increase, from the 20 percent which had been considered prudent 40 years before, was partly justifiable because the postwar welfare state provided some security and permitted the redirection of income from medical, unemployment, and other needs. Yet, in all of this, low income earners were almost totally bypassed. They were politically weak and there was substantial public opposition to public housing before the 1960s. While the NHA did have provisions for low income housing, they were only of minor benefit to low income earners. It was believed that filtering would solve the housing needs of low income people, but this theory was not, in practical terms, workable. Thus it can be argued that Canada before this point did not have a housing policy so much as it had an economic policy that included housing as one of its components. Nonetheless, by the 1960s, there was a lessening of hostility to public housing and government policies began to reflect these wider social realities.

Throughout, Alberta's response to these programmes was unique. It was unwilling to become involved in those it thought damaging to its overriding priorities and contrary to its view of the legitimate role of the state in economic and social life. While this demonstrated one of the consequences of divided jurisdiction in the housing field, it also reflected deeply felt regional and political considerations that came to the fore over housing. In 1919 the province saw the federal housing programme as potentially injurious to its interests, and given the problems that local governments in Alberta faced, it was only prudent to recognize that the federal programme might create further liabilities for the province. The financial solvency of local governments was considered a more basic concern than was building new houses or meeting the social objectives of postwar adjustment. In 1935, much the same reasoning applied in Alberta's nonparticipation in the DHA, although in this case it involved weighing the national housing programme against what Alberta had to surrender in order to participate. For Social Credit under Aberhart, the answer was relatively clear. The protection of farmers and the farm economy through debt legislation was more important than either the urban middle class, which wanted subsidized mortgages for new houses, or urban house builders and building supply merchants who wanted increased business. After 1945, the availability of NHA loans in Alberta was possible because a new dynasty had been formed after Aberhart's death, but it also demonstrated that Alberta was changing in more fundamental ways. After 1943, the province increasingly championed free enterprise and the authority of the market economy, which NHA loans did not threaten and, indeed, confirmed. Nonetheless, only after long resistance did Alberta's housing policy recognize that public housing need not challenge the market system, and this was effected after 1964. The suggestion can be hazarded that state subsidized housing for low income earners provided adequate housing and simultaneously mitigated demands for better wages as a route to solving the problem of affordability.

While state housing policies helped to provide adequate housing for an increased number of people in increasingly large cities, it left untouched the overall impact that such policies were having. The idealization of the single-family detached house profoundly shaped the urban environment and perpetuated a type of shelter that created problems of major significance but uncertain resolution. While the near bankruptcy of many local governments in Alberta during and after World War I was the consequence of poor tax planning and tax default in a period of speculation, it was also the result of installing on a large geographical scale the infrastructure required by modern serviced single-family detached houses. The efforts that followed to make urban areas more compact, such as moving houses closer to the core of towns and cities and resurveying subdivided urban land, were belated recognition of the problems inherent in such an approach to housing. The financial problems of urban areas were not so readily corrected, however, and were largely solved only through more expansion after World War II. In this phase, even greater infrastructure was required: not only did lots have to be serviced, they now had to be linked into the urban framework through a transportation network of unprecedented scale and impact, largely focused on the private automobile. Such a system met personal choice and could be accommodated given Alberta's relatively small but wealthy postwar population. Even so, the continued mythologizing of the single-family detached dwelling reinforced an approach to housing that continually stimulated problems of increasing scale and complexity. As Lewis Mumford wrote in 1938,

> The dwelling is in reality a very complex adaptation to an exceedingly complicated set of requirements, and it is quite likely that any simplified solution, expressible in purely mechanical terms, will not satisfy all the necessary conditions. What is important is to treat the geographic, economic, social, technical, and personal requirements on a single plane. Twentieth century technics cannot be fitted into laissez faire economics and seventeenth century taste. . . . the most spectacular advance is no advance until it is integrated.[2]

The rejection of such approaches, in part through dismissing the ethos of the modernists during the interwar years, was partly an effort to sustain an economic and political order. As well, however, its rejection asserted a particular view of comfort and attempted to sustain human values through a familiar and comforting definition of the home.

The 1970s and 1980s

With a new found concern and involvement by the provincial government, 1967 was a turning point in the history of housing in Alberta. The coming years provided unforseen opportunities for the exercise of this concern since Alberta was at the beginning of an economic boom that lasted just over a decade. The international oil crisis of 1973, sparked by the actions of the Organization of Petroleum Exporting Countries, drove oil prices to new heights. Alberta's economy boomed, resulting in housing shortages and rising prices. By 1976 the population of the province was almost 2 million, an increase of over 200,000 in five years and a half million over the previous 15 years. In contrast to similar occasions in the past, there was now a widespread expectation that government was able to and should solve the housing problems resulting from such growth. The mechanisms to permit effective government action on the housing front had been in place for almost ten years, and government seemed willing to respond, a measure of the change that had taken place.

By the late 1970s, there had been significant expansion of provincial housing programmes, mostly targeted at specific groups, all of whom were defined, in various ways, as disadvantaged. One priority, the provision of low cost houses, was met through a number of programmes including direct subsidies and low interest lending schemes. Between 1970 and 1975, almost 1,500 public housing units were constructed in Edmonton alone, which marked a significant departure from the policies of the decade before.[1] At the federal level, new programming approaches were also being implemented, and during the late 1960s, the interest rate on NHA mortgages was allowed to "go free," that is, to be set by market conditions, and after amendments to the *Bank Act*, the chartered banks began granting conventional loans for housing. NHA lending was now different from conventional lending in only two ways; it protected lenders through insurance, and set certain standards and inspection requirements.[2] In the years following, fluctuating interest rates had a disproportionate impact on Alberta because of the relatively high number of mortgaged homes in the province. In 1971, 60 percent of Alberta homes were mortgaged, the highest percentage in Canada.[3]

The NHA was further amended in 1974. New programmes were added and consumers were encouraged to be more involved in the design of the houses they were building. A Ministry of State for Urban Affairs was created, with a major emphasis on housing.[4] The Ministry's name signalled that housing problems continued to be defined as largely urban, a view that shaped the ministry's orientation. Some attention, however, was paid to nonurban housing. The amendments to the NHA in 1974 included new programmes for native and rural housing. Similar changes in housing policy also occurred in Alberta's programmes. By the mid 1970s, the province had broadened existing programmes or instituted new ones for Metis and northern housing, senior citizen housing, and assistance in the construction and purchase of low cost housing. With these developments came an increasingly specialized bureaucracy. In 1970, the Alberta Housing and Urban Development Corporation evolved into the Alberta Housing Corporation, and by 1977 provincial housing policy was operating along three fronts: programmes run by the Department of Housing and Public Works, the Alberta Housing Corporation, and the Alberta Home Mortgage Corporation.[5]

The 1970s demonstrated not only a shifting emphasis in government policy but an increasing variety of housing types as well. Apartments continued to grow in importance and high rise condominiums, co-op housing, and townhouses were constructed. Mobile homes also grew in popularity, and the province established a lending programme for mobile home purchasers and assisted in developing mobile home parks.[6] While the single-family detached dwelling remained the ideal, such developments helped to weaken the long held view that it was feasible for all families to own such a home. Expectations were lowered by rapid increases in housing prices, high national inflation rates, and rapid population growth. Land once again became a crucial determinant of housing costs in Alberta. While the overall initiative for land acquisition programmes was left with local governments,[7] the province began a small land banking project in 1968. Millwoods, one of the outline plan suburbs in Edmonton, was built on land assembled by the Alberta Housing Corporation, which then sold it to the city at cost or below market price.[8] Most cities, except Calgary, participated in similar programmes in an effort to reduce land costs and ensure that sufficient land was available for development in high growth areas. Land costs continued to rise, however, and, in response, new higher density developments were created and new approaches to land use emerged. Devices such as "zero lot" placement of houses and the use of smaller lots were permitted in an attempt to make housing affordable. The greatest housing crises were in Edmonton and Calgary where costs increased dramatically. From 1971 to 1975 housing costs rose 87 percent in Edmonton and 82 percent in Calgary, but other centres were also affected, especially in areas of major resource activity. Development of the oil sands at Fort McMurray had begun by the mid 1960s, but the oil crisis stimulated further development, making housing expensive and scarce. As Bill Yurko, the Minister of Housing and Public Works, observed in 1977, unless one bought a mobile home in Fort McMurray, "chances are rather small one can afford to buy a single-family dwelling. . . . at today's costs."[9] Yet, at the same time, there were significant improvements in housing in smaller centres generally and on farms. Lending programmes which targeted these groups were instituted, and economic conditions for farmers improved for a time as well. By 1973, many houses in rural areas were equipped with amenities and services similar to those found in the largest urban centres in Alberta.[10] This process was assisted in part by a policy of decentralization announced by the province in 1973. Intending to encourage the growth of smaller centres, locational incentives were offered to industry and lower interest rates were available for home mortgages.[11]

The economy began to decline by 1982–83 when the world recession hit particularly hard in Alberta. While a rapid drop in economic activity was not a unique event in Alberta, for many builders it was traumatic. They had basically operated in a boom environment since 1946 and the new realities of the early 1980s often brought hard lessons. It is still difficult to assess the significance of the boom of the 1970s in Alberta. Douglas Owram, in his history of the prairie economy, has commented that it was of "relatively short duration and from a historical perspective it is difficult to be certain whether it heralds a new era in Western Canadian development or merely another phase in the boom-bust cycles which have characterized the region's history."[12]

◆ ◆ NOTES

ABBREVIATIONS

BPSC	Bruce Peel Special Collections Library, University of Alberta
CAA	Canadian Architectural Archives, University of Calgary
CEA	City of Edmonton Archives
CMHC	Central (Canada) Mortgage and Housing Corporation
GAI	Glenbow Alberta Institute Archives
PAA	Provincial Archives of Alberta
PP	Premiers' Papers, Provincial Archives of Alberta
RAIC Journal	Royal Architectural Institute of Canada, *Journal*
RDDA	Red Deer and District Archives

NOTE REGARDING USE OF *CENSUS OF CANADA* STATISTICS ON HOUSING

The 1931 census noted that the 1901, 1911, and 1921 censuses had inconsistently applied the terms "dwellings," "dwelling houses," and "houses." For example, the term "dwelling" included each single detached house occupied by one family as well as each apartment in one apartment building. Further, the term included all places where people lived, including rooms in offices and stores, railway cars, and, among others, tents. From 1931, the census used a number of different categories, including "buildings containing dwellings," to address this lack of precision and other problems. Because of such difficulties, we have attempted to use these statistics in the most cautious fashion. For further discussion on interpretation and difficulties with 1921 and earlier censuses, see *Census of Canada, 1931*, vol. 5, pp. xviii–xxi.

INTRODUCTION

1. Douglas Owram, *The Economic Development of Western Canada: An Historical Overview* (Ottawa: Economic Council of Canada, Discussion Paper no. 219, 1982), 4–11; Alan Artibise, "The Urban West: The Evolution of Prairie Towns and Cities to 1930," *Prairie Forum* 4 (1979): 251–53.

2. *Edmonton Bulletin*, November 1, 1884.

3. Deryk Holdsworth, "Regional Distinctiveness in an Industrial Age: Some California Influences on British Columbia Housing," *The American Review of Canadian Studies* 12 (1982): 65.

4. A formative study on the diffusion of house styles was Fred B. Knif-

fen, "Folk Houses—Key to Diffusion," *Annals of the Association of American Geographers* 55 (1965): 549–77. Kniffen argued that house design was spread in the United States by migration from the eastern seaboard to areas further west and south. Among the best recent studies that explore this process is Allan Noble, *Wood, Brick and Stone* (Amherst: University of Massachusetts Press, 1984).

5. Robert Bastian, "The Prairie Style House: Spatial Diffusion of a Minor Design," *Journal of Cultural Geography* 1 (1980): 50–65. A criticism of the "social diffusion" argument is Dell Upton, "Towards a Performance Theory of Vernacular Architecture: Early Tidewater Virginia as a Case Study," *Folklore Forum* 12 (1979): 176.

6. Pierce F. Lewis, "Common Housing, Cultural Spoor," *Landscape* 19 (1975): 1–22.

7. Charlotte Vestal Brown, review of *American Architecture* by Marcus S. Whiffen & Frederick Koeper, *Winterthur Portfolio* 19 (1984): 292–95. Alan Gowans's work is a good beginning for an analysis of style in ordinary housing. He defines the bungalow, foursquare, and homestead houses as "stylistic forms" but subsequently simply calls them forms. His outline of historical styles provides an excellent and workable guide. Alan Gowans, *The Comfortable House: North American Suburban Architecture 1890– 1930* (Cambridge, Massachusetts: The MIT Press, 1986). Amos Ropoport's treatment of vernacular architecture as illustrative of historical process is also relevant since ordinary housing could be treated as a form of vernacular architecture which he describes as "a process, of how it comes to be, or as a product" illustrating man-environment relations. Amos Ropoport, "Vernacular Architecture and the Cultural Determinants of Form," in *Buildings and Society*, ed. A. King (London: Routledge and Kegan Paul, 1980), 285–86.) On the problems of using "style" to analyse ordinary housing, see Henry Glassie, "Eighteenth Century Cultural Process in Delaware Valley Folk Building," in *Common Places: Readings in American Vernacular Architecture*, ed. Dell Upton and John Michael Vlach (Athens, Georgia: The University of Georgia Press, 1986), 394–97.

8. Lewis Mumford, *The Culture of Cities* (1938; reprint, London: Secker and Warburg, 1946), 468.

9. See Allan Smith, "The Myth of the Self-made Man in English Canada, 1850–1914," *Canadian Historical Review* 58 (1978): 189–219.

10. One attempt to analyse the house in terms of these problems is Gwendolyn Wright, *Moralism and the Model Home: Domestic Architecture and Cultural Conflict in Chicago, 1873–1913* (Chicago: University of Chicago Press, 1980).

11. Richard Harris, "Housing in Canadian Cities: An Agenda and Review of Sources," *Urban History Review* 14 (1986): 259–60.

12. John Saywell, *Essays on Residential Construction in Canada* (Ottawa: Economic Council of Canada, Discussion Paper no. 24, 1975), 5.

13. This broad periodization reflects combined economic and policy factors in housing in Alberta. Douglas Owram has suggested that the economic history of the modern prairies can be divided into five periods: 1870-late 1890s (settlement frontier); 1900–1912 (Laurier boom); 1913–1929 (mature

wheat economy); 1930–1939 (Depression); and 1940-the 1960s. Owram, *The Economic Development of Western Canada*, 2–3.

1 SETTLEMENT AND EARLY HOUSING IN ALBERTA

1. Mary Cullen, "Highlights of Domestic Buildings in Pre-Confederation Ontario as Seen Through Travel Literature from 1763 to 1860," *APT Bulletin* 13 (1981): 28.

2. Virginia L. Hull, "A Geographical Study of the Impact of Two Ethnic Groups on the Rural Landscape of Alberta" (M.A. thesis, University of Alberta, 1964), 37.

3. G.B. Parlby, *The Family Farm in Alberta: Its Origins, Development and Future* (Edmonton: Alberta Department of Agriculture, Alberta Land Use Forum, 1974), 6.

4. John Lehr, "The Landscape of Ukrainian Settlement in the Canadian West," *Great Plains Quarterly* 1–2 (1982): 95.

5. John Lehr, "Mormon Settlements in Southern Alberta" (M.A. thesis, University of Alberta, 1971), 50–54.

6. Diamond Jenness, *The Indians of Canada*, 7th ed. (Toronto: University of Toronto Press in association with National Museum of Man, 1977), 90.

7. Edward Rogers, "Indian Life in Autumn," *The Beaver* Outfit 311–3 (1980): 58; David Mandelbaum, *The Plains Cree: An Ethnographic, Historical and Comparative Study* (Regina: Canadian Plains Research Center, 1979), 87–89, 327.

8. Oscar Lewis, *The Effects of White Contact Upon Blackfoot Culture with Specific Reference to the Role of the Fur Trade*, 2nd ed. (Seattle: University of Washington Press, 1966), 35–36.

9. Rogers, "Indian Life in Autumn," 58; Mandelbaum, *The Plains Cree*, 89, 225.

10. *Edmonton Bulletin*, May 24, 1884.

11. Ibid., September 6, 1884.

12. Ibid., May 24, 1884.

13. Donat Savoie, *The Amerindians of the Canadian North-West in the 19th Century as seen by Emile Petitot, Vol. II, The Loucheaux Indians* (Ottawa: Department of Indian Affairs, Northern Science Research Group, MDRP 10, 1970), 55, 57, 95.

14. Doug Babcock, "Fur Trade Architecture in Alberta: The First Century, 1778–1878" (Paper delivered at the Banff Conference on Log Structures in Canada, Banff, Alberta, October 27, 1977), 2, 5–10. There is little unanimity on the proper name for this system, and it is also known as pièce sur pièce, poteaux et pièce coulissante, poteaux sur sole, timber frame, and Manitoba or Red River frame.

15. Ibid., 5–11.

16. Ibid., 12–18.

17. Frank Gilbert Roe, "The Old Log House in Western Canada," *Alberta Historical Review* 6 (1958): 6.

18. Thomas Ritchie, "Plankwall Framing, A Modern Wall Construction

with an Ancient History," *Journal of the Society of Architectural Historians* 30 (1971): 68; William Wonders, "Log Dwellings in Canadian Folk Architecture," *Annals of The Association of American Geographers* 69 (1979): 196.

19. Harold Innis, *The Fur Trade in Canada* (Toronto: University of Toronto Press, 1973), 312.

20. Roe, "The Old Log House," 6.

21. Babcock, "Fur Trade Architecture," 8–9.

22. D. Moodie, "St. Albert Settlement: A Study in Historical Geography" (M.A. thesis, University of Alberta, 1965), 116. Post on sill was not the "official" construction method of the Roman Catholic Church in Alberta. The Rectory at Fort Saskatchewan, built in 1877, was horizontal log construction with dove tailed corners, all covered with siding (Peter Ream, *The Fort on the Saskatchewan*, 2nd ed. (n.p.: Metropolitan Printing, 1974), 54–55).

23. Angus Sherwood, "Building in the North," *APT Bulletin* 6 (1974): 2; Thomas Ritchie, *Canada Builds: 1867–1967* (Toronto: University of Toronto Press, 1967), 94–99.

24. Babcock, "Fur Trade Architecture," 19.

25. James MacGregor, *A History of Alberta*, rev.ed. (Edmonton: Hurtig Publishers, 1981), 67, 68.

26. Ibid., 65, 78; Irene Spry, ed., *The Papers of the Palliser Expedition* (Toronto: The Champlain Society, 1968), 173 n. 1.

27. Spry, *Papers of the Palliser Expedition*, 222.

28. Ibid., 220.

29. R.G. Ironside and E. Tomasky, "Agricultural and River Lot Settlement in Western Canada: The Case of Pakan (Victoria) Alberta," *Prairie Forum* 1 (1–2): 7, 9.

30. Moodie, "St. Albert Settlement," 114; Victoria Callihoo, "Early Life in Lac Ste. Anne and St. Albert in the Eighteen Seventies," *Alberta Historical Review* 1 (1953): 21; Sherwood, "Building in the North," 2.

31. Marcel Giraud, *The Metis in the Canadian West*, trans. George Woodcock, 2 vols. (Edmonton: University of Alberta Press, 1986), Vol. 2: 166.

32. Callihoo, "Lac Ste Anne and St. Albert," 21.

33. Roe, "The Old Log House," 3.

34. Wonders, "Log in Canadian Folk Architecture," 199–202.

35. William Wonders and Mark Rasmussen "Log Buildings of West Central Alberta," *Prairie Forum* 5 (1980): 197; Spry, *The Papers of the Palliser Expedition*, 22.

36. *Edmonton Bulletin*, November 1, 1884. A "mud roof" no doubt meant a sod roof.

37. Roe, "The Old Log House," 1.

38. Chester Martin, *Dominion Lands Policies* (1938, reprint edited and with an introduction by L.H. Thomas, Toronto: McClelland and Stewart, 1973), 183; Hugh Dempsey, ed., "The West of Edward Maunsell," *Alberta History* 34 (1986): 11.

39. *Edmonton Bulletin*, January 14, 1882; *Macleod Gazette*, October 18, 1888.

40. *Macleod Gazette,* July 4, August 22, and October 3, 1889, and March 17, 1899.

41. Helen Lee, *The Forest Industry in Alberta, 1870–1955* (Wetaskiwin: Reynolds Alberta Museum, Background Paper 19, 1984), 71–88.

42. Dempsey, "The West of Edward Maunsell," 11.

43. Canada, *Annual Report of the Department of the Interior for the Year 1902–03* (Canada Sessional Papers, no. 25, 1904, Part I), 27.

44. Sherwood, "Building in the North," 3.

45. Wonders and Rasmussen, "Log Buildings in West Central Alberta," 201; Dempsey, "The West of Edward Maunsell," 11.

46. Roe, "The Old Log House," 3–4, 7.

47. Maurice Clayton, "Canadian Housing In Wood" (Typescript, 1986), p. 3.32.1–2.

48. Wonders and Rasmussen, "Log Buildings in West Central Alberta," 204; John Lehr, *Ukrainian Vernacular Architecture in Alberta* (Edmonton: Historic Sites Service, Occasional Paper no. 1, 1976), 12.

49. Roe, "The Old Log House," 5.

50. Ibid., 5; Wonders and Rasmussen, "Log Buildings in West Central Alberta," 205.

51. Building Report, Northern Institute of Technology, Architectural Technology Section, 69.268/1/8, PAA; Wonders and Rasmussen, "Log Buildings in West Central Alberta," 207.

52. Percy Talbot, "Pioneering on Strawberry Plain. Early Days in Lacombe," *Alberta Historical Review* 3 (1955): 24–25; Roe, "The Old Log House," 7.

53. *Farm and Ranch Review,* August 20, 1912.

54. Dempsey, "The West of Edward Maunsell," 11; Wonders and Rasmussen, "Log Buildings in West Central Alberta," 208; Roe, "The Old Log House," 7.

55. K. Taggart, "The First Shelter of the Early Pioneers," *Saskatchewan History* 11 (1958): 86; Wonders and Rasmussen, "Log Buildings in West Central Alberta," 200; John Hudson, "Frontier Housing in North Dakota," *North Dakota History* 42 (1975): 13; Northern Institute of Technology, Architectural Technology Section, 69.268/1/8, PAA.

56. Roe, "The Old Log House," 8.

57. Roe, "The Old Log House," 1; *Edmonton Bulletin,* December 7, 1893; D. Stone, "The Process of Rural Settlement in the Athabasca Area, Alberta" (M.A. thesis, University of Alberta, 1971), 146.

58. Wonders, "Log in Canadian Folk Architecture," 203.

59. Wonders and Rasmussen, "Log Buildings in West Central Alberta," 212; Lehr, *Ukrainian Vernacular Architecture in Alberta,* 36.

60. Lehr, *Ukrainian Vernacular Architecture in Alberta,* 1, 7.

61. John Lehr, "The Log Buildings of Ukrainian Settlers in Western Canada," *Prairie Forum* 5 (1980): 184–90, 193.

62. Ibid., 186; Lehr, *Ukrainian Vernacular Architecture in Alberta,* 18.

63. Roe, "The Old Log House," 8–9.

64. Lehr, *Ukrainian Vernacular Architecture in Alberta,* 18; Lehr, "The Landscape of Ukrainian Settlement," 103.

65. Orest Martynowych, *The Ukrainian Bloc Settlement in East-Central Alberta 1890–1930: A History* (Edmonton: Historic Sites Service, Occasional Paper no. 10, 1985), 130.

66. Lehr, "The Log Buildings of Ukrainian Settlers," 190.

67. Martynowych, *Ukrainian Bloc Settlement*, 130.

68. Lehr, "The Log Buildings of Ukrainian Settlers," 190.

69. Ibid., 193.

70. Martynowych, *Ukrainian Bloc Settlement*, 128.

71. See floor plans in Lehr, "The Log Buildings of Ukrainian Settlers," 194–95.

72. Martynowych, *Ukrainian Bloc Settlement*, 131.

73. Lehr, *Ukrainian Vernacular Architecture in Alberta*, 21.

74. Martynowych, *Ukrainian Bloc Settlement*, 129–31.

75. *Farm and Ranch Review*, August 5, 1912.

76. Lehr, *Ukrainian Vernacular Architecture in Alberta*, 11.

77. R. Bauer, *One of Many* (Edmonton: Edmonton Imprimerie La Survivance Printing, 1965), 53.

78. Lehr, "The Landscape of Ukrainian Settlement," 96.

79. Martynowych, *Ukrainian Bloc Settlement*, 121.

80. Andriy Nahachewsky, *Ukrainian Dug-Out Dwellings in East Central Alberta* (Edmonton: Historic Sites Service, Occasional Paper no. 11, 1985), 113ff.

81. Martynowych, *Ukrainian Bloc Settlement*, 121.

82. Frank Gilbert Roe, "The Sod House," *Alberta Historical Review* 18 (1970): 2. On the Barr colonists, see Askton Reminiscences, 67.137, PAA.

83. Details on sod house construction are from: E. Slater McLeod, "Our Sod House," *The Beaver* Outfit 308: 2 (1977): 12–15; Roe "The Sod House," 1–7; D. Gates, "The Sod House," *Journal of Geography* 32 (1933): 353–58; Ritchie, *Canada Builds*, 103.

84. McLeod, "Our Sod House," 15.

85. Roe, "The Sod House," 7.

86. *Calgary Herald*, August 17, 1911.

87. See for example, *Calgary Herald*, April 3, 1889; *Lethbridge News*, July 5, 1899; *Edmonton Bulletin*, April 10, 1893.

88. *Alberta Statistical Review: 75th Anniversary Edition* (Edmonton: Alberta Bureau of Statistics, 1980), Table 2, p. 4.

89. *Calgary Herald*, April 12, 1911.

90. *Saturday News*, September 22, 1906.

91. Warren Caragata, *Alberta Labour: A Heritage Untold* (Toronto: James Lorimer and Company, 1979), 46.

92. *Calgary Herald*, July 4, and July 15, 1907.

93. Ibid., July 4, 1907.

94. Roe, "The Sod House," 1.

95. Ronald J. Goodfellow, "A Historical and Ecological Study of Southern Alberta" (Bachelor of Architecture thesis, University of British Columbia, 1968/69), 6–19.

96. Kathleen Strange, *With the West in Her Eyes* (Toronto: Macmillan Co. of Canada Ltd., 1945), 22.

97. *Farm and Ranch Review,* April 20, 1914.

98. Goodfellow, "Historical and Ecological Study of Southern Alberta," 6–21; Gladys Rowell, "Memoirs of an English Settler," *Alberta History* 30 (1982): 34.

99. *The Public Health Journal* 8 (1917): 53.

100. Owen Douglas Jones, "The Historical Geography of Edmonton, Alberta" (M.A. thesis, University of Toronto, 1962), 60.

101. Hudson, "Frontier Housing in North Dakota," 7; Taggart, "First Shelter," 81.

102. In a study of settlement between Lethbridge and Medicine Hat, Robin Mallett found only one sod house in the sample area. This area had easy access to rail transportation, making machined building materials easily obtainable, pointing again to the preference for milled lumber construction. Robin Barrie Mallett, "Settlement Process and Land Use Change—Lethbridge-Medicine Hat Area" (M.A. thesis, University of Alberta, 1971), 99.

103. Hudson, "Frontier Housing in North Dakota," 4–5.

104. Figures on pioneer houses in Saskatchewan indicate that milled lumber houses were commonest there. In 1955, the results of a questionnaire on pioneer conditions indicated that of 86 houses built before 1900, 17 were of lumber and 69 were of log or sod, while of 164 built after 1900, 95 were of lumber and 69 were of log or sod. The questionnaire was voluntary (Taggart, "First Shelter," 81).

105. Ritchie, *Canada Builds,* 161–65. See also J. T. Rempel, *Building with Wood and Other Aspects of Nineteenth Century Building in Ontario* (Toronto: University of Toronto Press, 1967).

106. *Farm and Ranch Review,* December 1907.

107. David Handlin, *The American Home: Architecture and Society 1815–1915* (Boston: Little Brown and Co., 1979), 68, and *passim.*

108. *Calgary Herald,* June 24, 1897.

109. *Farm and Ranch Review,* April 1905.

2 THE CONTEXT OF DESIGNING THE MODERN HOUSE

1. Paul Voisey, "In Search of Wealth and Status: An Economic and Social Study of Entrepreneurs in Early Calgary," in *Frontier Calgary: Town, City and Region, 1875–1914,* ed. Anthony W. Rasporich and Henry C. Klassen (Calgary: University of Calgary, McClelland and Stewart West, 1975), 221–41.

2. Henry Klassen, "Life in Frontier Calgary," in *Western Canada Past and Present,* ed. Anthony Rasporich (Calgary: University of Calgary, McClelland and Stewart West, 1975), 45.

3. Gerald Friesen, *The Canadian Prairies: A History* (Toronto: University of Toronto Press, 1984), 283–84.

4. *Calgary Herald,* June 29, 1911.

5. For the context of such ideas, see Smith, "The Myth of the Self-made Man in English Canada," 200–3.

6. *Calgary Herald,* November 16, 1910.

7. Ibid., November 15, 1911.

8. Ibid., April 9, 1912.

9. Ibid., June 29, 1911.

10. David Bercuson, ed., *Alberta Coal Industry, 1919* (Calgary: Alberta Records Publication Board, The Historical Society of Alberta, 1978), 31.

11. *Calgary Herald*, December 2, 1908.

12. *Farm and Ranch Review*, August 1907.

13. *Annual Report, Dependent and Delinquent Children 1915*, Alberta Department of the Attorney General, 38.

14. *Claresholm Review*, June 24, 1915; *Calgary Herald*, September 27, 1910.

15. Catherine Cleverdon, *The Woman Suffrage Movement in Canada* (1950; reprint with an introduction by Ramsay Cook, Toronto: University of Toronto Press, 1974), vi.

16. G. Leslie, "Domestic Service in Canada 1880–1920," in *Women at Work 1850–1930* J. Acton, P. Goldsmith, and B. Shepard, eds. (Toronto: Women's Press, 1974), 89–90; *Calgary Herald*, March 21, 1910.

17. *Calgary Herald*, July 29, 1907.

18. *Farm and Ranch Review*, October 1906.

19. See for example, ibid., April 12, 1913.

20. Colin Howell and Michael Smith, "Orthodox Medicine and the Health Reform Movement in the Maritimes, 1850–1885," *Acadiensis* 18 (1989): 62, 68–71.

21. Handlin, *The American Home*, 48, 53–59.

22. *Calgary Herald*, October 23, 1911.

23. *Farm and Ranch Review*, October 20, 1909.

24. *Calgary Herald*, September 24, 1910.

25. Gowans, *The Comfortable House*, 27–28.

26. P.H. Bryce, "History of Public Health in Canada," *Canadian Therapeutist and Sanitary Engineer* 6 (1910): 287–88, 291.

27. *Macleod Gazette*, April 4, 1889.

28. Ibid., September 18, 1890.

29. *Macleod Gazette*, April 4, 1889; General correspondence, 1893–94, Griesbach Papers, MS209 File 7, CEA.

30. *Macleod Gazette*, September 18, 1890.

31. Braithwaite to Griesbach, August 30, 1893, MS209 File 7, CEA; *Calgary Herald*, June 15, 1907; *Macleod Gazette*, December 9, 1898.

32. *Macleod Gazette*, December 9, 1898. On the situation in Calgary, see H. Klassen, "Social Troubles in Calgary in the Mid-1890s," *Urban History Review*, no. 3–74 (1974): 11.

33. *Canadian Engineer* 19 (1910): 687.

34. *Calgary Herald*, September 12, and October 22, 1910. Scientific theory, obviously honoured in the breach in Calgary, held that a cesspool should not be built within 100 feet of a dwelling. (*Canadian Architect and Builder*, May 1907, 85).

35. *Calgary Herald*, September 3, 1890, and April 5, 1893.

36. *Canadian Engineer* 27 (1914): 661–62.

37. *Hanna Herald*, March 30, 1916.

38. A.N. Reid, "Urban Governments in the North-West Territories:

Their Development and Machinery of Government," *Saskatchewan History* 7 (1954/56): 60.

39. *Calgary Herald*, September 9, 1910. See also *Lethbridge News*, October 1, 1890.

40. *Calgary Herald*, September 24, 1910.

41. N.D. Beck to Kinnard, June 23, 1903, Edmonton City Secretary's Papers, RG8/C.5/13, CEA, and Petition of Property Owners, April 26, 1904, RG8/C.10/01, CEA.

42. *Calgary Herald*, December 14, 1918.

43. Secretary Treasurer to Davidson, January 14, 1910, RG8/24/66, CEA; *Calgary Herald*, January 15, 1903, and March 13, 1912.

44. *Calgary Herald*, September 19, 1910.

45. *Conservation of Life*, 2 (1916): 88.

46. Thomas Adams, "Planning for Civic Betterment in Town and Country," *American City* 15 (1916): 50.

47. J. David Hulchanski, *The Origin of Urban Land Use Planning in Alberta 1900–1945* (Toronto: Centre for Urban and Community Studies, University of Toronto), Research Paper no. 119. Land Policy Paper no. 1, 1981, 3.

48. Maxwell Foran, "The Civic Corporation and Urban Growth, Calgary, 1884–1930" (Ph.D. diss., University of Calgary, 1981), 136.

49. Hulchanski, *The Origin of Urban Land Use Planning*, 5; Maxwell Foran, "The Mawson Report in Historical Perspective," *Alberta History* 28 (1980): 32; *Calgary Herald*, March 23 and June 15, 1911, and October 11, 1912.

50. Hulchanski, *The Origin of Urban Land Use Planning*, 5.

51. *Contract Record*, 25 (1911): 52.

52. Hulchanski, *The Origin of Urban Land Use Planning*, 22.

53. Foran, "The Mawson Report," 33; Hulchanski, *The Origin of Urban Land Use Planning*, 5.

54. *Saturday News*, March 11, 1911.

55. C. Youe, "Eau Claire, the Company and the Community," *Alberta History* 27 (1979): 3.

56. See for example, *Conservation of Life*, 2 (1916): 61–62; various articles in the *Canadian Engineer* 21 and 22 (1911–12).

57. Hulchanski, *The Origin of Urban Land Use Planning*, 12.

58. Foran, "The Mawson Report," 33–38.

59. Foran, "The Civic Corporation and Urban Growth," 142.

60. *Calgary Herald*, February 23, 1909.

61. On residential segregation on the prairies, see Friesen, *The Canadian Prairies: A History*, 285–86. A model study of residential segregation is Michael J. Doucet, "Working Class Housing in a Small Nineteenth Century Canadian City: Hamilton Ontario, 1852–1881," in *Essays in Canadian Working Class History*, eds. Gregory Kealey and Peter Warrian (Toronto: McClelland and Stewart, 1976), 83–105.

62. See *Calgary Herald*, October 5, and October 10, 1910.

63. Hulchanski, *The Origin of Urban Land Use Planning*, 8.

64. Youe, "Eau Claire," 2–3.

65. Klassen, "Life in Frontier Calgary," 45; Lawrence D. McCann, "Changing Morphology of Residential Areas in Transition" (Ph.D. diss., University of Alberta, 1972), 20.

66. *Calgary Herald*, March 15, 1911.

67. Foran, "The Mawson Report," 32.

3 DESIGNING THE MODERN HOUSE

1. John Warkentin, "Time and Place in the Western Interior," *ArtsCanada*, Autumn (1972): 21.

2. On Downing's plan books in Alberta, see Lorne Render, "Paper on Calgary Architecture," p. 11, M3816, GAI.

3. Michael J. Doucet and John C. Weaver, "Material Culture and the North American House: The Era of the Common Man," *Journal of American History* 72, Part II (1985–86): 574–75.

4. Richard Mattson, "The Bungalow Spirit," *Journal of Cultural Geography* 1 (1981): 77.

5. Correspondence between Shaw and O'Brian, January-April, 1913, Shaw Papers, A.S536B, File 2, GAI.

6. *Claresholm Review*, October 2, 1908; *Blairmore Enterprise*, July 11, 1913.

7. Pollard to Brennen, July 26, 1916, L.D. Pollard Papers, M53, File 33, CEA.

8. *Calgary Herald*, January 23, 1919; *Coleman Journal*, February 24, 1944.

9. Doucet and Weaver, "Material Culture and the North American House," 581–82.

10. *Calgary Herald*, February 22, 1908.

11. Bryan Melnyk, *Calgary Builds: The Emergence of an Urban Landscape 1905–1914* (Regina: Alberta Culture/Canadian Plains Research Center, 1985), 47–57.

12. *Calgary Herald*, July 15, 1912.

13. *Canadian Architect and Builder* 9 (1896): 39.

14. Ibid., 10 (1897):235, and 3 (1890): 55–57.

15. John Burchard and Albert Bush Brown, *The Architecture of America* (Boston: Little Brown and Co., 1961), 168.

16. *Calgary Herald*, April 22, 1912.

17. *Construction*, June 1909, 71, 75.

18. *Saturday News*, July 30, 1910.

19. *Canadian Architect and Builder* 3 (1890): 55–57.

20. *Construction*, June 1915, 219.

21. Ibid., September 1909, 65.

22. Holdsworth, "Regional Distinctiveness in an Industrial Age," 69; Gowans, *The Comfortable House*, 75.

23. Wright, *Moralism and the Model Home*, 231–53.

24. *Farm and Ranch Review*, September 5, 1912.

25. Doucet and Weaver, "Material Culture and the North American House," 583.

26. *Farm and Ranch Review*, January 20, 1910.

27. *Calgary Herald*, March 25, 1912.

28. *Construction*, June 1909, 75; *Calgary Herald*, May 17, 1913.

29. *Farm and Ranch Review*, September 1907.

30. *Calgary Herald*, April 22, 1912.

31. Ibid., April 29, 1912.

32. *Construction*, November 1910, 79; *Grande Prairie Herald*, July 17, 1917.

33. Mattson, "The Bungalow Spirit," 75–78. Illustrating the difficulties in defining bungalow form, Gowans defines them narrowly as houses with at least three of the four basic features of the Bengali prototype. (Gowans, *The Comfortable House*, 76–78.)

34. *Construction*, August 1908, 45–46.

35. Mattson, "The Bungalow Spirit," 80–81, 88–89.

36. *Construction*, August 1908, 49.

37. Mattson, "The Bungalow Spirit," 82–83.

38. *Construction*, August 1908, 45.

39. *Calgary Herald*, April 19, 1913; Mattson, "The Bungalow Spirit," 81.

40. *Farm and Ranch Review*, November 5, 1910.

41. Warkentin, "Time and Place in the Western Interior," 20.

42. On homestead form see Gowans, *The Comfortable House*, 94–99.

43. On foursquare form, see ibid., 84–93; Thomas Hanchett, "The Four Square House in the United States," in *Perspectives in Vernacular Architecture*, ed. Camille Wells (Annapolis, Maryland: Vernacular Architecture Forum, 1982), 51–53.

44. On approaches to styles see Alberta Culture, Historic Sites Service, *Sites Type Manual* (Edmonton: Alberta Culture, 1979); Noble, *Wood, Brick and Stone*; Gowans, *The Comfortable House*.

45. Doucet and Weaver, "Material Culture and the North American House," 582.

46. *Farm and Ranch Review*, March 5, 1918; *Eaton's Catalogue of House Plans*, House no. 667 (1917–18), T. Eaton Co. Catalogue Excerpts File, M1466, GAI.

47. *Farm and Ranch Review*, June 5, 1913.

48. *Canadian Architect and Builder*, 8 (1895): 104.

49. Ibid., 9 (1896): 188–90; City of Edmonton, "A Bylaw Respecting the Construction of Sewer Connections" (Bylaw 240, 1903).

50. Handlin, *The American Home*, 458.

51. *Canadian Architect and Builder*, June 1907, 104–5; *Construction*, May 1910, 3; *Canadian Engineer* 8 (1900): 457; *Calgary Herald*, March 25, 1912.

52. *Construction*, June 1915, 243; *Canadian Architect and Builder*, June 1907, 104–5.

53. "Allen House," RDDA.

54. Klassen, "Social Troubles in Calgary in the Mid-1890s," 13.

55. *Calgary Herald*, March 5, 1903.

56. In 1913 the Provincial Sanitary Engineer reported that in Edmonton,

9,275 "houses" were connected to the water mains and 5,738 houses were not connected, or roughly 40 percent. These figures are unclear. In 1921, the first time the number of houses was reported in the census, there were 11,888 single detached houses in the city, indicating that the total number of houses connected plus those not connected in 1913 exceeded the total number in 1921. Possibly, "lots" were meant, or possibly the total number of connections to all buildings, residential and nonresidential. The same discrepancy applies to the figures reported for Calgary and other places. In most cases, the number of water connections exceeded the number of sewer connections, although the meaning of "connection" remains unclear (Annual Report of Provincial Sanitary Engineer for 1913, reprinted in *The Canadian Engineer*, 27 (1914): 661–62).

57. Bercuson, *Alberta's Coal Industry 1919*, 117, 184–5, 221.

58. *Calgary Herald*, July 4, 1917; *Conservation of Life*, 4 (1918): 1–2.

59. *Calgary Herald*, July 8, 1910.

60. Ibid., August 25, 1910.

61. *Farm and Ranch Review*, November 20, 1912, and May 5, 1914.

62. On farm wells see *Farm and Ranch Review*, March 30, 1911. On conditions on Alberta farms and recommended sanitary systems, see ibid., November 20, 1913, and *Calgary Herald*, August 26, 1912.

63. *Canadian Architect and Builder*, 10 (1897): 235.

64. *Farm and Ranch Review*, December 5, 1912.

65. Ibid., March 5, 1910.

66. Ibid., December 5, 1912.

67. *Construction*, June 1915, 243.

68. *Farm and Ranch Review*, December 5, 1912.

69. Ibid.

70. *Calgary Herald*, March 25, 1912.

71. *Farm and Ranch Review*, September 15, 1912.

72. *Calgary Herald*, September 30, 1910.

73. *Canadian Architect and Builder*, February 1906, 59; *Calgary Herald*, September 30, 1910.

74. See *Farm and Ranch Review*, October 1906, and December 5, 1912; Alberta, *Annual Report of the Department of Agriculture for 1913*, 119.

75. *Public Health Journal* 8 (1917): 52.

76. *Calgary Herald*, June 2, 1909.

77. *Canadian Architect and Builder* 7 (1894): vii.

78. *Calgary Herald*, June 2, 1909; *Conservation of Life* 4 (1918): 16.

79. *Farm and Ranch Review*, April 5, 1910.

80. *Farm and Ranch Review*, March 5, 1910.

81. *Calgary Herald*, April 15, 1912.

82. *Canadian Architect and Builder*, June 1907, 104–5.

83. *Construction*, February 1912, 68; *Calgary Herald*, May 27, 1912.

84. *Calgary Herald*, April 15, 1912.

85. *Farm and Ranch Review*, September 20, 1911. Alabastine came in 21 colours and allowed one to get rid of wallpaper and Kalsomine since "tinted walls are now the vogue." It was said that it would not "rub-off," a questionable claim (ibid).

86. *Farm and Ranch Review*, June 5, 1913, and February 5, 1914.

87. *Calgary Herald*, April 22, 1912. Another consequence of the stress on sunlight was a decline in the popularity of heavy curtains and their replacement with sheer curtains.

88. *Farm and Ranch Review*, January 20, 1910.

89. *Conservation of Life* 4 (1918): 20–21; *Construction*, June 1915, 263–64; *Hanna Herald*, January 20, 1916.

90. *Farm and Ranch Review*, October 20, 1909.

91. Ibid., May 1908.

92. *Construction*, June 1915, 263.

93. *Calgary Herald*, March 23, 1911; *Farm and Ranch Review*, May 1908.

94. *Farm and Ranch Review*, October 20, 1909. Damp basements were corrected by installing fresh air ducts, sump wells, and the laying of weeping tile or gravel around the exterior of the basement at floor level (*Canadian Architect and Builder*, 12 (1899); Jack Manson, *Bricks in Alberta* (Edmonton: John Manson and the Alberta Masonary Institute, 1983), 26).

95. *Edmonton Bulletin*, November 5, 1881.

96. R. Cunniffe, *Calgary—In Sandstone* (Calgary: Historical Society of Alberta, 1969), 10; *Medicine Hat News*, August 2, 1894.

97. *Farm and Ranch Review*, September 5, 1912.

98. Bercuson, *Alberta's Coal Industry 1919*, viii, 74; "Allen House" RDDA.

99. *Job Reed's Letters: Life in Lethbridge, 1886–1906* (Lethbridge: Historical Society of Alberta, Whoop Up Chapter, 1979), 48; *Claresholm Review*, January 2, 1912.

100. *Calgary Herald*, June 26, 1909.

101. Ibid., November 18, 1909; Manager to Dennis, June 25, 1912, Canadian Pacific Railway Co. Papers, BN C2126. File 2, GAI; See also *Saturday News*, August 5, 1911.

102. H.F. Greenway, "Housing in Canada," *Census of Canada, 1931*, vol. 12, *Monographs*, 413.

103. *Canadian Architect and Builder* 12 (1899): 173, and May 1907, 84–5; *Calgary Herald*, July 8, 1912; *Construction*, October 1907, 59–60.

104. *Construction*, March 1908, 67.

105. *Macleod Gazette*, June 24, 1898; Correspondence May 5–July 17, 1900, MacDonald Papers, MS313, CEA.

106. *Calgary Herald*, March 25, 1912.

107. *Canadian Architect and Builder* 7 (1894): 152.

108. *Conservation of Life* 2 (1916): 35–41.

109. *Calgary Herald*, April 4, 1910.

110. Ibid., January 12, 1909.

111. *Calgary Herald*, April 22, 1916; *Farm and Ranch Review*, December 1907, and June 1909.

112. *Calgary Herald*, May 25, 1911.

113. Ibid., April 23, 1909.

114. Ibid., March 23, 1909.

115. Annie Jack, *The Canadian Garden: A Pocket Help for the Amateur* (Toronto: The Musson Book Company, 1910), 40.

116. *Calgary Herald*, March 1, 1911.

117. *Saturday News*, May 27, 1911; *Farm and Ranch Review*, January 20, 1910.

118. *Saturday News*, May 27, 1911; *Canadian Architect and Builder* 9 (1896): 38.

119. *Calgary Herald*, April 8, 1916.

120. Ibid., July 12, 1907.

121. Handlin, *The American Home*, 270.

122. *Farm and Ranch Review*, October 20, 1909.

4 PERMANENT HOUSING: COST, SUPPLY, AND BUILDING

1. Owram, *The Economic Development of Western Canada*, 14–15.

2. David Breen, "Calgary: The City and the Petroleum Industry Since World War II," *Urban History Review* 2-77 (1977): 59.

3. John Thompson, *The Harvests of War. The Prairie West, 1914–1918* (Toronto: McClelland and Stewart, 1978), 45 ff.

4. Saywell, *Housing Canadians*, 2.

5. *Census of Canada, 1951*, Vol. I, Table 1, p. 1–1. For this and subsequent citations to census statistics, see introductory note.

6. *Census of the Prairie Provinces, 1946*, Vol. 2, Table 9, p. 348.

7. *Census of Canada, 1921*, Vol. III, Table 12, p. 40.

8. Ibid., 1951, Vol. I, Table 1, p. 1–1.

9. M. Holden, "The Normans Come to Calgary," *Alberta History* 28 (1980): 26.

10. *Annual Report, Dependent and Delinquent Children 1912*, Alberta Department of the Attorney General, 39.

11. *Farm and Ranch Review*, March 5, 1910.

12. A.E. Grauer, *Housing: A Study Prepared for the Royal Commission on Dominion-Provincial Relations* (Ottawa: 1939), 32.

13. Statement Re: Delburne, March 20, 1912, Stewart Papers, M1180, GAI.

14. D.G. Wetherell and Associates Ltd., *Historical and Architectural Evaluation of the Beatty House, Rimbey* (Typescript, Edmonton: Historic Sites Service, 1990), 4–5.

15. *Edmonton Bulletin*, January 7, 1887, and July 3, 1893.

16. *Census of Canada, 1921*, Vol. III, Table 9, p. 26.

17. Caragata, *Alberta Labour*, 43; *Calgary Herald*, September 1, 1910.

18. *Annual Report, Dependent and Delinquent Children 1912*, 14.

19. *Calgary Herald*, December 3, 1907. In 1921 there were 351 row houses in Alberta. This may mean either the number of dwellings in row houses or the number of row houses. In either case, they were a minor percentage of dwelling units. No statistics on row houses or duplexes are available for an earlier period. (*Census of Canada, 1921*, Vol. III, Table 9, p. 26).

20. *Canadian Engineer*, January 19, 1911, 182–3; Melnyk, *Calgary Builds*, 72.

21. *Construction*, December 1909, 106.

22. Melnyk, *Calgary Builds*, 70–2; *Edmonton Journal*, July 5, 1985; Calgary Buildings: Apartments, clipping files, GAI; Letter from Sylvester, August 3, 1912, City of Calgary Papers, BE33.C151P, File 470, GAI.

23. Orr to Cook, October 25, 1890, Orr Letterbooks, M928, vol.1, no. 643, GAI; *Calgary Herald,* January 4, 1910 (Inspector Harrison's Building Report for 1909).

24. Richard Harris, "The Unremarked Homeownership Boom in Toronto," *Histoire sociale/Social History* 18 (1985): 433–37.

25. *Census of Canada, 1921,* Vol. III, Table 15, p. 54.

26. *Lethbridge News,* April 23, 1890, August 2, 1894, June 22, 1898, and October 4, 1899.

27. *Edmonton Journal,* October 12, 1948; Orr to Barber, March 31, 1894, M928, Vol. 5, no. 406, GAI; Orr to Ingram, March 29, 1897, M928, Vol. 5, no. 430, GAI; *Calgary Herald,* May 1, 1909; Maxwell Foran, "Land Speculation and Urban Development in Calgary 1884–1912" in *Frontier Calgary,* 209.

28. Saywell, *Housing Canadians,* 13; *Edmonton Journal,* October 12, 1948.

29. Speculation in land normally took the form of "futures" with "the buyer making a small down-payment, holding the remaining debt in the form of a mortgage" (R. Rees, "The Magic City on the Banks of the Saskatchewan. The Saskatoon Real Estate Boom 1910–1913," *Saskatchewan History* 27, no. 2 (1974): 3).

30. *Edmonton: Metropolis of Canada's Farther West* (Winnipeg: 1912) (promotional pamphlet).

31. *Calgary Herald,* December 17, 1907.

32. *Calgary Herald,* November 10, 1911.

33. See for example, *Calgary Herald,* March 1, 1909, and November 22, 1911, and *Saturday News,* November 13, 1909.

34. Carl Betke, "The Development of Urban Community in Prairie Canada: Edmonton, 1898–1921" (Ph.D. diss., University of Alberta, 1981), 328–30; *Saturday News,* March 16, 1907.

35. Foran, "Land Speculation and Urban Development in Calgary 1884–1912," 209; *Calgary Herald,* July 31, 1909.

36. *Calgary Herald,* March 30, 1918.

37. *Construction,* February 1919, 61–62.

38. L. Pollard to Arthur, April 26, 1917, L.D. Pollard Papers, M53, File 33, CEA.

39. *Edmonton Bulletin,* November 5, 1881, and January 21, 1882.

40. *Edmonton Bulletin,* January 7 and December 31, 1887; *Lethbridge News,* January 27, 1891.

41. Orr to Cook, October 25, 1890, Vol. 1, no. 643, M928, GAI.

42. *Edmonton Bulletin,* November 6, 1899; *Macleod Gazette,* March 3, 1899; *Calgary Herald,* December 20, 1900.

43. Costs were calculated from advertisements and articles in the *Calgary Herald,* March-June and September-November, 1905–1912. Issues cited are: April 15, and November 3, 1905; April 2, and May 6, 1907; July 31, 1909; May 13 and May 31, 1910.

44. The range of costs was determined from advertisements in the *Calgary Herald,* April-June and September-November, 1911. Issues cited are: March 15, June 29, November 9 and November 22, 1911. It was believed by 1914 that the ratio of the cost of serviced land to the total cost of a house

should not exceed 25 percent. Thus, a house costing $2,400 should ideally be built on fully serviced land costing no more than $600.

45. Data were gathered from *Calgary Herald*, April–June and September–November, 1905–1913. Citations are from: April 1, April 15, May 30, June 22, and November 3, 1905; May 6, June 5, and October 11, 1907; May 10, June 10, June 13, and September 30, 1910; March 6, April 5, April 13, May 26, June 13, and October 4, 1911. These figures for large houses roughly confirm those of Bryan Melnyk (*Calgary Builds*, 58, n. 93).

46. *Claresholm Review*, May 4, 1911.

47. *Calgary Herald*, December 7, 1905.

48. For Canadian building cycles see Saywell, *Housing Canadians*, 22–23.

49. Owram, "The Economic Development of Western Canada," 11, n. 25. The demand for capital in prairie Canada was high. From 1900 until 1912 the amount of capital invested in mortgages in the three prairie provinces was $200 million (*Calgary Herald*, January 22, 1912); a significant figure since from 1867 to 1900, $1,000 million had been invested in houses in all of Canada (Saywell, *Housing Canadians*, 83). From 1896 to 1910, the gross investment in prairie farm residential housing was an estimated $126.5 million (Kenneth Buckley, *Capital Formation in Canada, 1896–1930* (Toronto: McClelland and Stewart, 1974), 219, Table N).

50. *The Bulletin, Greater Edmonton Number* (n.p.: n.d [1911]), 64, 142, 148. Western Homebuilding Ltd. was formerly Edmonton Homebuilders Ltd.

51. Saywell, *Housing Canadians*, 87–90.

52. Orr to Hansen, August 30, 1894, M928, Vol. 4, no. 92, GAI.

53. *Lethbridge News*, April 23, 1890; Bond Papers, File 12, *passim*, MS1, CEA; *Calgary Herald, Supplement*, September 13, 1900.

54. *Calgary Herald*, January 23–27, 1912 (advertisements).

55. *Calgary Herald*, June 10, 1912.

56. *Calgary Herald*, May 1, 1909.

57. J. David Hulchanski, "The 1935 Dominion Housing Act: Setting the Stage for a Permanent Federal Presence in Canada's Housing Sector," *Urban History Review* 15 (1986): 27.

58. *Saturday News*, May 25, 1912.

59. *Calgary Herald*, April 13, and May 26, 1911, and April–November, 1910–1913, *passim*.

60. Caragata, *Alberta Labour*, 43.

61. *The Bulletin, Greater Edmonton Number*, 64.

62. *Calgary Herald*, July 6, 1912.

63. *Calgary Herald*, July 17, 1909.

64. There is no accessible information on the number of houses built by owners. The ready-cut house manufacturers claimed that 30 percent of a house's cost was labour. This was probably a high estimate. On child labour for a later period see Rebecca Coulter, "The Working Young of Edmonton, 1921–1931," in *Childhood and Family in Canadian History*, ed. Joy Parr (Toronto: McClelland and Stewart, 1982), 143–59.

65. For advertisements for builders in most Alberta towns, see *Calgary*

Herald, Supplement, September 13, 1900. For Pincher Creek see "Information Concerning House Builders at Pincher Creek," Sykes Papers, M2815, Sheet 1, GAI.

66. See for example, Orr to Stewart, October 30, 1890, M928, vol. 1, no. 652, GAI; O'Brian to Shaw, February 6, 1913, Shaw Papers, M1131, File 2, GAI.

67. *Calgary Herald,* December 20, 1900.

68. *Lethbridge News,* August 23, 1899; Secretary Treasurer to Semmens, October 11, 1910, Edmonton City Secretary's Papers, RG8/24/73, CEA; J.P. Dickin McGinnis, "Birth to Boom to Bust: Building in Calgary 1875–1914," in *Frontier Calgary,* 16.

69. *Calgary Herald,* August 12, 1912.

70. *Calgary Herald,* May 21, 1903; Caragata, *Alberta Labour,* 11, 23–25; *The Labour Gazette,* August 1903, 141–42.

71. See for example, *Calgary Herald,* August 6, 1903.

72. Ibid., October 1, 1910.

73. Ibid., March 18, 1911.

74. P.J. Smith, "Change in a Youthful City: The Case of Calgary Alberta," *Geography* 56 (1971): 10.

75. *Calgary Herald,* December 7, 1905.

76. Smith, "Change in a Youthful City," 10; *Calgary Herald,* October 21, 1911 and September 16, 1910; Maxwell Foran, "Land Development Patterns in Calgary, 1884–1945," in *The Useable Urban Past,* Alan F.J. Artibise and Gilbert A. Stelter, eds. (Toronto: Macmillan of Canada, 1979), 305.

77. David G. Bettison, John K. Kenward, and Larrie Taylor, *Urban Affairs in Alberta* (Edmonton: University of Alberta Press, 1975), 23–24; *Claresholm Review,* January 4, and April 25, 1912.

78. Quoted in John Weaver, "Edmonton's Perilous Course 1904–1929," *Urban History Review* 2–77 (1977): 23.

79. Permit Building Book, 1907–1909, Harrison to Mayor, January 2, 1909, BE33.C581E, Vol. 8, GAI; *Calgary Herald,* January 12, 1909.

80. *Calgary Herald,* March 23, 1911.

81. A. Randall to Picard, March 11, 1897, RG8/4; *Edmonton Journal,* June 14, 1904.

82. See *Calgary Herald,* May 14, 1903; *Lethbridge News,* January 19, 1900.

83. Calgary building regulations, tabulated history, Kirkham Papers, M1892, GAI.

84. *Calgary Herald,* February 8, and March 29, 1911.

85. Foran, "The Civic Corporation and Urban Growth," 141. On Winnipeg, see Alan Artibise, *Winnipeg: A Social History of Urban Growth, 1874–1914* (Montreal: McGill-Queen's University Press, 1975), 233–45.

86. *Contract and Engineering Review* 27 (1913), 43.

87. N. McIvor to E. Morehouse, April 2, 1921, Papers of the Alberta Association of Architects, 187/A/84–08, File CO.21C47, CAA.

88. *Calgary Herald,* August 30, 1907.

89. Hulchanski, *The Origin of Urban Land Use Planning,* 13.

90. Youe, "Eau Clair," 2; *Macleod Gazette*, October 2, 1903.

91. Bercuson, *Alberta's Coal Industry 1919*, 64, 114, 176–79, 183–84.

92. *Calgary Herald*, December 14, 1918.

93. Bercuson, *Alberta's Coal Industry 1919*, 94.

94. *Calgary Herald*, December 7, 1905.

95. Ibid., July 17, 1909.

96. Ibid., October 8, 1903.

97. *Lethbridge News*, October 8, 1890.

98. *Edmonton Bulletin*, April 8, 1882.

99. *Edmonton Journal*, October 12, 1948.

100. *Lethbridge News*, August 2, 1899, and April 23, 1890.

101. *Calgary Herald*, September 12, 1901.

102. Betke, "The Development of Urban Community," 480.

103. John Weaver, "Edmonton's Perilous Course, 1904–1929," 22; Elizabeth Bloomfield, "Community Ethos and Local Initiative in Urban Economic Growth: Review of a Theme in Canadian Urban History," *Urban History Yearbook 1983*, 61–64.

104. Grauer, *Housing*, 33.

105. See for examples, Thomas Adams in *Journal of the American Institute of Architects*, 7 (1919): 512–18; *Conservation of Life*, 6 (1920): 11–14.

106. Saywell, *Housing Canadians*, 4.

5 BUILDING MATERIALS

1. *Farm and Ranch Review*, August 1909.

2. John Jackson, "The House as a Visual Indicator of Social Status Change: The Example of London Ontario 1861–1915" (M.A. thesis, University of Western Ontario, 1973), 87ff.

3. Manson, *Bricks in Alberta*, 7, 27, 85, 119.

4. Ibid., 13–14, 119.

5. E.A. Doherty, *Residential Construction Practices in Alberta 1900–1971* (Edmonton: Alberta Department of Housing, 1984), 30.

6. B. Jansen, "The Community of Mountain View, Alberta: A Study in Community Development, 1890–1925" (M.A. thesis, University of Alberta, 1972), 69; *Construction*, December 1909, 101. The spread of brick buildings in Edmonton can be seen from the maps in W. Graham, "Construction of Large Scale Structured Base Line Maps of Central Edmonton for 1907, 1911 & 1914" (M.A. thesis, University of Alberta, 1984).

7. Manson, *Bricks in Alberta*, 85; *Calgary Herald*, March 12, 1912. The appeal of hard brick for grand buildings led to its continued use for large houses like the Shaw house in Edmonton (Magoon and Macdonald to L. Kelsey, June 2, 1913, Magoon and Macdonald Papers, 78.11, PAA). For a photograph of the Shaw house see *Edmonton's Lost Heritage* (Edmonton Historical Board, 1982), 34–35.

8. Manson, *Bricks in Alberta*, 16.

9. *Census of Canada, 1921*, Vol. III, Table 13, p. xxiv.

10. *Lethbridge News*, July 26, 1888, and September 24, 1890.

11. *Canadian Architect and Builder* 7 (1894): 34.

12. Cunniffe, *Calgary—In Sandstone*, 6.

13. Melnyk, *Calgary Builds*, 53.

14. Cunniffe, *Calgary—In Sandstone*, 19; *Lethbridge News*, August 23, 1899; Robert Dawe, "An Investigation into the Development of the Red Deer Community in Relation to the Development of Western Canada" (M.A. thesis, University of Alberta, 1954), 55. The Red Deer quarry closed in 1914.

15. *Calgary Herald*, March 12, 1912.

16. Goodfellow "A Historical and Ecological Study of Southern Alberta," p. 6.25; Letter to G. Fussler, October 15, 1906, Brown Papers, M145, GAI.

17. *Canadian Architect and Builder* 7 (1894), 152. See also Orr to Fitzgerald, June 8, 1892, M928, Vol. 3, no. 106, GAI.

18. *Calgary Herald*, September 18, 1908. Portland cement was a hydraulic cement, that is, it would harden under water.

19. *Census of Canada, 1921*, Vol. III, Table 5, p. 12. There were 57 concrete dwellings reported in 1911. These may have been apartments, flats and houses. For concrete block advertisements see *Claresholm Review*, April 22, and May 20, 1909.

20. *Edmonton Journal*, July 5, 1904.

21. Ritchie, *Canada Builds 1867–1967*, 239.

22. *Construction*, November 1907, 61.

23. *Calgary Herald*, March 12, 1912.

24. *Edmonton Bulletin*, January 7, 1887. On the dominance of frame buildings in Lloydminster in 1906 see Fred Acland, "Alberta, 1906," *Alberta History* 28 (1980):13. On Duhamel in 1902/03 see Canada, *Annual Report of the Department of the Interior for the Year 1902/03*, Report of the Commissioner of Immigration (Canada Sessional Papers, 1904, no. 25, Part II), 114.

25. Lee, *The Forest Industry in Alberta 1870–1955*, 56, 71–77, 88–90.

26. Youe, "Eau Clare," 4; Carr to Tull and Ardern Ltd., September 17, 1928, Bow River Lumber Company Papers, M1564, File 1, GAI.

27. *Edmonton Bulletin*, April 5, 1890.

28. Lee, *The Forest Industry in Alberta*, 71–88, 98.

29. *Calgary Herald*, December 23, 1907.

30. *The Bulletin, Greater Edmonton Number*, 151, 159; *The Labour Gazette*, April 1906, 1114–15.

31. Wonders, "Log in Canadian Folk Architecture," 201.

32. G.E. Mills and D.W. Holdsworth, *The B.C. Mills Prefabricated System: The Emergence of Ready-Made Buildings in Western Canada*, (Ottawa: Parks Canada Occasional Papers in Archaeology and History, no. 14, 1975), 168, n. 10.

33. *The Bulletin, Greater Edmonton Number*, 25, 37.

34. *The Prairie Illustrated*, April 18, 1891; *Calgary Herald*, July 4, 1910.

35. Price List, Edmonton Paint and Glass, 1916 and Price List, Edmonton Metal Works Ltd., 1915, Chown Hardware Co. Papers, 68.295/8/15a, PAA; *The Saturday News*, April 21, 1906; *The Farm and Ranch Review*, April 1907, and October 5, 1910.

36. *Calgary Herald,* February 22, 1908.

37. *The Westerner,* July 12, 1921.

38. *Calgary Herald,* February 22, 1908.

39. Doucet and Weaver, "Material Culture and the North American House," 578.

40. *The Labour Gazette,* April 1903, 757; *Calgary Herald,* March 5, 1903; *The Farm and Ranch Review,* May 1907.

41. Wood to Sinclair, October 4, 1907, Department of the Attorney General Papers, 66.166/783, PAA.

42. *The Saturday News,* May 4, 1907.

43. Lumber Combine, File 783, *passim,* 66.166, PAA.

44. *Calgary Herald,* July 31, 1908.

45. John Leaning, "Our Construction Heritage" (Extract from *Our Architectural Ancestry* (1983): 96 (CMHC Library)

46. Clayton, "Canadian Housing in Wood," p. 3.38.3–3.38.44.

47. Paul Sprauge, "The Origin of Balloon Framing," *Journal of the Society of Architectural Historians* 40 (1981): 311–19.

48. *Edmonton Bulletin,* June 5, 1886.

49. Ritchie, *Canada Builds,* 171.

50. "The Platform Method of Framing," *Habitat* 18 (1975):18–19.

51. David K. Butterfield and Edward M. Ledohowski, *Architectural Heritage: The Brandon and Area Planning District* (Winnipeg: Manitoba Culture, Heritage and Recreation, Historic Resources Branch, 1985), 25–30.

52. Mills and Holdsworth, *The B.C. Mills,* 130–32; M. Darnell, "Innovations in American Prefabricated Houses: 1860–1890," *Journal of the Society of Architectural Historians* 31 (1972): 51–55.

53. Mills and Holdsworth, *The B.C. Mills,* 129, 135, 140.

54. Thelma Dennis, *Albertans Built: Aspects of Houses in Rural Alberta to 1920* (Edmonton: University of Alberta Printing Services, 1986), 68.

55. Mills and Holdsworth, *The B.C. Mills,* 132.

56. *Choosing Your Home* (Vancouver: Cut to Fit Building Company/Fabricated Building Company, n.d. (ca. 1918), (catalogue) (GAI Library).

57. D. Schwartz, "Sears Sold Everything Else, So Why Not Houses?," *Smithsonian,* November 1985, 93, 98; Gowans, *The Comfortable House,* 48–50.

58. *Farm and Ranch Review,* October 5, 1910; *Calgary Herald,* August 19, 1911.

59. *Calgary Herald,* July 25, 1911, and August 12, 1911.

60. Clayton, "Canadian Housing in Wood," p. 3.38.2.

61. Roe, "The Old Log House," 1. For a description of such a house in 1918 in Kitscoty see F. Luczynski to Dominion Agencies, January 24, 1918, Dominion Agencies Ltd. Papers, 74.208, PAA.

62. Orr to Barker, December 27, 1895, M928, Vol. 4, no. 629, GAI; *Calgary Herald,* December 10, 1890.

63. *Calgary Herald,* October 18, and May 17, 1919.

64. *Canadian Architect and Builder* 12 (1899): 143.

65. *Canadian Architect and Builder* 7 (1894): 152; *Calgary Herald,* November 17, 1948.

66. A.E. Cox, Estimate, March 18, 1887, M2815, Sheet 2, GAI; "Notes Made During Survey," November 3, 1888, Goddard Papers, M421, GAI; *Farm and Ranch Review*, June 5, 1913.

6 HOUSING CONDITIONS, 1919–1945

1. Owram, *The Economic Development of Western Canada*, 19–31.

2. *Western Municipal News*, February, 1922. On the role of the home, see *Calgary Herald*, April 12, 1919, and April 11, 1931; *Edmonton Journal*, March 15, and April 5, 1919.

3. "Observations re Edmonton Zoning" August 29, 1929, Alberta Association of Architects Papers, 187A/84.08, CAA.

4. *Calgary Herald*, December 4, 1920.

5. *Census of Canada, 1921*, Vol. III, Table 9, p. 26; *Alberta Statistical Review 75th Anniversary*, Table 22, 13. In 1921, there were 136,125 dwellings in the province of which 132,575 were single detached houses; in 1931 this number had grown to 159,838 out of a total of 170,069 dwellings; and by 1941, 175,457 of a total of 193,456 dwellings in the province were single detached houses. The 1921 and 1931 statistics are not strictly comparable. See Note regarding use of Census of Canada statistics. The 1941 figures are likely the most accurate, because the definitions of apartments had become more precise.

6. *Alberta Statistical Review 75th Anniversary*, Table 21, 12. For 1921 national figures, see *Edmonton Journal*, May 20, 1922.

7. *Calgary Herald*, May 8, 1920, August 2, 1924, and March 28, 1925.

8. *Contract Record and Engineering Review*, October 30, 1918.

9. John McDonald, "Soldier Settlement and Depression Settlement in the Forest Fringe of Saskatchewan," *Prairie Forum* 6 (1981): 37–40.

10. *Eaton's Farm Buildings and Equipment* (1919), Soldier land settlement scheme catalogue, 66.184, PAA; *Farm and Ranch Review*, April 21, 1919.

11. Saywell, *Housing Canadians*, 157.

12. Report of the Committee of the Privy Council, February 20, 1919 (P.C. 374), 192.4/298, Saskatchewan Archives, Regina.

13. Ibid.

14. See for example *Calgary Herald*, June 7, and June 14, 1919, June 4, 1921; *Engineering and Contract Record* 33 (1919): 308–11.

15. *Social Welfare*, June 1, 1919.

16. *Conservation of Life*, January 1919, 1.

17. Hulchanski, *The Origin of Urban Land Use Planning*, 23.

18. *Calgary Herald*, March 2, 1919; *Edmonton Journal*, February 2, 1919.

19. *Calgary Herald*, January 8, 1920; *The Labour Gazette*, April 1919, 446.

20. On demands for lower labour costs, see *Western Canada Contractor*, 18 (1921): 14; *Calgary Herald*, June 25, 1921; *Edmonton Journal*, March 19, 1919.

21. *Calgary Herald*, May 24, 1919.

22. Ibid., December 7, 1918.

23. Ibid., January 6, 1919.

24. Ibid., January 13, 1919, January 17, and January 27, 1920. On one call for Alberta's participation, see *Edmonton Journal*, March 20, 1920.

25. *Calgary Herald*, July 5, 1919, January 12, and January 27, 1920; Minutes of Meeting re: Housing Scheme, January 20, 1922, City of Calgary Papers, BE33 C151P/1073, GAI.

26. *Town Planning and Conservation of Life*, 6 (1920): 25–27; Grauer, *Housing*, 36.

27. *Edmonton Journal*, July 9, 1921.

28. Saywell, *Housing Canadians*, 157; *National Municipal Review* 8 (1919): 354–59.

29. John Bacher, "Canadian Housing 'Policy' in Perspective," *Urban History Review* 15 (1986): 5.

30. *The Labour Gazette*, December 1934, 1102–3.

31. National Construction Council to Mayor, February 1, 1935, BE33 C151P/2055, GAI. Overall, rural people too seem to have accepted such principles. A contrary opinion came from a University of Alberta student who contended that housing reformers did not recognize that farm houses were "homes," regardless of their amenities, and urban people had no right to tell farmers about a proper lifestyle. These sentiments may have been those of a homesick student; farm organizations tirelessly told farmers that they should adopt modern conveniences and designs (*Farm and Ranch Review*, September 6, 1920).

32. *Calgary Herald*, September 28, 1918.

33. *Census of Canada, 1921*, Vol. III, Table 12, p. 40. There is no means of distinguishing apartments from houses in the census figures, but given the preponderance of single-family dwellings in Alberta, this should not invalidate the general figures on the size of houses.

34. *The Case for Alberta: Part I: Alberta's Problems and Dominion Provincial Relations* (Edmonton: King's Printer, 1938), 324–29; *Census of Canada, 1931*, Vol. 5, Table 65, p. 1030. A household was defined as a group of persons living together in a dwelling whether or not related by ties of kinship. Thus, it could include a lodger (Greenway, "Housing in Canada," 414).

35. *Census of Canada, 1931*, Vol. 5, Table 65, p. 1028. The analysis of households with families of two or more persons filters out one person families and gauges social conditions more precisely.

36. Letter to Miller, February 6, 1936, BE33 C151P/2055, GAI; *Census of Canada, 1931*, Vol. 5, Table 56, p. 978.

37. *Edmonton Journal*, April 3, 1919.

38. Ross to Greenfield, March 5, 1925, PP, File 302, PAA.

39. Correspondence, Edmonton Building Bylaws, 187A/184.08, File CO21C47, CAA; "Observations re Edmonton Zoning," September 16, 1929, 187A/84.08, File CO 29T684, CAA.

40. "Town Planning Progress in Alberta up to December 1931," [March 26, 1932], PP, File 247, PAA.

41. Wilson to Mayor, November 12, 1929, BE33 C151P/1684, GAI.

42. Alberta, *Annual Report of the Department of Public Health*, 1939,

18; Town of Beverly to M.D. of Tomahawk, June 30, 1932, M.D. of Tomahawk Papers, M966, File 36, GAI.

43. *Journal of the Town Planning Institute*, February 1930, 3–6. Hulchanski, *The Origin of Urban Land Use Planning*, 33–36.

44. See Wah May W. Chan, "The Impact of the Technical Planning Board on the Morphology of Edmonton" (M.A. thesis, University of Alberta, 1969), 3–7.

45. Jones, "The Historical Geography of Edmonton, Alberta," 117; H.L. Macleod, "Property, Investors and Taxes: A Study of Calgary Real Estate Investments, Municipal Finance and Property Tax Arrears, 1911–1919" (M.A. thesis, University of Calgary, 1977), 143.

46. Foran, "The Civic Corporation and Urban Growth," 299; *Edmonton Journal*, May 10, 1930.

47. *Western Municipal News*, July 1922, 187; *Canadian Engineer*, 48(1925): 475; Seymour to Young, May 6, 1931, Department of Municipal Affairs Papers, 71.4, PAA.

48. Bettison, Kenward, and Taylor, *Urban Affairs in Alberta*, 58; Hulchanski, *The Origin of Urban Land Use Planning*, 38–42; *Journal of the Town Planning Institute*, 1927, 206. In 1927, Edmonton hired landscape architects Morell and Nichols to prepare a city plan. It was never implemented.

49. Alberta, *Regulations in Regard to Subdivision of Land*, June 1, 1929; Hulchanski, *The Origin of Urban Land Use Planning*, 38–39.

50. Hulchanski, *The Origin of Urban Land Use Planning*, 42; Chan, "The Impact of the Technical Planning Board," 3.

51. Ferris to Wilson, November 9, 1951 (attachments), Department of Economic Affairs Papers, 68.328/287, PAA.

52. See for example *Journal of the Town Planning Institute*, January 1923, 9–16.

53. "Information Relative to Farmstead Planning" (Typescript) n.d. (ca. 1930), and Seymour to English, May 29, 1931, Department of Municipal Affairs Papers, 78.133/406, PAA.

54. *The UFA*, April 15, 1929.

55. David Breen, ed., *William Stewart Herron: Father of the Petroleum Industry in Alberta* (Calgary: Historical Society of Alberta, Alberta Records Publication Board, 1984), xxviii–xxxv.

56. "Annual Report of the Town and Rural Planning Advisory Board for 1929" (typescript), Legislative Assembly Papers, 70.414/1009, PAA.

57. On provisions for regional planning before 1929 in Alberta, see Bettison, Kenward, and Taylor, *Urban Affairs in Alberta*, 21, 51.

58. "General Report" (Town Planning), April 18, 1931, Department of Municipal Affairs Papers, 70.413/199, PAA.

59. A.A. den Otter, "A Social History of the Alberta Coal Branch" (M.A. thesis, University of Alberta, 1967), 115–17, 172–73; David Lake, "The Historical Geography of the Coal Branch" (M.A. thesis, University of Alberta, 1967), 42–47.

60. *Report of the Alberta Coal Commission 1925* (Edmonton: King's Printer, 1926), 260–61.

61. Ibid., 260–63.

62. *Report of the Royal Commission Respecting the Coal Industry of the Province of Alberta 1935* (Edmonton: King's Printer, 1936), 57–58.

63. *Coleman Journal*, June 23, 1939.

64. Friesen, *The Canadian Prairies: A History*, 296–300.

65. "Reports, Evidence Etc. re: The Report of the Royal Commission on the Conditions of the Halfbreed Population of the Province of Alberta, 1935–1936," p. 488 (typescript), 70.340, PAA.

66. Ibid., 635, 660, 684.

67. See for example ibid., testimony of Donald McLeod, MLA and Frank Falkener, MLA, 417–28.

68. David Williamson, "Valleyfield's First Settlers," *Alberta History* 30 (1982): 33–34.

69. Nix to Aberhart, August 3, 1936, PP, File 1187, PAA.

70. Strange, *With the West in Her Eyes*, 111.

71. Parlby, *The Family Farm in Alberta*, 6–7.

72. "Report on Sylvan Lake District, Alberta. A Guide for Intending Settlers," 88–193 (typescript, Department of the Interior, 1924), Dominion Land Survey Papers, 68.321/3, PAA.

73. B.H. Kristjanson and C.C. Spence, *Land Settlement in North-eastern Alberta, 1943* (Ottawa: Dominion Department of Agriculture in Cooperation with the Department of Political Economy, University of Alberta, 1947, Technical Bulletin 63), 39–40.

74. L.G. Thomas, "Okotoks: From Trading Post to Suburb," *Urban History Review* 8 (1970): 13–14; *Edmonton Journal*, April 26, 1930.

75. *Drumheller Review*, November 26, 1920; *Cardston News*, September 17, 1937; *Peace River Record*, June 19, 1936.

76. *Cardston News*, February 18, 1936.

77. Correspondence, Edmonton Health Department, April 1927, Edmonton City Commissioner's Papers, RG11/1/1, CEA.

78. *Prices in Canada and Other Countries, 1938* (Ottawa: Canada Department of Labour, 1938), 4.

79. City Commissioner to Pardee, June 3, 1929, RG11/2/4, CEA. These figures are confirmed through advertisements and listings of McCallum Agencies Ltd., Edmonton (See J.S. McCallum Papers, MS 14, Files 99–101 (1927–30) CEA).

80. Stenographer's Notebook, n.d.[1930], wage chart, 1919–1929, International Brotherhood of Electrical Workers, Local 348 Papers, BLI61B, GAI; "Building Trades, Edmonton, Salaries" (1930–68), Edmonton Building Trades Papers, 67.54, PAA; United Brotherhood of Carpenters and Joiners to Reid, April, 1934, PP, File 927A, PAA.

81. The Canadian Department of Labour used 18.5 percent as the appropriate percentage of income for shelter in 1938 (*Prices in Canada and Other Countries, 1938*, 4); *Edmonton Journal*, May 3, 1930.

82. *Census of Canada, 1931*, Vol. 5, Table 23, p. 60.

83. *The Case for Alberta*, 326.

84. Dunn to Mayor, August 8, 1929, BE33 C151P, File 1458, GAI.

85. Saywell, *Housing Canadians*, 171; Marshall to Aberhart, March 24, 1938, PP, File 1187, PAA. For construction figures giving type of construction, see *The Case for Alberta*, 336.

86. *Edmonton Journal*, August 24, 1937; R. Macdonald, "Progress in Housing and Health," *Canadian Public Health Journal* 29 (1938): 381. A substantial increase in the conversions of single-family dwellings to flats took place during the 1930s in Edmonton. (McCann, "Changing Morphology of Residential Areas," 28.)

87. Hill to Mayor, April 24, 1936, BE33 C151P, File 2055, GAI.

88. Ibid.

89. *RAIC Journal*, June 1940, 107; *Calgary Herald*, March 5, and March 8, 1940.

90. Interview with Robert A. Lott, September 5, 1978, Charles Ursenbach Papers, M4211, GAI.

91. *Claresholm Local Press*, January 16, 1941.

92. *RAIC Journal*, June 1941, 108.

93. Ibid., July 1943, 15; Letter 158, February 15, 1943, and Letter 201, August 1944, Watt Papers, BPSC.

94. Jill Wade, "Wartime Housing Ltd. 1941–1947: Canadian Housing Policy at the Crossroads," *Urban History Review* 15 (1986): 44.

95. *Alberta Facts and Figures* (Edmonton: Alberta, Bureau of Statistics, 1950) 365; Reports and correspondence, 1942/43, RG11/3/5, CEA.

96. Letter 201, August, 1944, Watt Letters, BPSC; *RAIC Journal*, July 1943, 115.

97. See for example, correspondence, PP, File 921B, PAA.

98. City Commissioners to Bylaws Committee, June 19, 1941, RG11/35/2, CEA.

99. See for example, *Claresholm Local Press*, December 24, 1942, September 16, 1943, and February 24, 1944.

7 GOVERNMENT HOUSING PROGRAMMES

1. Hulchanski, "The 1935 Dominion Housing Act," 22–23. For European models and Canadian housing reformers, see for examples, *Social Welfare*, May 1929, 169–71; *Journal of the Town Planning Institute*, December 1929, 115.

2. *The Labour Gazette*, May 1935, 412–13.

3. D.J. Matthews and L.B. Smith, *Report on Canada Mortgage and Housing Corporation* (Ottawa: Task Force on Central Mortgage and Housing Corporation, 1979), 5; Hulchanski, "The 1935 Dominion Housing Act," 26–27.

4. Hulchanski, "The 1935 Dominion Housing Act," 32–35.

5. Grauer, *Housing*, 43–44b, 60–60a.

6. Ibid. The NHA also provided for loans for repair of existing houses. This provision was not implemented until 1954.

7. Bacher, "Canadian Housing 'Policy' in Perspective," 5.

8. *The Labour Gazette*, September 1944, 1175, and December 1945, 1769–70.

9. Grauer, *Housing*, 42–43. The HIP was not part of the NHA. It was authorized by *The Home Improvement Loans Guarantee Act* (1937). A good study of its social context and provisions is Margaret Hobbs and Ruth Roach Pierson, "'A Kitchen That Wastes No Steps. . . .' Gender, Class and the

Home Improvement Plan, 1936–1940," *Histoire sociale/Social History* 21 (1988): 9–37. See also David G. Bettison, *The Politics of Canadian Development* (Edmonton: University of Alberta Press, 1975), 65.

10. *Edmonton Bulletin*, November 24, and December 11, 1936; *RAIC Journal*, March 1940, 48; *An Act to Exempt from Assessment Certain Improvements on Land*, Statutes of Alberta, 1937, c. 53.

11. City Commissioners Report, October 31, 1940, RG11/3/4, CEA.

12. *Canadian Engineer*, June 22, 1937, 13.

13. Maynard to Ilsley, March 8, 1945, Legislative Assembly Papers, 70.414/2204, PAA.

14. *An Act for the Security of Homeowners*, Statutes of Alberta, 1938, c. 29.

15. Copy of Petition of the Edmonton Chamber of Commerce For the Disallowance of Certain Acts. . . . May 11, 1938, and Lapointe to Governor General in Council, June 13, 1938; P.C. 1368, June 15, 1938, (copies), PP, File 1203, PAA.

16. Premier's copy of letter to Kroehmal, January 16, 1957, PP, File 2060, PAA.

17. *RAIC Journal*, April 1939, 91; Correspondence Re: Charter Amendments, Edmonton City Secretary's Papers, RG8/22/17, and RG11/22/21, CEA.

18. Graves to Housing Committee, October 15, 1929, BE33 C151P/1458; Brockington to Davison, July 19, 1929, BE33 C581E/35, GAI.

19. Foran, "The Civic Corporation and Urban Growth," 348–52, 352 n.4.

20. Correspondence re: housing scheme, 1938, RG11/22/17, CEA; *RAIC Journal*, October 1938, 234.

21. Correspondence re: Sunset Cottages, 1937, RG11/53/2–3, CEA; R.T. Williams, "The Story of Edmonton's Sunset Cottages 1937–1954" (Pamphlet); Deputy Minister to Reeves, October 2, 1944, 78.133/120C/22, Department of Municipal Affairs Papers, PAA.

22. *Edmonton Journal*, March 9, 1937; *RAIC Journal*, April, 1941, 74.

23. "Brief. . . . by Edmonton Builders Exchange, January 30, 1936," PP, File 908, PAA; *Coleman Journal*, November 17, 1938. For further examples, see correspondence, 1935–1939, PP, File 1187, PAA.

24. *RAIC Journal*, June 1941, 108.

25. *Calgary Herald*, March 5–March 12, 1940.

26. Aberhart to Urchack, June 8, 1941, Aberhart to Campbell, September 27, 1941, "Loans for Housing Purposes," June 24, 1942 (briefing note), PP, File 1187, PAA.

27. *Edmonton Bulletin*, December 5, 1944.

28. Maynard to Ilsley, February 21, 1945, 70.414/2204, PAA. In fact, Alberta had passed similar legislation in 1936 in respect to the DHA but it had not satisfied the lending institutions (Bettison, Kenward, and Taylor, *Urban Affairs in Alberta*, 76; Aberhart to Brown, June 2, 1936, PP, File 1187, PAA).

29. Wilson to Aberhart, September 23, 1935, and Aberhart to Wilson, September 25, 1935, PP, File 1187, PAA.

30. Carrigan to Wood, n.d.(1945), 68.328/100, PAA; *Invest in Home Security* (Edmonton Co-operative Building Association, 1947), 68.328/137, PAA; *How Can I Build a Home?* (Calgary Pioneer Co-operative Building Association, 1955), PP, File 1753, PAA; King to Orr, July 5, 1942, PP, File 1187, PAA.

31. Alberta, *Report of the Royal Commission on the Metropolitan Development of Calgary and Edmonton* (Edmonton, 1956), 24.

32. "Report of Hearings, Taxpayers Protective Association of Edmonton, Submission. . . ."(typescript) (Royal Commission on Dominion Provincial Relations, February 1938), 1–4.

33. Ibid., Testimony of A. Davison, 6147; *Edmonton Journal*, December 17, 1932.

34. Aberhart to MacDonald, September 14, 1942, PP, File 915, PAA.

8 MEANINGS OF MODERNITY: HOUSE DESIGN AND SERVICING

1. Cecil Burgess, "The Home,"(Radio Talk) (1930), Burgess Papers, File 72–28–22, UAA.

2. President's Report, 1924/25, Edmonton Home Economics Association Papers, 69.272/15, PAA; "Report on Homemaking," May 13, 1933, 69.272/17, PAA.

3. Cecil Burgess, "Hygiene in Architecture" (1920), File 72.28.8, UAA.

4. Catherine Bauer Wurster, "The Social Front of Modern Architecture in the 1930s," *Journal of the Society of Architectural Historians* 24 (1965): 48; Richard Pommer, "The Architecture of Urban Housing in the United States During the Early 1930s," ibid., 37 (1978): 263.

5. Cecil Burgess, "Recent Domestic Architecture" (Radio Talk), November 2, 1932, File 72–28–29, UAA.

6. *Calgary Herald*, April 11, 1931. The debate over modernism in Canada seems not to have been as bitter as it was in England (see Anthony Jackson, "The Politics of English Architecture: 1929–1951," *Journal of the Society of Architectural Historians*, 24 (1965): 97–107). Indeed, in Canada, for much of the interwar period modernism was simply ignored by the architectural profession (Alexander F. Gross, "Witness to the Passing of Victorian Architecture, The RAIC Journal, 1924–1938," *Society for the Study of Architecture in Canada, Bulletin* 12 (1989): 9–15).

7. Burgess, "Recent Domestic Architecture."

8. *Calgary Herald*, May 28, 1921; Critchley to Dempsey, June 24, 1965, transmittal letter with documents, M1505, GAI.

9. Minutes, Meeting of the Council of the Alberta Association of Architects, November 1, 1928, 187A/84–08, File CO.28C62, CAA; *Calgary Herald*, September 11, 1926.

10. Burgess, "Recent Domestic Architecture."

11. Burgess, "The Home."

12. Cecil Burgess, "Lecture at Edmonton Museum of Art," November 1934, File 72–28–38, UAA.

13. *Alberta's Natural Resources and Industries*, pp. 12–14 (Edmonton: King's Printer, 1941), Alberta Department of Trade and Industry Papers,

76.33/3, PAA; *Calgary Herald*, September 20, 1924; *RAIC Journal*, September 1935, 144, 149; *Calgary Albertan*, May 13, 1938; *Edmonton Journal*, March 23, 1929; Doherty, *Residential Construction Practices in Alberta, 1900–1971*, 40–1; Burgess, "Recent Domestic Architecture."

14. Northwestern Utilities to Griesbach, February 9, 1924, Griesbach Papers, MS 209, File 248, CEA; *Edmonton Journal*, September 19, 1925; *Calgary Herald*, September 28, 1929; Correspondence Re: Highwood Sarcee Oils Ltd. 1940, PP, File 693B, PAA.

15. *RAIC Journal*, January–February 1925, 34–37.

16. *Calgary Herald*, April 11, 1931.

17. Ibid., May 11, 1929, and May 30, 1925.

18. *Calgary Albertan*, May 13, 1938.

19. From 1916 to 1940 only 2,500 Delco light plants, the commonest type in the province, were sold in Alberta (BB.1 D345 File 2, Delco Light Papers, GAI).

20. *Calgary Herald*, May 26, 1928.

21. *Claresholm Review Advertiser*, December 27, 1918 (advertisement).

22. Burgess, "Hygiene in Architecture."

23. *Calgary Herald*, April 1, 1922. The series was sanctioned by the Alberta Association of Architects as a means of educating the public about the need for architect-drawn house plans (Minutes, Calgary Chapter of the Alberta Association of Architects, January 4, 1921, 187A/84–08, 3a/76.01, Ch. 1.1, CAA).

24. A concise guide to contemporary Canadian design ideas is Helen MacMurchy, *How to Build the Canadian House* (Ottawa: Department of Health, The Little Blue Book Home Series, King's Printer, 1927).

25. *Edmonton Journal*, May 10, 1924.

26. See for example, Burgess, "The Home." On concerns about the growth of public entertainment and society, see Donald G. Wetherell with Irene Kmet, *Useful Pleasures: The Shaping of Leisure in Alberta, 1896–1945* (Regina: Alberta Culture and Multiculturalism and Canadian Plains Research Center, 1990), 43–44, 66–69.

27. *Calgary Herald*, June 4, 1927, and April 26, 1930.

28. MacMurchy, *How to Build the Canadian House*, 7.

29. *RAIC Journal*, July 1935, 116–20.

30. "Report on Homemaking," May 13, 1933, 69.272/17, PAA.

31. *Calgary Herald*, June 4, 1927.

32. Burgess, "Recent Domestic Architecture," *Calgary Herald*, April 11, 1931.

33. *Farm and Ranch Review*, October 1, 1929; Strange, *With the West in her Eyes*, 50.

34. *Calgary Herald*, August 14, 1920.

35. Burchard and Bush Brown, *The Architecture of America*, 361.

36. *Canadian Engineer*, May 22, 1928, 557.

37. *Edmonton Journal*, June 12, 1926.

38. John Lehr, "Changing Ukrainian House Styles," *Alberta History*, Winter, 1975, 28–29; Lehr, "The Landscape of Ukrainian Settlement in the Canadian West," 101–3. A case study of the renovations to a traditional

Ukrainian dwelling is in Demjan Hohol, *The Grekul House: A Land Use and Structural History* (Edmonton: Historic Sites Service, Occasional Paper No. 14, 1985), 124–38.

39. McCann, "Changing Morphology of Residential Areas," 23.

40. Underwood to Markus, June 12, 1928, 187A/84–08, File CO28C62, CAA.

41. See for examples, *Calgary Herald,* April 26, and June 14, 1919.

42. *Edmonton Journal,* March 10, 1923; *Calgary Herald,* April 10, 1920.

43. *RAIC Journal,* February 1935, 32.

44. *Edmonton Journal,* April 17, 1926; "A Home of Your Own" (Calgary: Eau Claire and Bow River Lumber Co., n.d., ca. 1926, plan catalogue), GAI Library.

45. *Edmonton Journal,* March 1927, various articles.

46. Ibid., March 1928, various articles.

47. *Farm and Ranch Review,* March 5, 1918, and April 21, 1919.

48. *Calgary Herald,* August 14, 1920.

49. Warkentin, "Time and Place in the Western Interior," 21; also see for example, *Edmonton Journal,* April 5, 1930.

50. See Holdsworth, "Regional Distinctiveness in an Industrial Age," 72; *Early Domestic Architecture in Regina: Presentation Drawings and Plans* (Regina: Norman Mackenzie Art Gallery, 1982), 38–39.

51. Gowans, *The Comfortable House,* 105–20, 164–65, 182–90.

52. *Edmonton Journal,* March 22, 1930.

53. Peggy O'Connor Farnell, *Old Glenora* (Edmonton: Old Glenora Historical Society, 1984), 47.

54. *Edmonton Journal,* May 31, 1930.

55. Ibid., May 10, 1930.

56. For examples, see the designs awarded prizes in the 1938 Dominion Housing Competition sponsored under the DHA (*RAIC Journal,* April 1938, 81ff).

57. See Earnest A. Connally, "The Cape Cod House: An Introductory Study," *Journal of the Society of Architectural Historians* 19 (1960): 47–56.

58. One source for modernization concepts is articles and advertisements run by lumber companies. The Western Lumber Association produced a booklet, *Modernize with Lumber,* that was distributed free of charge on the prairies (copy in Red Deer District Archives). See also Hobbs and Pierson, "A Kitchen That Wastes No Steps," 21–23.

59. See for example, *The UFA,* October 15, 1928; *Edmonton Journal,* May 6, 1926, and April 12, 1930; *Calgary Herald,* November 21, 1925; Lionel F. Scott, *Fixing Up the House: A Guide to Practical Interior Decoration* (Toronto: Oxford University Press, Canadian Branch, 1933).

60. *Edmonton Journal,* April 5, 1930.

9 POSTWAR PROGRAMMES AND APPROACHES

1. *Alberta Statistical Review, 75th Anniversary,* Table 5, p. 6.
2. Owram, *The Economic Development of Western Canada,* 40–44.

3. *Alberta Statistical Review, 75th Anniversary*, Table 25, p. 14.

4. Lutes to Manning, January 30, 1945, PP, File 1187, PAA.

5. Litchfield to Robertson, February 5, 1945 (copy), PP, File 1866, PAA.

6. Hooke to Manning, September 27, 1945, PP, File 915, PAA.

7. Women's magazines are a good index of these hopes. See for example, house plans and articles in *The Canadian Home Journal*, 1941–1944. For *Canadian Homes and Gardens*, see Christina Cameron, *Index of Houses Featured in Canadian Homes and Gardens from 1925 to 1944* (Ottawa: Parks Canada, 1980).

8. "Post War Reconstruction Commission, Post War Survey" n.d. (1945), Department of Economic Affairs Papers, 68.328/179, PAA.

9. Roland Ward, "Country Residential Development in the Edmonton Area to 1973: A Case Study of Exurban Growth" (M.A. thesis, University of Alberta, 1977), 59.

10. Alberta Bureau of Statistics, *Alberta Facts and Figures* (Edmonton: 1950), 365; *Coleman Journal*, September 26, 1946.

11. Byrne to Hooke, February 5, 1946, PP, File 1403, PAA.

12. McClaskey to Manning, September 30, 1946, PP, File 1403, PAA.

13. Order in Council 1102/45 [Dawson Creek Huts], June 30, 1945; Manning to Ward, July 12, 1945, PP, File 1187, PAA; Clash to Manning, March 29, 1945, PP, File 915, PAA.

14. "Marketing Services Ltd." (typescript, n.d.), summary sheets, PP, File 1752A, PAA.

15. *Calgary Herald*, December 3, 1945; Fire Commissioners Office Special Inspection Report, December 3, 1947 (and clippings), Department of the Provincial Secretary Papers, 67.4/79C, PAA; Butterfield to Nance, February 25, 1948, Department of Social Services and Community Health Papers, 84.274/36, PAA.

16. Letter no. 235, November 20, 1945, Watt Papers, BPSC.

17. Hooke to Manning, January 27, 1950, Department of Agriculture Papers, 72.302/12/557, PAA.

18. McClaskey to Manning, September 30, 1946, PP, File 1403, PAA.

19. *RAIC Journal*, October 1948, 393.

20. *Housing in Canada 1946–1970. A Supplement to the 25th Annual Report of CMHC* (Ottawa: Central Mortgage and Housing Corporation, 1970), 6; *Report of the Federal Task Force on Housing and Urban Development* (Ottawa: 1969), 5.

21. *Housing and Urban Growth: Draft for Discussion. Paper no. 11* (Edmonton Regional Planning Commission, Edmonton Regional Growth Studies, 1976), 27.

22. R.G. Lillie, "Twenty Years of Housing: CMHC 1946–1968," *Habitat* 11, no. 1 (1968):12, and 11, no. 2 (1968): 13; J. V. Poapst, *Developing the Residential Mortgage Market* (Report for CMHC, 1973), Vol. 1, 2–3.

23. *Report of the Royal Commission on the Metropolitan Development of Calgary and Edmonton*, Chap. 4, 21.

24. Springer to Manning, May 24, 1968, Department of Municipal Affairs Papers, 75.530/22, PAA.

25. Barbara Wake Carroll, "Post War Trends in Canadian Housing Policy," *Urban History Review* 18 (1989): 64.

26. Albert Rose, *Canadian Housing Policies* (Toronto: Conference on Housing, University of Toronto, Background Paper no. 2, June, 1968), 36–37.

27. *Submission by Calgary House Builders Association to the Gordon Royal Commission on Canada's Economic Progress* (1955), 6, Craig Papers, M7478, GAI.

28. Cohos to Gerhart, January 29, 1968, 75.530/22, PAA.

29. Donald Harasym, "The Planning of New Residential Areas in Calgary, 1944–73" (M.A. thesis, University of Alberta, 1975), 101–2. Calgary had been considering this policy since 1947 (*Calgary Herald*, April 11, 1947).

30. *Submission by Calgary House Builders to Gordon Royal Commission*, November 25, 1955, 4, M7478, GAI.

31. Campbell to Manning, February 5, 1957, PP, File 2107, PAA.

31. Litchfield to Clark, May 25, 1944 (copy), PP, File 1866, PAA.

33. Bacher, "Canadian Housing 'Policy' in Perspective," 10.

34. *RAIC Journal*, July 1946, 175.

35. Manning to Clark, January 15, 1940, PP, File 1485, PAA.

36. Manning to Winters, September 30, 1949, PP, File 1866, PAA.

37. *Report of Royal Commission on Metropolitan Development of Calgary and Edmonton*, Chap. 4, 21–24; *The Labour Gazette*, 52 (1952): 1091. The other provinces which required local governments to pay the full 25 percent were Manitoba and Nova Scotia. For a different interpretation on Alberta's approach, see Bettison, Kenward, and Taylor, *Urban Affairs in Alberta*, 105.

38. D.J. Matthews and L.B. Smith, *Report on Canada Mortgage and Housing Corporation*, (Ottawa: Task Force on Canada Mortgage and Housing Corporation, 1979), 9.

39. Advisory Committee on Reconstruction, n.d. (1943), 68.328/168, PAA.

40. "Calgary: Churchill Park Scheme First in Alberta," *Urban Renewal and Public Housing in Canada* 2 (1966): 8.

41. Rose, *Canadian Housing Policies*, 34–35.

42. Bacher, "Canadian Housing 'Policy' in Perspective," 8.

43. *Report of Royal Commission on Metropolitan Development of Calgary and Edmonton*, Chap. 4, 21; "Housing in Calgary," 11, 13, (Social Planning Council of Calgary, 1968), Alberta Council on Child and Family Welfare papers, M6466, GAI.

44. *Alberta Statistical Review, 75th Anniversary*, Table 21, 12.

45. See for example, correspondence, PP, File 1756A, PAA.

46. Darroch to Manning, December 8, 1949, ibid.

47. See correspondence in PP, Files 1160, 1756A, and 1866, PAA.

48. "Report of Discussion Regarding. . . . Alberta's Housing Problem," (1950), 72.302/12/557, PAA.

49. *Alberta Rental Control Board, Annual Report, 1952*, 2, Department of Economic Affairs Papers, 68.328/199, PAA.

50. "[Report on] Wainwright," n.d. (1951), 68.328/197, PAA.

51. "Condensed Report, 1953," Alberta Rental Control Board, 68.328/199, PAA.

52. *Alberta Rental Control Board, Annual Report, 1952*, 3, 68.328/199, PAA.

53. See for example, 68.328/191, Vol. 1(a) and 1(b), PAA.

54. Ferris to Scott, November 20, 1952, 68.328/191, Vol. 1(b), PAA.

55. Ferris to Barnes, January 26, 1952, 68.328/201 Vol. 1(c), PAA.

56. "Condensed Report 1953," Alberta Rental Control Board, 68.328/199, PAA.

57. See for examples, Barnes to Ferris, February 11, 1953, 68.328/201(c), PAA; Property Owners' Association to Cabinet, February 19, 1953, PP, File 1930, PAA.

58. "Planning Report for the Town of Brooks" (1952), 8, Department of Municipal Affairs Papers, 68.199, PAA.

59. *Report of the Royal Commission on the Metropolitan Development of Calgary and Edmonton*, Chap. 3, 1–31.

60. Ibid.

61. Ibid., Chap. 4, 10–28.

62. Rose, *Canadian Housing Policies*, 47; Matthews and Smith, *Report on Canada Mortgage and Housing Corporation*, 8.

63. Letter to authors from L. Mueller, Alberta Mortgage and Housing Corporation, April 15, 1986; *The Government of the Province of Alberta Submission to the Honourable Paul Hellyer, Minister of Transport and the Federal Task Force on Housing and Urban Development* (Alberta Housing and Urban Renewal Corporation, November 1968), 1–2.

64. Deputy Minister to Gerhart, May 30, 1968, 75.530/22, PAA.

65. Matthews and Smith, *Report on Canada Mortgage and Housing Corporation*, 9.

66. *Alberta's Housing Profile* (Edmonton: Alberta Housing and Urban Renewal Corporation, 1968), 5.

67. Deputy Minister to Gerhart, May 30, 1968, 75.530/22, PAA.

68. Speech by Gerhart, September 1967, 75.530/22, PAA. See also *Report on Housing* (Alberta Housing and Urban Renewal Corporation, 1967), 2.

69. "Peace River: First Public Housing in Alberta," *Urban Renewal and Public Housing in Canada* 2 (1966): 5–6; *Municipal Affairs*, 1, Department of Municipal Affairs Papers, 75.530, PAA.

70. *Report of the Royal Commission on Consumer Problems and Inflation: Prairie Provinces Cost Study Commission* (Provinces of Alberta, Saskatchewan, Manitoba, 1968), 231.

71. Jean Burnet, *Next Year Country* (Toronto: University of Toronto Press, 1951), 57.

72. Willem Janssen, "The Impact of Public Institutions on Rural Housing Investment in the Prairie Provinces" (M.A. thesis, University of Saskatchewan, 1964), 110.

73. *Report on Public Works* (Alberta Post War Reconstruction Committee, March 1945), 13.

74. "Sewer and Water Installations" (July 31, 1956), PP, File 2055A,

PAA; Ross to Hogge, February 23, 1959, PP, File 2070B, PAA.

75. Mallett to Hogge, May 22, 1962, Department of Public Health Papers, 70.21, PAA.

76. J. Munger, *Housing and Environmental Conditions in the Prairie Provinces with Particular Emphasis on the Effects of Urbanization on Rural Housing and Public Facilities* (Saskatoon: Canadian Centre for Community Studies, University of Saskatchewan, 1966), 70, 97.

77. Martin O'Connell, *Canadian Standards of Housing in Indian Reserve Communities* (n.p.: A memorandum for the Indian-Eskimo Association of Canada, May, 1965).

78. "Housing in Northern Communities" (1969), Department of Energy and Natural Resources Papers, 76.502, Box 8, PAA.

79. *Opportunity Housing: A Review and Evaluation of the Indian and Metis Housing Programme* (Edmonton: Alberta Opportunity Corporation, 1968), 4–6. See also Fred Hatt, *Appendix A: Metis of the Lac la Biche Area, Community Opportunity Assessment* (Edmonton: Human Resources Research and Development, Executive Council, 1967), 23–26.

80. Fimrite to Premier and Ministers, August 22, 1968, Department of Agriculture Papers, 72.302/54/2855, PAA.

81. *Final Report* (Edmonton: Alberta Post War Reconstruction Committee, 1945), 25.

82. "Resolution on Rural Electrification," January 1946, PP, File 1513, PAA; "The History of Rural Electrification in Alberta," (1952), and "Rural Electrification" n.d., Department of Utilities and Telecommunications Papers, 83.333/1, PAA.

83. *Census of Canada, 1951*, Table 36, p. 36–35.

84. "Rural Housing," February 10, 1948, Department of Municipal Affairs Papers, 78.133/75/578, PAA.

85. *Building Research in Canada*, June 30, 1955, 14; Prairie Rural Housing Committee, *Heating the Farm Home* (1950), and *Farm Houses* (1949).

86. *Census of Canada, 1961*, Table 35, p. 35–2, and Table 40, p. 40–42.

87. "Brief. . . . on Improvement of Rural Housing in Alberta," August 1966, Department of Public Works Papers, 79.387/10, PAA.

88. Burnet, *Next Year Country*, 21.

89. *Alberta's Housing Profile*, 13.

90. 3,635 loans under the act were made for new houses, and 4,762 for renovation of houses in Alberta. This was the highest percentage of loans in the prairies, but since there were 68,209 farm dwellings in 1961, only a small percentage of farmers were receiving loans. (Munger, *Housing and Environmental Conditions in the Prairie Provinces*, 67.)

91. Farmers Union of Alberta, "Farm Homes" (Radio Broadcast September 27, 1963), Farmers' Union of Alberta Papers, 77.151/2/20, PAA.

92. Putnam to McWilliams, August 12, 1959, 72.302/31/1764, PAA; Ballantyne to Ruste, February 25, 1969, 72.302/142/6481, PAA.

93. "Brief. . . . on Improvement of Rural Housing in Alberta," August, 1966, 79.387/10, PAA.

94. Correspondence: Sunset Cottages, Edmonton City Commissioner's Papers, RG11/53/3, CEA; clipping file, "Lions Club," CEA.

95. Circular Letter to Municipalities, April 15, 1954, PP, File 1780, PAA.

96. Manning to Weeks, May 1, 1958, PP, File 2127B, PAA. See also "Homes for the Aged, Alberta," (1960), Department of Public Welfare Papers, 68.308/3, PAA.

97. "Housing for Senior Citizens. . . . ," n.d. (ca. 1960), 3, 9–10, 68.308/3, PAA; J. Austin, "Alberta Houses its Senior Citizens," *Habitat*, 4 (1961):8–10; Alberta News Release, October 17, 1962, RG11/15/7, CEA.

98. Litchfield to Mansur, May 2, 1949 (copy), PP, File 1866, PAA.

10 REDESIGNING THE RESIDENTIAL LANDSCAPE

1. Noel Dant "A Brief History of the Planning Statutes of Alberta" (n.d.), pp. 4–6, Department of Municipal Affairs Papers, 70.393, PAA. A good study of the impact of the 1950 amendments is Chan, "The Impact of the Technical Planning Board," 13–17.

2. "Devon" clipping files, PAA; *RAIC Journal*, January 1949, 34; *Calgary Herald*, October 17, 1947.

3. "Economic Survey of Drayton Valley" (1959), PP, File 2055B, PAA.

4. "Skid Shack City," *The Star Weekly*, April 16, 1955.

5. "Drayton Valley" (clippings, 1953–57), clipping files, PAA; Makale, Holloway and Associates, *Town of Drayton Valley, Alberta: General Plan* (1967), 15, Department of Housing and Public Works Papers, 80.299, PAA.

6. Alberta, *Annual Report of the Department of Municipal Affairs, 1954*, xii. The area taken in by some of these planning commissions was large. In 1952 the Calgary District Planning Commission took in 2,300 square miles (*RAIC Journal*, February 1953, 37).

7. *Planning in Alberta: Proceeding of the Alberta Planning Conference, June 18, 19, 1954* (Edmonton: Community Planning Association of Canada, Alberta Branch, 1954), 22.

8. *Urban Residential Land Development* (Edmonton: Alberta Land Use Forum, Summary Report no. 4, 1974), 5; "Red Deer," *City Magazine* 2 (1976): 19–20.

9. H. Diemer, "Annexation and Amalgamation in the Territorial Expansion of Edmonton and Calgary" (M.A. thesis, University of Alberta, 1975), 55, 382–92. On the politics of annexation at Edmonton, see R. Hatfield, "The Metropolitan Development of Edmonton: The City, The Province, and the Strategy of Neglect" (M.A. thesis, University of Alberta, 1982), 88–91.

10. Letter to Cole, January 29, 1958, Department of Municipal Affairs Papers, 83.431/5/100/352, PAA.

11. *Report of the Royal Commission on the Metropolitan Development of Calgary and Edmonton*, Chap. 11, 7–11.

12. Ward, "Country Residential Development in the Edmonton Area," 59–72.

13. Harasym, "Planning New Residential Areas in Calgary," 10–23.

14. Interview with Noel Dant, April 3, 1979, Tape 3, CEA.

15. Harasym, "Planning New Residential Areas in Calgary," 59.

16. Robert Graden, "The Planning of New Residential Areas in Edmonton, 1950–1976" (M.A. thesis, University of Alberta, 1979), 42–44, and Harasym, "Planning New Residential Areas in Calgary," 157.

17. Graden, "Planning New Residential Areas in Edmonton," 36–37. In resurveying the Sherbrook subdivision in Edmonton, originally laid out on a gridiron, density was increased from 15.4 persons per acre to 24 persons per acre (ibid., 37).

18. *The Labour Gazette*, September 1944, 1175.

19. Graden, "Planning New Residential Areas in Edmonton," 11–12.

20. Harasym, "Planning New Residential Areas in Calgary," 153.

21. *RAIC Journal*, February 1947, 61–62.

22. "Royal Bank Letter," *RAIC Journal*, June 1945, 129.

23. Litchfield to Robertson, February 1945, (copy), PP, File 1866, PAA.

24. Graden, "Planning New Residential Areas in Edmonton," iv-vi, 49.

25. *Edmonton Journal*, January 12, 1961.

26. Graden, "Planning New Residential Areas in Edmonton," 4.

27. Quoted in Ibid., 87.

28. Ibid.

29. Harasym, "Planning New Residential Areas in Calgary," 201.

30. Graden, "Planning New Residential Areas in Edmonton," 93–94, 114–15.

11 POSTWAR HOUSING AND DESIGN

1. Warkentin, "Time and Place in the Western Interior," 21.

2. *Review of Housing in Canada* (Ottawa: Central Mortgage and Housing Corporation, 1958), VI-6.

3. Warkentin, "Time and Place in the Western Interior," 21. It should be recalled that this horizontal quality in ordinary housing had also been integral to bungalow design from the beginning of the century.

4. See articles in *RAIC Journal*, August 1950, and July 1954.

5. *Choosing a House Design* (Ottawa: Central Mortgage and Housing Corporation, 1957), 8.

6. Peter Blake, *The Master Builders* (New York: W.W. Norton and Co., 1976), 316.

7. Trevor Boddy, *Modern Architecture in Alberta* (Regina: Alberta Culture and Multiculturalism and Canadian Plains Research Center, 1987), 27–28.

8. Burchard and Bush-Brown, *The Architecture of America*, 465.

9. *Edmonton Journal*, May 25, 1966.

10. "A Report on Row Housing" (1953), RG11/15/90, CEA.

11. *Edmonton Journal*, December 15, 1960.

12. *Farm Homes* (Winnipeg: Prairie Rural Housing Committee, 1949), 4.

13. *Farm Notes*, August 22, 1952 (Alberta Department of Agriculture).

14. *RAIC Journal*, August 1947, 261–63.

15. *Farm and Ranch Review*, November 1946.

16. Susan Kent, "The Effects of Television Viewing: A Cross Cultural Perspective," *Current Anthropology* 26 (1985): 126.

17. See for example, *RAIC Journal*, August 1947, 261–63; *Farm Notes*, September 30, 1949.

18. *67 Homes for Canadians* (Ottawa: Central Mortgage and Housing Corporation, 1947), 76–77.

19. *Alberta's Economic Prospects* (Alberta Department of Economic Affairs, 1955), 19.

20. *Final Report* (Edmonton: Alberta Post War Reconstruction Committee, 1945), 287.

21. *Builders' Bulletin*, April 26, 1947 (Central Mortgage and Housing Corporation).

22. "Camrose Planning Report. . . . ," November 1955, Alberta Department of Municipal Affairs Papers, M1854, GAI.

23. McCann, "Changing Morphology of Residential Areas," 78.

24. *RAIC Journal*, August 1949, 231, 234–36. Maurice Clayton, formerly with CMHC, believes the primary influence on apartment design in Canada was Swedish design. Personal communication with authors.

25. *Edmonton Residential Land Use Staging, 1967–1971* (City of Edmonton, Research Report no. 5, 1964), 4.

26. *RAIC Journal*, February 1945, 37.

27. Jacqueline Hayter, "Residential Mobility and the Function of Selected High Rises in Central Edmonton" (M.A. thesis, University of Alberta, 1973), 48–63, 212. On the role of high rises in increasing residential space in the central area of Edmonton, see Michael Bannon, "The Evolution of the Central Area of Edmonton, Alberta, 1946–1966" (M.A. thesis, University of Alberta, 1967), 18–19.

28. Carl Condit, *American Building Materials and Techniques from the Beginning of the Colonial Settlements to the Present* (Chicago: University of Chicago Press, 1968), 192–94.

29. Alvin Rosenburg, *Condominium in Canada* (Toronto: Canada Law Book Co. Ltd., 1969), 1–3.

30. D. Manderscheid, "Some Problems with the Condominium Law in Alberta" (Master of Laws thesis, University of Alberta, 1983), 2.

31. *RAIC Journal*, April 1952, 121.

32. "A Report on Row Housing," RG11/15/90, CEA.

33. Turner to Mayor, April 8, 1953, RG11/15/90, CEA.

34. Smith to Gerhart, December 29, 1967, 75.503/22, PAA.

35. *Alberta Industrial Newsletter*, September 1961, 2.

36. "Mobile Home Parks in the Urban Environment" (City of Edmonton, Research Report no. 7, 1968), 5.

37. Isbister to Glidden, October 21, 1964, 78.133/87B, PAA.

38. *Mobile Home Report* (Alberta Housing Corporation, October 1970), 7, 25–26.

39. N.B. Giffen, "The Mobile Home in the Edmonton Area—An Overview of Current and Future Use" (M.A. thesis, University of Alberta, 1976), 33–44, 72–73.

40. *Mobile Home Report*, 4–7.

1. *RAIC Journal*, February 1946, 44; Minutes, June 3, 1944, United Brotherhood of Carpenters and Joiners of America, Local 1325 Papers, 62.112, PAA.

2. Dant to Mayor, August 10, 1950, RG11/15/87, CEA.

3. *Review of Housing in Canada* (1958), vi-6.

4. "Advisory Committee on Reconstruction, Sub Committee on Post War Reconstruction Projects," 68.328/168, PAA.

5. Litchfield to Clark, May 25, 1944 (copy), PP, File 1866, PAA.

6. *Calgary Herald*, October 17, 1947.

7. *1963 Town 'n' Country Catalogue* (Beaver Lumber Company) (GAI Library); *The Art of Modern Living Homes by ATCO* (ca. 1966), 75.530/22, PAA.

8. Reprinted in *Calgary Herald*, April 29, 1947.

9. Saywell, *Housing Canadians*, 198.

10. Maxwell Foran, "Calgary, Calgarians and the Northern Movement of the Oil Frontier, 1950–1970," in *The Making of the Modern West*, ed. A.W. Rasporich (Calgary: University of Calgary Press, 1984), 126–27.

11. See for example *RAIC Journal*, April 1942, 53–54.

12. Alberta, *Annual Report of the Department of Public Health 1955*, 56.

13. See for example, *Maclean Building Catalogue, Western Edition* (1952), McLaurin Papers, 66.206/14/102, PAA.

14. *Alberta Industrial Newsletter*, October 1960, 6.

15. "Report of Discussion Regarding Alberta's Housing Problem," (1950), 72.302/2/537, PAA.

16. *RAIC Journal*, August 1953, 213–17.

17. "The Platform Method of Wall Framing," *Habitat* 18 (1975): 19.

18. "Revision to Building Code," May 5, 1960, RG11/15/98, CEA.

19. H.B. Dickens and A.T. Hansen, "Canadian National Building Code: Its Development and Use," *Habitat* 18 (1975): 8–9; *RAIC Journal*, April 1948, 111–16.

20. "Submission by Calgary House Builders. . . . to the Federal Task Force on Housing and Urban Development, 1968," Werry Papers, 84.405/98, PAA.

21. *Building Research in Canada* (National Research Council of Canada), June 30, 1956, 74.

22. Alberta, *Annual Report of the Department of Public Health, 1954*, 65; "Memorandum of the Proceeding of the Conference. . . . National Building Code," (June 1955), 83.341/5/100/295(2), PAA.

23. Bylaw Committee Report, no. 12, May 5, 1960, RG11/15/78, CEA.

24. Duke to Commissioners, January 20, 1953, RG11/15/90, CEA.

25. "Memorandum of Proceeding of Conference. . . . National Building Code," (June 1955), 83.341/5/100/295(2), PAA.

26. *Building Research in Canada*, December 31, 1953, 179–81.

27. Fowler to Kerstens, November 10, 1971, 83.431/5/100/295(2), PAA.

28. *RAIC Journal*, December 1950, 411.

29. *RAIC Journal*, November 1934, 161; *Calgary Herald*, February 11, 1921; Interview with Robert A. Lott, September 5, 1978, James Moyle Oral History Program, M4211, GAI.

30. Cecil Burgess, "The Housing Problem," (1940), File 72–28–48, UAA.

31. The general contractor had begun to appear in Ontario by the late 1920s (*RAIC Journal*, December 1955, 462–63). Large scale building had occurred in Alberta before 1945, for example, during the boom years of 1909–1913.

32. *Towards More Stable Growth in Construction: Report on Cyclical Instability in Construction* (Ottawa: Economic Council of Canada, 1974), pp. S-7–S-8.

33. Interview with Robert A. Lott, September 5, 1978, M4211, GAI.

34. *Building Research in Canada* 2 (1956): 77–78; *Review of Housing in Canada* (1958), VI-1.

35. *Review of Housing in Canada* (1958), V-1.

36. Sam Gitterman, "Industrialized Building" (A Report Prepared for CMHC, typescript), 9.

37. *Review of Housing in Canada* (1958) VI-3.

38. The National House Builders Association, Alberta Section to Manning, n.d. [September, 1948], PP, File 1757, PAA.

39. *Calgary Herald*, October 9, 1948.

40. *Submission by the Calgary House Builders Association to the Gordon Royal Commission on Canada's Economic Prospects, November 25, 1955*, Craig Papers, M7478, GAI; United Brotherhood of Carpenters and Joiners of America, Local 1325, Edmonton, Brief . . . , March 26, 1957, United Brotherhood of Carpenters and Joiners of America, Local 1325 Papers, 67.88/181, PAA.

41. Max Foran and Heather MacEwan, *Calgary: Canada's Frontier Metropolis* (Sponsored by the Calgary Chamber of Commerce, Windsor Publications, 1982), 304, 339.

42. *Industry and Resources, 1973* (Edmonton: Alberta Bureau of Statistics), 87.

43. Membership List, 1956, Edmonton Home Builders Association, (EHBA Office).

44. *Towards More Stable Growth in Construction*, p. S-10.

45. Rose, *Canadian Housing Policies*, 37.

13 BUILDING, TRENDS, AND DESIGN IN ALBERTA

1. *Housing and Urban Growth: Draft for Discussion, Paper No. 11* (Edmonton Region Growth Studies, Edmonton Regional Planning Commission, 1976), 47.

2. Mumford, *The Culture of Cities*, 466.

POSTSCRIPT: THE 1970S AND 1980S

1. Yurko to Hawrelak, June 27, 1975, Yurko Papers, 79.94, PAA.

2. *Housing in Canada, 1946–1970: A Supplement to the Annual Re-*

port of *Central Mortgage and Housing Corporation* (Ottawa: 1970), 9–10.

3. *Human Settlement in Canada* (Ottawa: Ministry of State for Urban Affairs, 1976), 18.

4. "Housing and Housing Policy," *Canadian Encyclopedia*, 2nd ed. (Edmonton: Hurtig Publishers, 1988), Vol. 2, 840–41.

5. Bairstow to Swan, May 16, 1977, Alberta Home Mortgage Corporation Papers, 85.270/3, PAA.

6. Speech by Yurko, April 9, 1976, 79.94/4, PAA.

7. Letter to Donnachie, January 27, 1969, Department of Municipal Affairs Papers, 75.530/22, PAA.

8. *Edmonton Journal*, July 18, 1987.

9. Yurko to Tesolin, January 31, 1977, 79.94/3, PAA.

10. Parlby, *The Family Farm in Alberta*, 21–24.

11. *Human Settlement in Canada*, 75.

12. Owram, *The Economic Development of Western Canada*, 46.

◆ ◆ COMMENT ON SOURCES

The sources that this study drew upon were wide but often scattered. The Calgary and Edmonton newspapers periodically carried housing sections. Much of the featured material was syndicated, providing valuable guidance to the ideas that people were exposed to, but local information about housing and local advertisements by realtors and builders also appeared. Small town newspapers rarely featured plans or articles about housing and very rarely reported on house building or housing conditions in the town or district. The most important rural magazine in Alberta before World War II was the *Farm and Ranch Review*, published in Calgary. It was a valuable source of information about rural housing and house planning. Other useful periodicals of national or regional focus include various municipal affairs journals and planning journals, such as the *Journal of the Town Planning Institute* and *The Western Municipal News*. The *Journal of the Royal Architectural Institute of Canada* provided solid references about building and design in Canada. Even more important for construction practices were building journals, including *Canadian Architect and Builder, Construction,* and *Contract Record and Engineering Review,* and, for the west, *The Western Canada Contractor* (titles vary).

The *Census of Canada* provided a basic and indispensable range of statistical information on housing, although the use of these figures is complicated and caution must be exercised because of inconsistent definitions. Other printed government records that contained information on housing, although often incidentally, were reports of provincial royal commissions and public inquiries, such as those on Alberta's coal industry in 1919, 1925, and 1935, the Royal Commission on the Metropolitan Development of Calgary and Edmonton in 1956, and the inquiry into the conditions among the Metis in 1935–36. Alberta's submissions to federal royal commissions, such as the Rowell Sirois in 1938, and reports prepared for such commissions also contained useful material. For the postwar period, the numerous publications of Central Mortgage and Housing Corporation (later Canada Mortgage and Housing Corporation) and Alberta Housing and Urban Renewal Corporation (later Alberta Housing Corporation) were useful.

Manuscript sources concerned exclusively with housing were rare. Civic papers for small towns have rarely survived, although extensive collections exist for Edmonton at the City of Edmonton Archives and for Calgary at the Glenbow-Alberta Institute Archives. These records provided important material on housing conditions, health, planning, construction, and bylaws. Assessment records and building permits also exist for some periods and towns, although they were not used here because of the complexity of using them consistently for the whole province. Provincial records such as the Premiers' Papers and the records of the Departments of Municipal Affairs, Economic Development, Agriculture, and Health contained much significant material. These records provided a range of information on planning, rent control, senior citizens' housing, mobile homes, housing conditions, sanitation and servicing, and, among others, building codes. Few private manuscript collections relating to housing were found. The papers of L.D. Pollard, an Edmonton builder, held at the City of Edmonton Archives and Samuel Shaw's papers, held at Glenbow, were unique in providing a view of the work of small builders. Descriptions of actual construction methods were infrequently recorded, possibly because knowledge was gained through the working of tradition, innovation, or on-the-job training. Similarly, people, especially of the working and middle classes, rarely left records about their houses. Perhaps the house was so accepted as a part of the physical world and bore so many similarities to those nearby that few people thought it merited description. In such cases, photographic evidence was valuable and, given the destruction of the historical built environment in Alberta in the past four decades, it is sometimes the only method that remains of visualizing buildings in their context. Photographs do, however, tend to focus on better quality houses and rarely reflect the full range of housing in the province. Architects rarely designed ordinary housing in Alberta. Their papers, when they exist, usually included some blueprints and occasionally some presentation drawings, but most often only for corporate clients. They rarely contained correspondence or other material. The Cecil Burgess papers at the University of Alberta Archives were an exception. Burgess was professor of architecture at the University of Alberta after 1913, and his papers provided valuable material in the form of transcripts of radio talks, lecture notes, clippings, and a limited amount of correspondence. The papers of the Alberta Association of Architects at the Canadian Architectural Archives, University of Calgary, contained valuable contextual material concerning the profession in Alberta and about building and construction.

SECONDARY LITERATURE ON HOUSING

The secondary literature on housing in Alberta or prairie Canada is scant indeed. There are few synthetic studies of housing in Canada. John Saywell's *Essays on Residential Construction in Canada* (Ottawa: Economic Council of Canada, Discussion Paper no. 24, 1975) remains the best, although it is primarily directed to economic and policy considerations. A more localized study is Bryan Melnyk, *Calgary Builds: The Emergence of an Urban Landscape 1905–1914* (Regina: Alberta Culture and Canadian Plains Research Center, 1985) which contains one chapter on housing in Calgary to 1914. Given the breadth of the topic of housing, the tendency in studies in Canada has been to focus on specific aspects of the topic. History of common twentieth century houses is generally neglected in Canada, although there are a number of studies about nineteenth century Ontario and Quebec houses and housing. Canadian architectural history, such as Alan Gowans, *Building*

Canada: An Architectural History of Canadian Life (Toronto: Oxford University Press, 1966) treats common housing in western Canada only incidentally. However, his *The Comfortable House* (Cambridge, Massachusetts: The MIT Press, 1986) is a valuable guide through the maze of styles and forms of ordinary North American housing. Design and architecture are approached differently by architectural historians and geographers, the two disciplines most consistently interested in the evolution of buildings. The traditions of architectural history have directed attention to the evolution and meaning of historical styles, which tended to confine the field to major buildings. The discipline is shifting, however, to a more socially integrated approach. Geographers have produced valuable work on diffusion of house forms, but have tended to ignore style in favour of studies of form, layout, and construction in an effort to understand population movement and its impact on the landscape. The pioneer work by the American geographers Fred Kniffen and Henry Glassie was formative in shaping the approach geographers have taken to the topic, and one of the best recent studies is Alan Noble, *Wood, Brick and Stone* (Amherst: University of Massachusetts Press, 1984). Much of the research produced by geographers focuses on folk buildings. An example relevant to Alberta is John Lehr's ground breaking work on Ukrainian folk styles in Alberta, notably *Ukrainian Vernacular Architecture in Alberta* (Edmonton: Alberta Culture, Occasional Paper no. 1, 1976) and "The Log Buildings of Ukrainian Settlers in Western Canada," *Prairie Forum* 5 (1980). The various occasional papers of Historic Sites Service, Alberta Culture and Multiculturalism on Ukrainian buildings in Alberta provided additional valuable material for one folk variant. Two additional studies on the connection between folk building techniques and ethnicity are William Wonders and Mark Rasmussen, "Log Buildings of West Central Alberta" (*Prairie Forum* 5 (1980) and William Wonders, "Log Dwellings in Canadian Folk Architecture" (*Annals of the Association of American Geographers* 69 (1979). There are also many recollections about pioneering that often contain references to housing. A synthetic and well illustrated study of pioneer housing in Alberta is Thelma Dennis, *Albertans Built: Aspects of Housing in Rural Alberta to 1920* (Edmonton: University of Alberta Printing Services, 1986). A fine series of studies on Manitoba rural housing published under the general title *Architectural Heritage* (Winnipeg: Manitoba Culture, Heritage and Recreation, 1982–85) provide some regional context for housing on the prairies.

More general studies of the history of construction and construction techniques include a useful study by E.A. Doherty, *Residential Construction Practices in Alberta 1900–1971* (Edmonton: Alberta Department of Housing, 1984). A basic study of building technology and servicing in Canada remains Thomas Ritchie, *Canada Builds 1867–1967* (Toronto: University of Toronto Press, 1967). A good study on one aspect of prefabrication is G.E. Mills and D.W. Holdsworth, *The B.C. Mills Prefabricated System: The Emergence of Ready-Made Buildings in Western Canada* (Ottawa: Parks Canada, 1975). A well balanced overview that links construction materials and practices with other aspects of housing in North America is Michael Doucet and John Weaver, "Material Culture and the North American House:

The Era of the Common Man, 1870–1920," *Journal of American History* 72, part II (1985–86). The American literature on building is more extensive, but a standard work is Carl Condit, *American Building Materials and Techniques from the Beginning of the Colonial Settlements to the Present* (Chicago: University of Chicago Press, 1968). A study that could serve as a model on the impact of bylaws and regulations on housing is M.J. Daunton, *House and Home in the Victorian City: Working Class Housing, 1850–1914* (London: Edward Arnold, 1983).

Other studies have concentrated on economic aspects of housing. Difficulties in using the historical statistics on housing have often entailed a preliminary effort to make the statistical base consistent. The pioneering work in the economic history of housing in Canada is O.J. Firestone, *Residential Real Estate in Canada* (Toronto: University of Toronto Press, 1951), while Kenneth A.H. Buckley, *Capital Formation in Canada* (Toronto: McClelland and Stewart, 1974, Carleton Library, first published in 1955) treats housing along with other aspects of capital formation. Another study is J. Pickett, "Residential Capital Formation in Canada, 1871–1921," *Canadian Journal of Economics and Political Science* 29 (1963):40–53.

No historical study of Alberta government housing policy exists, although two volumes are important for the provincial context. David G. Bettison, *The Politics of Canadian Urban Development* (Edmonton: University of Alberta Press, 1975) and David G. Bettison, John Kenward, and Larrie Taylor, *Urban Affairs in Alberta* (Edmonton: University of Alberta Press, 1975) contain a wealth of information and analyses on all aspects of federal and Alberta policy on urban development, including housing. There are also a number of articles and studies on the history of Canada Mortgage and Housing Corporation, many of which appear in the publications of the corporation. In addition, *Urban History Review* 15 (1986), guest edited by J. David Hulchanski, contains an important series of articles. An account of Canadian housing policy is Albert Rose, *Canadian Housing Policies, 1935–1980* (Toronto: Butterworth and Co., 1980). Rose's primary concern is with developments after World War II. A British study that relates state policy to social aspects of housing is John Burnett, *A Social History of Housing, 1815–1970* (London: David Charles, 1978), while one analysis of American housing policy is Barry Checkoway, "Large Builders, Federal Housing Programmes and Postwar Suburbanization," *International Journal of Urban and Regional Research* 4 (1980).

Studies of the design and conceptualization of the house in its social context are limited in Canada. Comparative studies include David Handlin, *The American Home: Architecture and Society 1815–1915* (Boston: Little Brown and Co., 1979). Through a study of the ideas that shaped housing, Handlin's book is among the best treatments of American housing. Two books by Gwendolyn Wright, *Moralism and the Model Home: Domestic Architecture and Cultural Conflict in Chicago, 1873–1913* (Chicago: University of Chicago Press, 1980) and *Building the Dream. A Social History of Housing in America* (New York: Pantheon Books, 1981) are useful; the latter is mainly concerned with the place of the house in utopian thinking. Two solid studies on design of ordinary houses are Deryk Holdsworth, "Regional

Distinctiveness in an Industrial Age: Some California Influences on British Columbia Housing," *The American Review of Canadian Studies* 12 (1982) and Richard Mattson, "The Bungalow Spirit" *Journal of Cultural Geography* 1 (1981).

Another approach to understanding the context of housing is through the history of planning. A good outline of planning developments in Alberta is J. David Hulchanski, *The Origins of Urban Land Use Planning in Alberta, 1905–1945* (Toronto: Centre for Urban and Community Studies, University of Toronto, 1981). There are a number of graduate theses on postwar planning in Alberta, and those notable for housing include L. McCann, "Changing Morphology of Residential Areas in Transition" (Ph.D. dissertation, University of Alberta, 1972), a fine study of changes in Edmonton's built environment. Also useful are Donald Harasym, "The Planning of New Residential Areas in Calgary, 1944–1973" (M.A. thesis, University of Alberta, 1975) and Robert Graden, "The Planning of New Residential Areas in Edmonton, 1950–1976" (M.A. thesis, University of Alberta, 1979).

Lastly, studies on tenure, segregation, ownership, and class aspects of housing are limited. The exceptions are Richard Harris's preliminary work on tenure and affordability, especially two articles in *Histoire sociale/Social History*, "The Unremarked Homeownership Boom in Toronto" (1985) and "Working Class Ownership and Housing Affordability Across Canada in 1931" (1986). For discussion and references on other articles and sections of books dealing with residential segregation, ownership, and working class housing in Ontario and Montreal, see Richard Harris, *Class and Housing. Tenure in Modern Canada* (Toronto: Centre for Urban and Community Studies, University of Toronto, Research Paper No 113, 1984).

◆ ◆ BIBLIOGRAPHY OF CITED
SECONDARY SOURCES

Acland, Fred. "Alberta, 1906." *Alberta History* 28 (1980).

Alberta Culture, Historic Sites Service. *Sites Type Manual.* Edmonton: Alberta Culture, 1979.

Alberta Facts and Figures. Edmonton: Alberta, Bureau of Statistics, 1950.

Alberta Statistical Review Annual: 75th Anniversary Edition. Edmonton: Alberta Bureau of Statistics, 1980.

Artibise, Alan. *Winnipeg: A Social History of Urban Growth, 1874–1914.* Montreal: McGill-Queen's University Press, 1975.

———. "The Urban West: The Evolution of Prairie Towns and Cities to 1930." *Prairie Forum* 4 (1979).

Babcock, Doug. "Fur Trade Architecture in Alberta: The First Century, 1778–1878." Paper delivered at the Banff Conference on Log Structures in Canada, Banff, Alberta, October 27, 1977.

Bacher, John. "Canadian Housing 'Policy' in Perspective." *Urban History Review* 15 (1986).

Bannon, Michael. "The Evolution of the Central Area of Edmonton, Alberta, 1946–1966." M.A. thesis, University of Alberta, 1967.

Bastian, Robert. "The Prairie Style House: Spatial Diffusion of a Minor Design." *Journal of Cultural Geography* 1 (1980).

Bauer, R. *One of Many.* Edmonton: Edmonton Imprimerie La Survivance Printing, 1965.

Bercuson, David, ed. *Alberta Coal Industry, 1919.* Calgary: Alberta Records Publication Board, The Historical Society of Alberta, 1978.

Betke, Carl. "The Development of Urban Community in Prairie Canada: Edmonton, 1898–1921." Ph.D. diss. University of Alberta, 1981.

Bettison, David G. *The Politics of Urban Development.* Edmonton: University of Alberta Press, 1975.

Bettison, David G., Kenward, John, and Taylor, Larrie. *Urban Affairs in Alberta.* Edmonton: University of Alberta Press, 1975.

Blake, Peter. *The Master Builders.* New York: W.W. Norton and Co., 1976.

Bloomfield, Elizabeth. "Community Ethos and Local Initiative in Urban Economic Growth: Review of a Theme in Canadian Urban History." *Urban History Yearbook 1983.*

Boddy, Trevor. *Modern Architecture in Alberta.* Regina: Alberta Culture and Multiculturalism and Canadian Plains Research Center, 1987.

Breen, David. "Calgary: The City and the Petroleum Industry Since World War II." *Urban History Review* 2–77 (1977).

————, ed. *William Stewart Herron: Father of the Petroleum Industry in Alberta*. Calgary: Alberta Records Publication Board, The Historical Society of Alberta, 1984.

Bryce, P.H. "History of Public Health in Canada." *Canadian Therapeutist and Sanitary Engineer* 6 (1910).

Buckley, Kenneth. *Capital Formation in Canada, 1896–1930*. Toronto: McClelland and Stewart, 1974.

Burchard, John, and Bush Brown, Albert. *The Architecture of America*. Boston: Little Brown and Co., 1961.

Burnet, Jean. *Next Year Country*. Toronto: University of Toronto Press, 1951.

Butterfield, David K. and Ledohowski, Edward M. *Architectural Heritage: The Brandon and Area Planning District*. Winnipeg: Manitoba Culture, Heritage and Recreation, Historic Resources Branch, 1985.

Callihoo, Victoria. "Early Life in Lac Ste. Anne and St. Albert in the Eighteen Seventies." *Alberta Historical Review* 1 (1953).

Cameron, Christina. *Index of Houses Featured in Canadian Homes and Gardens from 1925 to 1944*. Ottawa: Parks Canada, 1980.

Caragata, Warren. *Alberta Labour: A Heritage Untold*. Toronto: James Lorimer and Company, 1979.

Carroll, Barbara Wake. "Post War Trends in Canadian Housing Policy." *Urban History Review* 18 (1989).

Chan, Wah May. "The Impact of the Technical Planning Board on the Morphology of Edmonton." M.A. thesis, University of Alberta, 1969.

Clayton, Maurice. "Canadian Housing In Wood." Typescript, 1986.

Cleverdon, Catherine. *The Woman Suffrage Movement in Canada*. 1950; reprint with an introduction by Ramsay Cook, Toronto: University of Toronto Press, 1974.

Connally, Earnest A. "The Cape Cod House: An Introductory Study." *Journal of the Society of Architectural Historians* 19 (1960).

Condit, Carl. *American Building Materials and Techniques from the Beginning of the Colonial Settlements to the Present*. Chicago: University of Chicago Press, 1968.

Coulter, Rebecca. "The Working Young of Edmonton, 1921–1931," in *Childhood and Family in Canadian History*, ed. Joy Parr. Toronto: McClelland and Stewart, 1982.

Cullen, Mary. "Highlights of Domestic Buildings in Pre-Confederation Ontario as Seen Through Travel Literature from 1763 to 1860." *APT Bulletin* 13 (1981).

Cunniffe, R. *Calgary—In Sandstone*. Calgary: Historical Society of Alberta, 1969.

Darnell, M. "Innovations in American Prefabricated Houses: 1860–1890." *Journal of the Society of Architectural Historians* 31 (1972).

Dawe, Robert. "An Investigation into the Development of the Red Deer Community in Relation to the Development of Western Canada." M.A. thesis, University of Alberta, 1954.

Dempsey, Hugh, ed. "The West of Edward Maunsell." *Alberta History* 34 (1986).

den Otter, A.A. "A Social History of the Alberta Coal Branch." M.A. thesis, University of Alberta, 1967.

Dennis, Thelma. *Albertans Built: Aspects of Houses in Rural Alberta to 1920*. Edmonton: University of Alberta Printing Services, 1986.

Dickens, H.B. and Hansen, A.T. "Canadian National Building Code: Its Development and Use." *Habitat* 18 (1975).

Dickin McGinnis, J.P. "Birth to Boom to Bust: Building in Calgary 1875–1914" in *Frontier Calgary: Town, City, and Region 1875–1914*, A. Rasporich and H. Klassen, eds. Calgary: University of Calgary: McClelland and Stewart West, 1975.

Diemer, H. "Annexation and Amalgamation in the Territorial Expansion of Edmonton and Calgary." M.A. thesis, University of Alberta, 1975.

Doherty, E.A. *Residential Construction Practices in Alberta 1900–1971*. Edmonton: Alberta Department of Housing, 1984.

Doucet, Michael J. "Working Class Housing in a Small Nineteenth Century Canadian City: Hamilton Ontario, 1852–1881" in *Essays in Canadian Working Class History*, eds. Gregory Kealey and Peter Warrian. Toronto: McClelland and Stewart, 1976.

Doucet, Michael J. and Weaver, John C. "Material Culture and the North American House: The Era of the Common Man." *Journal of American History* 72, Part II (1985–86).

Early Domestic Architecture in Regina: Presentation Drawings and Plans. Regina: Norman Mackenzie Art Gallery, 1982.

Edmonton's Lost Heritage. Edmonton Historical Board, 1982.

Farnell, Peggy O'Connor. *Old Glenora*. Edmonton: Old Glenora Historical Society, 1984.

Foran, Maxwell. "Calgary, Calgarians and the Northern Movement of the Oil Frontier, 1950–1970" in *The Making of the Modern West*, ed. A.W. Rasporich. Calgary: University of Calgary Press, 1984.

———. "The Civic Corporation and Urban Growth: Calgary, 1884–1930." Ph.D. diss., University of Calgary, 1981.

———. "Land Development Patterns in Calgary, 1884–1945" in *The Useable Urban Past*, Alan F.J. Artibise and Gilbert A. Stelter, eds. Toronto: Macmillan of Canada, 1979.

———. "Land Speculation and Urban Development in Calgary 1884–1912" in *Frontier Calgary: Town, City, and Region 1875–1914*, A. Rasporich and H. Klassen, eds. Calgary: University of Calgary: McClelland and Stewart West, 1975.

———. "The Mawson Report in Historical Perspective." *Alberta History* 28 (1980).

Foran, Maxwell, and MacEwan, Heather. *Calgary: Canada's Frontier Metropolis*. Sponsored by the Calgary Chamber of Commerce, Windsor Publications, 1982.

Friesen, Gerald. *The Canadian Prairies: A History*. Toronto: University of Toronto Press, 1984.

Gates, D. "The Sod House." *Journal of Geography* 32 (1933).

Giffen, N.B. "The Mobile Home in the Edmonton Area—An Overview of Current and Future Use." M.A. thesis, University of Alberta, 1976.

Giraud, Marcel. *The Metis in the Canadian West.* trans. George Woodcock, 2 vols. Edmonton: University of Alberta Press, 1986.

Glassie, Henry. "Eighteenth Century Cultural Process in Delaware Valley Folk Building" in *Common Places: Readings in American Vernacular Architecture,* eds. Dell Upton and John Michael Vlach. Athens, Georgia: The University of Georgia Press, 1986.

Goodfellow, Ronald J. "A Historical and Ecological Study of Southern Alberta." Bachelor of Architecture thesis, University of British Columbia, 1968/69.

Gowans, Alan. *The Comfortable House: North American Suburban Architecture 1890–1930.* Cambridge, Massachusetts: The MIT Press, 1986.

Graden, Robert. "The Planning of New Residential Areas in Edmonton, 1950–1976." M.A. thesis, University of Alberta, 1979.

Graham, W. "Construction of Large Scale Structured Base Line Maps of Central Edmonton for 1907, 1911 & 1914." M.A. thesis, University of Alberta, 1984.

Grauer, A.E. *Housing: A Study Prepared for the Royal Commission on Dominion-Provincial Relations.* Ottawa: 1939.

Greenway, H.F. "Housing in Canada." *Census of Canada, 1931,* Vol. XII, Monographs.

Gross, Alexander F. "Witness to the Passing of Victorian Architecture, The RAIC Journal, 1924–1938." *Society for the Study of Architecture in Canada, Bulletin* 12 (1989).

Hanchett, Thomas. "The Four Square House in the United States" in *Perspectives in Vernacular Architecture,* ed. Camille Wells. Annapolis, Maryland: Vernacular Architecture Forum, 1982.

Handlin, David. *The American Home: Architecture and Society 1815–1915.* Boston: Little Brown and Co., 1979.

Harasym, Donald. "The Planning of New Residential Areas in Calgary, 1944–73." M.A. thesis, University of Alberta, 1975.

Harris, Richard. "Housing in Canadian Cities: An Agenda and Review of Sources." *Urban History Review* 14 (1986).

———. "The Unremarked Homeownership Boom in Toronto." *Histoire sociale/Social History* 18 (1985).

Hatfield, R. "The Metropolitan Development of Edmonton: The City, The Province, and the Strategy of Neglect." M.A. thesis, University of Alberta, 1982.

Hayter, Jacqueline. "Residential Mobility and the Function of Selected High Rises in Central Edmonton." M.A. thesis, University of Alberta, 1973.

Hobbs, Margaret and Pierson, Ruth Roach. "'A Kitchen That Wastes No Steps. . . .' Gender, Class and the Home Improvement Plan, 1936–1940." *Histoire sociale/Social History* 21 (1988).

Hohol, Demjan. *The Grekul House: A Land Use and Structural History.* Edmonton: Historic Sites Service, Occasional Paper No. 14, 1985.

Holden, M. "The Normans Come to Calgary." *Alberta History* 28 (1980).

Holdsworth, Deryk, "Regional Distinctiveness in an Industrial Age: Some California Influences on British Columbia Housing." *The American Review of Canadian Studies* 12 (1982).

Housing in Canada, 1946–1970. A Supplement to the Annual Report of Central Mortgage and Housing Corporation. Ottawa: 1970.

Howell, Colin and Smith, Michael. "Orthodox Medicine and the Health Reform Movement in the Maritimes, 1850–1885." *Acadiensis* 18 (1989).

Hudson, John. "Frontier Housing in North Dakota." *North Dakota History* 42 (1975).

Hulchanski, J. David. "The 1935 Dominion Housing Act: Setting the Stage for a Permanent Federal Presence in Canada's Housing Sector." *Urban History Review* 15 (1986).

———. *The Origin of Urban Land Use Planning in Alberta 1900–1945.* Toronto: Centre for Urban and Community Studies, University of Toronto. Research Paper no. 119. Land Policy Paper no. 1, 1981.

Hull, Virginia L. "A Geographical Study of the Impact of Two Ethnic Groups on the Rural Landscape of Alberta." M.A. thesis, University of Alberta, 1964.

Human Settlement in Canada. Ottawa: Ministry of State for Urban Affairs, 1976.

Innis, Harold. *The Fur Trade in Canada.* Toronto: University of Toronto Press, 1973.

Ironside, R.G. and Tomasky, E. "Agricultural and River Lot Settlement in Western Canada: The Case of Pakan (Victoria) Alberta." *Prairie Forum* 1, no. 1 and 2 (1976).

Jackson, Anthony. "The Politics of English Architecture: 1929–1951." *Journal of the Society of Architectural Historians,* 24 (1965).

Jackson, John. "The House as a Visual Indicator of Social Status Change: The Example of London Ontario 1861–1915." M.A. thesis, University of Western Ontario, 1973.

Jansen, B. "The Community of Mountain View, Alberta: A Study in Community Development, 1890–1925." M.A. thesis, University of Alberta, 1972.

Janssen, Willem. "The Impact of Public Institutions on Rural Housing Investment in the Prairie Provinces." M.A. thesis, University of Saskatchewan, 1964.

Jenness, Diamond. *The Indians of Canada.* 7th ed. Toronto: University of Toronto Press in association with National Museum of Man, 1977.

Job Reed's Letters: Life in Lethbridge, 1886–1906. Lethbridge: Historical Society of Alberta, Whoop Up Chapter, 1979.

Jones, Owen Douglas. "The Historical Geography of Edmonton, Alberta." M.A. thesis, University of Toronto, 1962.

Kent, Susan. "The Effects of Television Viewing: A Cross Cultural Perspective." *Current Anthropology* 26 (1985).

Klassen, H. "Social Troubles in Calgary in the Mid-1890s." *Urban History Review,* no. 3–74 (1974).

———. "Life in Frontier Calgary" in *Western Canada Past and Present,* ed. Anthony Rasporich. Calgary: University of Calgary, McClelland and Stewart West, 1975.

Kniffen, Fred B. "Folk Houses—Key to Diffusion." *Annals of the Association of American Geographers* 55 (1965).

Kristjanson, B.H. and Spence, C.C. *Land Settlement in Northeastern Alberta, 1943.* Ottawa: Dominion Department of Agriculture in Co-operation with the Department of Political Economy, University of Alberta, 1947, Technical Bulletin 63.

Lake, David. "The Historical Geography of the Coal Branch." M.A. thesis, University of Alberta, 1967.

Leaning, John. "Our Construction Heritage." Extract from *Our Architectural Ancestry*, 1983. (CMHC Library).

Lee, Helen. *The Forest Industry in Alberta, 1870–1955.* Wetaskiwin: Reynolds Alberta Museum, Background Paper 19, 1984.

Lehr, John. "Changing Ukrainian House Styles." *Alberta History*, Winter, 1975.

————. "The Landscape of Ukrainian Settlement in the Canadian West." *Great Plains Quarterly* 1–2 (1982).

————. "The Log Buildings of Ukrainian Settlers in Western Canada." *Prairie Forum* 5 (1980).

————. "Mormon Settlements in Southern Alberta." M.A. thesis, University of Alberta, 1971.

————. *Ukrainian Vernacular Architecture in Alberta.* Edmonton: Historic Sites Service, Occasional Paper no. 1, 1976.

Leslie, G. "Domestic Service in Canada 1880–1920" in *Women at Work 1850–1930*, J. Acton, P. Goldsmith, and B. Shepard, eds. Toronto: Women's Press, 1974.

Lewis, Oscar. *The Effects of White Contact Upon Blackfoot Culture with Specific Reference to the Role of the Fur Trade.* 2nd ed. Seattle: University of Washington Press, 1966.

Lewis, Pierce F. "Common Housing, Cultural Spoor." *Landscape* 19 (1975).

Lillie, R.G. "Twenty Years of Housing. CMHC 1946–1968." *Habitat* 11, no. 1 (1968), and 11, no. 2 (1968).

MacGregor, James. *A History of Alberta.* rev.ed. Edmonton: Hurtig Publishers, 1981.

Macleod, H.L. "Property, Investors and Taxes: A Study of Calgary Real Estate Investments, Municipal Finance and Property Tax Arrears, 1911–1919." M.A. thesis, University of Calgary, 1977.

Mallett, Robin Barrie. "Settlement Process and Land Use Change—Lethbridge-Medicine Hat Area." M.A. thesis, University of Alberta, 1971.

Mandelbaum, David. *The Plains Cree: An Ethnographic, Historical and Comparative Study.* Regina: Canadian Plains Research Center, 1979.

Manderscheid, D. "Some Problems with the Condominium Law in Alberta." Master of Laws thesis, University of Alberta, 1983.

Manson, Jack. *Bricks in Alberta.* Edmonton: John Manson and the Alberta Masonary Institute, 1983.

Martin, Chester. *Dominion Lands Policies.* 1938, reprint edited and with an introduction by L.H. Thomas, Toronto: McClelland and Stewart, 1973.

Martynowych, Orest. *The Ukrainian Bloc Settlement in East-Central Alberta 1890–1930: A History.* Edmonton: Historic Sites Service, Occasional Paper no. 10, 1985.

Matthews, D.J. and Smith, L.B. *Report on Canada Mortgage and Housing Corporation*. Ottawa: Task Force on Central Mortgage and Housing Corporation, 1979.

Mattson, Richard. "The Bungalow Spirit." *Journal of Cultural Geography* 1 (1981).

McCann, L. "Changing Morphology of Residential Areas in Transition." Ph.D. diss., University of Alberta, 1972.

McDonald, John. "Soldier Settlement and Depression Settlement in the Forest Fringe of Saskatchewan." *Prairie Forum* 6 (1981).

McLeod, E. Slater. "Our Sod House." *The Beaver* Outfit 308:2 (1977).

Melynk, Bryan. *Calgary Builds: The Emergence of an Urban Landscape 1905–1914*. Regina: Alberta Culture/Canadian Plains Research Center, 1985.

Mills, G.E. and Holdsworth, D.W. *The B.C. Mills Prefabricated System: The Emergence of Ready-Made Buildings in Western Canada*. Ottawa: Parks Canada Occasional Papers in Archaeology and History, no. 14, 1975.

Moodie, D. "St. Albert Settlement: A Study in Historical Geography." M.A. thesis, University of Alberta, 1965.

Mumford, Lewis. *The Culture of Cities*. 1938; reprint, London: Secker and Warburg, 1946.

Munger, J. *Housing and Environmental Conditions in the Prairie Provinces with Particular Emphasis on the Effects of Urbanization on Rural Housing and Public Facilities*. Saskatoon: Canadian Centre for Community Studies, University of Saskatchewan, 1966.

Nahachewsky, Andriy. *Ukrainian Dug-Out Dwellings in East Central Alberta*. Edmonton: Historic Sites Service, Occasional Paper no. 11, 1985.

Noble, Allan. *Wood, Brick and Stone*. Amherst: University of Massachusetts Press, 1984.

Owram, Douglas. *The Economic Development of Western Canada: An Historical Overview*. Ottawa: Economic Council of Canada, Discussion Paper no. 219, 1982.

Parlby, G.B. *The Family Farm in Alberta: Its Origins, Development and Future*. Edmonton: Alberta Department of Agriculture, Alberta Land Use Forum, 1974.

"The Platform Method of Wall Framing." *Habitat* 18 (1975).

Pommer, Richard. "The Architecture of Urban Housing in the United States During the Early 1930s." *Journal of the Society of Architectural Historians* 37 (1978).

Ream, Peter. *The Fort on the Saskatchewan*. 2nd ed. n.p.: Metropolitan Printing, 1974.

Rees, R. "The Magic City on the Banks of the Saskatchewan. The Saskatoon Real Estate Boom 1910–1913." *Saskatchewan History* 27, no. 2 (1974).

Reid, A.N. "Urban Governments in the North-West Territories: Their Development and Machinery of Government." *Saskatchewan History* 7 (1954/56).

Rempel, J.T. *Building with Wood and Other Aspects of Nineteenth Century Building in Ontario*. Toronto: University of Toronto Press, 1967.

Ritchie, Thomas. *Canada Builds: 1867–1967*. Toronto: University of Toronto Press, 1967.

———. "Plankwall Framing, A Modern Wall Construction with an Ancient History." *Journal of the Society of Architectural Historians* 30 (1971).

Roe, Frank Gilbert. "The Old Log House in Western Canada." *Alberta Historical Review* 6 (1958).

———. "The Sod House." *Alberta Historical Review* 18 (1970).

Rogers, Edward. "Indian Life in Autumn." *The Beaver* Outfit 311-3 (1980).

Ropoport, Amos. "Vernacular Architecture and the Cultural Determinants of Form" in *Buildings and Society*, ed. A. King. London: Routledge and Kegan Paul, 1980.

Rose, Albert. *Canadian Housing Policies*. Toronto: Conference on Housing, University of Toronto, Background Paper no. 2, June, 1968.

Rosenburg, Alvin. *Condominium in Canada*. Toronto: Canada Law Book Co. Ltd., 1969.

Rowell, Gladys. "Memoirs of an English Settler." *Alberta History* 30 (1982).

Savoie, Donat. *The Amerindians of the Canadian North-West in the 19th Century as Seen by Emile Petitot, Vol. II, The Loucheaux Indians*. Ottawa: Department of Indian Affairs, Northern Science Research Group, MDRP 10, 1970.

Saywell, John. *Essays on Residential Construction in Canada*. Ottawa: Economic Council of Canada, Discussion Paper no. 24, 1975.

Schwartz, D. "Sears Sold Everything Else, So Why Not Houses?" *Smithsonian*, November 1985.

Sherwood, Angus. "Building in the North." *APT Bulletin* 6 (1974).

Smith, Allan. "The Myth of the Self-made Man in English Canada, 1850–1914." *Canadian Historical Review* 58 (1978).

Smith, P.J. "Change in a Youthful City: The Case of Calgary Alberta." *Geography* 56 (1971).

Sprauge, Paul. "The Origin of Balloon Framing." *Journal of the Society of Architectural Historians* 40 (1981).

Spry, Irene, ed. *The Papers of the Palliser Expedition*. Toronto: The Champlain Society, 1968.

Strange, Kathleen. *With the West in Her Eyes*. Toronto: Macmillan Co. of Canada Ltd., 1945.

Stone, D. "The Process of Rural Settlement in the Athabasca Area, Alberta." M.A. thesis, University of Alberta, 1971.

Talbot, Percy. "Pioneering on Strawberry Plain: Early Days in Lacombe." *Alberta Historical Review* 3 (1955).

Taggart, K. "The First Shelter of the Early Pioneers." *Saskatchewan History* 11 (1958).

Thomas, L.G. "Okotoks: From Trading Post to Suburb." *Urban History Review* 8 (1970).

Thompson, John. *The Harvests of War: The Prairie West, 1914–1918*. Toronto: McClelland and Stewart, 1978.

Upton, Dell. "Towards a Performance Theory of Vernacular Architecture: Early Tidewater Virginia as a Case Study." *Folklore Forum* 12 (1979).

Vestal Brown, Charlotte. Review of *American Architecture* by Marcus S. Whiffen & Frederick Koeper. *Winterthur Portfolio* 19 (1984).

Voisey, Paul. "In Search of Wealth and Status: An Economic and Social Study of Entrepreneurs in Early Calgary" in *Frontier Calgary: Town, City, and Region, 1875–1914*, ed. Anthony W. Rasporich and Henry C. Klassen, eds. Calgary: University of Calgary, McClelland and Stewart West, 1975.

Wade, Jill. "Wartime Housing Ltd. 1941–1947: Canadian Housing Policy at the Crossroads." *Urban History Review* 15 (1986).

Ward, Roland. "Country Residential Development in the Edmonton Area to 1973. A Case Study of Exurban Growth." M.A. thesis, University of Alberta, 1977.

Warkentin, John. "Time and Place in the Western Interior." *ArtsCanada*, Autumn (1972).

Weaver, John. "Edmonton's Perilous Course 1904–1929." *Urban History Review* 2-77 (1977).

Wetherell, Donald G, with Kmet, Irene. *Useful Pleasures: The Shaping of Leisure in Alberta, 1896–1945*. Regina: Alberta Culture and Multiculturalism and Canadian Plains Research Center, 1990.

Williamson, David. "Valleyfield's First Settlers." *Alberta History* 30 (1982).

Wonders, William. "Log Dwellings in Canadian Folk Architecture." *Annals of The Association of American Geographers* 69 (1979).

Wonders, William, and Rasmussen, Mark. "Log Buildings of West Central Alberta." *Prairie Forum* 5 (1980).

Wright, Gwendolyn. *Moralism and the Model Home: Domestic Architecture and Cultural Conflict in Chicago, 1873–1913*. Chicago: University of Chicago Press, 1980.

Wurster, Catherine Bauer. "The Social Front of Architecture in the 1930s." *Journal of the Society of Architectural Historians* 24 (1965).

Youe, C. "Eau Claire, the Company and the Community." *Alberta History* 27 (1979).

◆ ◆ INDEX